Play the Open Games as Black

What to do when White avoids the Ruy Lopez

John Emms

First published in the UK by Gambit Publications Ltd 2000
Reprinted 2001, 2006
Copyright © Gambit Publications Ltd 2000

ISBN 1 901983 27 7

DISTRIBUTION:
Worldwide (except USA): Central Books Ltd, 99 Wallis Rd, London E9 5LN. Tel +44 (0)20 8986 4854 Fax +44 (0)20 8533 5821.
E-mail: orders@Centralbooks.com
USA: Continental Enterprises Group, Inc., 302 West North 2nd Street, Seneca, SC 29678, USA.

For all other enquiries (including a full list of all Gambit chess titles) please contact the publishers, Gambit Publications Ltd, 6 Bradmore Park Rd, Hammersmith, London W6 0DS, England. E-mail: info@gambitbooks.com
Or visit the GAMBIT web site at http://www.gambitbooks.com

Edited by Graham Burgess
Typeset by Petra Nunn
Printed in Great Britain by CPI Bath Press Ltd., Bath, Somerset.

10 9 8 7 6 5 4 3

Gambit Publications Ltd
Managing Director: GM Murray Chandler
Chess Director: GM John Nunn
Editorial Director: FM Graham Burgess
German Editor: WFM Petra Nunn

Contents

Symbols

+	check
++	double check
#	checkmate
!!	brilliant move
!	good move
!?	interesting move
?!	dubious move
?	bad move
??	blunder
Ch	championship
Cht	team championship
Wch	world championship
Ech	European Championship
Ct	candidates event
IZ	interzonal event
Z	zonal event
OL	olympiad
jr	junior event
wom	women's event
mem	memorial event
qual	qualifying event
rpd	rapidplay game
corr	correspondence game
tt	team tournament
sim	simultaneous display
1-0	the game ends in a win for White
½-½	the game ends in a draw
0-1	the game ends in a win for Black
(n)	nth match game
(D)	see next diagram

Bibliography

Books

Nunn's Chess Openings, John Nunn, Graham Burgess, John Emms and Joe
    Gallagher (Everyman/Gambit 1999)
Encyclopaedia of Chess Openings Volume C (Šahovski Informator 1997)
The Bishop's Opening, T.D. Harding (Batsford 1973)
The Complete Vienna, Mikhail Tseitlin and Igor Glazkov (Batsford 1995)
The King's Gambit, Neil McDonald (Batsford 1998)
Winning With the King's Gambit, Joe Gallagher (Batsford 1992)
Play the King's Gambit: Volume 1 King's Gambit Accepted, Y. Estrin and
    I.B. Glazkov (Pergamon 1982)
The Scotch Game, Peter Wells (Batsford 1998)
New Ideas in the Four Knights, John Nunn (Batsford 1993)
The Italian Game, Tim Harding and George Botterill (Batsford 1977)
The Two Knights Defence, Yakov Estrin (Batsford 1983)
Understanding the Open Games (Except Ruy Lopez), Andy Soltis,
    Edmar Mednis, Jack Peters and William Hartston (RHM 1980)
101 Chess Opening Surprises, Graham Burgess (Gambit 1998)
A Startling Chess Opening Repertoire, Chris Baker (Cadogan 1998)
The Oxford Companion to Chess, David Hooper and Kenneth Whyld
    (Oxford University Press 1996)

Periodicals

Informator
ChessBase Magazine
The Week in Chess
British Chess Magazine
Chess Monthly

Introduction

It's just typical isn't it? You've got your favourite defence to Ruy Lopez all sorted out, be it the Schliemann, the Zaitsev, the Open, the Marshall or any one of numerous Anti-Spanish systems. But what actually happens? How often do you actually get your intended defence? I imagine your answer could well be "not very often, because most of my opponents surprise me earlier on with a menacing-looking gambit or some other peculiar opening". If you hear yourself thinking just that, then you're just the sort of chess-player this book is aimed at. *Play the Open Games as Black* is primarily a book for players who have a defence to the Lopez, but are annoyed by all those other little variations that White can play. And we are talking about a real A-Z of openings here. From the Allgaier Gambit through to the Zukertort-Burger Variation, there are countless different variations considered in this book, with (hopefully) at least one more than satisfactory line against each of them for Black.

When writing this book I've tried as hard as possible to provide a black repertoire for both the aggressive and also the more positionally minded player. Against many openings there will be a choice of two or possibly

three lines to play. When I have only included one defence, then it's because I'm confident that its reliability and diversity should be enough to satisfy Black.

What is an Open Game?
Perhaps I should clarify the definition of *Open Games*. In general terms, *open games* are types of positions which are typified by clear lines, relatively few pawns and great activity for the pieces. More specifically, *Open Games* means the group of openings that begin 1 e4 e5. In this book I present a repertoire for Black against all Open Games, with the exception of the Ruy Lopez.

Characteristics of Open Games
Open Games are distinguished by rapid development, open lines, early exchanges in the centre, early attacks on the king and plenty of tactical play. This is the main reason that 1 e4 e5 openings are so well suited to white and black players of the attacking persuasion. I would add that Open Games are very popular among junior players, who can benefit greatly by sharpening their tactical skills in tactical openings. Many of the best players begin in this fashion.

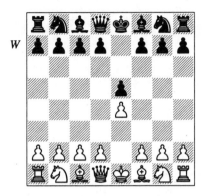

If we take a look at the diagram above, we can see already that both sides can develop their queen and king's bishop onto active squares. Indeed, one of the very first tricks we discover is contained in the moves ♕h5, ♗c4 and hopefully ♕xf7#! If White were to play an early d4 as well, then the c1-bishop will also come into play very quickly. If Black replies with ...exd4, then already we see the centre starting to clear and become more open.

How this book is set out

In Chapters 1-6 we deal with all White's second-move alternatives to 2 ♘f3, the most important of which are the Vienna Game (2 ♘c3) and the 'romantic' King's Gambit (2 f4). The King's Gambit in particular is an opening that often frightens off prospective

1...e5 players. Hopefully a study of Chapters 4-6 should have Black licking his lips in anticipation of his next King's Gambit challenge!

Chapters 7-13 deal with offbeat lines such as the Ponziani, the Göring Gambit and the Belgrade Gambit, along with the more respected Four Knights Game. Probably the most significant chapter in this section is the one on the Scotch Opening, which has become more popular at all levels since its big seal of approval from Garry Kasparov.

Finally Chapters 14-18 deal with the Italian Game and my recommendation of the daring Two Knights Defence. In these chapters the variations are very rich in tactical play and we experience the delights of studying such lines as the legendary Max Lange.

Before we start on our long trek through the variations, I would say that the main thing to remember is that these openings are just as much fun for Black as they are for White. So much so, perhaps, that we could see all those white players running back to their Ruy Lopez!

Finally, I would like to thank Graham Burgess and John Nunn for some much-needed advice and Mike Read for his analytical help.

1 Rare Second Moves for White

1 e4 e5 *(D)*

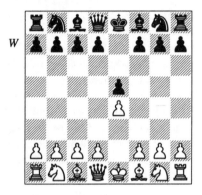

In this first chapter we deal with a considerable catalogue of wild and not so wonderful second-move alternatives for White. Against most of these openings there is no real need to learn a 'book' response; simple sensible play by Black should be sufficient to reach a very playable middlegame. It's unlikely that any of these lines are going to become fashionable (if they were going to make it at all, they would have done so by now). There is one possible exception, the relatively new Portuguese Opening (Line G), though even this is unlikely to become as popular as its mirror image (1 d4 d5 2 ♗g5!?).

Anyway, without further ado, here's the list of second moves considered in this chapter:

A:	**2 ♘e2**	8
B:	**2 c3!?**	8
C:	**2 d3**	9
D:	**2 g3?!**	9
E:	**2 c4**	9
F:	**2 a3!?**	10
G:	**2 ♗b5!?**	10

A)

2 ♘e2

This is Alapin's Opening. The idea is to support the advance f2-f4, but Black can react quickly in the centre. After 2...♘f6 3 f4 ♘xe4 4 d3 ♘c5 5 fxe5 d5! 6 d4 ♘e6, 7 ♘f4 c5 8 ♘c3 cxd4 9 ♘cxd5 ♘c6 left Black better in Alapin-Rubinstein, Vienna 1908. 7 c3 is stronger, but Black can still secure a comfortable game with 7...c5 8 ♗e3 ♘c6.

B)

2 c3

This move, aiming for a kind of Accelerated Ponziani, isn't so bad and it was once played by Paul Morphy. Once again Black's best response is to react aggressively in the centre:

a) 2...d5 3 exd5 (if White plays 3 ♘f3, then 3...dxe4 4 ♘xe5 ♕d5 is equal, while 3...♘c6 transposes to Chapter 8) 3...♕xd5 4 d4 ♘c6 5 ♘f3 exd4 (5...♗g4!?) 6 cxd4 ♗g4, and we reach a position discussed in Chapter 9, Line A.

b) 2...♘f6 3 d4 ♘xe4 (3...d5 is also playable; for example, 4 exd5 exd4 {or 4...♕xd5} 5 ♕xd4 ♕xd5) 4 dxe5 and now Morphy-Bottin, Paris 1858 continued 4...♗c5? 5 ♕g4 ♘xf2? 6 ♕xg7 ♖f8 7 ♗g5 f6 8 exf6 ♖xf6 9 ♗xf6 ♗e7 10 ♕g8+ 1-0. Much stronger for Black is the liberating 4...d5. After 5 exd6 ♘xd6 6 ♘f3 ♗e7 7 ♗d3 ♘c6 8 0-0 ♗g4 Black had no problems in MacLeod-Delmar, USA 1889.

C)

2 d3

After this innocuous move, Black has many reasonable moves, including 2...♘c6 and 2...♗c5. After 2...♘f6 3 ♘f3 ♘c6 we reach Chapter 7, while White's only way to make things a little exciting is via 2...♘f6 3 f4!? ♘c6:

a) 4 ♘c3 ♗b4! 5 fxe5 ♘xe5 6 ♘f3 ♕e7 7 ♗f4 ♘g6 8 ♗g5 d5 was fine for Black in Vorotnikov-Berkovich, Moscow 1990.

b) 4 ♘f3 *(D)*.

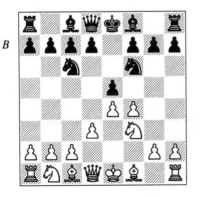

Older theory led me to believe that 4...d5!? was strong for Black, based on the idea 5 fxe5 dxe4! 6 exf6 exf3 7 ♕xf3 ♘d4! 8 ♕e4+ ♗e6 9 fxg7?! ♗xg7 10 ♘a3 0-0, when Black has an awesome position. However, the simple 5 exd5! is a tougher nut to crack, and I can't come up with anything useful after 5...♘xd5 6 fxe5 ♗g4 7 c3!, as both 7...♘xe5 8 ♕a4+ ♕d7 9 ♕e4! and 7...♗xf3 8 ♕xf3 ♘xe5 9 ♕e4 ♕e7 10 d4 seem to favour White. Going back to the position after 4 ♘f3, it's now clear to me that Black should cut out any nonsense with 4...exf4! 5 ♗xf4 and only then 5...d5!, when Black may already be a bit better, e.g. 6 e5 ♘h5 7 ♗g5 ♗e7 8 ♗xe7 ♕xe7.

D)

2 g3

With 2 g3 White is aiming to fianchetto his bishop without any preparatory moves. This could easily transpose into other lines after, for instance, 2...♘f6 3 ♗g2 d5 4 exd5 ♘xd5 5 ♘c3 (see Chapter 3). However, Black has a much stronger reply in the immediate 2...d5!; for example, 3 exd5 ♕xd5 4 ♘f3 ♗g4 5 ♗e2 (5 ♗g2 loses to 5...e4 6 ♘c3 exf3!) 5...♘c6 6 ♘c3 ♕d7 and Black will continue with ...0-0-0, leaving White's bishop looking rather silly on e2.

E)

2 c4

This looks plain ugly, but before I condemn it out of hand I have to admit there is some reasoning to the move. White aims to achieve a clamp in the centre and intends to follow up with moves such as ♘ge2, g3, ♗g2 and d3, as in Botvinnik's system in the English Opening. However, Black is better placed here to exploit the weakness of the d4-square. Following 2...♘c6 3 ♘c3 ♗c5 4 d3 d6 5 ♘ge2 ♘ge7, intending ...f5, it's White who has to think about how to equalize.

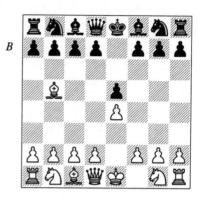

F)

2 a3

The one positive thing you could say about 2 a3, is that it's not as bad as it looks, as a2-a3 generally has at least some value in Open Games. Naturally Black has many reasonable ways to play, and depending on your own repertoire as White, you have the choice of 2...♘f6, 2...♘c6, 2...♗c5 or even 2...f5!?. One word of warning to would-be Scotch Game players, though. After 2...♘f6 3 ♘c3 d5?! 4 exd5 ♘xd5, White has the move 5 ♕h5!, which, in contrast to the similar line 1 e4 e5 2 ♘f3 ♘c6 3 d4 exd4 4 ♘xd4 ♕h4!?, is much stronger as 2 a3 has eliminated ...♘b4 ideas. If one wants to play as in the Scotch, then the move-order 3...♘c6 4 ♘f3 d5 should be preferred (see Chapter 12).

G)

2 ♗b5 (D)

This is the so-called Portuguese Opening. The idea behind this bizarre-looking move is to get the bishop 'out of the way' and prevent an early advance of Black's d-pawn, while retaining flexibility about where to develop the g1-knight. For example, if Black were to try to steer the game into Lopez territory with 2...a6 3 ♗a4 ♘c6, then White could surprise him with 4 f4!?, or 4 ♘e2, planning 0-0 and f4. I wouldn't worry about 2 ♗b5 too much. It hasn't travelled too well, so unless you're planning to play some chess on your holidays in Portugal, you're quite unlikely to come across it. I should add, however, that it's recently received some good reviews in the popular chess press, so we'll have to treat it with some respect. Indeed, I would go as far as to say that White has excellent chances of equality in this line!

2...c6

Attacking the bishop and thus gaining a tempo. Why not indeed?

3 ♗a4

The only sensible choice. Obviously 3 ♗c4 would run into an early ...d5.

3...♘f6 4 ♘c3 (D)

The other main choice for White in this position is 4 ♕e2. Black should continue with 4...♗c5 5 ♘f3, when 5...0-0 6 0-0 d6 is solid, while 5...d5!? led to one of shortest black wins between two titled players. Vescovi-I.Sokolov, Malmö 1995 continued 6 exd5 0-0 7 ♘xe5 ♖e8 8 c3 ♗xf2+! 9 ♔f1 ♗g4 10 ♕xf2 ♖xe5 11 ♔g1 ♕e7 and White threw in the towel. Not the best publicity job for this opening.

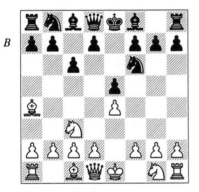

4...b5!?

This move is the 'main line', but I rather like the look of the natural 4...♗c5, playing as in the Italian Game, but with colours reversed. This seems to give Black a very comfortable game; for example:

a) 5 ♘ge2 ♘g4!? (5...0-0 6 0-0 d5 7 exd5 cxd5 8 d4 exd4 9 ♘xd4 ♗g4 looks equal) 6 d4 exd4 7 ♘xd4 ♕h4! 8 g3 ♕h3 and White has some trouble completing his development.

b) 5 ♘f3 b5 6 ♗b3 d6 7 d3 a5! and we've actually reached a well-known position in the Giuoco Piano (1 e4 e5 2 ♘f3 ♘c6 3 ♗c4 ♗c5 4 c3 ♘f6 5 b4 ♗b6 6 d3 d6 7 a4), but with colours reversed. Theory holds this position to be level; for example, 8 a4 b4 9 ♘e2 0-0 10 ♘g3 ♘bd7 11 0-0 ♗a7 12 c3 bxc3 13 bxc3 d5 is equal. This position was reached, with colours reversed, in Psakhis-Schüssler, Lugano 1988.

5 ♗b3 b4

Once again Black should consider 5...♗c5!?, with lines similar to the note above.

6 ♘a4 ♘xe4 7 ♘f3

7 ♕e2 d5 8 d3 ♘f6 9 ♕xe5+ ♗e7 10 ♗f4 0-0 11 ♘f3 c5 12 0-0 ♘c6 13 ♕c7 ♕xc7 14 ♗xc7 ♗a6 was slightly better for Black in Nogueira-Pereyra Arcija, Mar del Plata 1996. Black has some annoying pressure on the queenside.

7...d5

Giving back the pawn is the safest way. White has reasonable compensation for the pawn after 7...d6 8 d4 exd4 9 ♕xd4 d5 10 0-0, as it's hard for Black to finish his kingside development.

8 d3 ♘f6 9 ♘xe5 ♗d6 10 d4 0-0 11 0-0 ♘bd7

We've reached a roughly level position. 12 ♘xc6 can be answered by 12...♕c7, regaining the pawn. Instead Damaso-Tisdall, Manila OL 1992 continued 12 ♗f4 ♗xe5 13 dxe5 ♘e8 14 ♖c1 ♗b7 15 c3 ♕e7 16 ♖e1 ♘c7 17 ♕h5 ♘e6 18 ♗d2 a5 with a balanced middlegame.

2 The Centre Game and the Danish Gambit

1 e4 e5 2 d4 exd4 *(D)*

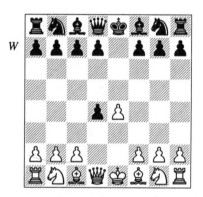

The Centre Game (1 e4 e5 2 d4 exd4 3 ♕xd4) came to prominence in the late 19th century. When it was utilized (mainly by Paulsen and Schallopp) in the 1881 Berlin Tournament, in twelve games White scored a very creditable eight points. However, once the early shock had warn off, Black soon found ways of dealing with White's opening, which does after all flout the general principle of not moving your queen early in the opening.

That said, it would be dangerous to dismiss the Centre Game as merely trash. The first time I realized that this opening should be taken with any degree of seriousness was when a young

Russian by the name of Alexander Morozevich scored a sensational 9½/10 in the very last Lloyds Bank Masters in London in 1994. On the way he used the Centre Game to beat Grandmaster Mark Hebden in under 30 moves, quite an achievement in itself considering Hebden has played 1...e5 all his life.

The Danish Gambit (1 e4 e5 2 d4 exd4 3 c3) started to become popular at the beginning of the 20th century and was a particular favourite of Jacques Mieses, who scored some spectacularly quick wins with it. White sacrifices either one or two pawns in order to obtain an advantage in development and attacking chances against the black king. Despite the fact that virtually no modern grandmasters venture to play the Danish Gambit, the compensation if Black accepts is very reasonable and it's certainly risky to try to hang on to the two-pawn advantage. Its lack of popularity has probably more to do with the fact that Black, if he wishes, has a chance to transpose into the Göring Gambit Declined (see Chapter 9). As we shall see later, this variation is known to be quite inoffensive at the very best.

A Quick Summary of the Recommended Lines

As both the Centre Game and the Danish Gambit are seen very infrequently (if my memory serves me right, I've yet to face the Centre Game in a serious game), I'm recommending only one line against each (although defenders against the Danish have the option of transposing to the Göring). Line A is a study of Black's main defence to the Centre Game, concentrating on lines with ...♗e7, rather than the also playable ...♗b4. Despite the slight extravagance of moving the queen so early, it's hard to believe that White can be worse, but Line A shows that in fact it is White who seems to be chasing equality.

Line B concentrates on Black's main defence to the Danish, which has been known for many years now. Black immediately sacrifices one of the two pawns back and offers a second pawn as well. White can either accept this and transpose into a level ending, or decline and reach a complex middlegame position.

The Theory of the Centre Game and the Danish Gambit

1 e4 e5 2 d4 exd4

Now we discuss the following variations:

A: 3 ♕xd4   13
B: 3 c3   15

A)
3 ♕xd4 *(D)*

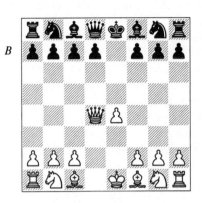

3...♘c6 4 ♕e3

This is by far the most popular queen retreat, although there is something to be said for 4 ♕a4, treating the position like a Scandinavian Defence, but with the extra tempo for e2-e4. Having said that, Black can easily reach a comfortable position after 4...♘f6 5 ♗g5 ♗e7 6 ♘c3 0-0 7 ♘f3 d6 8 0-0-0 ♗d7 9 ♕c4 h6 10 ♗h4 ♗e6 11 ♕e2 ♘d7 12 ♗xe7 ♕xe7, as in Szabolcsi-P.Lukacs, Budapest 1994. 4...♗c5 also looks sensible; for example, 5 ♘f3 ♘f6 6 ♗g5 h6 7 ♗h4 d6 8 ♘c3 ♗d7 9 ♗b5 a6 10 ♗xc6 ♗xc6 11 ♕c4 g5! 12 ♗g3 b5 and Black was fine in Bellon-Rivera, Santa Clara Guillermo Garcia mem 1998.

4 ♕d2 is a suggestion of Bronstein, with a plan of ♗d3, f4, ♘f3, 0-0, b3 and ♗b2. This works very well if Black has no moves, but otherwise 4...♘f6 5 ♗d3 d5 is a reasonable antidote.

4...♘f6 5 ♗d2

This move-order discourages lines with ...♗b4, but as I'm recommending 5...♗e7 this doesn't really matter. We transpose to the main line following 5 ♘c3 ♗e7 6 ♗d2, while after 5 ♘c3 ♗e7, 6 ♘c4 0-0 7 ♗d2 d6 reaches the note to Black's 6th move. Also possible is 6 ♕g3, but 6...♘b4! 7 ♗d3 d6 8 ♕xg7 (8 ♘f3?? ♘h5 is very embarrassing for the white queen) 8...♖g8 9 ♕h6 ♖xg2 favours Black.

Another line I should mention here is 5 e5!? ♘g4 6 ♕e4, when 6...♘gxe5!? 7 f4 d5 8 ♕e2 ♗g4 9 ♘f3 ♗c5 looks good for Black. In addition to this possibility, Black can play the liberating continuation 6...d5! 7 exd6+ ♗e6 and now:

a) 8 dxc7 ♕d1+! (8...♕xc7 also appears good, but the text-move gets the nod, just because of its aesthetic and possible surprise value) 9 ♔xd1 ♘xf2+ 10 ♔e1 ♘xe4 and Black will round up the c7-pawn.

b) 8 ♗a6 ♕xd6 9 ♗xb7 ♕b4+ 10 ♕xb4 ♘xb4 11 ♘a3 ♖b8 12 ♗f3 ♗c5 13 ♗xg4 ♗xg4 with good counterplay for the pawn, V.Scherbakov-Ravinsky, Moscow 1955.

5...♗e7 6 ♘c3 d5

6...0-0 7 ♗c4 is also important, since this position can be reached via the move-order 5 ♘c3 ♗e7 6 ♗c4 0-0 7 ♗d2. Then 7...d6 8 0-0-0 ♗e6 9 ♗xe6 fxe6 10 ♕h3 ♕c8 looks roughly equal. After 11 ♘ge2 b5! 12 ♘g3 ♘e5 13 ♗e1 ♔h8 14 ♘ce2 c5 Black's attack proved to be quite dangerous in

the game Borge-L.B.Hansen, Danish Ch 1996.

7 exd5 ♘xd5 *(D)*

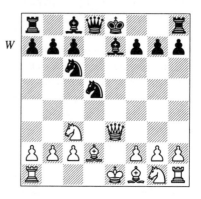

8 ♕g3

Perhaps White's safest bet is the simple 8 ♘xd5. *ECO* gives Black an edge after 8...♕xd5 9 ♘e2 ♗g4 10 ♘f4 ♕d7 11 f3 0-0-0 12 0-0-0 (12 fxg4? ♗h4+ 13 ♔d1 ♖he8 14 ♕d3 ♕xg4+ 15 ♗e2 ♖xe2! 16 ♕xe2 ♕xf4 17 ♔c1 ♘d4 is winning for Black) 12...♗f5 13 ♗d3 but it's very difficult to believe this position is anything but dead level.

8...♘cb4!

The only recent high-profile Centre Game occurred in Adams-Anand, Linares PCA Ct (6) 1994, which continued 8...♘xc3 9 ♗xc3 ♗f6 10 ♗xf6 ♕xf6 11 0-0-0 0-0 12 ♘f3, and then 12...♗f5?! 13 ♕f4 ♖ae8 14 ♗d3 ♗xd3 15 ♕xf6 gxf6 16 ♖xd3 gave White an edge due to Black's poor kingside structure. 12...♗e6 is an improvement for Black, but this may all be academic due to the text-move. Another enticing idea is 8...♗d6!? 9 ♕xg7 ♗e5 10 ♕h6 ♘cb4!? (this is Hübner's recommendation; in his opinion White stands better after 10...♘xc3 11 ♗xc3 ♗xc3+ 12 bxc3 ♕e7+ 13 ♕e3 ♕xe3+ 14 fxe3, whereas Nunn's assessment is equality after 14...0-0 15 ♘f3 ♖e8 16 ♔f2 ♘e5; the truth is probably somewhere in between) 11 ♗b5+ (Black is better after 11 ♘xd5 ♘xc2+ 12 ♔d1 ♘xa1 13 ♗c4 ♗e6 and 11 ♗d3 ♘xd3+ 12 cxd3 ♘b4) 11...♗d7, when it's true that White is in big trouble after 12 ♗xd7+? ♕xd7 13 ♘xd5 ♘xc2+ 14 ♔d1 ♕xd5 15 ♔xc2 ♕c4+. Unfortunately 12 ♗g5! looks a much stronger move, against which I can find no reasonable response.

9 ♘xd5

9 0-0-0 ♘xc3 10 bxc3 ♘xa2+ 11 ♔b1 ♗e6 can only be good for Black; for example, 12 c4 ♘b4 13 ♗e2 c5! 14 ♗xb4 ♕b6 15 ♕xg7 ♕xb4+ 16 ♔c1 ♖f8 and White's king has no cover. 9 ♖c1 guards the immediate threat, but Black must be better after a simple developing move such as 9...0-0.

9...♕xd5 10 ♗xb4

Now is not the time for greediness with 10 ♕xc7?. This gluttony can be punished by 10...♗g4! (threatening ...♖c8 and ...♕e5+, etc.) 11 ♗xb4 ♗xb4+ 12 c3 ♖d8! 13 ♗b5+ ♕xb5 14 cxb4 0-0 and White will be lucky to reach the endgame alive.

10...♕e4+ 11 ♘e2 ♕xb4+ 12 ♕c3

Black's bishop-pair guarantees him a small edge, Blanco Fernandez-Otero, Villa Clara 1995.

B)

3 c3 dxc3

The more solidly inclined have a fail-safe option here with 3...d5, which transposes to Chapter 9 after 4 exd5 ♕xd5 5 cxd4 ♘c6 6 ♘f3 ♗g4.

4 ♗c4

White sacrifices a second pawn. 4 ♘xc3 ♘c6 5 ♘f3 transposes to Chapter 9.

4...cxb2 5 ♗xb2 (D)

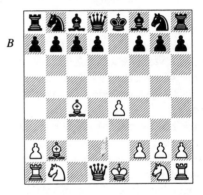

5...d5!

Naturally Black can also try to hold on to his two-pawn advantage, but this entails some risk. The text-move is the most reliable method of meeting the Danish Gambit. Black immediately offers back the pawns.

6 ♗xd5 ♘f6 7 ♘c3

Playing in true gambit fashion. The major alternative here is 7 ♗xf7+ ♔xf7 8 ♕xd8 ♗b4+ 9 ♕d2 ♗xd2+ 10 ♘xd2, leading to an endgame position equal in both material and position. However, the presence of two-pawn majorities on either wing unbalances the position sufficiently for both players to be able to play for a win. After 10...♖e8, 11 f3 ♘c6 12 ♖c1 ♗e6 13 a3 ♖ad8 left Black well coordinated in Nyholm-Tartakower, Baden-Baden 1914. Keres gives the alternative 11 ♘gf3 ♘c6 12 0-0, when 12...♗g4 gives a roughly level position.

7...♗e7

It goes without saying that Black must be a little careful here. For example, 7...♘xd5 8 ♘xd5 c6? allows 9 ♘f6+!.

8 ♕b3

Hector-Schüssler, Malmö 1985 continued 8 ♕e2!? ♘xd5 9 ♘xd5 c6! 10 ♘xe7 ♕xe7 11 ♗xg7 ♖g8 12 ♗b2 ♖xg2 13 ♕e3, and after 13...♕g5 14 ♕xg5 ♖xg5 15 ♘f3 ♖g4 16 0-0-0 Black had succeeded in exchanging queens and the onus was on White to prove he had something for the pawn. When I first looked at this game I thought that Black could improve with the sneaky 13...♗f5, when 14 0-0-0 ♕xe4 15 ♕xe4+ ♗xe4 16 ♖e1 f5! and 14 exf5 ♕xe3+ 15 fxe3 ♖xb2 clearly favour Black. However, White has the equally sneaky 14 ♔f1!, when 14...♗xe4 15 ♖e1 f5 16 ♕d4 looks very dangerous. However, 13...♖g4!? 14 f3 ♖g2 looks possible.

8...♘xd5 9 ♘xd5 c6

This knight must be shifted. 9...0-0? 10 ♕g3 is extremely unpleasant for Black.

10 ♘xe7 ♕xe7 11 ♗xg7

Otherwise Black will play ...0-0 and remain a pawn to the good.

11...♖g8 12 ♗b2 ♕xe4+ 13 ♘e2 *(D)*

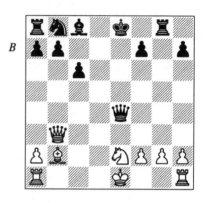

13...♘a6!

An improvement over the timid 13...♕e7?! 14 0-0! ♗e6 15 ♕a4 ♖g4 16 f4 ♗d5 17 ♘g3 ♕c5+? (17...♕e3+ is better) 18 ♔h1, when White's king has been driven to safety while Black's is in deep trouble, I.Firnhaber-Zuckmann, corr 1976.

The text-move, 13...♘a6, is a multipurpose move, preparing ...♕b4+, ...♘b4 and ...♘c5. For example, 14 0-0-0 ♘c5 15 ♕a3 ♗f5! 16 ♕xc5 ♕b1+ 17 ♔d2 ♕xb2+ 18 ♔e1 ♗e6 is clearly better for Black. White can prevent the knight entering the game, but only at a cost of removing the bishop from the long diagonal with 14 ♗a3. However, after 14...b5, preparing ...♗e6, the onus is still on White to prove he has something for the pawn.

3 The Vienna Game (and the Bishop's Opening)

1 e4 e5 2 ♘c3 *(D)*

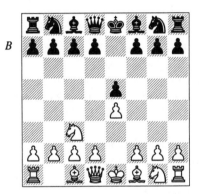

The Vienna Game is an especially powerful weapon at club level. On a personal level, I always had problems when I faced it as a junior, so much so that I started playing with the white pieces myself. I think the reason for its success is that many players do not really know the theory very well (perhaps it's quite far down on the 'things to do' list behind 'learn the Ruy Lopez', 'find a defence to the Giuoco Piano' and 'watch TV'). Another interesting point is that the some of so-called main defences are actually more favourable for White than the so-called rare defences. My recommended line of 2...♘f6 3 ♗c4 ♘c6 4

d3 ♗b4! only makes it into the 'unusual lines' section of *The Complete Vienna* (Tseitlin and Glazkov), along with 4...♘a5!?, and yet at grandmaster level, these two defences are considered Black's most reliable.

The point is that Black really needs to know what he's doing against the Vienna, otherwise it's very easy to drift into a bad position early on. Even playing normal-looking developing moves may not be enough. Look how easy it is for White in the following miniature.

Lane – S. Jackson
British Ch (Plymouth) 1989

1 e4 e5 2 ♗c4 ♘f6 3 d3 ♘c6 4 ♘c3

The game starts as a Bishop's Opening, but now transposes to the Vienna. In the theory section I recommend 4...♗b4!, pinning the c3-knight and preparing ...d5. The move chosen here also looks very natural, but it allows White just what he wants.

4...♗c5 5 f4 d6 6 ♘f3

Now we have another transposition, this time to the King's Gambit Declined (which can be reached via 1 e4 e5 2 f4 ♗c5 3 ♘f3 d6 4 ♘c3 ♘f6 5

♗c4 ♘c6 6 d3). It's no wonder Black often gets confused against this opening! Theory states that White has a slight advantage in this line. Moreover, it's easy for White to play and just as easy for Black to go wrong. Just witness what happens here.

6...♗g4

Again this looks the most natural.

7 ♘a4! ♗xf3 8 ♕xf3 ♘d4 9 ♕d1 b5 *(D)*

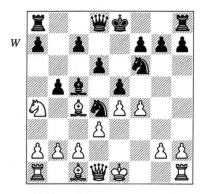

10 ♗xf7+!

This is all still theory.

10...♔xf7 11 ♘xc5 exf4?

You can understand why Black didn't want to delve into the complexities of 11...dxc5 12 fxe5 ♘d7 13 c3 ♘e6 14 0-0+ ♔e8 15 d4. Nevertheless, this is the best chance (although theory still prefers White).

12 ♘b3 ♘e6 13 0-0 g5 14 g3! fxg3 15 ♗xg5!

Now the attack down the f-file will be unbearable.

15...gxh2+ 16 ♔h1 ♘xg5 17 ♕h5+ ♔e7 18 ♕xg5 ♖f8 19 ♘d4 *(D)*

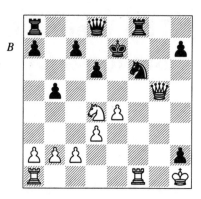

Black is totally busted. Why play the Ruy Lopez when you can reach such a position after only 19 moves?

19...♕e8 20 e5 dxe5 21 ♕xe5+ ♔d7 22 ♕f5+ ♔d6 23 ♖ae1 1-0

I scored many similar victories with the Vienna in my youth. I even succeeded in bamboozling a young Vishy Anand with it. However, as I progressed to playing high-class opposition on a regular basis, the flaws of the opening started to show. Players' choices of openings are very often influenced by an individual game and the following game made a great impression on me. In a way the roles are reversed from the previous game. White plays natural moves and doesn't make any obvious errors, but is still convincingly outplayed.

Emms – Condie
British Ch (Southampton) 1986

1 e4 e5 2 ♗c4 ♘f6 3 ♘c3 ♘c6 4 d3 ♗b4! 5 ♘f3 d5 6 exd5 ♘xd5 7 0-0

♗xc3 8 bxc3 ♗g4 9 ♖e1 0-0 10 ♗d2 ♖e8 *(D)*

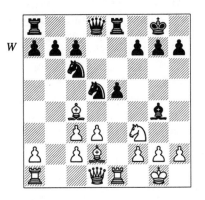

White has the two bishops, but in return Black is wonderfully centralized and has acquired the so-called 'small centre' (the e5-pawn versus the d3-pawn). This extra space makes Black's game-plan very straightforward. Simply more centralization!

11 ♖b1 ♘b6 12 ♗b3 ♕f6 13 ♖e4 ♗h5 14 ♕e2 ♗g6 15 ♖e3 ♖e7 16 ♗c1 ♕d6 17 ♘h4 ♘d5 18 ♘xg6 hxg6 19 ♗xd5 ♕xd5 20 ♖b3 ♖ae8 21 f3 b6 22 ♕e1 ♘a5 23 c4 ♕d6 24 ♖b1 ♘c6 *(D)*

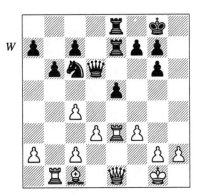

25 c3 f5

Now I've really set my stall out for defence, but Black's pieces are totally harmonious. The rest of the game was not a happy experience.

26 ♖b5 ♘b8 27 ♖d5 ♕f6 28 c5 ♖e6 29 cxb6 axb6 30 ♖b5 ♘a6 31 ♗a3 c5 32 c4 e4!? 33 fxe4 fxe4 34 ♗b2? exd3! 35 ♗xf6 ♖xe3 36 ♕h4 d2 37 ♖b1 ♖e1+ 38 ♔f2 ♖xb1 39 ♗xg7 ♔xg7 0-1

Now I'm sure that objectively White is no worse after the opening moves, and I'm also sure that my play in the middlegame could be improved somewhat, but after this game, I never really believed in this variation any more. Black's play just seemed too simple and too effective. You could argue that this is only one variation of the Vienna, but I'm confident what I'm recommending against 3 g3 and the 3 f4 will also stand Black in good stead.

A Quick Summary of the Recommended Lines

Line A (2 ♘c3 ♘f6 3 g3) is White's most positional approach to the Vienna. I've advocated the popular 3...d5 against this system this system. In my opinion, lines with ♘f3 (Line A2) present Black with slightly more problems than ones with ♘e2 (Line A1). Line A2 is also important as it can also be reached via the Four Knights Game.

In Line B I've recommended the move-order 2 ♘c3 ♘f6 3 ♗c4 ♘c6 4 d3 ♗b4!, which caused me so many problems when I ventured to play the Vienna. White has three main choices, with Lines B2 and B3 posing Black more questions than the less popular B1.

Line C deals with 2 ♘c3 ♘f6 3 f4 d5. Here, Lines C1 and C2 don't cause Black any problems at all. However, Line C3 is extremely tricky and has even caught out very experienced players. Finally, C4 gives us the main variation of the Vienna (2 ♘c3 ♘f6 3 f4 d5 4 fxe5 ♘xe4 5 ♘f3). Here I've recommended the reliable 5...♗c5, which seems to give Black a reasonably comfortable position.

The Theory of the Vienna Game

1 e4 e5 2 ♘c3

Closely related to the Vienna Game is the Bishop's Opening, which on another occasion would deserve a chapter on its own, if it weren't for the fact that all my recommendations transpose into other variations. After 2 ♗c4 ♘f6 we have the following lines:

a) 3 ♘c3 directly transposes to the Vienna (see Line B).

b) 3 d4 exd4 4 ♘f3 (4 e5 d5! is good for Black) 4...♘c6 gives us the Two Knights Defence (see Chapters 15-17).

c) 3 f4 ♘xe4 (for 3...exf4 see Chapter 5) 4 d3 ♘d6 5 ♗b3 and now Black can play:

c1) After 5...e4 Larsen gives 6 dxe4 ♘xe4 7 ♗xf7+ ♔xf7 8 ♕d5+ ♔e8 9 ♕xe4+ ♕e7 10 ♘c3 c6 as better for Black, although if White is going to play 3 f4, he might as well go all-in with 6 ♘c3 exd3 7 ♕xd3.

c2) 5...exf4 6 ♗xf4 ♗e7 7 ♘f3 0-0 8 0-0 ♘e8! 9 ♘c3 c6 10 ♕d2 d5 11 ♖ae1 ♗f6 and, with the b3-bishop blocked out of the game, it's hard to see any compensation for the pawn.

d) 3 ♕e2 ♘c6 4 c3 ♗c5 looks very comfortable for Black, since the white queen has committed herself too early.

e) 3 d3 ♘c6 4 f4 (4 ♘c3 transposes to Line B, and 4 ♘f3 to Chapter 14, Line C) 4...d5!? (after 4...exf4, for 5 ♘f3 d5 6 exd5 ♘xd5 and 5 ♗xf4 d5 6 exd5 ♘xd5 see note 'c' to White's 4th move in Chapter 5 and 5 ♘c3 ♗b4 leads to the note to White's 5th move in Line B) 5 exd5 ♘xd5 6 fxe5 (or 6 ♕e2 ♗e6 7 fxe5 ♘d4!) 6...♗c5 (6...♘xe5 7 ♕e2 is annoying) 7 ♘f3 ♗g4 and Black has good play for the pawn.

2...♘f6 *(D)*

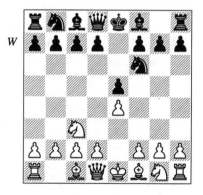

Now we look at White's three main choices:

A: 3 g3   21
B: 3 ♗c4   24
C: 3 f4   30

A)

3 g3 (D)

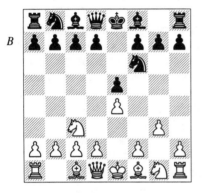

3...d5 4 exd5 ♘xd5 5 ♗g2 ♘xc3
5...♗e6 is playable, but the text-move is considered to be more reliable.

6 bxc3 ♗d6
Bolstering the e-pawn and preparing to castle is Black's most reliable way to play this position. If you're looking for more adventure, then 6...♗c5 may be worth a try. Despite its lack of popularity it looks quite playable; for example:

a) After 7 ♕h5!?, 7...♕f6 8 ♘f3 ♘c6 9 0-0 g6 10 ♕h6 ♗g4 11 ♘g5! ♗f5 12 ♘e4 ♗xe4 13 ♗xe4 was better for White in Arnason-Emms, Kopavogur 1994. After the game I decided that the simple 7...0-0 is more accurate;

for example, 8 ♘f3 ♘d7 and Black hasn't anything to fear from White's early queen move.

b) 7 ♘f3 e4!? 8 ♘d4!? (8 ♕e2 0-0! 9 ♘e5 ♕f6 10 ♗xe4 ♗xf2+! is good for Black; Tseitlin and Glazkov give only "8 ♘g5! ♕xg5 9 d4", but it's hard to believe that White has enough for the pawn after 9...♕f6 10 dxc5 ♕xc3+ 11 ♗d2 ♕c4!) 8...♗xd4 9 cxd4 ♕xd4 10 ♗a3, when White's raking bishops give him some compensation for the pawn. In Forster-Rocko, Plzen 1995 Black was soon in trouble after 10...♗d7?! 11 0-0 ♕a4 12 ♕c1 ♗c6 13 ♖b1 ♘a6 14 ♗h3 f6 15 ♗e6!, but 10...♘c6, planning ...♗f5 and/or ...♕a4, looks a sterner test of White's sacrifice.

c) 7 ♘e2 ♘c6 and now:

c1) 8 ♖b1 ♗e6! 9 0-0 (9 ♖xb7 ♗d5 10 ♗xd5 ♕xd5 11 0-0 ♗b6 traps the rook) 9...♗d5! (the exchange of bishops leaves White with weak light squares around his king) 10 d4 ♗b6 11 ♗a3 ♗xg2 12 ♔xg2 ♕d5+ 13 f3 0-0-0 and Black was doing very well in Corkett-Wells, British Ch (Plymouth) 1989. This was the game that first attracted me to 6...♗c5.

c2) 8 0-0 0-0 (ideally Black would like to follow Peter Wells's plan with 8...♗e6, which works well after 9 d3 ♗d5 or 9 ♖b1 ♗d5; however, my initial enthusiasm for this line was dampened somewhat by the discovery of the more direct 9 d4! exd4 10 cxd4 ♘xd4 11 ♗b2! ♘xe2+ 12 ♕xe2, when Black is in some trouble; e.g., 12...0-0 13

♗xg7!) 9 ♖b1 ♗b6 10 ♗a3 ♖e8 11 d3 ♗g4 12 h3 ♗e6 13 c4 ♖b8 14 ♔h2 ♕d7 and despite the prevention of ...♗d5, Black has quite a playable position, Erenska Radzewska-Sosnowska, Polish Cht 1981.

After 6...♗d6 we will look at two options for White:

A1: 7 ♘e2   22
A2: 7 ♘f3   22

A1)

7 ♘e2 0-0 8 0-0 ♘d7 9 d3 *(D)*

With White's knight placed on e2, he doesn't really have the set-up to justify advancing with 9 d4. In contrast to 7 ♘f3 lines, there's not enough pressure on Black's e5-pawn. After 9...c6 10 f4 exf4 11 ♗xf4 Black can hope to exploit the weak squares on the queenside with 11...♘b6!.

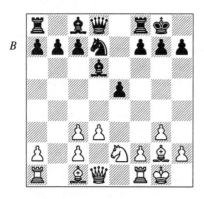

9...c6

Blocking the diagonal in this manner is Black's most solid choice. Tseitlin and Glazkov recommend 9...♖b8, with the plan of exchanging bishops

by ...b6 and ...♗b7. If this could be achieved, then Black would stand well, but 10 c4! b6 11 ♘c3 ♗b7 12 ♘d5! cuts across Black's plan, and maintains a small advantage for White.

10 f4 exf4 11 ♗xf4 ♘e5 12 ♖b1 ♖b8 13 c4

Spassky-Karpov, Tilburg 1979 now continued 13...♗g4 14 h3 ♗xe2 15 ♕xe2 ♘g6 16 ♗xd6 ♕xd6 17 ♕f2 f5 18 c5 ♕c7 19 ♖be1 with a minute plus for White. Black should instead consider 13...♘g6 14 ♗xd6 ♕xd6, which looks quite comfortable for Black.

A2)

7 ♘f3 0-0 8 0-0

This move keeps White's options open. After 8 ♖b1 Black should probably answer with 8...♘c6, which will transpose to the main line. If White wants to play lines with d2-d3, then it's probably more accurate to castle first, as the immediate 8 d3 gives Black the option of 8...♗d7!?, intending ...♗c6. For example, 9 0-0 ♗c6 10 a4 (or 10 ♖e1 ♘d7 11 ♖b1 b6 12 d4 exd4 13 cxd4 ♖e8 with a comfortable position for Black, Balashov-V.Kovačević, Karlovac 1979) 10...♘d7 11 d4 exd4 12 cxd4 ♗e4 13 c4 c5 14 d5 ♖e8 and Black is fine, Averbakh-Kholmov, USSR Ch 1964.

8...♘c6 *(D)*

8...♘d7 is another main move for Black here, but 8...♘c6 fits in with Black's repertoire quite nicely, as this position can also be reached via the Glek Variation of the Four Knights

Game (see note 'a' to White's 4th move in Chapter 13).

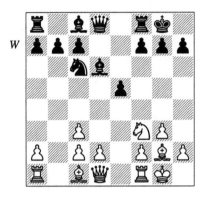

9 ♖b1

Adding pressure to the b7-pawn. The immediate 9 d4 is likely to transpose into the main line after either 9...h6 or 9...♖e8. An independent idea for White is to continue with the restrained 9 d3 ♗g4, and now:

a) 10 h3 ♗d7!? (or 10...♗h5 11 ♖b1 ♖b8 12 g4 ♗g6 13 ♘g5 ♕d7 14 ♗e3 b6 15 h4 h6 16 h5 ♗xh5 17 gxh5 hxg5 18 ♗xg5 with an unclear position, Gallagher-Campora, Biel 1996) 11 ♖b1 ♖b8 12 ♖e1 ♖e8 13 d4 h6 with equality, Makarychev-Vasiukov, Moscow 1981.

b) 10 ♗e3 f5!? 11 ♕b1 ♖b8 12 ♕b5 ♔h8 13 ♖fe1 f4 and Black has some attacking chances on the kingside, Conquest-Van der Sterren, Bern 1993.

9...♖b8

Lending support to the b7-pawn, although it's also possible to do without this move. 9...♖e8 10 d4 h6 11 ♖e1 (or

11 ♗e3 ♖b8 12 ♘d2 ♘a5 13 ♕h5 b6 14 ♖fe1 ♗b7 15 ♗xb7 ♖xb7 and Black is even a little better, Glek-Hector, Copenhagen 1995) 11...exd4 12 ♖xe8+ ♕xe8 13 cxd4 b6 14 ♖b3 ♗b7 15 ♖e3 ♕f8 resulted in a roughly balanced position in Glek-Hort, Bundesliga 1994/5.

10 d4 ♖e8

Along with 10...h6, this move was recommended by Tseitlin and Glazkov. For some reason 10...♗g4 has been a popular move here, but White has good chances to keep the advantage after both the simple 11 h3 ♗xf3 12 ♗xf3 and even 11 ♕d3. If Black wants to prevent something coming to g5, then 10...h6!? is sensible, with the following lines:

a) 11 ♖e1 ♕f6 12 ♘d2 and now 12...exd4? lost material to 13 ♗xc6 in Shaked-Morović, Groningen FIDE KO Wch 1997, but 12...♗f5! 13 ♘e4 ♕g6 is more than satisfactory for Black.

b) The immediate 11 ♘d2 may be more to the point. Now 11...♘a5, preventing ♘c4, worked for Black in Van Mil-Van der Sterren, Antwerp 1996. After 12 dxe5 ♗xe5, this game continued 13 ♖b5 ♗xc3 14 ♖d5 ♕e7 15 ♘b1? (15 ♘e4 looks better) 15...♗b4 16 a3 ♗c5 and Black consolidated his extra pawn. However, I can't find anything convincing against the stronger 13 ♕h5!, which plans to answer 13...♗xc3? with 14 ♘e4 ♕d4 15 ♕f3! winning a piece. Because of this it seems safer to develop with 11...♗f5.

Glek-Rozentalis, Bundesliga 1994/5 continued 12 ♘c4 ♕f6 13 ♘e3 exd4 (13...♗h7!? deserves attention) 14 ♘xf5 ♕xf5 15 cxd4 ♖fd8 16 ♗e3 (16 a3!?) 16...♘b4 17 c3 ♘d5 18 ♗d2 c6 19 ♖e1 b5 20 ♗e4 ♕f6 21 h4 b4 22 ♗xd5 cxd5 23 cxb4 ♕xd4 24 ♗e3 ♕xd1 25 ♖exd1 ♖xb4 26 ♖xb4 ♗xb4 27 ♗xa7 ♖a8 28 ♗e3 ♖xa2 29 ♖xd5 ♖a5 30 ♖d8+ ♔h7 31 ♔g2 ½-½.

11 ♘g5!?

Despite being given a '?!' by Tseitlin and Glazkov, I believe this to be the critical test of Black's position. Other moves don't make much impression:

a) 11 ♖e1 exd4 12 ♘xd4 ♘xd4 13 cxd4 b6 14 ♗e3 ♗f5 15 ♗c6 ♗d7 16 ♕f3 ♗xc6 17 ♕xc6 ♖e6 left Black without any problems in Nasybullin-P.Nikolić, Erevan OL 1996.

b) 11 ♘d2 ♘a5! compares favourably to the variation 10...h6 11 ♘d2 ♘a5, as here ...♖e8 is certainly more useful than ...h6. For example, 12 dxe5? ♗xe5 13 ♕h5 can be answered with the simple 13...g6!.

11...♗f5 12 ♗d5 ♗g6 (D)

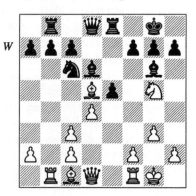

13 h4!

Much stronger than 13 ♖xb7? ♖xb7 14 ♗xc6 ♖b1! 15 ♗xe8 ♕xe8, when, despite the extra pawn, White is struggling. Krasenkov-Kupreichik, USSR Ch 1986 continued 16 ♕e2 h6 17 ♘e4 ♕e6 18 ♘xd6 cxd6 19 f4 ♕xa2 20 dxe5 dxe5 21 fxe5 a5, when Black's a-pawn gives him excellent winning chances.

13...♗e7

Now after 14 ♖b5!? (14 ♕f3 ♗xg5! 15 ♗xg5 ♕d7 16 h5 e4 17 ♗xc6 bxc6 18 ♕e2 ♗f5 is OK for Black) the game W.Watson-Dawson, British Ch (Brighton) 1984 continued 14...exd4? 15 h5! ♗xg5 16 hxg6 hxg6 17 ♗xc6 ♗xc1 18 ♖d5 and White won. However, both 14...♗xg5 15 ♗xg5 ♕d7! and 14...a6!? 15 h5 ♗xg5 16 hxg6 hxg6 17 ♗xc6 axb5 18 ♗xe8 ♗xc1 19 ♗xf7+ ♔xf7 20 ♕xc1 ♕d5 are much stronger possibilities for Black.

In conclusion, 6...♗d6 is a very reliable way of meeting the g3 Vienna. Lines with ♘e2 tend to be quiet and don't really threaten Black. 7 ♘f3 leads to sharper play, but it seems to me that 8...♘c6 is a fully viable option for Black. Both 10...h6 and 10...♖e8 are playable, while 9...♖e8 also seems reasonable for Black. Moreover, Black can also try the underused 6...♗c5, which needs more practical tests.

B)

3 ♗c4 ♘c6 4 d3

Overprotecting e4 and opening the line of the c1-bishop, so that it can support the f2-f4 push. 4 d3 is by far the most common move here. Other ideas can be dealt with very quickly.

a) 4 ♘f3 ♘xe4! transposes to Line A, Chapter 14.

b) After 4 ♘ge2?! Black can employ the standard fork trick 4...♘xe4!, when both 5 ♗xf7+ ♔xf7 6 ♘xe4 d5 and 5 ♘xe4 d5 6 ♗d3 dxe4 7 ♗xe4 ♗c5 leave Black with an edge.

c) 4 f4 ♘xe4! 5 ♘f3 (5 ♘xe4 d5 and 5 ♗xf7+ ♔xf7 6 ♘xe4 d5 7 ♘g5+!? ♔g8 8 ♕h5 ♕e7! are obviously fine for Black) 5...♘xc3 (also sufficient is 5...♘d6 6 ♗d5 exf4 7 d4 ♗e7 8 ♗xf4 0-0, when White did not have enough compensation for the pawn in Myers-Gligorić, Lugano OL 1968) 6 dxc3 ♕e7! (an annoying move for White as the natural 7 0-0 runs into 7...♕c5+) 7 b4 d6 8 0-0 ♗e6 9 ♗xe6 ♕xe6 10 b5 ♘d8 11 fxe5 dxe5 12 ♘xe5 ♗d6 13 ♘f3 0-0 and although White has regained his material, his own weakened pawn-structure leaves him worse, Kuindzhi-Razuvaev, USSR Ch 1973.

4...♗b4! (D)

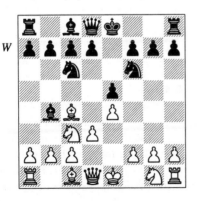

Now White has a choice of continuations:

B1: 5 ♘f3	25
B2: 5 ♗g5	26
B3: 5 ♘e2	28

5 f4 is seen very rarely as 5...exf4 6 ♘f3 d5! gives Black a very comfortable position. After 7 exd5 ♘xd5 8 0-0 ♗xc3 (8...♘xc3 9 ♕e1+! ♕e7 10 bxc3 ♗d6 looks equal) 9 bxc3 0-0 10 ♗xd5 ♕xd5, 11 ♔h1 g5! left Black clearly better in Prasenjit-Shetty, Calcutta 1999. White should recapture the pawn with 11 ♗xf4, although 11...♕c5+ 12 ♔h1 ♕xc3 13 ♗xc7 ♗g4 is still slightly better for Black.

B1)

5 ♘f3

This move, once a favourite of Bent Larsen, has fallen into disuse after the discovery of Black's 8th move.

5...d5 6 exd5 ♘xd5 7 0-0 (D)

7 ♗d2 will probably transpose to the main line after 7...♗xc3 8 bxc3 ♗g4 9 0-0 0-0.

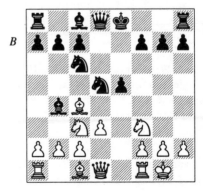

7...♗xc3

The most sensible choice. Black can grab a pawn here with 7...♘xc3 8 bxc3 ♗xc3, but in doing so is forced to face a violent attack after 9 ♘g5 (or even 9 ♗a3!?).

8 bxc3 *(D)*

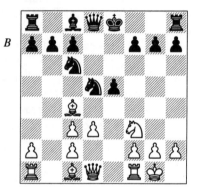

8...♗g4!

This ordinary pinning move takes the entire sting out of White's position and killed much of the enthusiasm I once had for 5 ♘f3. If instead 8...0-0 White can keep the initiative with 9 ♘g5!; for example, 9...h6 10 ♘e4 f5 11 ♗a3 ♖e8 12 ♕h5 and Black faces serious problems holding his position together.

9 ♖e1

In Larsen-Timman, Bugojno 1982, White allowed his pawns to be shattered with 9 ♕e1, but after 9...♗xf3 10 gxf3 0-0 11 ♔h1 ♕d6 12 ♖g1 ♖ad8 Black was in control.

9...0-0

Much safer than 9...♘xc3?! 10 ♕d2 ♗xf3 11 ♕xc3 ♗d5 12 ♖xe5+! ♘xe5

13 ♕xe5+ ♗e6 14 ♕xg7, when Black is in big trouble.

10 ♗d2 ♖e8 11 ♖b1 ♘b6 12 ♗b3 ♕f6 13 ♖e4 ♗h5 14 ♕e2 ♗g6 15 ♖e3 ♖e7

We are following Emms-Condie, British Ch (Southampton) 1986. White has the bishop-pair, but Black's space advantage gives him a very comfortable position (see the introduction to this chapter for the rest of the game).

B2)

5 ♗g5

White continues to fight for the d5-square by pinning the f6-knight. Tseitlin and Glazkov recommended this move.

5...h6 *(D)*

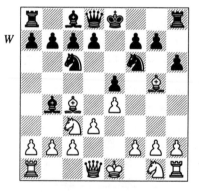

6 ♗xf6

The most consistent choice. After 6 ♗h4 Black can take the initiative with 6...g5! 7 ♗g3 d5. W.Watson-Emms, British Ch (Eastbourne) 1990 continued 8 exd5 ♘xd5 9 ♘e2 (9 ♕h5 ♗e6 10 ♘ge2 ♕d7 simply leaves the queen

looking silly on h5) 9...♗e6 10 ♗b5
♗xc3+ 11 bxc3 ♘f4 12 ♗xc6+ bxc6
13 0-0 0-0 14 f3 f5 15 c4 ♘g6 and the
space on the kingside gave me a pleasant position.

6...♗xc3+

This is an important in-between move, as the immediate recapture with 6...♕xf6 allows White to play 7 ♘e2!, both supporting the f4 advance and protecting c3. After a subsequent 0-0 White will threaten both ♘d5 and f4.

7 bxc3 ♕xf6 8 ♘e2 d6

Another option for Black here is to re-route his knight immediately with 8...♘e7. The idea of this move is to try to transpose to normal lines without allowing White the option of pinning the knight with ♗b5. After 9 0-0 g5, this transposition is achieved following 10 d4 d6, while 10 ♘g3 h5!? 11 ♘xh5 ♕h6 12 g4 ♘g6 13 ♕f3 ♘f4 14 h3 d6 15 ♖ab1 c6 16 ♘xf4 gxf4 17 ♔g2 ♔e7 gave Black long-term compensation for the pawn in Mieses-Fritz, Dusseldorf 1908. White could also consider 9 ♕d2 g5 10 h4!?.

9 0-0 (D)

9 ♕d2 g5 10 d4 ♘e7 11 dxe5 dxe5 12 ♖d1 ♘g6 13 ♗b5+ c6 14 ♗c4 ♘h4 15 0-0 0-0 gave Black no problems in Milner-Barry – Alekhine, London 1932.

9...g5 10 d4

10 ♖b1 got White nowhere in the game Lastin-Nenashev, Calcutta 1998, after 10...♘e7 11 f3 h5! 12 ♕d2 h4 13 ♕e3 b6 14 d4 ♘g6 15 dxe5 dxe5 16 ♖bd1 0-0 17 ♖d2 ♗b7 18 ♖fd1 ♖ad8

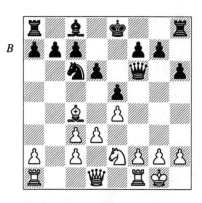

19 g3 ♖xd2 20 ♖xd2 ♔g7 21 ♖d3 ♗c8 22 ♔g2 ♖h8, when, if anything, Black was a little better.

However, 10 ♗b5!? is an interesting alternative. Given that the black knight can become an important player after ...♘e7-g6, then there is some logic in preparing to exchange it. After 10...♗d7 11 ♖b1 h5 12 ♕d2 h4 13 f3 ♕g7 14 h3 f6 15 d4 ♘d8 16 dxe5 ♗xb5 17 ♖xb5 fxe5 18 c4 b6 19 ♘c3 White was slightly better in Schlechter-Leonhardt, Bad Pistyan 1912. Perhaps Black should release the pin immediately with 10...0-0, which induces White to exchange immediately with 11 ♗xc6. Following 11...bxc6 12 ♖b1 ♕g6, Black can obtain sufficient counterplay with ...f5.

10...♘e7 11 ♕d2

Another move here is 11 f3, with the long-term plan of g3 and f4. However, Black can dissuade White from this plan by lunging forward with the h-pawn. Following 11...h5! 12 g3 h4 White played the dismal 13 g4 and after 13...♘g6 Black was already better in H.Jonkman-Bezgodov, Pardubice 1996. However, it's difficult to suggest an improvement for White, especially as the logical 13 f4 runs into 13...gxf4 14 gxf4 ♖g8+ 15 ♔h1 ♕g6! and Black wins.

11...♞g6 12 ♖ad1 *(D)*

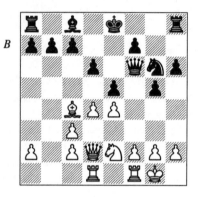

We have been following Mi.Tseitlin-Naumkin, Moscow 1988, which continued 12...♞f4?! 13 g3 ♞h3+ 14 ♔g2 ♕g6 15 f3 0-0 16 ♕e3 b6 17 ♔h1 ♔h8 18 ♖d2 and White held a small advantage. However, Black's knight manoeuvre to h3 is not particularly impressive and takes up a lot of time. At first I liked the idea of 12...0-0 13 f3 ♝e6, but after a while it dawned on me that following 14 ♝b3!, White will prepare f4 with g3, and I can't find a convincing plan against this. Therefore Black should content himself with 12...♔f8, planning ...h5-h4, or simply the immediate 12...h5 13 f3 h4, when the position is evenly balanced (but unbalanced, if you get my meaning).

B3)
5 ♞e2 *(D)*

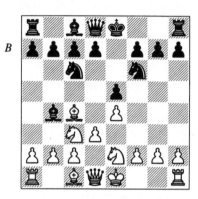

With this move, White supports the knight on c3 and plans a quick 0-0 and f4. Once again Black's most challenging option is to advance immediately in the centre.

5...d5 6 exd5 ♞xd5 7 0-0

White's other main option here is 7 ♝xd5 ♕xd5 8 0-0, which gives up the bishop-pair, but on the other hand gains time by attacking the black queen. Normally Black retreats the queen with 8...♕d8 (although 8...♕a5 9 a3 0-0 10 ♝e3 ♝xc3 11 ♞xc3 was also fine for Black in Spielmann-Réti, Dortmund 1928) and after the natural 9 f4 we have two possibilities:

a) 9...exf4 (the safe choice) 10 ♝xf4 0-0 11 ♕e1 ♝g4 (11...♞e7 12 ♕f2 ♝g4 13 a3 ♝xe2 14 ♞xe2 ♝d6 15 ♖ae1 ♝xf4 16 ♞xf4 ♕d7 17 ♖e4 ♞g6 18 ♞xg6 hxg6 19 ♖fe1 ♖fe8 was also dead equal in Balashov-Nunn, Dortmund 1987) 12 ♕g3 ♝xe2 13 ♞xe2 ♞d4 14 ♞xd4 ♕xd4+ 15 ♔h1

½-½ Mitkov-Flear, French Cht 1995. After 15...♗d6 16 ♗xd6 ♕xd6 17 ♕xd6 cxd6 18 ♖ae1 ♖fe8 there's not much play left in the position, unless you're a wizard at rook and pawn endings.

b) 9...0-0!? (this is riskier, but the rewards may be greater) 10 f5 ♘d4 11 ♘g3 ♗c5 12 ♔h1 f6 13 ♘ce4 ♗b6 14 c3 ♘c6 15 ♘h5 ♖f7 happened in Bzowski-M.Maciejewski, Wisla 1992, with a double-edged position which is quite typical for the 5 ♘e2 line. White has some pressure on the kingside, but Black can defend with ...♔h8 and ...♘e7, and meanwhile, White's weak d3-pawn could become subjected to an attack.

7...♗e6

Overwhelmingly the most popular choice, but after 7...♘xc3 8 bxc3 ♗c5, Black didn't stand badly following 9 ♘g3 0-0 10 ♖e1 ♕h4 in D.Ledger-Kennaugh, British Ch (Torquay) 1998. White could instead try 9 d4!?, as after 9...exd4 10 cxd4 ♘xd4 11 ♘xd4 ♕xd4 12 ♕e2+ White has obvious compensation for the pawn.

8 ♗xd5

Once again this has traditionally been the principal move, but more recently other attempts have been tried for White here.

a) 8 ♗b3 0-0 9 ♔h1 (9 ♘e4 ♗e7 transposes to line 'b') 9...♘d4 (9...♖e8 10 f4 ♗xc3 11 bxc3 f6 (11...♗g4!?) 12 ♗d2 ♔h8 13 f5 ♗g8 14 ♘g3 a5 15 ♕g4 is perhaps slightly more comfortable for White, I.Rogers-Parker, British

League (4NCL) 1997/8) 10 ♘xd4 exd4 11 ♘xd5 ♗xd5 12 ♗d2 a5 13 ♖e1 ½-½ Kiss-Gyimesi, Nagykanizsa 1994.

b) 8 ♘e4 ♗e7 9 ♗b3 (9 f4?! exf4 10 ♘xf4? loses material to 10...♘xf4 11 ♗xf4 ♕d4+ 12 ♔h1 ♗xc4) 9...0-0 10 f4 exf4 11 ♘xf4 ♘xf4 12 ♗xf4 ♘d4 with equality, Belkhodja-Hebden, French Cht 1988.

8...♗xd5 9 f4 0-0 (D)

For a while I was attracted to the idea of 9...♕d7, planning to castle queenside, thus drawing much of the sting out of White's f5 advance. However, it seems that the loss of tempo suffered after 10 ♘xd5! ♕xd5 is too much of a burden on Black's position. After 11 fxe5 0-0-0 12 c3 ♗e7 13 d4 ♘xe5 14 ♘f4 ♕d7 15 ♕b3 White's position is favourable.

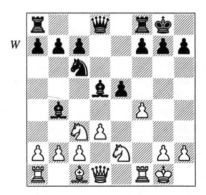

10 f5

The most challenging move. Using the f-pawn as a spearhead, White plans to build up gradual pressure against the black king. Black must be prepared to meet this challenge, while hoping that his control over the central squares and the queenside will offer him enough counterplay.

10...♗xc3!?

A difficult decision to make. Black gives up the bishop-pair and cedes the d4-square as a possible outpost. However, Black's dark-squared bishop can become a problem piece and offloading it compromises White's queenside pawn-structure. The other main option here is the immediate 10...f6:

a) 11 ♘g3 ♗f7 12 ♗e3 ♗a5 13 ♔h1 ♗b6 14 ♗d2 a5 15 a3 ♘d4 16 ♖c1 ♕e7 17 ♘ce4 c5 18 ♕g4 ♖fd8 19 ♗e3 a4 20 ♖f2 ♖a6 led to a finely balanced position in Mitkov-Motwani, Erevan OL 1996. White has the usual kingside pressure, but Black is well placed defensively and is able to create counterplay on the other wing.

b) Another option is to eliminate Black's light-squared bishop with 11 ♘xd5. Emms-Eames, London 1997 continued 11...♕xd5 12 ♘g3 ♗c5+ 13 ♔h1 ♖ad8 14 ♘e4 ♗b6 15 ♗d2 and now, instead of my opponent's 15...♘d4?, which lost material to 16 c4! ♕c6 17 c5 ♗xc5 18 ♖c1 b6 19 b4, Black should offer the exchange of bishops with 15...♗a5!.

11 bxc3 f6 12 ♘g3

The advance 12 c4?! is premature. After 12...♗f7 13 ♖b1 (or 13 ♗a3 ♗h5! 14 ♗xf8 ♘d4! with advantage to Black because 15 ♖e1? loses after 15...♘xe2+ 16 ♖xe2 ♗xe2 17 ♕xe2 ♕d4+!) 13...♗h5! 14 ♕e1 (14...♘d4 was the threat) 14...♗xe2 15 ♕xe2 b6

16 ♗e3 (Emms-Parker, Cambridge 1996) and now 16...♕d6 17 ♖f3 ♘d4 18 ♗xd4 ♕xd4+ 19 ♕f2 ♖fd8 gives Black any advantage that's going, because White's pawns on f5 and a2 may become weak in the double rook ending.

12...♖e8

A.Ledger-Twyble, British League (4NCL) 1998/9 continued 13 ♕g4 ♔h8 14 a4 ♕d7 15 ♗a3 ♖ad8 16 ♖ae1 and now unclear complications arose after 16...e4.

C)

3 f4

This is the main line of the Vienna, but Black has an effective reply.

3...d5! *(D)*

Black must decline the pawn, as 3...exf4? gives Black a miserable game after 4 e5 ♕e7 5 ♕e2!, when the knight must make an unhappy retreat to g8. Also unplayable is 3...♗b4? 4 fxe5 ♗xc3 5 dxc3 ♘xe4 6 ♕g4!, while 3...d6 4 ♘f3 ♘c6 5 ♗b5 leaves Black very passively placed.

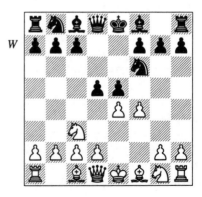

4 fxe5

This is the overwhelmingly most popular choice here, but other moves do exist, and Black needs to know what do against these alternatives.

a) 4 ♘f3 gets White nowhere after 4...dxe4 5 ♘xe5 ♗d6 6 d4 exd3 7 ♗xd3 0-0 8 0-0 ♘bd7, when Black is at least equal.

b) 4 d3 *(D)* has been tried by David Bronstein, although this could probably be classified as one of his less successful opening experiments. Black should simply respond with 4...exf4, when the position resembles a kind of King's Gambit where Black has successfully engineered an early ...d5 break. White has three possible choices here, but is struggling to equalize in all of them.

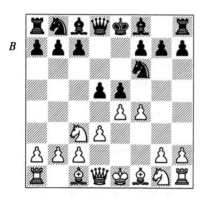

b1) 5 e5 d4! 6 ♘ce2 ♘d5 7 ♘xf4 ♗b4+ 8 ♔f2 ♘c6 9 ♘f3 0-0 and Black was clearly better in Lombardy-Smyslov, Teesside 1975.

b2) 5 ♗xf4 ♗b4 6 exd5 ♘xd5 7 ♗d2 ♗xc3 8 bxc3 0-0 9 ♘f3 ♖e8+ 10

♗e2 ♕e7 and once again White is struggling, Spielmann-Em.Lasker, St Petersburg 1909.

b3) 5 exd5 (probably the best out of a bad choice) 5...♘xd5 6 ♘xd5 ♕xd5 7 ♗xf4 ♗d6 8 ♗xd6 ♕xd6 9 ♕d2 0-0 10 ♘f3 ♗g4 and Black was slightly better in Bronstein-Matanović, Vienna Echt 1957.

c) 4 exd5 and now:

c1) 4...exf4 (aiming to transpose to a good line of the King's Gambit) 5 ♘f3 (acquiescing; 5 ♗b5+ c6 6 dxc6 bxc6 7 ♗e2 ♗d6 was better for Black in Suttles-Smyslov, Venice 1974) 5...♘xd5 6 ♘xd5 ♕xd5 7 d4 ♗e7 8 c4 (following 8 ♗e2?! g5 White will struggle to regain his pawn) 8...♕e4+ 9 ♔f2 ♗f5 (9...♗g4 10 ♗d3 ♗h4+ 11 ♔f1! looks unclear) 10 ♗e2 (10 c5 ♘c6! 11 ♗b5 ♕d5 12 ♗xf4 0-0-0 13 ♗e3 ♗f6 14 ♕a4 ♗e4 15 ♗xc6 ♕xc6 16 ♕xc6 ♗xc6 gave Black the advantage in Kieninger-Eliskases, Stuttgart 1939, while *ECO* gives 10 ♕a4+ ♘c6 11 ♗d2 0-0-0 12 ♖e1 ♕c2 13 ♕xc2 ♗xc2 14 ♗xf4 ♖he8 with a small plus to Black) 10...♘c6 11 ♖e1 0-0-0 12 ♗f1 ♕c2+ 13 ♕xc2 ♗xc2 with an equal endgame, Novikov-Borisenko, USSR 1956.

c2) 4...♘xd5!? (keeping a Vienna flavour) 5 fxe5 (safer is 5 ♘xd5 ♕xd5 6 fxe5, when both 6...♕xe5+ 7 ♕e2 ♕xe2+ 8 ♗xe2 and 6...♕e4+!? 7 ♗e2 ♗g4 8 ♔f1 ♗xe2+ 9 ♕xe2 ♕xc2 10 d4 ♕xe2+ 11 ♔xe2 look equal) 5...♘xc3 6 bxc3 ♕h4+ 7 ♔e2 ♗g4+ 8 ♘f3 ♘c6 9 d4 0-0-0 10 ♗d2 (10 ♕e1 may be stronger, although Black can choose between 10...♕h5 and 10...♖xd4!? 11 cxd4 ♘xd4+ 12 ♔d1 ♘xf3 13 ♕xh4 ♘xh4+) 10...♗xf3+?! (10...♖xd4!) 11 gxf3 (not 11 ♔xf3? ♖xd4! 12 cxd4 ♘xd4+ 13 ♔e3 ♗c5 14 ♔d3 ♖d8 15 ♔c3 ♘f3 and Black has a winning attack) 11...♘xe5 12 dxe5? (12 ♕e1!) 12...♗c5 13 ♕e1 ♕c4+ 14 ♔d1 ♕xc3 and Black won quickly in the game Hamppe-Steinitz, Vienna 1859.

4...♘xe4 (D)

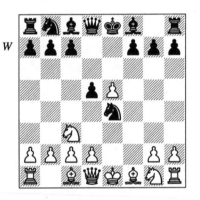

Here White has four principal possibilities:

C1: 5 ♕e2?! 32
C2: 5 ♕f3 32
C3: 5 d3 33
C4: 5 ♘f3 34

C1)
5 ♕e2?! ♘c6!
This logical move virtually refutes 5 ♕e2.
6 ♘f3
6 ♘xe4 ♘d4! is good for Black.
6...♗f5 7 ♕b5

This idea doesn't work, but having played 5 ♕e2, White feels honour-bound to go through with it. Besides, 7 d3 ♘xc3 8 bxc3 d4 9 g3 dxc3 10 ♗g2 ♗c5 was clearly better for Black in Pel-Van den Doel, Dieren 1998.
7...a6! 8 ♕xd5
Critical is 8 ♕xb7, but this fails after 8...♘b4 9 ♘xe4 ♗xe4! 10 ♘d4 ♗c5 11 ♘c6 ♕h4+ 12 g3 ♘xc2+ (Tseitlin and Glazkov give 12...♗f3 13 ♗d3 ♘xc2+? 14 ♗xc2 ♕c4 as winning for Black, which it would be if it weren't for 15 ♕xa8+ ♔d7 16 ♗f5#!) 13 ♔d1 ♕g4+ 14 ♗e2 ♕c8 15 ♕xc8+ ♖xc8 and Black is attacking both rooks, so one must go.
8...♘b4 9 ♕xd8+ ♖xd8 10 ♗d3 ♘xd3+ 11 cxd3 ♖xd3 12 ♘h4 ♘xc3 13 ♘xf5 ♘b5
Black is comfortably better, K.Berg-Spassky, Bundesliga 1986/7.

C2)
5 ♕f3 ♘c6
Once again this move, which plans to meet 6 ♘xe4? with 6...♘d4, seems the most logical response to White's early queen move. Black does have alternatives, however, including bolstering the knight with 5...f5. One possible continuation is 6 d3 ♘xc3 7 bxc3 d4 8 ♕g3 ♘c6 9 ♗e2 ♗e6 10 ♗f3 ♕d7 11 ♘e2 0-0-0 12 0-0 ♗c5 13 c4 and now in Vorotnikov-Kapengut, USSR 1975 great complications developed after 13...♗xc4 14 ♘f4 ♘xe5!? 15 dxc4 d3+ 16 ♔h1 dxc2.
6 ♗b5 ♘xc3 7 bxc3 ♕h4+

If Black prefers to keep the queens on, then 7...♗e7 is a reasonable alternative, although after 8 d4 0-0 9 ♗d3 f6, White can force a draw with 10 ♕h5 g6 11 ♗xg6 hxg6 12 ♕xg6+ ♔h8 13 ♕h6+ ♔g8, as in Hromadka-Em.Lasker, Mährisch-Ostrau 1923.

8 g3 ♕e4+ 9 ♕xe4 dxe4 10 ♗xc6+ bxc6 11 ♘e2 *(D)*

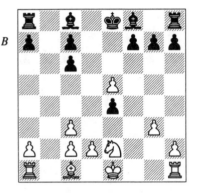

This position is given as equal in *NCO*, while Tseitlin and Glazkov think that Black is clearly better. My own view is probably somewhere in between. If nothing else, the two bishops offer Black good practical chances. Here are two possible continuations:

a) 11...♗a6 12 ♖f1 c5 13 ♖f4 ♗b7 14 c4 g6 15 ♖b1 ♗c6 16 ♘c3 f5! 17 exf6 ♗d6 18 ♖f2 ♔f7 19 ♗a3 ♖he8 20 ♔e2 a6 with a deceptive position. At first sight White is simply a pawn up, but the more you look at the position, the more difficult it is to suggest a useful plan for White. Indeed Vulfson-Lilienthal, Kuibyshev 1942 saw Black take over the operation after 21

♘d5 ♖ab8 22 ♖ff1 ♖xb1 23 ♖xb1 ♖e5 24 ♘f4 ♖f5 25 ♖f1 ♗a4 26 ♖c1 ♗xf4 27 gxf4 ♖h5. Here White blundered with 28 ♗xc5?? ♖xc5, but in any case, he was already in trouble.

b) 11...♗h3 12 ♘f4 ♗g4 13 d4 was played in the game Hromadka-Bogoljubow, Mährisch-Ostrau 1923 and here Tseitlin and Glazkov recommend 13...exd3 14 cxd3 0-0-0 15 d4 c5 16 h3 ♗f5 17 ♗e3 cxd4 18 cxd4 ♗b4+ 19 ♔f2 g5 20 ♘e2 h6, which is slightly better for Black.

C3)
5 d3

This move contains more than just a touch of poison. Black has to be aware of certain tricks in this line.

5...♘xc3

Instead:

a) White's main trap is seen when the plausible 5...♕h4+? runs into 6 g3 ♘xg3 7 ♘f3 ♕h5 8 ♘xd5!, when White is clearly better; for example:

a1) 8...♘xh1 9 ♘xc7+ ♔d8 10 ♘xa8 ♗e7 11 ♗g2 ♗h4+ 12 ♔f1 ♘c6 13 d4 is much better for White (*NCO*).

a2) 8...♗g4 9 ♗g2 ♘xh1 10 ♘xc7+ ♔d8 11 ♘xa8 ♘c6 12 d4 ♗xf3 13 ♕xf3 ♕xf3 14 ♗xf3 ♘xd4 15 ♗g5+ ♔c8 16 0-0-0! ♗c5 17 ♗xh1 ♔b8 18 b4 ♘e6 19 bxc5 ♘xg5 20 ♖d7 ♔xa8 21 ♖xb7 and a grandmaster scalp was claimed in Hon-Van der Sterren, London Lloyds Bank 1992.

b) Another tricky line occurs after 5...♗b4, which is fine for Black, so long as he is happy with an equal ending or a forced draw. After 6 dxe4 ♕h4+ 7 ♔e2 ♗xc3 8 bxc3 ♗g4+ 9 ♘f3 dxe4 10 ♕d4 ♗h5! White has two options:

b1) 11 ♔e3 ♗xf3, when 12 gxf3 ♕e1+ 13 ♔f4 ♕h4+ is a perpetual check, while 12 ♗b5+ c6 13 gxf3 cxb5 14 ♕xe4+ ♕xe4+ 15 ♔xe4 ♘d7 leads to an equal ending.

b2) 11 ♕d2 ♕g4 12 h3 ♕f4+ 13 ♔e1 ♕g3+ 14 ♕f2 ♕xf2+ 15 ♔xf2 exf3 16 gxf3 ♘d7, when White's weak pawns are more important than the bishop-pair.

6 bxc3 d4 7 ♘f3 dxc3

After 7...♘c6 the position should transpose to the main line with 8 ♗e2 dxc3 9 0-0. The alternative 8 cxd4 ♗b4+! 9 ♗d2 ♗xd2+ 10 ♕xd2 ♘xd4 11 c3 ♘xf3+ 12 gxf3 ♕d5! is considered slightly better for Black (*NCO*).

8 ♗e2 ♘c6

Another respectable option for Black is 8...♗e7; for example, 9 0-0 ♗e6 10 ♕e1 ♘c6 11 ♕xc3 (11 ♕g3 can be answered by the simple 11...♖g8, followed by ...♕d7 and ...0-0-0) 11...0-0 12 ♗e3 f6 13 d4 ♔h8 14 ♖ad1 fxe5 15 dxe5 ♗b4 16 ♕b2 ♕e7 with an unclear position, Sax-Plaskett, Lugano 1986.

9 0-0 ♘d4

This is probably the safest way to reach a playable position. It looks tempting to throw in a check, but White's results have been quite good after 9...♗c5+ 10 ♔h1 0-0 11 ♕e1 ♘d4 12 ♗d1!, when both 12...f6 13 ♕xc3 ♗b6 14 ♗a3 and 12...♘xf3 13

♗xf3 ♖e8 14 ♕g3 slightly favour White.

10 ♘g5 ♗c5 11 ♔h1 0-0 12 ♗h5 ♗e6 13 ♘e4 ♗e7 14 ♘xc3

Black is fully developed and has no genuine problems. Both 14...♕d7 and 14...f6 are roughly equal.

C4)
5 ♘f3 (D)

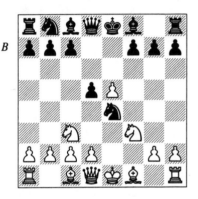

The most popular continuation. White simply gets on with the process of completing kingside development.

5...♗c5!

Black has other good moves, but this is the most active continuation. White must do something about the immediate threat of 6...♘f2.

6 ♕e2

The other way to prevent ...♘f2 is with 6 d4, but then Black can keep on the active path with 6...♗b4 7 ♗d2 ♗g4! 8 ♘xe4 dxe4 9 ♗xb4 exf3:

a) 10 ♕d2 ♕d5 (this was suggested in *NCO*; after 10...♘c6 11 ♗c3 ♕d5 12 h3 ♗e6 13 gxf3 0-0-0 I prefer

Black, Ljubojević-Ciocaltea, Skopje OL 1972) 11 0-0-0 (11 ♗c3 ♘c6 transposes to the previous bracket) 11...♘c6 12 c4 (L'Hoste-Boudre, Val Maubuée 1990) and now 12...fxg2! 13 ♗xg2 ♕xc4+ is good for Black.

b) 10 gxf3 ♕h4+ 11 ♔e2 ♘c6! is also pleasant for Black. J.Sørensen-Flear, Hastings 1988/9 continued 12 fxg4 ♕xg4+ 13 ♔f2 (alternatively, 13 ♔e3 ♕g5+) 13...♕f4+ 14 ♕f3? (14 ♔g2 ♘xb4 is only slightly better for Black) 14...♕xd4+ 15 ♔g2 ♕xb4 and Black had a large advantage.

6...♗f2+ 7 ♔d1 ♘xc3+ 8 dxc3

The other recapture, 8 bxc3, has been either condemned or ignored, but as far as I can see it seems no worse (although no better) than the text-move. After 8...♗c5 9 d4 ♗e7 10 ♕f2 ♗f5 there have been two examples:

a) 11 ♕g3 0-0 12 ♗d3 ♗xd3 13 cxd3 ♖e8 14 ♖f1 f6 15 ♗h6 ♗f8 16 ♘h4 ♘d7 17 ♔d2 ♔h8! and White's weak king on d2 eventually told in Swanson-Fernandez Garcia, Lucerne OL 1982.

b) After 11 ♖b1!?, 11...♕c8?! 12 ♕g3 0-0 13 ♗h6 ♗g6 14 h4! gave White a promising attack in Uritzky-Kogan, Tel-Aviv 1996. Black should probably keep the queen on d8 and play simply with 11...b6. Then 12 ♕g3 0-0 13 ♗h6 ♗g6 14 h4 can be answered with 14...gxh6 15 h5 ♗g5!.

8...♗b6

Also possible is 8...♗h4, planning ...♗e7 to give the kingside more cover.

Janošević-Baratić, Yugoslavia 1977 continued 9 ♗f4 ♗e7 10 ♔d2 0-0 11 ♖d1 c5 12 ♔c1 ♕a5 13 ♔b1 ♘c6 (13...♗e6 14 ♗g5 ♘c6 15 ♗xe7 ♘xe7 16 ♘g5 looks roughly level) 14 ♕e1 (Gligorić proposed 14 ♕b5, but then Tseitlin and Glazkov's suggestion of 14...♕c7!? 15 ♖xd5 ♗e6 looks interesting) 14...♗e6 15 ♕g3 d4 16 c4 ♖fe8 (16...b5!? 17 ♗h6 g6 18 ♗xf8 ♖xf8 gives Black an attack for the exchange) 17 a3 a6 18 ♗d3 b5 19 ♘g5 ♗xg5 20 ♗xg5 and now 20...♘xe5! 21 ♕xe5 bxc4 gives Black a strong attack.

9 ♗g5

ECO stops here with an assessment of 'slightly better for White', but with the white king on d1, it's very difficult to agree with this judgement. It's true that White can 'castle by hand', but the time required to do this allows Black to catch up in development (at least), and besides, Black has no weaknesses in his position.

9...♕d7 10 ♔d2 h6 *(D)*

Here *NCO* gives 11 ♗e3 0-0 as 'unclear', which seems about right; for example, 12 ♖d1 ♕a4 13 a3 c5 14 ♔c1 ♗e6 and Black is certainly no worse in any pawn-storm race. Instead Boog-Godena, Geneva 1993 continued 11 ♗h4 ♕a4 12 ♕b5+ ♕xb5 13 ♗xb5+ c6 14 ♗d3 0-0 15 ♘d4 ♘d7 16 e6?! (16 ♖ae1 is stronger) 16...♘e5 17 ♖ae1? (now White must play 17 exf7+) 17...f6! 18 ♗f5 ♖e8 19 b3 c5 and the e6-pawn dropped off.

4 The King's Gambit: Introduction and Rare 3rd Moves for White

1 e4 e5 2 f4 *(D)*

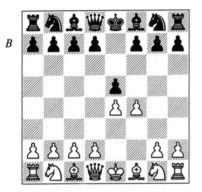

The King's Gambit is an opening with an immense history, and was a favourite of the attacking legends of the 19th century, such as Adolf Anderssen and Paul Morphy. In those days defensive techniques of the top players were not yet developed enough to cope with White's swashbuckling attacks. Witness the following encounter, known as the 'Immortal Game', where it looks like the chess comes from another planet as well as another lifetime. For detailed analysis of this game, see *The Mammoth Book of the World's Greatest Chess Games*.

Anderssen – Kieseritzky
London 1851

1 e4 e5 2 f4 exf4 3 ♗c4 ♕h4+ 4 ♔f1 b5 5 ♗xb5 ♘f6 6 ♘f3 ♕h6 7 d3 ♘h5 8 ♘h4 ♕g5 9 ♘f5 c6 10 g4 ♘f6 11 ♖g1 cxb5 12 h4 ♕g6 13 h5 ♕g5 14 ♕f3 ♘g8 15 ♗xf4 ♕f6 16 ♘c3 ♗c5 17 ♘d5 ♕xb2 18 ♗d6 ♗xg1 19 e5 ♕xa1+ 20 ♔e2 ♘a6 21 ♘xg7+ ♔d8 *(D)*

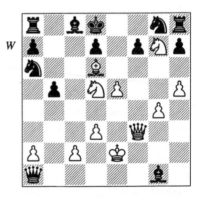

22 ♕f6+!! ♘xf6 23 ♗e7# (1-0)

However, time passed and as accuracy and analysis started to overtake boldness, the King's Gambit suffered and took a long backward step out of the limelight.

In recent times it has made a recovery and is beginning to appear in the games of leading players once more, including the likes of Nigel Short and Alexander Morozevich. Mention should also be made of Joe Gallagher, who is one of the leading King's Gambit players of recent times and whose book, *Winning With the King's Gambit*, has done much to popularize the opening at club level.

Players tend to play the King's Gambit in a different way now. Gone are the days where White always goes for an all-out attack, sacrificing virtually all of his pieces in the hope of a spectacular mate. On just as many occasions we see White trying to regain the pawn, stifle Black's activity and then nurture the advantage of a better pawn-structure in the endgame. Nevertheless, that lunge with the f-pawn on move two still sends a shiver down the spine of even the most seasoned 1...e5 player.

At club and tournament level it's possible for the well-prepared King's Gambiteer to score very well. Nigel Davies points out that many players, when faced with this bold opening, immediately feel uncomfortable and their instinctive reaction is one of passivity. This of course is just what White wants. In the King's Gambit the onus is on Black to be just as courageous as White. Armed with an attitude of 'show me what you've got' and

'fortune favours the brave', I believe that Black must grab the pawn and then hang on to his hat!

If you haven't guessed by now, then I should tell you that I'm advocating 2...exf4! (the King's Gambit Accepted) as Black's best reply to the King's Gambit. In this chapter we will concentrate on rare third moves for White; Chapter 5 discusses the Bishop's Gambit (3 ♗c4) and finally Chapter 6 deals with the King's Knight Gambit (3 ♘f3).

A Quick Summary of the Recommended Lines

Of White's third move alternatives, Lines A and B can be dealt with very easily. Line D is rather passive and the only one that gives Black any real concern is the tricky 3 ♘c3!? (Line C).

The Theory of Rare Third Moves For White

1 e4 e5 2 f4 exf4 *(D)*

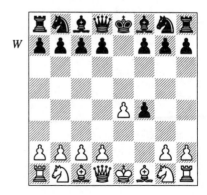

Apart from 3 ♗c4 and 3 ♘f3, we shall consider these four moves:

A: 3 d4?!   38
B: 3 ♕f3   39
C: 3 ♘c3!?   40
D: 3 ♗e2   42

A)

3 d4?!

This is called the Centre Gambit by Estrin and Glazkov in their book *Play the King's Gambit*. In an ideal world White will follow up with ♗xf4, take control of the centre, develop the rest of his pieces and castle. Unfortunately for White, Black has some moves too, and one of these happens to be a very disruptive queen check!

3...d5! *(D)*

3...♕h4+ 4 ♔e2 d5 will usually transpose, but I believe that 3...d5 gives White slightly fewer options.

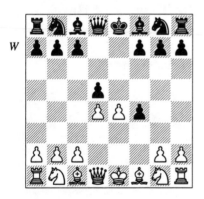

4 exd5 ♕h4+ 5 ♔e2

5 ♔d2?! led to a crushing victory for Black in Jacobs-Formanek, Lewisham 1981, which continued 5...♘f6 6

c4 ♕f2+ 7 ♕e2+ ♘e4+! (an unusual event in the opening; three checks in a row!) 8 ♔d3 ♗f5 9 ♘d2 ♘c6!! 10 dxc6 0-0-0 11 cxb7+ ♔b8 12 ♕xf2 ♘xf2+ 13 ♔e2 ♘xh1 14 ♔f3 ♖xd4 15 ♘b3 ♗e4+ 16 ♔xf4 ♗d6+ 17 ♔e3 ♖d1 18 ♔xe4 ♖e8+ 19 ♔f3 ♖xf1+ 0-1.

Naturally 5 g3? is bad owing to 5...fxg3 6 ♘f3 g2+! 7 ♘xh4 gxh1♕.

5...♘f6 6 ♘f3 ♗g4 7 ♕e1

If White tries to hold on to his d-pawn, then Black should simply develop as quickly as possible and then try to plant a check on the e-file. For example, 7 c4 ♗d6 8 ♕b3 0-0 and it would take a very brave (or foolish) player to accept the pawn on b7.

7...♕xe1+

This move-order is more accurate than 7...♗xf3+, which allows 8 ♔xf3+! ♕xe1 9 ♗b5+.

8 ♔xe1 ♗xf3 9 gxf3 ♘xd5 *(D)*

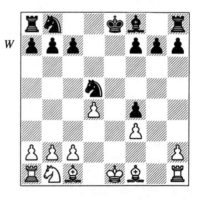

Tartakower suggested that 10 c4 gives White enough compensation for the pawn after 10...♘b4 11 ♔d1. However, in *Play the King's Gambit*,

Estrin and Glazkov improved on Black's play with 10...♘e3, claiming that Black has the advantage. This assessment seems to hold true; for example, 11 ♗xe3 fxe3 12 ♔e2 ♘c6 13 ♔xe3 0-0-0 14 ♗h3+ ♔b8 15 d5 ♗c5+ 16 ♔f4 ♗d6+ 17 ♔e3 ♖he8+ 18 ♔f2 ♘b4 and the threats start to mount.

B)

3 ♕f3

According to Estrin and Glazkov, this slightly eccentric move was originally the idea of the Hungarian player Breyer, who is perhaps better known for his solid defence in the Closed Ruy Lopez, and for his slightly controversial aphorism "after 1 e4, White's game is in its last throes!". I would think his saying is more accurate when applied to 3 ♕f3.

3...♘c6! *(D)*

Other moves such as 3...d5 and 3...♕h4+!? are also playable, but I prefer the simplicity of this idea. Black plans to develop both knights before striking back in the centre with ...d5. Note that with the white queen on f3, the c2-pawn is now a little sensitive, and Black is ready to pounce at any moment with ...♘b4.

4 c3

Logically preparing to play d4, after which White will hope to capture on f4 with the c1-bishop. Other moves fail to cause Black any problems.

a) 4 ♘e2 d5! 5 exd5 ♘b4 6 ♘a3 ♘xd5 7 ♘xf4 ♘xf4 8 ♕xf4 ♗d6 is probably a little better for Black.

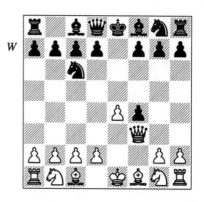

b) 4 ♕xf4 d5! and now 5 exd5 ♘b4 6 ♕e4+ ♕e7 7 ♗b5+ ♗d7 8 ♗xd7+ ♔xd7 9 ♕xe7+ ♗xe7 10 ♘a3 ♘xd5 leaves Black with a healthy-looking endgame. Perhaps White should instead choose to close the centre with 5 e5!?, but Black still has many reasonable ways to continue; for example, 5...f6, or 5...♘ge7!? 6 d4 ♘b4 7 ♘a3 ♗f5.

4...♘f6 5 d4 d5 6 e5

Bogoljubow gives 6 exd5?! ♗g4! 7 ♕xf4 ♗d6 8 ♕e3+ (8 ♕g5 h6 9 ♕xg7? ♖h7! traps the white queen) 8...♘e7 as being good for Black.

6...♘e4 7 ♗xf4

White cannot spend too long dithering over the capture of this pawn. Spielmann-J.Møller, Gothenburg 1920 continued 7 ♗b5?! ♕h4+ 8 ♔f1 g5 9 ♘d2 and now 9...♗f5! would have left Black with the advantage.

7...♗e7

Also deserving attention is 7...f6!?, and now:

a) 8 ♗b5 ♗e7 9 exf6 ♗xf6 10 ♘e2 0-0 11 0-0 g5! 12 ♗xc6 bxc6 13

♗e5 (Spielmann-Tarrasch, Gothenburg 1920) and now 13...♗a6! looks promising for Black.

b) 8 ♗d3 ♗f5 9 exf6 ♕xf6 10 ♗xc7?! (10 ♘d2 is safer and approximately equal) 10...♘xd4! (a surprisingly strong tactic) 11 cxd4 ♗b4+ 12 ♘c3 (12 ♔d1 ♗g4 13 ♕xg4 ♘f2+, 12 ♔e2 ♕xd4 13 ♕xf5 ♕xb2+ 14 ♔d1 ♘f2+ and 12 ♔f1 0-0 are all good for Black) 12...♘xc3 and now Alderson-Boyd, corr 1970 finished abruptly with 13 ♕xf5? ♘e4+, but even after the stronger 13 ♗xf5 ♘e4+ 14 ♔e2 ♕xd4 15 ♖d1 ♕xb2+ 16 ♔f1 0-0! Black is well on top.

c) 8 exf6! (probably the safest way to continue) 8...♘xf6 9 ♗d3, with a roughly equal position.

8 ♘d2 f5 9 exf6 ♘xf6 10 ♗d3 0-0 11 ♘e2

11 ♘h3 looks ugly. Black was definitely better after 11...♗g4 12 ♕e3 ♕d7 13 0-0 ♖ae8 in Spielmann-Grünfeld, Baden-Baden 1925.

11...♗g4 *(D)*

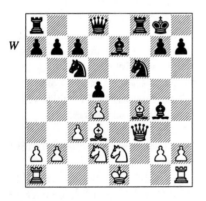

Black's slight lead in development and pressure down the open f-file assure him of a more comfortable position:

a) 12 ♕f2? ♘h5 13 g3 ♘xf4 14 gxf4 ♗h4 15 ♘g3 ♕e7+ 16 ♔f1 ♗h3+ 17 ♔g1 ♕d6 18 f5 ♘e7 19 ♕e3 ♘xf5 20 ♗xf5 ♗xf5 and Black is in total control, Drimer-Unzicker, Hastings 1969/70.

b) 12 ♕e3 ♗d6 (12...♖e8!?) 13 ♗xd6 ♕xd6 14 ♘f3 ♖ae8 and again White is suffering due to being behind in the development race.

c) 12 ♕g3 (this move, exerting pressure on c7, may be White's best chance) 12...♗xe2!? (more enterprising than 12...♖c8, which looks equal) 13 ♗xc7 (13 ♗xe2? ♘h5! 14 ♗xh5 ♗h4 wins for Black) 13...♕xc7!? 14 ♕xc7 ♗xd3 with an interesting position where Black's three minor pieces give good value for the queen and pawn. Note that after the very greedy 15 ♕xb7? ♖fc8! 16 ♕b3 ♖ab8 Black achieves a clear advantage.

C)

3 ♘c3!?

This is the so-called Mason Gambit, which is perhaps not the best objective choice at move 3, but it does contain surprise value and certainly gets Black thinking for himself. White leaves himself wide open to the check on h4, and it would be quite rude not to oblige, so...

3...♕h4+

This check is far more disruptive to White if the king is forced to go to e2, as opposed to the square f1, which is available in the Bishop's Gambit and the Petroff Gambit.

4 ♔e2 d5!?

While it's patently obvious that 3...♕h4+ is the best approach, the objective merits of this move are not so clear. I give it as the main line because traditionally it has been the most popular choice, but there are signs that not everyone would agree to its suitability and one can always find an argument for keeping one's central pawns! So what are Black's alternatives? Here's some more food for thought:

a) 4...d6 (this has been condemned as too passive, but it looks sensible enough to me) and now:

a1) 5 ♘d5?! ♕d8! 6 d4 ♘f6 7 ♘c3 (7 ♘xf6+ ♕xf6 8 ♘f3 g5 also looks good for Black) 7...d5 8 e5 ♘e4 9 ♗xf4 ♘c6 10 ♘xe4 dxe4 (10...♗g4+!) 11 ♔e3 ♗e7 12 ♔xe4 0-0 13 d5 ♘b4 14 c4 ♕d7 15 g4 0-1 was the crazy game A.David-Romanishin, Turin 1998, although in my opinion White resigned way too early here. Surely having your king on e4 is an everyday hazard of playing the King's Gambit?

a2) More normal would be 5 ♘f3, when 5...♗g4 6 d4 g5 7 ♘d5 ♔d8 has been assessed as unclear, but Black could instead go all the way back with the very cheeky 5...♕d8!?. Black's argument for this seeming indulgence is the following: one of the two tempi White has gained has been spent on playing the horrendous move ♔e2. If this positioning of the king were to be

corrected at some point with the reasonable move ♔f2, then we would reach a normal King's Gambit position with White's king on f2 rather than e1, the consequences of which are difficult to ascertain.

b) 4...♕e7!? (this also looks quite good) 5 d4 ♘f6 6 e5 d6 7 ♘f3 dxe5 8 dxe5 g5 9 ♔e1 g4 10 ♗xf4 gxf3 11 ♕xf3 c6 12 ♗c4 ♗g7 13 ♔d2 ♘g4 and Black went on to win in C.Bauer-Bacrot, Enghien-les-Bains 1999. The onus is on White to come up with something here as well.

5 ♘xd5 (D)

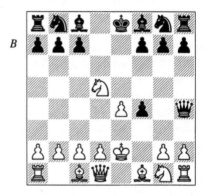

5...♗d6

The main alternative for Black is to play 5...♗g4+!? 6 ♘f3 ♘c6, the only problem I can see being that best play probably leads to a draw.

a) 7 d4?! 0-0-0 8 ♗xf4 f5! 9 ♔e3 ♗xf3 10 gxf3 ♘f6 11 ♘xf6 ♖xd4 12 ♕e1 ♕xf6 favours Black, according to McDonald in *The King's Gambit*.

b) 7 c3 0-0-0 8 ♕e1 ♕xe1+ 9 ♔xe1 and now I prefer 9...f5 to 9...♖e8 10 d4

♖xe4+ 11 ♔f2, which Glazkov gives as equal.

c) 7 ♘xc7+ (and why not?) 7...♔d8 8 ♘xa8 ♘e5 and now:

c1) 9 d4? ♘xf3 10 gxf3 ♗xf3+! 11 ♔xf3 ♕h5+ 12 ♔f2 ♕xd1 wins.

c2) 9 ♕e1!? (as far as I know this has not been suggested before, but it's the first move my greedy computer comes up with) 9...♘xf3 10 ♕xh4+ ♘xh4+ 11 ♔e1 with a very difficult position to assess. Black can round up the knight with ...♔c8-b8, but meanwhile White can probably win the f4-pawn, leaving a material imbalance of two minor pieces versus a rook and two pawns.

c3) 9 h3 ♗xf3+ (or 9...♗h5!? 10 d4! ♘xf3 11 gxf3 ♗xf3+ 12 ♔xf3 ♕h5+ 13 ♔g2 ♕xd1 14 ♗d3 ♕h5 15 ♗xf4 ♘e7 16 ♖hf1 and now instead of 16...f5, as in Jago-Thomas, corr 1954, Black should play 16...♘g6! with an unclear position) 10 gxf3 ♕g3 and now 11 d4 forces Black to take a draw with 11...♕xf3+ 12 ♔e1 ♕g3+ 13 ♔e2 ♕f3+.

6 ♘f3 ♗g4 7 d4 ♘c6 *(D)*

This position is critical for the assessment of 4...d5. White has three main choices:

a) 8 ♗d3!? ♕h5 9 c3 0-0-0 transposes to line 'c'.

b) 8 e5? 0-0-0! 9 ♗xf4 (9 exd6 ♖xd6 gives Black a very dangerous attack; McDonald then gives 10 c4 ♘f6 11 ♗xf4 ♘xd5 12 ♗xd6? ♖e8+ 13 ♗e5 ♘xe5 14 dxe5 ♖xe5+ 15 ♔d2 ♕h6+ 16 ♔c2 ♘e3+ and Black wins,

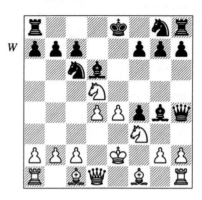

W

but as White can improve with 12 cxd5, 11...♗xf3+! 12 ♔xf3 ♖xd5! 13 cxd5 ♕g4+ is more clear-cut) 9...♘ge7 10 ♗g3 (10 c4 ♗b4 11 a3 ♘xd5 12 cxd5 ♖xd5 13 ♔e3 ♗xf3 14 ♕xf3 g5 is very good for Black – McDonald) 10...♕h6 11 ♘xe7+ ♗xe7 12 c3 f6 13 e6 f5 14 ♕a4 ♕xe6+ 15 ♔f2 ♕h6 16 ♔g1 ♖he8 and Black is in control, Lyell-Flear, British Ch (Plymouth) 1989.

c) 8 c3! 0-0-0 9 ♔d3 ♕h5 (Black could consider 9...♕h6!?) 10 ♔c2 ♘f6 (10...f5?! 11 e5! looks good for White) 11 ♘xf6 gxf6 with a position that is difficult to assess. Black's pawn-structure is pretty ugly, but his pieces are active and his king is slightly safer than White's.

In conclusion I would say that 3 ♘c3 is quite a tricky alternative to the main lines and players may wish to examine the other ideas suggested for Black at move 4.

D)

3 ♗e2 *(D)*

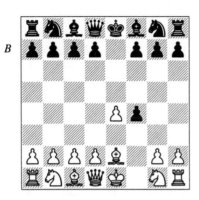

B

This continuation has been called both the Petroff Gambit and the Lesser Bishop's Gambit. White's idea is similar to the Bishop's Gambit, except that the bishop is less prone to attack by ...d5. On the other hand, Black can achieve the ...d5 break far more easily and the bishop is quite passive on e2, so this is hardly a serious attempt by White to achieve an advantage.

3...d5

This has generally been the prescribed antidote to 3 ♗e2, but if Black wishes to steer clear of the beaten track then there are other moves at his disposal. One such move that may be worth a second look is an immediate counterattack in the centre by means of 3...♘f6!?:

a) 4 ♘c3 d5 5 e5 ♘e4 6 ♘f3 ♘c6 7 d3 ♘xc3 8 bxc3 d4 9 0-0 dxc3 10 d4 (10 ♗xf4!?) 10...♗g4 11 ♗b5 ♕d5 12 ♗xc6+ bxc6 13 ♗xf4 c5 and Black was very comfortably placed in Shaw-Wells, London (Lloyds Bank) 1993.

b) 4 e5 looks more critical. Then 4...♘e4 5 ♘f3 d6 6 d3 ♘g5 7 ♗xf4

♘e6! 8 ♗g3 dxe5 9 ♘xe5 ♘d7 10 0-0 ♘xe5 11 ♗xe5 ♗c5+ 12 ♔h1 0-0 looks roughly level to me.

4 exd5 ♘f6 5 ♘f3

This looks like White's best move. After 5 c4?! c6!, 6 d4?! ♗b4+ 7 ♔f1 cxd5 8 ♗xf4 dxc4 9 ♗xb8? ♘d5! 10 ♔f2 ♖xb8 led to a quick win for Black in Tartakower-Capablanca, New York 1924. 6 ♘c3 is better, but I still prefer Black after 6...cxd5 7 cxd5 ♘xd5.

Tartakower recommended the odd-looking 5 ♘c3 ♘xd5 6 ♗f3, but following the simple 6...♘xc3 Black must surely be better after either 7 dxc3 ♕xd1+ 8 ♔xd1 ♗d6 or 7 bxc3 ♕h4+.

5...♘xd5 *(D)*

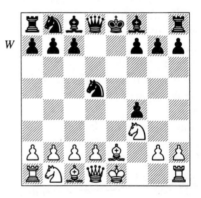

W

6 c4

This move minimizes Black's options. 6 0-0 allows Black to protect his extra pawn by 6...♗d6! 7 c4, and then:

a) The untried 7...♘e7!? is interesting, preparing to bolster the f4-pawn with ...♘g6.

b) 7...♘f6 8 d4 0-0 9 ♘c3 (9 c5 ♗e7 10 ♗xf4 regains the pawn but gives Black the important d5-square as an outpost; nevertheless, this still may be White's best hope) 9...c5! 10 d5 ♖e8 (10...a6?! 11 ♘g5 h6 12 ♘ge4 ♘xe4 13 ♘xe4 was slightly in White's favour in Shaw-McMichael, London (Lloyds Bank) 1993) and now:

b1) 11 ♘e1?! g5! 12 ♔h1 h6 13 ♘d3 ♘bd7 14 a3 ♘e5 15 ♘f2 ♗f5 and Black is in complete control, Thiel-Beikert, 2nd Bundesliga 1991.

b2) White should probably try to get rid of the d6-bishop with 11 ♘b5, although after 11...♗g4 12 ♔h1 a6 13 ♘xd6 ♕xd6 14 ♘g1 ♗xe2 15 ♘xe2 g5 Black has still managed to keep his extra pawn won on move 2.

6...♘e7 7 d4 ♘g6 8 ♘c3 c5 (D)

In general this move can be useful, as it helps Black achieve a foothold on the central squares and prevents any chance of White playing c5 to chase the bishop from d6. However, Black has a couple of important alternatives here:

a) 8...c6 9 ♕d3 ♗e7 10 ♗d2 ♘d7 11 0-0-0 ♘f6 12 ♖hf1 0-0 13 ♘e5 ♘xe5 14 dxe5 ♕xd3 15 ♗xd3 ♘g4 16 ♗xf4 g5 17 h3 gxf4 18 hxg4 ♗xg4 19 ♖d2 was unclear, but certainly no

worse for Black, in Arnason-Nei, Tallinn Keres mem 1983.

b) 8...♗d6!? is a recommendation by Csom. He gives the line 9 h4 h5 10 ♘e4 ♗f5 as being slightly better for Black. I would add to this that 9 0-0 0-0 10 c5 ♗e7 and 9 ♘e4 0-0 10 0-0 ♖e8 11 ♗d3 ♗g4 12 ♘xd6 ♕xd6 also shouldn't worry Black.

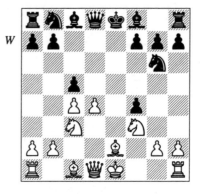

9 dxc5 ♕xd1+ 10 ♗xd1 ♗xc5

J.Cobb-Ferguson, British Ch (Swansea) 1995 now continued 11 ♘d5 ♘a6 12 a3 0-0 13 b4 ♖e8+ 14 ♗e2 ♗d6 15 ♔f2 ♘c7 16 ♘c3, when White has some compensation, but whether it's worth the pawn is very much open to debate.

5 The King's Gambit: The Bishop's Gambit

1 e4 e5 2 f4 exf4 3 ♗c4 *(D)*

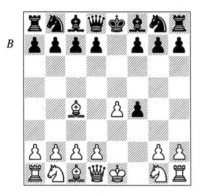

B

Bobby Fischer showed a fondness for 3 ♗c4, which has the advantage over the King's Knight's Gambit of being much less developed theorywise. White provocatively allows Black a queen check on h4. However, as I've stated before, this check looks more disruptive than it is, as the f1-square is a reasonable home for the king and White can then hope to gain time by exploiting the position of the black queen. Another positive feature of the Bishop's Gambit is that it dissuades Black from defending the f4-pawn with ...g5. Unlike in the King's Knight Gambit, the move ...g4 no longer attacks the knight, so it loses much

of its sting. So normally an early ...g5 can here be answered favourably with h4.

A Quick Summary of the Recommended Lines

On move 3 I'm recommending the main line for Black (3...♘f6), which concentrates on rapid development and a counterstrike in the centre with ...d5. After the normal 4 ♘c3 I'm advocating two different systems, both the rare but underrated 4...♗b4 (Line A) and the popular 4...c6 (Line B). Line A can become very sharp and the well-prepared player could be well rewarded here. Line B has been Black's traditional response to the Bishop's Gambit. Of the material here, Line B1 is fun, but shouldn't cause Black too much concern. As far as I can see, White's only real chance to achieve an advantage is with Line B22, although I believe Black has enough resources here too. Added to this, Black has an opportunity earlier on to steer the game into relatively uncharted territory. In general, much of the theory of the Bishop's Gambit is still rather undeveloped, making it a happy hunting ground for the hard-working player.

The Theory of the Bishop's Gambit

1 e4 e5 2 f4 exf4 3 ♗c4 ♘f6! *(D)*

The main choice. Black immediately puts pressure on the e4-pawn and prepares ...d5. It should be said that the obvious-looking 3...♕h4+, while still playable, loses some appeal here. White's king sits safely on f1 and White can then gain time with ♘f3. Garry Kasparov was once forced to play the Bryan Counter-Gambit (3...♕h4+ 4 ♔f1 b5?!) in a theme game against Nigel Short; he lasted all of fifteen moves and was not a happy person at the end of the game. It's true that Black has better ideas on move four, but I think you get the gist of what I'm saying.

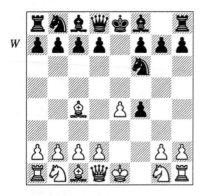

4 ♘c3 *(D)*

The most natural move, defending e4 and discouraging ...d5. Other moves are less good:

a) 4 e5?! d5! 5 ♗b3 ♘e4 6 ♘f3 ♗g4 7 0-0 ♘c6 and Black is simply a pawn up with a good position to boot, Anderssen-Morphy, Paris 1858.

b) 4 ♕e2 ♗c5! 5 ♘f3 (Estrin and Glazkov give 5 e5 0-0 6 ♘f3 d5 7 ♗b3 ♘c6 8 c3 d4! and 5 c3 ♗xg1 6 ♖xg1 0-0 as good for Black) 5...♘c6 6 ♘c3 0-0 7 d3 ♘d4! 8 ♘xd4 ♗xd4 9 ♗xf4 ♗xc3+ (9...d5!? 10 ♘xd5 ♘xd5 11 ♗xd5 ♗xb2 12 ♖b1 ♗c3+ 13 ♗d2 ♗xd2+ 14 ♕xd2 c6 15 ♗b3 ♕e7 16 0-0 ♗e6 looks about equal) 10 bxc3 d5 11 ♗b3 (11 ♗xd5 ♘xd5 12 exd5 ♖e8 13 ♗e3 ♕xd5 is clearly in Black's favour) 11...dxe4 12 0-0 exd3 13 cxd3 ♘d5 14 ♗e5 ♗e6 and White doesn't have enough play for the pawn.

c) 4 d3 was briefly used by the Polgar sisters, but it shouldn't cause Black any particular concern after 4...♘c6 5 ♗xf4 (5 ♘f3 d5 6 exd5 ♘xd5 7 ♗xd5 ♕xd5 8 ♗xf4 ♗g4 9 0-0 0-0-0 gave Black an edge in Balinov – Brinck-Claussen, Copenhagen 1989) 5...d6 6 exd5 ♘xd5 7 ♕e2+ (7 ♗d2?! ♗c5 8 ♕f3 ♕e7+ 9 ♘e2? ♘d4 10 ♕e4 ♘xc2+ gave Black a winning position in Spielmann-Chigorin, Nuremberg 1906, while 7 ♗xd5 ♕xd5 8 ♘f3 ♗g4 9 0-0 0-0-0 10 ♕d2 ♗c5+ 11 ♔h1 f6 is better for Black, Alapin-Chigorin, St Petersburg 1881) 7...♗e7 (or 7...♗e6!?, planning to answer 8 ♗xd5 ♕xd5 9 ♗xc7 with 9...♖c8!) 8 ♗xd5 ♕xd5 9 ♘c3 ♕a5 10 ♘f3 0-0 11 0-0 ♗g4 and Black's bishop-pair gives him an edge, Spielmann-Schlechter, Nuremberg 1906.

We now look at two playable ideas for Black.

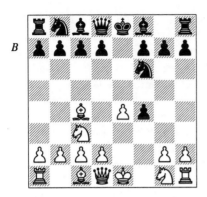

A: 4...♗b4!?   47
B: 4...c6   49

A)

4...♗b4!?

This natural developing move has been largely neglected in favour of 4...c6, but there is no evidence to suggest that it is in any way inferior. Black gets ready to castle and prepares to answer e5 with the classic counter-strike ...d5. In many ways you could say Black is playing *à la* Lopez and similarly White is playing a 'Schliemann' Attack(!). It's just a case of measuring how important the extra tempo for White is over the normal 1 e4 e5 2 ♘f3 ♘c6 3 ♗b5 f5.

5 e5

Attacking the f6-knight must be the critical test of Black's fourth move, but White does have two decent alternatives:

a) 5 ♘f3 0-0 and now:

a1) 6 ♘d5 ♘xd5 7 exd5 ♖e8+ 8 ♔f2 and now 8...d6 9 d4 ♕f6?? 10 c3 ♗a5 11 ♕a4 was a very bad day at the office for a chess genius in de Rivière-Morphy, Paris 1863. However, there's no real need for Black to worry unduly about this line. Substitute 8...d6 with 8...♗f8 9 d4 d6 10 ♗xf4 ♗g4 11 ♖f1 ♘d7, and Black has a rock-solid position, while the scope of White's light-squared bishop is severely hampered by his own pawn on d5.

a2) 6 0-0 ♘xe4! 7 ♘xe4 (7 ♘d5 c6! 8 ♘xb4 ♕b6+ 9 d4 ♕xb4 10 ♗b3 d5 also gives Black a pawn for nothing much) 7...d5 8 ♗xd5 ♕xd5 9 d3 ♗f5 and Black is at least OK.

a3) 6 e5 d5! (naturally) 7 ♗b3 ♗xc3 8 dxc3 ♘h5 9 ♕xd5 ♕xd5 10 ♗xd5 c6 11 ♗c4 ♗g4 12 0-0 ♘d7 13 ♖e1 ♖ae8 and the weakness of the e5-pawn gives Black the advantage, O.Jackson-Adams, Sheffield 1991.

b) 5 ♘ge2!? makes some sense, since now the f4-pawn is pretty much bagged. After 5...0-0 6 0-0 Black should once again simplify with the fork trick 6...♘xe4!. Zso.Polgar-Sanz Alonso, Leon 1989 continued 7 ♘xe4 d5 8 c3 ♗e7 9 ♗d3 dxe4 10 ♗xe4 c5 11 ♘xf4 ♘d7 12 ♕f3 ♖b8 13 ♘d5 ♗d6 14 d4 cxd4 15 cxd4 ♘b6 with a roughly level position.

5...d5!

Here the placing of the bishop on c4, and the loss of tempo over the Schliemann line of 1 e4 e5 2 ♘f3 ♘c6 3 ♗b5 f5 4 exf5 e4, actually helps Black. In the Schliemann, 5 d4 would not be an option because it attacks no bishop.

6 ♗b5+!

This is better than 6 exf6 dxc4 7 fxg7 ♖g8, as Black's queenside pawn-structure is an improvement over the main line.

6...c6 7 exf6 cxb5 *(D)*

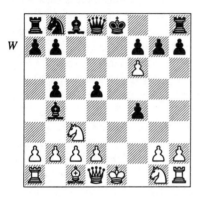

8 fxg7

It looks reasonably natural to grab this pawn and force the rook to move, but there is a line of reasoning for leaving the pawn on f6. A critical alternative for White is 8 ♕e2+!? ♗e6 9 ♕xb5+ ♘c6:

a) 10 ♕xb7 and now 10...♖c8 11 ♘f3 ♕xf6 transposes to line 'b', while 10...♘d4 11 ♘b5 ♘xc2+ 12 ♔d1 ♖c8 13 fxg7 ♖g8 gives us the note to White's 11th move in the main line.

b) 10 ♘f3 ♕xf6!? (Estrin and Glazkov give 10...♗xc3 11 bxc3 ♕c7 12 fxg7 ♖g8 13 c4 0-0-0 14 ♗b2 d4 as unclear) 11 ♕xb7 ♖c8 12 ♘xd5 ♕f5 13 ♘c7+ (13 ♘xb4 ♕e4+ 14 ♔d1 ♕xb4 15 ♕xb4 ♘xb4 16 c3 ♘d3 gives White an extra pawn, but Black has some kind of light-square bind). Now Paulsen-Kolisch, London 1861

continued 13...♖xc7? 14 ♕xc7 ♕e4+ 15 ♔d1 0-0 16 d3 ♕g6 17 ♕xf4 and White consolidated his extra material. However, if Black plays 13...♔d8! 14 ♘xe6+ ♕xe6+ 15 ♔f1 (or 15 ♔d1 ♕g6!?) 15...♕c4+, things are still far from clear.

8...♖g8 9 ♕e2+ ♗e6 10 ♕xb5+

Alternatively:

a) 10 ♘h3?! ♕h4+ 11 ♕f2 ♕xf2+ 12 ♘xf2 (McDonald-Law, British Ch (Hove) 1997) and now according to McDonald the simple 12...♖xg7 gives Black the advantage.

b) 10 ♘f3 ♘c6 11 d4 ♕f6 12 0-0 (12 ♕xb5 0-0-0 13 ♗d2 ♖xg7 seems to favour Black) 12...♗xc3 (12...♘xd4!? is also possible; 13 ♘xd4 ♕xd4+ 14 ♔h1 ♕c4 15 ♕f2 ♗xc3 16 bxc3 ♖xg7 17 ♗xf4 is very difficult to assess, but it's probably not worse for Black) 13 bxc3 a6 14 a4!? bxa4 15 ♖xa4 b5 16 ♖a1 ♖xg7 17 ♘e1!? (17 ♘e5 ♘xe5 18 dxe5 ♕g6 19 ♗xf4 appears equal) 17...♘xd4! and now instead of 18 cxd4? ♕xd4+ 19 ♕f2 ♕xa1 20 ♘d3 f3 21 g3 ♕a4 22 ♗b2 ♖g6 23 ♗d4 ♕c4 24 ♕e3 ♖g4, which was winning for Black in Chandler-Emms, London tt 1997, White should play 18 ♕f2!, after which the position remains incredibly murky.

10...♘c6 11 ♘f3 *(D)*

Instead 11 ♕xb7 ♖c8 (alternatively, 11...♘d4!?, when White might try 12 ♔d1) 12 ♘f3 ♖xg7 13 0-0 ♗h3 gave Black the initiative in the game O.Castro-Karpov, Stockholm jr Wch 1969.

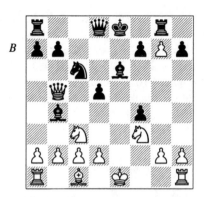

B

The position after 11 ♘f3 is still very complicated. It's true that Black's pawn-structure could be better, but the bishop-pair and chances to attack down the half-open g-file should give Black reason to feel reasonably confident. Here are a couple of practical examples (we've been waiting more than a century for more recent ones!):

a) 11...♖xg7 12 0-0 ♕d7 13 d4 0-0-0 14 ♗xf4 ♖dg8 15 ♖f2 and White is a little better, Chigorin-Englisch, Vienna 1882.

b) 11...♕d7 12 d4 a6! 13 ♕a4 (perhaps 13 ♕e2 is stronger) 13...♖xg7 14 0-0 ♗d6 15 ♘e2? ♗h3! 16 ♘e1 (or 16 ♖f2 ♕g4!) 16...♗xg2! 17 ♘xg2 ♕h3 18 ♖f2 f3 19 ♘g3 ♗xg3 20 hxg3 ♖xg3 and White had to resign in Rosenthal-Bird, Vienna 1873. Not especially good play from White, but this is an illustration of the counterplay Black can achieve down the half-open g-file.

B)

4...c6 *(D)*

This is Black's main choice at move 4. Logically, Black attempts to break in the centre with ...d5.

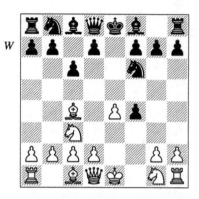

W

White now has two main options:
B1: 5 d4!?   50
B2: 5 ♗b3   52

Let's first consider less important moves:

a) Once again 5 e5 is answered by 5...d5!.

b) 5 ♘f3!? b5 6 ♗b3 b4 7 e5 (7 ♘e2 ♘xe4 8 d3 ♘c5 9 ♗xf4 d5 10 0-0 ♗e7 leaves White without enough compensation, Peixoto-Sanz Alonso, Loures 1997) 7...bxc3 8 exf6 ♕xf6 9 bxc3 ♗a6 10 ♔f2 ♗e7 11 d4 0-0 12 ♕d2 (De Wit-Overeem, Haarlem 1996) and here Black should return the pawn with 12...d5! 13 ♕xf4 ♘d7, when if anything Black has the advantage due to his better pawn-structure.

c) 5 ♕f3 d5! 6 exd5 ♗d6 with the alternatives:

c1) 7 d4 0-0 8 ♗xf4 ♗g4 9 ♕g3 ♖e8+ 10 ♔f1 ♗xf4 11 ♕xf4 cxd5 12

♗d3 ♘c6 and White had no compensation for his poor king position in Winkelman-Horowitz, Philadelphia 1936.

c2) 7 d3 ♗g4 8 ♕f2 0-0 9 ♗xf4 ♖e8+! 10 ♔f1 b5 11 ♗b3 b4 12 ♘ce2 ♘xd5 13 ♗xd5 cxd5 is clearly better for Black (Estrin and Glazkov).

c3) 7 h3 0-0 8 ♘ge2 g5 9 0-0 b5 10 ♗b3 b4 11 ♘a4 cxd5 12 ♗xd5 g4 13 ♕b3 ♘xd5 14 ♕xd5 f3! 15 ♕xa8 fxe2 16 ♖e1 ♖e8 17 d3 ♕h4 18 ♗e3 ♖xe3 19 ♕d5 ♖xh3 0-1 was a very nice game (from Black's point of view at least) in Szilagyi-S.Szabo, corr 1973.

c4) 7 ♕e2+! ♗e7 transposes to line 'd'.

d) 5 ♕e2 d5! 6 exd5+ ♗e7 and now:

d1) 7 d4 0-0 8 ♗xf4 cxd5 9 ♗b3 ♗b4 10 0-0-0 ♗xc3 11 bxc3 ♘e4! and Black was well placed in Enders-Möhring, Salzwedel 1982.

d2) 7 d6! ♕xd6 8 d3 0-0 9 ♗d2 b5 10 ♗b3 a5 11 a4 b4 12 ♘e4 ♘xe4 13 ♕xe4 ♗f6 14 0-0-0 ♗g4 15 ♗xf4 ♕d7 with an unclear position, J.Polgar-Benjamin, Buenos Aires 1992.

B1)
5 d4!?
This move is almost the exclusive property of Heikki Westerinen. White's idea is to answer 5...d5 with 6 exd5 cxd5 7 ♗b5+, leaving the bishop more active than on b3. However, Black can cut across this plan by putting immediate pressure on e4 with...

5...♗b4! 6 e5

This is virtually forced. 6 ♕f3 d5 7 exd5 0-0!? 8 ♘ge2 cxd5 9 ♗d3 ♗g4 10 ♕xf4 ♗xe2 11 ♔xe2 ♖e8+ 12 ♗e3 ♘c6 13 ♖af1 ♕d7 14 ♘d1 ♗d6 15 ♕h4 ♘e4 16 c3 f5 was very comfortable for Black in Hartmann-Spassky, Bundesliga 1985/6.

6...♘e4 (D)

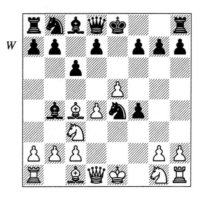

Now White has two main lines:

B11: 7 ♔f1!?   50
B12: 7 ♕h5   51

After 7 ♕f3 Keres analysed 7...d5 8 exd6 0-0 9 ♘e2 ♕h4+ 10 g3 fxg3 11 hxg3 ♕g4 12 ♕xg4 ♗xg4 13 ♗d3 ♖e8 as being good for Black.

B11)
7 ♔f1!?
Westerinen has tried this extravagant move a few times, with mixed success.

7...♘xc3 8 bxc3 d5!
White's idea is to meet 8...♗xc3!? with 9 ♗a3!, which can lead to great complications. Whilst these are not

necessarily bad for Black, it seems pointless to enter them when 8...d5 is such a good and safe alternative.

9 exd6 ♗xd6 10 ♕e2+

Alternatively:

a) 10 ♕f3 ♕f6 11 ♘e2 ♗e6 12 ♗b3 g5 13 ♖b1 ♗f5 14 ♗a4 ♕e7 15 ♘g3 ♗g6 16 ♗d2 ♔d8 17 ♖e1 ♕d7 18 ♘e4 g4 19 ♕f2 ♗xe4 20 ♖xe4 ♕f5 21 ♖e1 ♘d7 left Black very well placed in Westerinen-Hector, Gausdal 1989.

b) 10 ♕h5!? ♕f6 11 ♘f3 0-0 12 ♖b1 ♘d7 13 ♘g5 ♕g6 14 ♕xg6 hxg6 15 ♘e4 ♗c7 16 ♗a3 ♘b6! 17 ♗d3 (or 17 ♗xf8 ♘xc4 18 ♗e7 f5!) 17...♖d8 and Black's extra pawn still gives him the edge, Westerinen-Wedberg, Malmö 1988.

10...♔f8 11 ♘f3 ♗g4! 12 ♕e4 ♗xf3 13 ♕xf3 ♕c7 14 ♗d2 ♘d7

We are following the game Westerinen-Adams, Manila OL 1992. After 15 ♔g1 c5 16 ♗d5 ♖b8 17 ♖f1 ♘f6 18 ♗e4 g5 19 ♗f5 ♖g8 20 ♕f2 h6 21 h4 ♕c6 22 ♕f3 ♕xf3 23 ♖xf3 ♖e8 White had no compensation at all for the pawn and Black eventually converted his advantage into victory.

B12)

7 ♕h5 (D)

7...g6

Also possible for Black here is 7...d5 8 exd6 0-0 9 ♘ge2:

a) 9...♘f6 10 ♕h4 ♗xd6 11 ♗xf4 ♗xf4 12 ♕xf4 and White is slightly better, Westerinen-Flear, Oviedo rpd 1992.

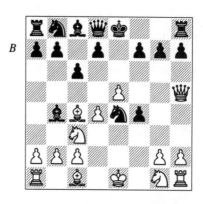

b) 9...♘d7! 10 ♗xf4 ♘df6 11 ♕h4 ♘xd6 12 ♗xd6 ♗xd6 13 0-0 ♗e7 (or 13...♗e6 14 ♗xe6 fxe6 15 ♘e4 e5 16 ♘xd6 ♕xd6 17 ♕g3 ♖fe8 18 ♖ad1 ♕e6 19 c4 exd4 20 ♘xd4 ♕e3+ 21 ♕xe3 ♖xe3 ½-½ Westerinen-Salo, Finnish Cht 1992) 14 ♕f4 ♗g4 15 h3 ♗h5 with equality, Westerinen-Wedberg, Espoo Z 1989.

8 ♕f3

After 8 ♕h6? McDonald gives the line 8...♘xc3 9 bxc3 ♗xc3+ 10 ♔d1 ♗xa1?! 11 ♕g7 ♖f8 12 ♗a3 d6 13 ♗xd6 ♘d7 14 ♗xf8 ♘xe5!, with great complications, before stating that Black can spoil all the fun with the clinical 8...d5!.

8...♕h4+

McDonald also points out that with the insertion of ...g6, playing in the same way as against 7 ♕f3 is not so profitable for Black. After 8...d5 9 exd6 0-0 10 ♘ge2, 10...♕h4+ 11 g3 fxg3 12 hxg3 ♕g4 allows White to make use of the weak dark squares with 13 ♕e3!, when 13...♖e8 runs into 14 ♖xh7! ♔xh7 15 ♗xf7, threatening mate on h6 and the rook on e8. However, 10...♘xd6 11 ♗d3 and only then 11...♕h4+ looks like a reasonable alternative for Black.

9 ♔f1 *(D)*

After 9 g3? fxg3 10 ♗xf7+ ♔e7 11 hxg3 ♕xg3+ 12 ♕xg3 ♘xg3 13 ♖h3 ♔xf7 14 ♖xg3 d5 Black was a pawn up with a good ending in Westerinen-Ernst, Helsinki 1991.

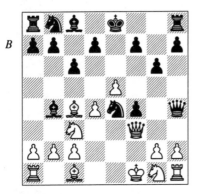

9...d5

9...♘g3+? is a little too greedy. Westerinen-Pakkanen, Helsinki 1992 continued 10 hxg3 ♕xh1 11 ♗xf4 ♗xc3 12 ♗xf7+!! ♔xf7 13 e6+ ♔xe6 14 ♗e5 ♕h5 15 ♕f6+ ♔d5 16 ♕d6+ ♔e4 17 bxc3 ♖f8+ 18 ♗f4 ♖xf4+ 19 ♕xf4+ ♔d5 20 g4 and Black resigned as he must give up his queen to avoid mate.

10 exd6 ♘xc3 11 bxc3 ♗xd6 12 g3

Ernst suggests 12 ♕e4+ ♕e7 13 ♕xe7+ ♔xe7 14 ♘e2, but after 14...g5 White still has some work to do even to reach a level position.

12...♕g4 13 ♗xf4 ♗xf4 14 ♖e1+

We are following Westerinen-Hector, Östersund Z 1992, which continued 14...♔d8 15 gxf4 ♖e8 16 ♗xf7 ♖f8 17 ♕xg4 ♗xg4 18 ♗e6 ♖xf4+ 19 ♔g2 ♗xe6 20 ♖xe6 ♔d7 21 ♖e3 ♘a6 22 ♘f3 ♖af8 23 ♖he1 ♘c7 with equality. Black can also try 14...♔f8; for example, 15 gxf4 ♗f5!? 16 ♕e3 ♘d7! 17 ♕e7+ ♔g7 18 ♕xf7+ ♔h6, with great complications.

B2)

5 ♗b3 d5 6 exd5 cxd5 7 d4 ♗d6 *(D)*

A major alternative for Black here is the pinning move 7...♗b4!?, whereby Black concentrates on possession of the light squares, particularly e4 and c4, rather than trying to hang on to f4. After 8 ♘f3 0-0 9 0-0 ♗xc3 10 bxc3 I've found two practical examples:

a) 10...♗e6 11 ♗xf4 ♘e4 12 ♕d3 ♘c6 13 ♘d2 ♘xd2 14 ♗xd2 ♕d7 15 ♖f4 ♘e7 16 ♖e1 ♖fe8 17 h3 ♖ac8 18 ♖f2 b5 19 ♖e5 a5 20 a3 a4 21 ♗a2 ♖b8 22 ♖h5 ♘g6 23 ♕f3 ♖bd8 and neither side can make any real progress, Westerinen-Raetsky, Hafnarfjördur 1998. This game is notable for the fact that even Westerinen, the greatest advocate of 5 d4, has recently switched his allegiance to 5 ♗b3.

b) 10...♕c7 11 ♖e1 ♘c6 12 ♕h4!? ♘e7! 13 ♗xf4 ♕xc3 14 ♗d2 ♕c7 15 ♘e5 ♘f5 16 ♕f4 ♗e6 17 ♗b4 ♖fc8 18 g4 ♘d6 19 ♖ae1 gave White some compensation for the pawn in Morozevich-Anand, Moscow rpd 1995, although whether it's enough is a matter for debate. Anand now continued 19...♘fe4?!, which allowed the young Russian star to increase the pressure further by 20 c4! dxc4 21 ♗c2, with White eventually winning the game after 21...♘f6 22 g5 ♘h5 23 ♕f3 g6 24 ♘xg6! hxg6 25 ♗xg6 fxg6 26 ♖xe6 ♕f7 27 ♕d5 ♘f5 28 ♖xf5!. Instead, Vaïsser suggests 19...a5! to be a better defence. After 20 ♗xd6 ♕xd6 21 g5 ♘e8! Black can look to the future with some confidence.

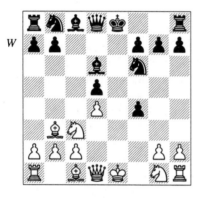

Here we have a further split in ideas. White can play either:

B21: 8 ♘ge2 53
B22: 8 ♘f3 54

B21)

8 ♘ge2

The old move, planning to regain the pawn on f4 as quickly as possible.

8...0-0 9 ♗xf4!?

In 1964 Bobby Fischer analysed this variation for the American magazine *Chess Life*. Grabbing the pawn with the text-move is Fischer's attempt at

an improvement over the older 9 0-0 g5! 10 ♘xd5 ♘c6, which seems to be OK for Black; for example:

a) 11 c3 ♘xd5 12 ♗xd5 ♘e7 13 ♗e4 f5 14 ♗d3 b6 15 ♗d2 ♘g6 16 ♕b3+ ♔g7 and Black was clearly better in the game Spielmann-Bogoljubow, Mährisch-Ostrau 1923.

b) 11 h4 (this is stronger) 11...h6 12 hxg5 hxg5 13 ♘ec3 (Tartakower assessed this position as equal) 13...♗f5 and now:

b1) 14 ♗e3 ♖e8 15 ♗f2 ♘g4 16 ♕d2 ♔g7 17 ♘e2 ♖xe2!! 0-1 was the brilliant conclusion to Baron-Negre, corr 1990. After 18 ♕xe2 ♕h8 19 ♖fe1 ♘ce5!! 20 dxe5 ♕h2+ 21 ♔f1 ♕h1+ 22 ♗g1 ♘h2+ 23 ♔f2 ♗c5+, Black wins everything.

b2) 14 g3!? ♖c8!? 15 gxf4 g4 16 ♔g2?! (16 ♘e3 seems to be stronger) 16...♘xd5 17 ♗xd5 ♗b4 and Black has good play for the pawn, Heinemann-E.Meier, Germany 1988.

9...♗xf4 10 ♘xf4 ♖e8+ 11 ♘fe2 ♘g4 12 ♘xd5 ♗e6 13 h3

13 ♘df4 ♗xb3 14 axb3 ♕f6! looks promising for Black.

13...♘h6! *(D)*

Fischer analysed 13...♗xd5 14 hxg4 ♗xg2 15 ♖h2! – it seems that White is better here; e.g., 15...♗f3 16 ♕d3 ♖xe2+ 17 ♖xe2 ♗xe2 18 ♕xe2 ♕h4+ 19 ♕f2 ♕xf2+ 20 ♔xf2 and, with a powerful bishop on b3, White has a better endgame, Berry-Day, corr 1974.

After the text-move (13...♘h6), it seems to me that Black has at least enough for the pawn. For example:

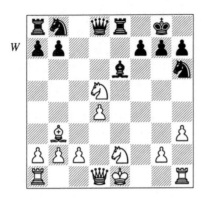

a) 14 c4? ♗xd5 15 cxd5 ♕h4+ 16 ♔f1 ♘f5! 17 ♕d3 ♕g5 18 ♖h2 ♖e3 19 ♕c2 (19 ♕b5 ♖xe2 20 ♕xb7 ♘g3+ 21 ♔g1 ♕e3#) 19...♘c6!! 20 h4 (20 dxc6 ♖xe2!! 21 ♕c3 ♘g3+ 22 ♔g1 ♕f4 and 20 ♕c4 ♖xe2! 21 ♔xe2 ♖e8+ lead to winning attacks for Black) 20...♕g4 21 ♗c4 (21 dxc6 ♖xe2 22 cxb7 ♘g3+ 23 ♔g1 ♕xd4# is mate, while 21 ♖e1 ♖xe2 22 ♖xe2 ♘g3+ 23 ♔e1 ♘xd4 is also winning for Black) 21...♘cxd4 22 ♘xd4 ♘g3+ 0-1 (due to 23 ♔g1 ♕xd4 24 ♕f2 ♘e4) Maior-ielli-Bucciardini, corr 1988.

b) 14 ♘df4 ♗xb3 15 axb3 ♘f5! (15...♕h4+?! 16 ♔d2 ♘c6 17 c3 is not so good) 16 ♔f2 (16 c3? ♘g3 17 ♖g1 ♕h4 18 ♔d2 g5! wins for Black) 16...♕h4+ 17 ♔g1 ♖e4 (17...♘c6!?) 18 ♕d2 ♘xd4 19 ♘xd4 ♕xf4 20 ♕xf4 ♖xf4 leading to an equal end-game.

In conclusion, it seems that White needs an improvement here; otherwise Black obtains at least an equal position, and possibly more. Perhaps White should reinvestigate 9 0-0.

B22)
8 ♘f3

This move has found favour with Nigel Short. White simply develops his pieces on their best squares and will only worry about retrieving the f4-pawn after castling.

8...0-0!

This looks more accurate than 8...♘c6 9 0-0 ♗e6 10 ♘g5!, which gave White an edge in Short-P.Nikolić, Wijk aan Zee 1997.

9 0-0 ♗e6 10 ♘e5

Alternatively:

a) 10 ♘g5?! ♗g4! 11 ♕d3 h6 12 ♘f3 ♘c6 13 a3 ♗xf3 and now 14 gxf3 ♕b6 15 ♘xd5 ♘xd5 16 ♗xd5 ♘xd4 17 ♔h1 ♖ad8 was clearly better for Black in Westerinen-Gunnarsson, Rey-kjavik 1997, while 14 ♖xf3 ♕b6 is not much of an improvement.

b) 10 ♘b5!? ♘c6 11 ♘xd6 ♕xd6 and now 12 ♕d2?! ♘h5 13 ♕f2 f6 14 c3 g5 15 ♗c2 ♖ae8 gave Black the ad-vantage in Jonkman-Xie Jun, Vlissin-gen 1997. Perhaps White should play 12 ♘g5!?, but even then Black can stir things up with 12...♗g4 13 ♕d3 ♘b4! 14 ♕b5 ♗d7 15 ♕a5, when the white queen is strangely situated.

10...♗xe5

Black can also continue in a solid fashion with 10...♘c6, although after 11 ♘xc6 bxc6 12 ♗xf4, 12...♗e7 13 ♕d3 ♕d7 14 ♗g5 ♗g4 15 ♖ae1 ♗h5 16 ♗a4 ♖fe8 17 ♕f5 left White a shade better in Maus-Gausel, Gausdal 1993. 12...♕c7 may be a better way to continue for Black, although it is possible for White to deviate earlier with 11 ♗xf4!?.

11 dxe5 ♘g4 (D)

11...♕b6+ 12 ♔h1 ♘e4 13 ♘xe4 dxe4 14 ♖xf4 looks slightly better for White, as Black has problems with his e4-pawn.

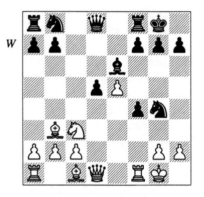

An important position for the assessment of 7...♗d6. As far as I can see, White has three playable alternatives.

a) 12 ♖xf4 ♕b6+ 13 ♕d4 ♕xd4+ 14 ♖xd4 ♘c6 15 ♖f4 ♘gxe5 16 ♘xd5 ♖fd8 17 ♘e3 ♘d4 leading to a level ending, Skrobek-Lukacs, Pamporovo 1981.

b) 12 ♕e1!? d4 13 ♘e4 ♗xb3 14 axb3 ♘xe5 15 ♗xf4 ♘bc6 16 ♕g3 with some compensation for the pawn, Eberth-Gacso, Aggtelek 1993.

c) 12 ♘xd5!? and now:

c1) 12...♗xd5 13 ♗xd5! (Bangiev gives 13 ♕xg4 ♗xb3 14 axb3 ♕d4+ 15 ♔h1 ♕xe5 16 c3 ♘c6 17 ♗xf4 ♕e6 as equal) 13...♕b6+ (else White just has the advantage of two bishops against two knights in an open position) 14 ♔h1 ♘f2+ 15 ♖xf2 ♕xf2 16 ♗xb7 ♘d7 17 ♗xa8 ♖xa8 18 ♗xf4 ♕xf4 19 ♕xd7 ♕xe5 20 c3 and White has chances to convert his extra pawn into victory.

c2) 12...♘c6 (this looks best) 13 ♗xf4 ♗xd5 14 ♕xg4 ♗xb3 15 axb3 ♕d4+ 16 ♔h1 ♕xb2 with an unclear position.

In conclusion, I would say that 8 ♘f3 looks like the most dangerous move in the 4...c6 line. I wouldn't be surprised if there are more developments in this last line. One good thing from Black's point of view is that there's always Anand's 7...♗b4 to fall back on, if things are looking shaky in the 7...♗d6 lines.

6 The King's Gambit: The Knight's Gambit

1 e4 e5 2 f4 exf4 3 ♘f3 *(D)*

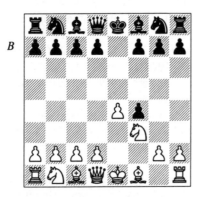

The King's Knight's Gambit is White's most popular form of the opening. By playing 3 ♘f3, White rules out ...♛h4+ (at least for the time being) and prepares to castle kingside. This leads to some of the most exciting variations there are in chess theory. White has a seemingly endless list of different types of gambits, many with strange-sounding names. The good news for Black is that with the repertoire I'm advocating, many of these lines can be avoided, and most of the ones that can't are quite unsound anyway! That said, it's not all doom and gloom for White, and Black is advised to study this chapter very carefully.

A Quick Summary of the Recommended Lines

Given the slightly unstable nature of the theory, where one new move can easily mean a reassessment of an entire variation, I've decided to recommend two defences, the Classical Variation with 3...g5 (Line A), for the bold and willing, and the Becker Defence with 3...h6 (Line B), for the slightly more reserved.

Line A1 is relatively unexplored and this is certainly worthy of some serious study. A2 gives us the old Hanstein and Greco-Philidor Gambits, which have fallen into disuse in recent times. White's main choice remains 4 h4, which can lead to the wild but ultimately unsound Allgaier Gambit (Line A31) or the much more popular Kieseritzky Gambit (Line A32). The Kieseritzky remains the sternest test of 3...g5, but as far as I can see, all Black's defences are holding up very well.

The Becker Defence (Line B) sees Black trying to transpose into favourable variations of Line A, without allowing the Allgaier and Kieseritzky Attacks. On the other hand, 3...h6 allows White other possibilities, including 4 b3!? (Line B1) and variations with an early g3 and/or h4 (Lines B21 and B22). However, Black also seems to be holding his own here, so the Becker Defence remains a viable and simple alternative to 3...g5.

The Theory of the King's Knight Gambit

1 e4 e5 2 f4 exf4 3 ♘f3

Here we will look at two defences for Black:

A: 3...g5   57
B: 3...h6   73

A)
   3...g5 *(D)*

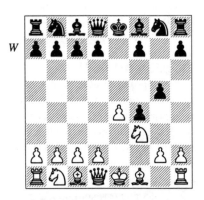

This is probably the most critical response to the King's Gambit. White is told in no uncertain terms that Black intends to hang on to the pawn. White now has three main tries:

A1: 4 d4   57
A2: 4 ♗c4   59
A3: 4 h4   64

The only other real alternative to be aware of is 4 ♘c3!?, which has some transpositional qualities. Black can then play:

a) 4...♗g7 5 d4 transposes to Line A1, and may be Black's safest course.

b) 4...g4!? 5 ♘e5 ♕h4+ 6 g3 fxg3 7 ♕xg4 and now:

b1) 7...g2+ 8 ♕xh4 gxh1♕ and now 9 ♘d5 gives White a dangerous attack for the rook; for example, 9...♘a6? 10 d4 (10 ♘f6+!?) 10...♗e7?? 11 ♕xe7+!! ♘xe7 12 ♘f6+ 1-0 Taylor-NN, Thorpe sim 1874. However, 9 ♕h5! is most convincing.

b2) 7...♕xg4 8 ♘xg4 is better for White than the similar line looked at in Line A1, as ♘c3 is more useful than d4. Here I would say that White has definite compensation for the pawn.

If this is the case, then 4 ♘c3 is a serious alternative to the main lines. Note that 4...♘c6 is the Vienna Gambit, which is outside our repertoire.

A1)
   4 d4

This is called the Rosentreter Gambit. White invites Black to play an early ...g4, when a knight move would allow a disruptive check on h4.

   4...g4 *(D)*

Black accepts the challenge. It's also possible to play it safe with 4...h6, transposing into the Becker Defence (see Line B), or perhaps the more flexible 4...♗g7:

a) 5 h4 h6 transposes to the Becker Defence (Line B2).

b) 5 ♗c4 d6 6 0-0 h6 gives us the Hanstein Gambit (Line A22).

c) 5 ♘c3!? d6 6 g3 g4 (6...h6 once more takes us to the Becker Defence) 7 ♘h4 f3 8 ♗e3 ♘e7!? (8...♘c6 9 ♕d2 ♘ce7 10 0-0-0 c6 11 ♗d3 ♕a5 was unclear in Furhoff-Aleksandrov, Stockholm 1995) 9 ♕d2 ♘g6 and now 10 ♘xg6?! hxg6 11 0-0-0 ♘c6 12 ♘d5 ♗e6 13 ♗b5 a6 14 ♗a4 ♗xd5 15 exd5 b5 16 dxc6 bxa4 17 ♖de1 ♔f8 18 ♕a5 ♖h5 turned out well for Black in Furhoff-Petran, Budapest 1994, but 10 ♘f5!? looks more testing.

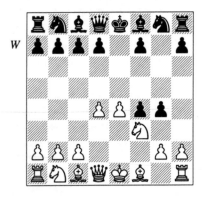

5 ♗xf4

White can also allow the check with 5 ♘e5!? ♕h4+ 6 g3 fxg3 7 ♕xg4, and now:

a) 7...g2+!? (winning a rook, but as so often in the King's Gambit, this is only the start and not the end of the story) 8 ♕xh4 gxh1♕ 9 ♘c3 d6 (a measure of Black's difficulties despite the extra rook can be seen in the pretty line 9...♗e7 10 ♕h5 ♘c6 11 ♘xf7 ♘f6?? 12 ♘d6++ ♔d8 13 ♕e8+ ♖xe8

14 ♘f7# (1-0) Bird-NN, Britain sim 1869) 10 ♘xf7 and now:

a1) 10...♔xf7? 11 ♕h5+ ♔g7 12 ♔f2!? (trying to trap the queen; 12 ♕g5+ ♔f7 13 ♕h5+ forces a draw, because 13...♔e7? 14 ♗g5+ is winning for White) 12...h6 13 ♗c4! (after 13 ♗g2 Black has the defensive resource 13...♘f6!) 13...♔h7 14 e5! and Black faces an awesome attack.

a2) 10...♗e7! 11 ♕h5 and now 11...♘f6 12 ♘xd6++ ♔d8 13 ♘f7+ ♔e8 is a draw by perpetual check (Levenfish). Note that the winning attempt 11...♗h4+? 12 ♕xh4 ♔xf7 is very strongly met by 13 ♕h5+! ♔f8 14 ♔f2!.

b) 7...♕xg4! (this simple move gives Black a safe edge) 8 ♘xg4 d5 9 ♘e3 dxe4 10 hxg3 ♘c6 and White doesn't have enough compensation for the pawn.

5...gxf3 6 ♕xf3 d6!?

The supposed refutation to White's play is contained in 6...d5, with the line continuing 7 exd5 ♘f6 8 ♗b5+ c6 9 ♗e5 ♗g7 10 dxc6 bxc6 11 ♗xc6+ ♘xc6 12 ♕xc6+ ♗d7 13 ♕f3 0-0 14 0-0 ♘e8, when Black's piece is worth more than White's three pawns. However, a recent correspondence game has forced a major reassessment of this line after the discovery of 7 ♗e5!. Coco-Tuisko, corr 1995 continued 7...f6 (7...dxe4 8 ♕xe4 ♕e7? 9 ♘c3! f6 10 ♘d5 wins for White) 8 ♕h5+ ♔e7 9 ♘c3 c6 10 exd5 ♕e8 (or 10...♕b6 11 ♗c4 ♕xb2 12 0-0! ♕xc3 13 d6+ ♔d8 14 ♗xg8 ♕e3+ 15 ♔h1

♘d7 16 ♗xf6+! ♘xf6 17 ♕f7 and White wins) 11 ♕h4 ♔d7 12 0-0-0 ♗h6+ (12...fxe5? 13 dxe5 ♔c7 14 d6+ ♔d7 15 g3, planning ♗h3+, wins) 13 ♔b1 ♕f8 14 ♗e2 ♔d8 15 ♖hf1 ♘d7 16 ♕g3 ♘xe5 17 dxe5 c5 18 e6 and White had a devastating position. Perhaps there are some improvements for Black along the way, but even so, White seems to have a very dangerous initiative.

7 ♘c3 ♘c6 8 ♗c4

After 8 0-0-0 ♕h4! 9 g3 ♗g4 10 ♕f2 ♕h5 Black is ready to castle queenside and consolidate his extra piece.

8...♕h4+!?

In his notes to the game Fedorov adorns Black's last move with a '?!' sign, claiming that Black should grab more material by 8...♘xd4 9 ♗xf7+ ♔xf7 10 ♕h5+ ♔g7. Fedorov gives the line 11 0-0 ♘f6! 12 ♗h6+ ♔g8 13 ♕g5+ ♔f7 14 ♕h5+ ♔e6 15 ♕h3+ ♔e7 16 ♕h4 ♘f5!, but, as McDonald points out, it would take a brave player to follow this line as Black. McDonald also points to 11 0-0-0 as a possible improvement for White, giving the line 11...♘e6 12 ♗e5+, while 11...♘c6 12 ♖d3 looks dangerous for Black.

9 ♗g3 ♕f6 10 ♕xf6 ♘xf6 11 0-0
(D)

Now in Fedorov-Adams, Pula Echt 1997, Black returned the extra piece with 11...♘xd4?, but after 12 ♖xf6 ♗e6 White could have kept a considerable advantage with 13 ♘d5 0-0-0 14 c3 ♘c6 15 ♖af1.

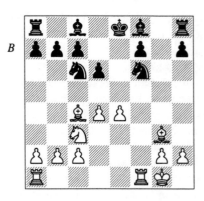

Instead of Adams's move, 11...♗e7! seems to be critical. Fedorov gives 12 e5, with the continuation 12...♘d7 13 ♗xf7+ ♔d8 14 ♖ad1 with unclear play, but McDonald improves on this (from Black's point of view) with 12...dxe5 13 dxe5 ♘a5!, when 14 exf6 is met by 14...♗c5+ and 15...♘xc4. White can keep the attack moving with 14 ♗xf7+ ♔xf7 15 ♘e4, but in my opinion it's unlikely there's enough play there for the sacrificed piece.

In conclusion, I would say that the Rosentreter is one of the least explored lines of the King's Knight's Gambit and so there could well be a reward for home analysis here. Black should bear in mind the 'cop-out' possibility with 4...♗g7.

A2)

4 ♗c4

In the early days of the King's Gambit this logical move, which hits the Achilles' Heel at f7 and prepares to castle, was White's most popular choice. However, in recent years it has been seen as the poor relation to 4 h4, which immediately attacks Black's pawn-wedge.

4...♗g7! *(D)*

It's this move, more than anything, which has caused the decline in use of 4 ♗c4. Rather than heading into the unfathomable complications of the Muzio Gambit with 4...g4 5 0-0!, Black plays it safe, and yet he can still count on the advantage of that extra pawn on f4. In order to attack this structure, White must make some committal decisions.

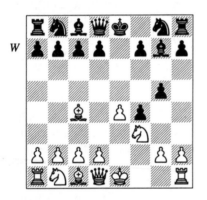

White has a choice between:

A21: 5 h4   60
A22: 5 0-0   62

The former is an attempt to undermine Black's pawn-chain, while the latter continues developing.

5 d4 will probably transpose to A21 or A22 after 5...d6 6 0-0 (or 6 h4).

A21)
5 h4

This gives us the so-called Greco-Philidor Gambit.

5...h6 6 d4 d6 7 c3

Alternatively:

a) 7 ♘c3 (this leaves the d4-pawn vulnerable) 7...♘c6 8 ♘e2 ♕e7 9 ♕d3 ♗d7 10 ♗d2 0-0-0 11 ♗c3 (11 0-0-0 can be answered by 11...♘f6 12 hxg5 ♘xe4!) 11...♖e8 12 d5 ♘e5 13 ♘xe5 dxe5 14 0-0-0 ♘f6 and Black is clearly better, Anderssen-Neumann, Berlin 1866.

b) 7 ♕d3 ♘c6 8 hxg5 hxg5 9 ♖xh8 ♗xh8 10 e5 (the point of White's 7th move; White threatens ♕h7) 10...♗g7 (10...♔f8 also looks good, and may well transpose) 11 ♕h7 (11 ♘c3 ♘h6 12 exd6 cxd6 13 ♘d5 ♔f8 14 ♘xg5 ♕xg5 15 ♗xf4 ♕h4+ gave Black the advantage in Rosenthal-Neumann, 1869) 11...♔f8 12 ♘c3 (12 ♕h5 ♘h6 13 exd6 ♘xd4! 14 ♘xd4 ♗g4 15 ♕h2 ♕xd6 16 ♘e2 ♖e8 17 ♘d2 ♘f5 and White resigned in Remakulus-Brglez, corr 1980 due to the twin threats of ...♘g3 and ...♘d4) 12...♘h6 13 ♗d3 ♘b4 14 ♗e4 d5 15 ♗d3 g4 and Black is on top, Anderssen-Neumann, Berlin 1865.

7...♘c6

Here we have a further split:

A211: 8 ♕b3?!   60
A212: 8 0-0   61

A211)
8 ♕b3?!

This gives Black the chance to move swiftly onto the counterattack, by attacking the e4-pawn.

8...♕e7! 9 0-0 ♘f6! 10 hxg5 hxg5 11 ♘xg5 ♘xd4! 12 ♗xf7+

Or 12 cxd4 ♘xe4! and White's in big trouble. After 13 ♘xe4 ♗xd4+ 14 ♘f2 ♕h4 Black wins at once. More resilient is 13 ♘h3, but even then Black keeps a very strong attack with 13...♗xd4+ 14 ♔h2 ♘g5.

12...♔d8 *(D)*

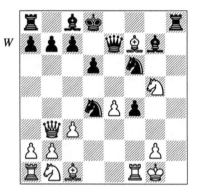

It appears that White has no good move here; for example:

a) 13 ♕d1 ♘xe4 14 ♖e1 ♕xg5 15 ♖xe4 ♕h4 16 ♕a4 ♘f3+ 17 ♔f1 ♕h1+ 18 ♔e2 ♕xg2+ 19 ♔d3 ♘e5+ 20 ♖xe5 dxe5 0-1 Mandoll-Buczko, corr 1983.

b) After 13 cxd4 ♘xe4 14 ♗xf4 (14 ♘f3 ♗xd4+ 15 ♘xd4 ♕h4 is winning for Black) 14...♗xd4+ 15 ♗e3, 15...♘g3! looks the most decisive way to win, e.g.:

b1) 16 ♖e1 ♕xg5 17 ♗xd4 (alternatively, 17 ♘d2 ♖h1+ 18 ♔f2 ♘f5 19 ♖xh1 ♗xe3+ 20 ♔e1 ♗xd2+ 21 ♔d1 ♘d4) 17...♖h1+ 18 ♔f2 ♕f4+ 19 ♕f3 ♕xd4+.

b2) 16 ♗xd4 ♖h1+ 17 ♔f2 ♖xf1+ 18 ♔xg3 ♕xg5+ 19 ♔h2 ♕h4+.

This line has not been seen recently and unless White can come up with a major improvement then it will remain very much dormant.

A212)

8 0-0 *(D)*

This is certainly better than 8 ♕b3, although once again Black shouldn't have to worry too much.

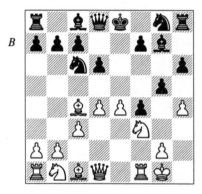

8...♘f6!?

This is certainly not the only way to play. Black also has:

a) 8...♕e7, after which White should not play 9 ♕b3?!, transposing to Line A211, but should attempt to gain space on the queenside, in preparation for Black's king castling that way. Berglund-Muller, corr 1988 continued 9 a4 ♗d7 10 a5 0-0-0 11 b4 ♘b8 12 b5 ♘f6 13 e5 ♘e8 with an unclear position.

b) 8...♗g4 9 ♕b3! (9 ♕d3!? is possible) 9...♘a5!? and now:

b1) 10 ♗xf7+ ♔f8 11 ♕a3 ♔xf7 12 ♕xa5 ♔g6!? (after 12...♗xf3, 13 ♖xf3 c5! 14 ♕xd8 ♖xd8 15 d5 ♗e5 16 g3 g4 17 ♖f1 f3 was very good for Black in Groeneveld-Jerabek, corr 1991, but 13 ♕d5+ may be stronger) 13 ♘bd2 c5 14 ♕b5 ♕d7 15 ♕d3 cxd4 16 cxd4 d5 17 e5+ ♗f5 18 ♕e2 ♘e7 and Black was better in Tebb-Ferguson, British League (4NCL) 1996/7.

b2) 10 ♕a4+!? c6 11 ♗d3 b5!? 12 ♕c2 ♗xf3 13 ♖xf3 ♘f6 was unclear in Zaremba-Mus, corr 1991.

9 hxg5 ♘h5!?

This is new. Previously Black had relied on 9...♘xe4, when *ECO* gives 10 ♖e1 d5 11 ♗d3 hxg5 12 ♗xe4 dxe4 13 ♖xe4+ ♔f8 with an advantage to Black. However, 10 ♗d5! looks stronger. Jerabek-McLeod, corr 1988 continued 10...♘xg5 11 ♗xf4 0-0 12 ♘bd2 ♗e6 13 ♗xg5 hxg5 14 ♗xe6 fxe6, and now 15 ♕b3! would have led to an equal position.

10 g6!?

10 gxh6 ♖xh6 gives Black plenty of play down the h-file. Hjartarson gives the line 11 ♕b3 ♕d7 12 ♘g5? ♘xd4! 13 cxd4 ♗xd4+ 14 ♖f2 ♘g3 and Black wins.

10...fxg6

Yoos-Hjartarson, Reykjavik 1996 now continued 11 ♘h2?! ♖f8 12 b4 a6 13 a4 ♗d7 14 ♗a3 ♘g3 15 ♖e1 ♕h4 and Black held a clear advantage. Hjartarson claims that White has compensation for the pawn after the superior 11 ♘bd2, but here I have to side with McDonald, who cannot find a

reasonable plan for White, and suspects that Black is doing well. After all, his king is probably safer and he has managed to keep the all-important pawn wedge on f4. And added to that, he's a pawn up!

A22)

5 0-0

This is the Hanstein Gambit.

5...h6 6 d4 d6 (D)

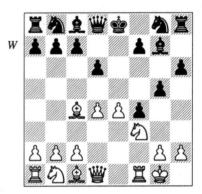

7 c3

Or:

a) Black has two good replies to 7 ♘c3:

a1) 7...♗e6 8 ♗xe6 fxe6 9 ♕d3 ♕d7 10 h4 ♘c6 11 d5 exd5 12 exd5 ♘e5 13 ♘xe5 ♗xe5 14 ♘b5 ♘e7 15 c4 0-0 16 hxg5 hxg5 and Black is a safe pawn up, Grabarczyk-Krasenkow, Polish Ch 1996.

a2) 7...♘c6 8 ♘d5 ♘ce7 9 g3 (or 9 ♘c3 f5 10 exf5 ♘xf5 11 ♖e1+ ♘ge7) 9...♘xd5 10 ♗xd5 ♘f6 11 gxf4 ♘xd5 12 exd5 g4 13 ♘e1 ♗f5 and Black's minor pieces are far better than White's,

Gi.Hernandez-P.Schlosser, Cienfuegos Capablanca mem 1997.

b) Black also need not fear the immediate 7 g3 ♗h3 8 ♖f2 ♘c6! in view of the following lines:

b1) 9 gxf4 g4 10 d5 ♘a5! 11 ♗b5+ c6 12 dxc6 bxc6 13 ♘d4 cxb5 14 ♘xb5 ♔f8 15 ♘1c3 ♘b7 16 ♕d5 ♕d7 17 ♗e3 ♘f6 and Black's extra piece told in Mors-Tanis, corr 1991.

b2) 9 ♗b5 fxg3 (9...♘f6 10 d5 a6 11 ♗xc6+ bxc6 is also good) 10 hxg3 ♗d7 11 ♘c3 ♘f6 and Black is clearly better. Keith-Niemand, corr 1988 continued 12 ♘xg5? hxg5 13 ♗xg5 ♘g4! 14 ♖xf7 (14 ♗xd8 ♖h1+!) 14...♕xg5 0-1.

7...♘c6 8 g3

White's only way to seek play is to attack Black's pawn wedge. 8 h4 gives us the Greco-Philidor Gambit.

8...♗h3 (D)

Naturally Black doesn't pass up the offer of developing his bishop with tempo.

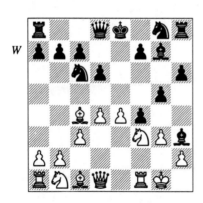

9 gxf4

Offering the exchange is the only way to play for the initiative. Black is doing well after other moves:

a) 9 ♖f2 ♘f6 10 gxf4 ♘xe4 11 ♖e2 (or 11 ♕e1 d5 12 ♘bd2 f5 13 ♗f1 ♗xf1 14 ♘xf1 g4 with a clear plus, Chigorin-Alapin, Ostend 1905) 11...d5 12 fxg5 ♕d7! preparing ...0-0-0 and ...♕g4+, with a virtually decisive attack.

b) 9 ♖e1 fxg3 10 hxg3 ♕d7, followed by ...0-0-0, when Black has a good extra pawn.

9...♕d7!

Once again activity is the key for Black. This move has long been known to be better than 9...♗xf1 10 ♕xf1, which gives White some compensation for the exchange.

10 ♖f2

After 10 f5 Black finally takes the exchange with 10...♗xf1 11 ♕xf1 ♘f6, and now:

a) 12 ♗b5 a6 13 ♗a4 ♘xe4 14 d5 ♕xf5 15 dxc6 ♕c5+ 16 ♔g2 b5 17 ♗c2 ♕xc6 with a clear advantage, Robuck-Niemand, corr 1988.

b) 12 e5 dxe5 13 ♘xe5 ♘xe5 14 dxe5 ♘d5 15 ♕f3 0-0-0 16 f6 ♗f8 and Black was winning in Skov-Devocelle, corr 1988.

c) 12 ♗d3 0-0-0 13 b4 g4 14 ♘fd2 ♖de8 15 b5 ♘a5 16 ♗a3 b6 and once again Black's material advantage counts, Bascetta-Pane, corr 1985.

10...♘f6 11 ♕e1

Alternatively:

a) 11 ♕d3!? 0-0-0 12 ♗b5 and now 12...♕g4+? 13 ♔h1 gxf4 14 ♘g1 f3 15 ♘xh3 ♕xh3 16 ♖xf3 ♕h4 17 ♘d2 ♘g4 18 ♕e2 gave White a plus in Hakola-Lehtinen, corr 1988, but the natural 12...♖he8! looks much stronger, after which White again has trouble supporting his centre.

b) 11 ♘xg5 hxg5 12 fxg5 ♕g4+ 13 ♕xg4 ♘xg4 14 ♗xf7+ (14 ♖xf7 ♘xd4! 15 ♖xg7 ♘f3+ 16 ♔h1 ♘f2# is mate) 14...♔e7 15 ♖f4 ♘xd4! 16 ♗c4 ♖af8 and Black went on to win in Boylu-Muller, corr 1992.

11...0-0-0 12 ♗b5

An example of how fragile White's centre is can be seen quite graphically in the line 12 e5 dxe5 13 ♘xe5 ♘xe5 14 fxe5 ♕g4+ 15 ♔h1 ♘e4 16 ♖e2 ♗xe5! and Black was winning in Issler-Eggman, corr 1966, as 17 dxe5 allows 17...♖d1! 18 ♕xd1 ♘f2+.

12...♖he8 *(D)*

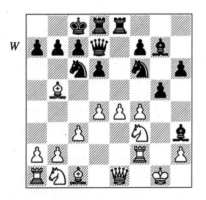

13 ♘bd2

Once again 13 e5 allows Black a devastating counterattack in the centre. After 13...♕g4+ 14 ♔h1 dxe5 we have:

a) 15 dxe5 ♘e4! 16 ♕xe4 ♖d1+ 17 ♘e1 ♖xe5! and Black wins.

b) 15 ♗xc6 bxc6 16 ♘xe5 ♖xe5! 17 fxe5 ♘e4 18 ♖e2 ♕f3+ 19 ♔g1 ♗xe5! and White is helpless against all the threats to his king, as 20 dxe5 loses to 20...♖d1 21 ♕xd1 ♕g4+ 22 ♔h1 ♘f2+ (Estrin).

13...gxf4 14 ♔h1 ♘xe4! 15 ♘xe4 d5

Black regains the piece with a clear advantage (Glazkov). It seems that White needs an improvement at move 11 or 12 to make this line playable again.

A3)

4 h4

This is currently White's most popular move. Black is forced to make an immediate decision over his g-pawn.

4...g4 *(D)*

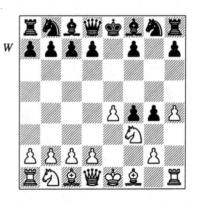

Now White has a major decision to make:

A31: 5 ♘g5   65
A32: 5 ♘e5   66

The former is the wild but probably unsound Allgaier Gambit, while the latter is the more respectable Kieseritzky Gambit.

A31)
5 ♘g5 h6!
In this case the proof of the pudding is most certainly in the eating. And here Black 'eats' the white knight.

6 ♘xf7 ♚xf7 *(D)*

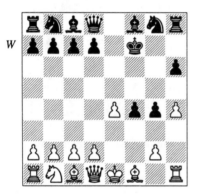

7 ♗c4+

This check is the most logical follow-up, but it's possible White may have other moves, which, while not being objectively better, may force Black to defend with more accuracy.

a) 7 ♕xg4?! (this simply allows Black to develop with gain of tempo) 7...♘f6 8 ♕xf4 (or 8 ♗c4+ d5! 9 ♕xf4 ♗d6 10 ♗xd5+ ♚g7 11 ♕f3 ♘xd5 12 exd5 ♕e8+ 13 ♚d1 h5! and White can already resign on account of ...♗g4) 8...♗d6 9 ♕f2 (9 ♕f5? ♗g3+ 10 ♚d1 d5! traps the white queen) and now 9...♚g7 looks good for Black.

b) 7 d4!? and now:

b1) 7...d6!? 8 ♗xf4 ♗g7 9 ♗c4+ ♚e8 10 0-0 ♘c6 11 ♗e3 ♕xh4 12 ♖f7 ♖h7 13 e5 ♘a5 14 ♗d3 ♚xf7 15 ♕f1+ ♚e7 16 ♗xh7 ♗e6 17 ♘d2 ♖f8 and White's attack was repelled in Morozevich-Kasparov, Paris rpd 1995. It should be noted that this actually arose from the move-order 1 e4 e5 2 f4 exf4 3 ♘f3 d6 (the Fischer Defence) 4 d4 g5 5 h4 g4 6 ♘g5!? (6 ♘g1 is the main line) 6...h6!? (6...f6 is considered stronger) 7 ♘xf7 ♚xf7.

b2) 7...f3 8 gxf3 (8 ♗c4+ d5 9 ♗xd5+ ♚g7 transposes to the main line) 8...d5 9 ♗e3 (or 9 e5 h5 10 ♗e3 ♘h6 11 ♗d3 ♘f5 12 ♗g5 ♗e7 13 fxg4 ♗xg5 14 hxg5 hxg4 15 ♖xh8 ♕xh8 16 ♕xg4 ♕h4+ 17 ♕xh4 ♘xh4 and Black went on to win in Gunsberg-Chigorin, Vienna 1903) 9...♗e7 10 e5 ♗xh4+ 11 ♚d2 c5 12 c3 ♘c6 with a clear advantage to Black, Gunsberg-Schlechter, Vienna 1903.

c) 7 ♘c3!? is a tricky move. White hopes to transpose into the Hamppe Allgaier Gambit after 7...♘c6. This version of the gambit, which often arises via a Vienna move-order of 1 e4 e5 2 ♘c3 ♘c6 3 f4 exf4 4 ♘f3 g5 5 h4 g4 6 ♘g5 h6 7 ♘xf7 ♚xf7, is considered less unfavourable to White than the normal Allgaier, as ♘c3 is more useful than ...♘c6. However, there is no need for Black to oblige in this way:

c1) 7...f3 8 gxf3 ♗e7 9 ♗c4+ d5 10 ♘xd5 ♗xh4+ 11 ♚f1 ♚g7 was considered unclear by Keres.

c2) Playing *à la* Kasparov with
7...d6 looks a reasonable idea, as it's
not clear how useful ♘c3 is in this
line. Following 8 d4 ♗g7 9 ♗c4+
♔e8! 10 ♗xf4 ♘c6, Black's pieces
are starting to coordinate well.

7...d5!

Black sacrifices a pawn back in order to open lines for development and
gain time by attacking the bishop later
on.

8 ♗xd5+ ♔g7 9 d4

9 ♗xb7!? should be mentioned, if
only because after 9...♗xb7 10 ♕xg4+
♔f7 11 ♕h5+, Black's only way to
avoid a perpetual is 11...♔e6 12 ♕f5+
♔d6. After 13 d4 ♘d7 14 ♗xf4+ ♔e7
Black survives ... just!

9...f3 10 gxf3 ♘f6 11 ♘c3

After 11 ♗b3 ♘c6 12 c3, Black can
sacrifice back with 12...♕d6! 13 e5
♘xe5 14 dxe5 ♕xe5+, and now it's
Black who is on the offensive.

11...♗b4 12 ♗c4 gxf3

I also like the look of simple development with 12...♘c6 13 ♗e3 ♖e8.

**13 ♖g1+ ♘g4 14 ♕xf3 ♕xh4+ 15
♖g3 ♖f8 16 ♗f4**

Marco-Schlechter, Vienna 1903
now continued 16...♕f6? 17 ♖xg4+
♔h7 18 ♗g8+! with an unclear position. 16...♔h7 is better, although after
17 0-0-0! ♗xc3 18 bxc3 ♘h2 19 ♗e5!
♘xf3 20 ♖g7+ ♔h8 21 ♖g8+ ♔h7 22
♖g7+ White escapes with a draw. Perhaps best of all is Korchnoi's suggestion of 16...♗e7!, preparing ...♗g5. In
this case it's difficult to see where
White's compensation lies.

A32)
  5 ♘e5 ♘f6! *(D)*

I have no reservations about recommending this move, the Berlin Defence, which is regarded as one of
Black's best and most reliable defences
to the Kieseritzky.

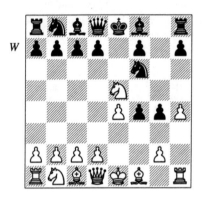

White now has two main lines:

A321: 6 ♗c4   67
A322: 6 d4   71

On first impression 6 ♘xg4?! looks
like a sensible move, but in fact White
is going after the wrong plan and the
wrong pawn. As Neil McDonald
pointed out in *The King's Gambit*, the
g4-pawn is a "positional nonentity"
and merely blocks counterplay down
the g-file, whereas the f4-pawn can be
used by Black as a possible spearhead
in a counterattack. After 6...♘xe4
Black's position already looks quite
promising. One line goes 7 d3 ♘g3 8
♗xf4 ♘xh1 9 ♕e2+ (or 9 ♗g5 ♗e7
10 ♕e2 h5! 11 ♕e5 f6 12 ♗xf6 d6 13
♕e4 ♗xg4 14 ♗xh8 ♔d7 15 ♗d4

♗xh4+ 0-1 Hebden-Stean, Marbella Z 1982) 9...♕e7 10 ♘f6+ ♔d8 11 ♗xc7+ ♔xc7 12 ♘d5+ ♔d8 13 ♘xe7 ♗xe7 ("and Black should win" – Fischer) 14 ♕g4 d6 15 ♕f4 ♖g8! 16 ♕xf7 (Morphy-Anderssen, Paris (13) 1858) and now Maroczy gives 16...♖f8! 17 ♕xh7 ♘g3 18 ♘d2 ♗f5, when Black's assortment of pieces should overcome the queen.

A321)
6 ♗c4
Until the discovery of 6 d4, this was White's most popular move. The threat to f7 virtually forces Black's reply.
6...d5 7 exd5 ♗d6 (D)
It was a toss-up between advocating this move or the equally playable 7...♗g7. In the end this one got the vote on account of more attacking possibilities against the white king.

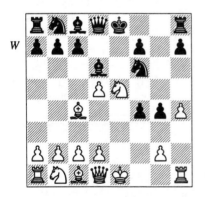

At this point there is a further split in variations. White can try:

The former is the bizarre Rice Gambit; the latter is the main line.

A3211)
8 0-0?!
This move introduces the infamous Rice Gambit. Mr Rice was a very generous sponsor, which led to whole tournaments being based around his opening (it would be most interesting to see Kasparov, Karpov and the rest have a go at this one). As Gallagher so accurately put it "White sacrifices a piece and castles into a raging attack, but according to theory, he miraculously holds the balance." Gallagher goes on to advise White to stay well away from it (he recommends 8 d4). It's unlikely Black will face it very often, but of course, we have to study it ... just in case!
8...♗xe5 9 ♖e1 ♕e7 10 c3 ♘h5 (D)
Black has two serious alternatives:

a) 10...f3!? 11 d4 ♘e4 12 ♖xe4 ♗h2+ 13 ♔xh2 ♕xe4 14 g3 0-0 and now:

a1) 15 ♗f4 (this was the starting position in a theme match between Lasker, who was playing White, and Chigorin; the final score was 3½-2½ to Black!) 15...♖e8 16 ♘d2 ♕g6 17 ♗f1 ♗f5 18 ♘c4 ♘d7 19 ♗xc7 ♘f6 20 ♘e5 ♕h6 and Black is better, Lasker-Chigorin, Brighton (4) 1903.

a2) 15 ♗d3 ♕xd5 16 ♕d2 ♖e8 (16...♕h5!?) 17 ♕h6 ♖e2+ 18 ♗xe2 fxe2 19 ♕e3 ♕e6 20 ♕g5+ ♕g6 21 ♕e3 ♗d7 (21...♕e6 forces White to take the draw) 22 ♕xe2 ♘c6 23 ♘a3

Re8 24 ♗e3 ♘e7 25 Rel ♘f5 26 ♕f2 ♘d6 27 ♗c1 Rxe1 28 ♕xe1 ♕d3 29 ♕e3 ♕f1 30 ♕g5+ ♔h8 31 ♕d8+ ♗e8 32 ♗f4 ♕e2+ 33 ♔g1 h6 34 d5 ♔g7 35 ♕xc7 ♕e1+ 36 ♔g2 ♕e2+ 37 ♔g1 ½-½ Forgacs-Marco, Monte Carlo Rice Gambit Special 1904.

b) 10...g3 11 d4 ♘g4 12 ♗xf4 (12 ♘d2 ♘e3! favours Black, Marshall-Swiderski, Monte Carlo (6) 1904) 12...♗xf4 13 Rxe7+ ♔xe7 14 ♕f3 ♗e3+ 15 ♔h1 f5 16 ♘a3 ♘f2+ 17 ♔g1 ♘g4+ 18 ♔h1 and here Black should probably accept the draw by perpetual check. Swiderski-Marshall, Monte Carlo (1) 1904 went instead 18...f4?! 19 ♘c2 ♘f2+ 20 ♔g1 ♗g4 21 d6+! and White went on to win.

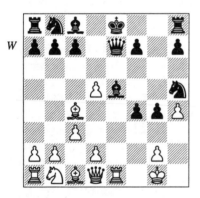

11 d4 ♘d7 12 dxe5

12 ♗b5 ♔d8 13 ♗xd7 ♗xd7 14 Rxe5 ♕xh4 15 Rxh5 ♕xh5 16 ♗xf4 Re8 was the starting position of another theme event between Marshall and Napier in London in 1905. Black won this encounter by the heavy margin of 4½-½, although at least this time it was fair to both players, who alternated colours (Napier was slightly more fortunate to get three Blacks).

12...♘xe5 (D)

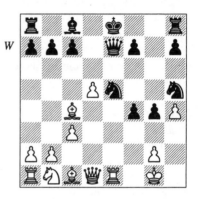

I can't find any practical examples of this position, but it has been analysed in depth by the likes of Capablanca and Keres. A summary of the analysis goes like this: 13 b3!? 0-0 14 ♗a3 ♘f3+! 15 gxf3 ♕xh4 16 Re5! (16 ♘d2 ♕g3+ 17 ♔h1 ♕f2 18 Rg1 ♕h4+ 19 ♔g2 ♕h3+ 20 ♔f2 ♕h2+ 21 ♔f1 ♘g3+ wins for Black) 16...♗f5 (16...♕g3+ draws immediately) 17 ♘d2 (17 Rxf5 ♕g3+ 18 ♔h1 Rfe8 19 ♘d2 appears to be another draw) 17...♕g3+ 18 ♔f1 ♕h2 19 ♗xf8 g3 20 ♗c5 g2+ 21 ♔e1 ♕h4+ 22 ♔e2 ♘g3+ 23 ♔f2 ♘e4+ 24 ♔xg2! (24 ♔e2?? allows a snap mate with 24...♘xc3#) 24...♗h3+ 25 ♔h1 and once again it's a draw by perpetual check.

So in conclusion the main line of the Rice Gambit may well lead to a draw, although at least Black has all the fun. If Black is playing for the win and cannot find any improvement here, then alternatives at move 10 should be revisited.

A3212)

8 d4 *(D)*

This is White's usual move.

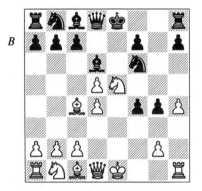

8...♘h5!? *(D)*

In practice Black's move-order to reach the main line has been 8...0-0 9 0-0 and only then 9...♘h5. Previously it was thought that White couldn't grab the pawn with 9 ♗xf4, but more recently a correspondence game has forced a change in assessment. Grasso-Pampa, corr 1995 continued 9 ♗xf4 ♘h5 10 g3 f6 (10...♘xf4!? 11 gxf4 h5 12 ♕d3 ♕f6 13 ♘d2 ♕xf4 14 0-0-0 ♔g7 was unclear in Balogh-Réti, Kosice 1918) 11 ♘xg4! (this line was earlier discredited due to 11 ♘d3? ♘xg3 12 ♗xg3 ♗xg3+ 13 ♔f1 ♕e8 and Black had a clear advantage in Pillsbury-Chigorin, Vienna 1903, but Grasso's move seems to be much better) 11...♕e8+ 12 ♔d2 ♘xf4 13 gxf4

♗xf4+ 14 ♔c3 and White's king is on a walkabout, but then again Black's isn't that much safer and White does have that extra pawn. It's a very murky position, but if I couldn't lean on the fence then I would probably fall on White's side.

Luckily 8...♘h5 avoids this line. The only drawback is that White has some extra options at move 9.

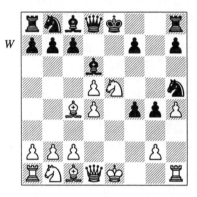

9 0-0

Alternatively:

a) 9 ♘c3 ♕e7! and now:

a1) 10 ♗b5+ c6 11 dxc6 bxc6 12 ♘d5 ♕e6 13 ♘c7+ ♗xc7 14 ♗c4 ♕e7 15 ♗xf7+ ♕xf7! 16 ♘xf7 ♔xf7 and the three pieces are worth more than the queen.

a2) 10 ♔f2 ♗xe5 11 ♖e1 ♘d7 12 ♗b5 ♕xh4+ 13 ♔g1 0-0 and Black went on to win in Murey-Hebden, Paris 1988.

a3) 10 0-0 ♗xe5 11 d6 (11 ♗b5+ c6 12 dxc6 bxc6 13 ♘d5 ♕xh4 14 dxe5 0-0! and 11 ♘b5 0-0 12 dxe5 a6 are both good for Black, while 11 dxe5? fails to 11...♕c5+) 11...♗xd6 12 ♖e1 ♗e6 13 ♗xe6 fxe6 14 ♕xg4 ♘f6 15 ♕h3 ♔f7 and Black is winning, Woudsma-Meijere, Dieren 1998.

b) 9 ♗b5+!? (Gallagher suggests that this may well be White's best move) 9...c6!? (this succeeded in an Anderssen brilliancy and certainly put players off 9 ♗b5+, but of course in the age of computer-assisted analysis, all old classics have to be reassessed; if you're not confident about the following rook sacrifice then 9...♔f8!? looks worth a go – after 10 ♘xg4 ♘g3 11 ♖h2 ♕e7+ 12 ♘e5 ♗xe5 13 dxe5 ♕c5!, Black wins material, while 10 ♘c3 ♘g3 11 ♖g1 ♕f6 12 ♘e2 ♘xe2 13 ♕xe2 h5 14 g3 f3 15 ♖f1 a6 16 ♗d3 ♘d7 17 ♘xd7+ ♗xd7 ended in a win for Black in Dufresne-De Koning, corr 1867) 10 dxc6 bxc6 (Black could try to avoid the following note with 10...♘xc6!?) 11 ♘xc6 (Gallagher suggests 11 ♗c4!?, giving 11...♗xe5 12 dxe5 ♕a5+ 13 ♘c3 0-0 as unclear) 11...♘xc6 12 ♗xc6+ ♔f8! 13 ♗xa8 ♘g3 14 ♖h2 (Kasparov gives 14 ♔f2 ♘xh1+ 15 ♕xh1 g3+ 16 ♔e1 ♕e7+ 17 ♔d1 ♗g4+ 18 ♗f3 ♗xf3+ 19 gxf3 ♖g8 20 ♕g2 ♕xh4 21 ♔e2 ♕h2 22 ♔f1 h5, but even this is far from clear) 14...♗f5 15 ♗d5 ♔g7 16 ♘c3 ♖e8+ 17 ♔f2 ♕b6 18 ♘a4 ♕a6 19 ♘c3 ♗e5!! 20 a4? ♕f1+!! (I'm sure this bit was extremely pleasurable) 21 ♕xf1 ♗xd4+ 22 ♗e3 ♖xe3 23 ♔g1 ♖e1# (0-1) Rosanes-Anderssen, Breslau (4) 1862.

9...0-0!

This is the tricky transposition. In general Black has played 9...♕xh4 here, but the ending arising after 10 ♕e1! ♕xe1 11 ♖xe1 is certainly more favourable for White than the main text.

10 ♘xg4 ♕xh4 11 ♘h2

11 ♘e5? fails to 11...♘g3 12 ♖e1 f6 13 ♘f3 (or 13 ♘d3 ♕h1+ 14 ♔f2 ♘e4+ 15 ♔f3 ♕h5+ 16 ♔xe4 ♗f5#) 13...♕h1+ 14 ♔f2 ♘e4+ 15 ♖xe4 ♕xd1 and White has lost his queen, Hebden-Lima, Hastings 1988/9.

11...♘g3 12 ♖e1 ♗f5!

This simple developing move assures Black of some advantage. Black's idea is to follow up with ...♘d7 and then double rooks on the e-file. It's as simple as that, although before this move was unleashed many still thought this position was good for White. This was partly because direct attempts from Black see him coming off second best; for example, 12...f3? 13 ♘xf3 ♕h1+ 14 ♔f2 ♘e4+ 15 ♔e3 ♕h6+ 16 ♔d3 ♕g6 17 ♖xe4 ♗f5 18 ♘bd2 ♖e8 19 ♔c3 ♗xe4 20 ♘xe4 ♕xe4 21 ♕h1! and now it's White's turn to attack. Olesen-K.Kristensen, Copenhagen 1995 continued 21...f6 22 ♗d3 ♕e7 23 ♕h5 ♘d7 24 ♗h6 c5 25 dxc6 bxc6 26 ♔d2 ♖ad8 and now 27 ♖e1! ♕f7 28 ♗c4 ♕xc4 29 ♕g4+ would have won.

13 ♘d2

Or 13 ♗d3 ♘d7 14 ♗xf5 ♘xf5 (with the idea of ...♘xd4!) 15 ♘f3 ♕h5 16 c4 ♖ae8 and Black builds up relentlessly.

13...♘d7 14 ♘df3 ♕h5 15 ♗e2 ♖ae8

de la Villa-Am.Rodriguez, Bayamo 1991 continued 16 c4 ♖e4! 17 ♗d2 ♖fe8 18 ♗d3 ♖xe1+ 19 ♗xe1 ♗xd3 20 ♕xd3 ♘e2+ 21 ♔f1 ♖e3! and Black had a clear advantage. Perhaps White should look again at alternatives on move 9.

A322)
6 d4

This move began to rise in popularity once it was discovered that an exchange of pawns on e4 and f4 could actually be favourable for White.

6...d6 7 ♗d3 ♘xe4 (D)

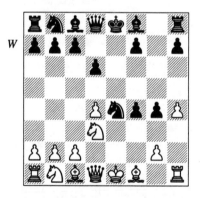

Now White has a further choice of moves:
A3221: **8 ♗xf4** 71
A3222: **8 ♕e2** 72

A3221)
8 ♗xf4 ♗g7

As we will see below, Black's 12th move has breathed new life into this

variation for Black. Previously 8...♕e7 had been beginning to show signs of taking over as the main move. The point is that after 9 ♕e2, Black reaches Line A3222. However, more recently White has been preventing this transposition by Gallagher's suggestion 9 ♗e2!?.

9 c3

The stem game for this line continued 9 ♘c3 ♘xc3 10 bxc3 c5! 11 ♗e2 cxd4 12 0-0 ♘c6 13 ♗xg4 0-0 14 ♗xc8 ♖xc8 15 ♕g4 (Spassky-Fischer, Mar del Plata 1960) and now Fischer recommends 15...♔h8 as giving Black a clear plus.

9...0-0 10 ♘d2 ♖e8 11 ♘xe4 ♖xe4+ 12 ♔f2 (D)

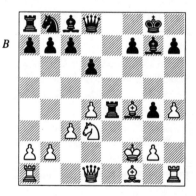

12...c5!

It was a long time before this logical and aggressive move saw the light. Hitherto only 12...♕f6 had been mentioned, but then White can consolidate with 13 g3 ♗h6 14 ♕d2!, preparing ♗g2 and a future attack down the f-file. The advantage of the text-move is that it prepares to open up the centre while White's king is still looking for safety.

13 dxc5 dxc5 14 g3

The earlier game J.de Wit-Van der Sterren, Dutch Cht 1994/5 saw White on the end of an even bigger mauling. After 14 ♕d2 c4! 15 ♘b4 ♕b6+ 16 ♔g3 ♗e6 17 ♘d5 ♕c5 18 ♖d1 ♘c6 19 b4 cxb3 20 axb3 ♖d8 21 c4 ♖xf4! White was forced to throw in the towel.

14...♕b6 15 ♗g2

McDonald mentions that 15 ♔g2 is more resilient, although more tellingly, he adds that after 15...♘c6 "it is clear that everything has gone wrong for White."

15...c4+ 16 ♔f1 ♖e8 17 ♘b4 ♘a6!

White is totally lost; for example:

a) 18 ♕a4 ♗f5 19 ♖e1 ♖xe1+ 20 ♔xe1 ♘xb4 21 ♕xb4 ♖e8+ 22 ♔d1 ♕f2!.

b) 18 ♘d5 ♕xb2 19 ♘e7+? ♖xe7 20 ♕d8+ ♗f8 21 ♗h6 ♕xa1+ 22 ♔f2 ♕b2+! 23 ♔f1 ♕b1+ 24 ♔f2 ♕b6+.

c) 18 ♘xa6 ♗f5! 19 ♘b4 ♖ad8! 20 ♘d5 (20 ♕a4 loses after 20...a5!) 20...♖xd5! 21 ♗xd5 ♗d3+ and White resigned due to 22 ♔g2 ♕xb2+ 23 ♔g1 ♗xc3 in Matsuura-Van Riemsdijk, Brazilian Ch 1995.

In conclusion, this is yet another line which needs some serious repair work for White.

A3322)
8 ♕e2

This forces Black's reply and plans eventual queenside castling.

8...♕e7 9 ♗xf4 ♘c6!

Black can also play 9...♗g7, but practical play has so far shown that it's more accurate to develop the queenside first and prepare to castle queenside. On the other hand it's not totally obvious where the dark-squared bishop should go yet, as there remains an option to play ...h5 and ....♗h6.

10 c3 ♗f5 (D)

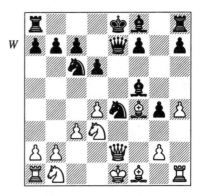

11 ♘d2

I haven't seen 11 d5!? mentioned anywhere, which is a bit surprising as it does at least contain a direct threat. I don't like the look of 11...♘d8, so I think Black should choose between 11...♘a5 and sacrificing a pawn with 11...♘e5!? 12 ♘xe5 dxe5 13 ♕b5+ ♗d7 14 ♕xb7 ♖d8. Following 15 ♗e3 ♘g3 16 ♖g1 ♘xf1 17 ♔xf1 ♗g7 18 ♗xa7 0-0, Black prepares to launch a very quick attack with ...f5.

11...0-0-0 12 0-0-0

12 ♘xe4 ♕xe4 13 ♕xe4 ♗xe4 leaves Black with an extra pawn in an endgame. It's true that the kingside

pawn-structure will mean that the extra pawn will be difficult to exploit, but at least it will be Black doing all the trying.

12...♖e8 13 ♖e1?!

It's very easy for White to fall into a number of traps here:

a) 13 g3? ♘xc3! 14 ♕xe7 ♘xa2+ 15 ♔b1 ♖xe7 16 ♔xa2 ♗xd3 17 ♗xd3 ♘b4+ 18 ♔b3 ♘xd3 and Black went on to win in Hajek-Buresch, corr 1962. 13...♘xc3 has the same effect against 13 ♕e3.

b) 13 d5? ♘xc3! 14 ♕xe7 ♘xa2+ 15 ♔b1 ♘xe7 16 ♔xa2 ♘xd5 and Black regains the piece, leaving him a few pawns up.

c) 13 ♘c4 ♕d7 (13...♘xc3?! 14 ♕xe7 ♘xa2+ 15 ♔b1 ♗xe7 16 ♔xa2 is now only unclear) 14 ♘e3 h5 and Gallagher admits that White doesn't have enough for the pawn.

d) 13 ♘xe4 (this is probably the best of a bad bunch) 13...♕xe4 14 ♕xe4 ♗xe4 15 ♘f2 f5 and Black has the extra pawn in the endgame, although once again it will be difficult to convert this advantage into victory.

13...♕e6!

Suddenly the attack on a2 causes White acute problems. These cannot be solved by either 14 ♘xe4 ♕xa2! or 14 ♔b1? ♘xd2+ 15 ♗xd2 ♕xe2 16 ♗xe2 ♖xe2.

14 a3 ♕a2 15 ♕d1 (D)

Or 15 g3 ♗g7 16 ♘xe4 ♖xe4 17 ♕xe4 ♗xe4 18 ♖xe4 ♕b3 and Black went on to win in Maes-Winants, Huy 1992.

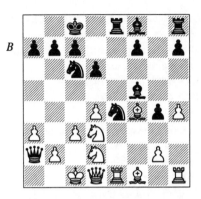

Black is clearly better. D.Holmes-Hebden, British Ch (Plymouth) 1989 concluded with 15...h5 16 g3 (16 ♕b3 is probably more resilient) 16...♗g7 17 ♖h2 ♘xc3! 18 bxc3 ♕xa3+ 19 ♔c2 ♗xd4 20 ♕a1 (20 cxd4 ♘b4+ 21 ♔b1 ♗xd3+ 22 ♗xd3 ♕a2+ 23 ♔c1 ♘xd3#) 20...♘b4+ 0-1. Once again the ball is in White's court.

B)

3...h6 (D)

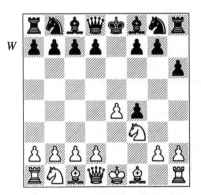

The Becker Defence. Black hopes to reach the main lines without allowing the Allgaier and Kieseritzky Gambits. However, this move-order does allow White other possibilities. White has two main tries at move 4:

B1: 4 b3   74
B2: 4 d4   75

Other moves tend to transpose:

a) 4 ♗c4 g5 5 0-0 ♗g7 gives us the Hanstein Gambit.

b) 4 ♘c3 and now 4...d6 5 d4 g5 or 4...g5 5 d4 ♗g7 transposes to B2.

B1)

4 b3!?

An attractive idea. White dissuades Black from playing ...g5 and so Black must search for another plan. The drawback of this move is that, while the bishop looks good on b2, its real home should be the c1-h6 diagonal, where it attacks a certain pawn on f4. From Black's point of view, he must try to reach a line of the King's Gambit where he can show that ...h6 is more useful than the move b3.

4...d5

Logically starting a counterattack in the centre. Another way to attack the e4-pawn is with 4...♘f6!?. While the Schallopp Defence proper (1 e4 e5 2 f4 exf4 3 ♘f3 ♘f6) hasn't a very good reputation, the insertion of b3 and ...h6 unquestionably helps Black here. For example, after 5 e5 ♘e4! both 6 d4 and 6 d3 can now be answered by the embarrassing 6...♗b4+ (with the pawn on b2 this could obviously be answered by c3). Shaw-Nunn,

Isle of Man 1994 continued instead with 6 ♕e2 ♘g5 7 ♗b2 ♘c6 8 d4 ♘xf3+ 9 ♕xf3, but after 9...♕h4+! 10 g3 ♘xd4! 11 ♕e4 (11 ♗xd4 fxg3) 11...fxg3 12 ♕xd4 g2+ 13 ♕xh4 gxh1♕ Black was in a winning position. Of course White can also defend the e4-pawn with 5 ♕e2, but then after 5...d5! 6 exd5+ ♗e7 7 ♗b2 0-0 8 ♘c3 ♖e8 we reach the note to White's 8th move, which looks favourable to Black.

5 exd5 ♘f6 6 ♗b2 ♗e7 7 ♘c3 0-0 8 ♗c4

This is Fedorov's suggested improvement over 8 ♕e2?!, which he played in Fedorov-Svidler, Pula Echt 1997. That game continued 8...♘bd7?! 9 0-0-0 ♖e8 10 ♕f2! ♘g4 11 ♕d4 and now 11...♗c5!? 12 ♕xf4 ♘f2 13 ♗b5 ♘xd1 14 ♖xd1 would have left White with reasonable compensation for the exchange. However, Black can play the stronger and more direct 8...♖e8!, preparing to recapture on d5. After 9 0-0-0 ♘xd5 10 ♕e5 ♘xc3 11 dxc3 ♗d6 12 ♕h5 White didn't have enough for the pawn in Hebden-Pein, London 1987. Gallagher goes on with 12...♘c6 (instead of Pein's 12...♘d7) 13 ♗c4 ♕f6 14 ♖he1 ♗d7 and Black keeps the advantage.

8...♘bd7

Also interesting is 8...♗c5, planning to answer 9 d4 with 9...♗b4, or 8...a6!? 9 a4 and only then 9...♗c5.

9 0-0 ♘b6 10 ♘d4 ♘bxd5

Black could try to retain the f-pawn here with 10...♗d6, or else 10...c5!?.

11 ♘xd5 ♘xd5 12 ♕f3 c6 13 ♖ae1 ♗f6

After 14 ♗xd5 ♕xd5 15 ♕xd5 cxd5 16 ♖xf4 ♗d7 an equal endgame has been reached.

In conclusion it would seem that 4 b3 doesn't present a great threat; both 4...d5 and 4...♘f6!? are fully playable for Black.

B2)

4 d4

This is White's main choice.

4...g5 (D)

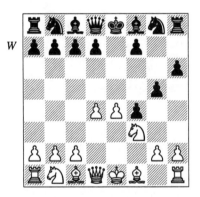

Here White has two main ideas:
B21: 5 h4 75
B22: 5 ♘c3 76

Alternatively:

a) 5 ♗c4 ♗g7 6 0-0 d6 gives us the Hanstein Gambit.

b) 5 g3 fxg3 6 h4?! (6 hxg3 ♗g7 7 ♘c3 transposes to Line B22) 6...g4 7 ♘g1 d5! 8 ♘c3 dxe4 9 ♘xe4 ♗e7 10 ♗f4 ♘f6 11 ♘xf6+ ♗xf6 12 ♕e2+ ♔f8 13 0-0-0 ♘c6 and Black had a clear plus in Brynell-Bjarnason, Copenhagen 1985.

B21)

5 h4 ♗g7 6 hxg5

Or 6 g3 d5! 7 exd5 g4 8 ♘e5 ♕xd5 9 ♖h2 ♗xe5 10 ♖e2 ♘c6 11 ♗xf4 ♕xd4, with a clear advantage to Black, according to Korchnoi.

6...hxg5 7 ♖xh8 ♗xh8 8 g3

This is the point of the continuation with an early h4. Black is not given enough time to consolidate his pawn wedge.

8...d5 (D)

This counterattack in the centre is certainly the critical move. After the more careful 8...d6 9 gxf4 gxf4 10 ♗xf4 ♗g4 11 ♗e3 ♘c6 12 ♗e2 ♕d7 13 ♘c3 f5 a level position was reached in the game Kennaugh-Kosten, Bozen 1992.

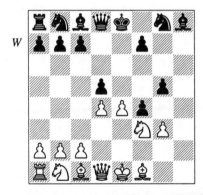

9 gxf4

9 exd5? ♕e7+! 10 ♗e2 g4 11 ♘e5 f3 12 ♗b5+ ♗d7 13 ♕d3 ♗xe5 14 dxe5 ♕xe5+ 15 ♔f2 ♗xb5 16 ♕xb5+

♘d7 17 ♗f4 ♕d4+ 18 ♗e3 ♕h8 gave Black a winning position in Krajkowsky-Alexander, corr 1963.

9...g4 10 ♘g5 f6 11 f5

White's only way to continue is to go headlong into the complications of this piece sacrifice. 11 ♘h3 dxe4 12 ♗e3 ♔f8 13 ♘f2 f5! was clearly better for Black in the game Gerlach-Beisser, corr 1968.

11...fxg5 12 ♕xg4 ♗xd4 13 ♘c3 ♗xc3+ 14 bxc3 ♕e7

Perhaps 14...♕f6!?, hitting c3, may be a better way to defend.

15 ♗xg5 ♕xe4+ 16 ♕xe4+ dxe4 17 ♗c4 (D)

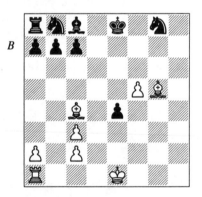

This is a very strange position. Black is a whole piece up and has even managed to trade queens, but all his remaining pieces are in their undeveloped state. Meanwhile White has a couple of raking bishops and a dangerous passed f-pawn to continue the initiative. Estrin considered 17...♔f8 18 f6 ♘d7 19 f7 ♘gf6 20 0-0-0 and 17...♘e7 18 f6 ♘g6 19 f7+ ♔f8 20

0-0-0 ♘c6 21 ♖h1 as too dangerous for Black, and preferred the safe option 17...♗xf5 18 ♗xg8, which he assessed as equal, although surely Black's extra pawn must give him a slight edge here.

B22)
5 ♘c3 (D)

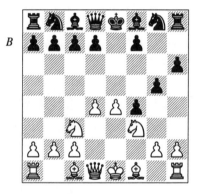

5...d6

Black can also consider the move-order with 5...♗g7, when after 6 g3 fxg3, 7 hxg3 d6 reaches the main line, while 7 h4!? is answered powerfully with 7...g4 8 ♘g1 d5! (revealing the point of delaying moving the d-pawn). Gallagher-Nunn, Islington 1990 continued 9 exd5 ♘e7 10 ♘ge2 c6 11 ♗g2 cxd5 12 ♗f4 ♘bc6 13 ♕d2 ♕a5 and Black held the advantage. So it seems that 5...♗g7 may avoid lines with g3 followed by h4 (whether Black wants to avoid this is open to question – see the note to White's 7th move below).

6 g3 fxg3

Another possibility for Black here is to return the gambited pawn with 6...♗g7!? 7 gxf4 g4 and now:

a) 8 ♗e3 (this move looks dubious) 8...gxf3 9 ♕xf3 h5 10 ♖g1 ♗g4 11 ♕g2 ♘c6 12 h3 ♗xd4 13 ♗xd4 ♘xd4 14 hxg4 ♕h4+ 15 ♔d2 hxg4 16 ♕xg4 ♕f2+ 17 ♗e2 ♘f6 18 ♕g3 ♘xe4+ and White had to resign in Furhoff-Hjartarson, Stockholm 1997.

b) 8 ♘g1 ♕h4+ 9 ♔e2 ♘c6 10 ♗e3 and now:

b1) 10...g3?! (this is the move given in most texts) 11 ♘f3 ♗g4 12 ♔d2! ♗xf3 13 ♕xf3 ♗xd4 (13...♘xd4 14 ♕xg3 is much better for White – Bhend) 14 ♗xd4 ♘xd4 15 ♕xg3 ♕xg3 16 hxg3 and the endgame favours White, J.Berry-Velker, corr 1978.

b2) 10...♗d7! 11 d5 (11 ♗g2 0-0-0 12 ♕d2 f5!? looks appealing as 13 e5 dxe5 14 fxe5 ♘xe5! 15 dxe5 ♗c6! appears good for Black) 11...♘ce7 12 ♔d2 f5 13 ♗g2 fxe4 14 ♗xe4 0-0-0 and I prefer Black, F.Larsen-Leeuwen, corr 1991.

7 hxg3

Also critical is 7 h4!? g4 8 ♘g1. Now after 8...g2! 9 ♗xg2 ♗e7 10 h5 ♗h4+ 11 ♔e2, 11...♗g5 12 ♗xg5 ♕xg5 13 ♕d2 ♕xd2+ 14 ♔xd2 is given in many texts as slightly better for White, but McDonald's 11...♘c6! ("it would be strange if White stood better here" – McDonald) looks a good bet. After 12 ♘d5 ♗g5 13 ♗xg5 hxg5! and 12 ♗e3 ♗g5 13 ♗xg5 ♕xg5, I know I'm starting to sound like a broken record, but once again

White is struggling to justify being a pawn down.

7...♗g7 8 ♗c4 *(D)*

8 ♘xg5? is just unsound. Black is winning after 8...hxg5 9 ♖xh8 ♗xh8 10 ♕h5 ♗xd4 11 ♗xg5 ♗f6 12 ♕h7? ♗xc3+! 13 bxc3 ♕xg5.

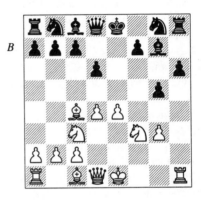

8...♗g4

After 8...♘c6?, 9 ♗e3 ♗g4 10 0-0 ♘f6 11 ♕d3 occurred in Fedorov-Notkin, St Petersburg 1996. Apparently neither player was aware of 9 ♘xg5! (Gallagher) which is just good for White after 9...hxg5 10 ♖xh8 ♗xh8 11 ♕h5!.

9 ♖f1!?

Or 9 0-0 ♗h5 10 ♕d3 ♗g6 11 ♗d2 ♘e7 and I prefer Black, Furhoff-Garde, Sweden 1994.

9...♕d7

Black has to show some care over his f7-pawn. The neglectful 9...♘c6 is punished by 10 ♗xf7+! ♔xf7 11 ♘xg5+ ♔e8 12 ♕xg4 hxg5 13 ♕e6+ ♘ge7 14 ♕f7+ ♔d7 15 ♕xg7, when White is clearly better (McDonald).

10 ♕d3 ♗h5!

A clever defensive move, adding vital protection to f7 and thus preparing to develop the g8-knight on e7.

11 ♗d2

11 ♗e3!? ♘f6 12 0-0-0 ♘g4 13 ♗d2 ♘c6 14 ♘d5 a6 15 ♔b1 ♘e7 16 ♖de1 gave White sufficient compensation for the pawn in Riemersma-Hommeles, Leeuwarden 1993, but perhaps Black can develop as in the main line, with ...a6, ...♘c6 and ...♘ge7.

11...a6 12 0-0-0 ♘c6 13 ♘d5 ♘ge7 *(D)*

Gallagher-P.Jürgens, Bad Wörishofen 1994 continued 14 ♖de1 ♗g6 15 ♗c3 0-0 16 ♕d2 b5 17 ♗b3 a5 and Black had more than consolidated his extra pawn. McDonald suggests that White should double rooks on the

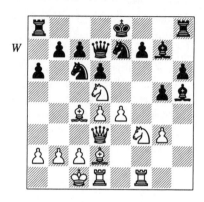

f-file with 14 ♖f2 and gives 14...g4!? 15 ♘f4 ♗g6 16 ♘xg6 fxg6 17 ♗f7+ ♔d8 18 d5, assessing the position as unclear. Of course Black could also play as in the game with ...♗g6 followed by ...0-0. Obviously White has a space advantage, but Black, as always, can count on that extra pawn.

7 2 ♘f3 ♘c6: Rare Third Moves for White

1 e4 e5 2 ♘f3 ♘c6 *(D)*

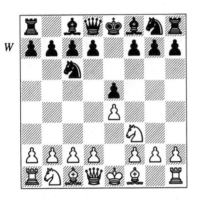

We have now reached White's most common choice on the second move. 2 ♘f3 attacks the e5-pawn and prepares kingside castling. It should come as no surprise to you that I'm recommending 2...♘c6, Black's most popular and reliable answer to 2 ♘f3 (strangely enough this defence has no name). In later chapters we deal with all of White's main tries (except the Ruy Lopez), but before we start, we should briefly examine unusual responses for White on move 3.

3 d3

White signals his intentions to play a reversed Philidor. Other moves include:

a) After 3 g3, 3...♘f6 4 ♘c3 transposes to the Glek Four Knights (see note 'a' to White's 4th move in Chapter 13), while Black could also consider 3...♗c5 or the cheeky 3...f5!?, angling for a reversed Vienna where White's extra move of g3 is not particularly relevant.

b) 3 c4?! has even less point here than when played on move 2, as White's knight is committed to the f3-square. Black can secure a very comfortable position with 3...♗c5 (or 3...f5!?) 4 d3 ♘ge7 5 ♘c3 d6, planning a later ...f5.

c) 3 ♗e2 ♘f6 and now for 4 ♘c3 see note 'b' to White's 4th move in Chapter 13, while 4 d3 d5 5 ♘bd2 transposes to the main line. 4 d4!? exd4 5 e5 ♘e4 6 0-0 d5 7 ♘xd4 ♘xd4 8 ♕xd4 ♗c5 9 ♕d3 0-0 was equal in Basman-Hebden, British Ch (Edinburgh) 1985.

3...♘f6 4 ♗e2

White can also play the position as a reversed Pirc with 4 g3 d5:

a) 5 exd5 ♕xd5! 6 ♗g2 ♗g4 7 h3 ♗h5 8 g4 ♗g6 9 0-0 0-0-0 10 ♘c3 ♕e6 was slightly better for Black in the game Heissler-D.Werner, Bundesliga 1996/7.

b) 5 ♘bd2 ♗c5 6 ♗g2 0-0 7 0-0 ♖e8 8 c3 and now perhaps the simplest way to achieve a good position is with the simple 8...dxe4 9 dxe4 a5, preventing White from expanding by playing b4.

4...d5 5 ♘bd2 ♗c5 6 0-0 0-0 7 c3 a5 *(D)*

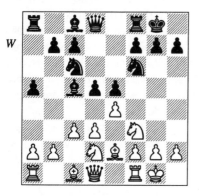

8 a4

As one would expect, despite the extra move, it's White who has to think about equalizing. Another option here, which is popular in the Philidor, is to expand slowly on the queenside with 8 b3, but once again Black can reach a

comfortable position by playing natural moves. 8...♖e8 9 a3 h6 10 ♗b2 dxe4 11 dxe4 ♘h5 is one way to continue.

8...♖e8 9 exd5

After 9 ♕c2 Black can slowly improve his position with moves such as ...h6 and ...♗e6.

9...♘xd5 10 ♘e4 ♗f8 11 ♖e1 h6 *(D)*

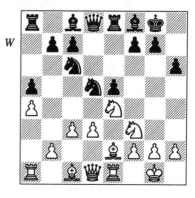

Black has a slight advantage. The game Svetushkin-Miles, Alushta 1999 continued 12 ♕b3?! ♗e6! 13 ♕xb7 ♘b6 14 ♕xc6 ♗d5, trapping the white queen.

8 The Ponziani Opening

1 e4 e5 2 ♘f3 ♘c6 3 c3 *(D)*

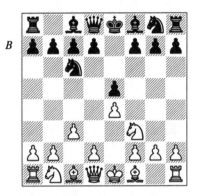

The Ponziani had a promising introduction to chess at the highest level, when it was utilized by both players in an 1846 match between Daniel Harrwitz and Bernhard Horwitz. The Ponziani was played in each of the first six games and the score-line ... 6-0 to White! However, despite this auspicious beginning, the Ponziani (or the 'Ponz' as it's affectionately called by some), has never really made it at the top level, and even accounting for fickle fashion, it really is unlikely to. Perhaps the most accurate description I can give is that it's as harmless as it sounds. White's idea is based on sound general principles of controlling the centre, but it ignores the more pressing concern of development, and because of this it's actually Black who is allowed the first strike in the centre.

A Quick Summary of the Recommended Lines

I've advocated two possible variations for Black against the Ponziani. Line A (3...d5) is for those who enjoy immense complications and are quite happy to sacrifice a pawn in the opening, while Line B is a more reliable antidote, for those of a more solidly inclined nature. The only problem I can see with Line B is that the main line gives a rather stale endgame position, in which it's difficult to drum up winning chance (this applies to both sides). However, there are chances for Black within the sidelines to create a more complex position. Line A requires much more study, but once again Black will be rewarded for his hard work.

The Theory of the Ponziani Opening

1 e4 e5 2 ♘f3 ♘c6 3 c3

We will look at both recommendations in turn:

A: 3...d5   82
B: 3...♘f6   87

A)

3...d5 *(D)*

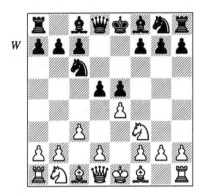

From this position White has two principal moves:

A1: 4 ♕a4   82
A2: 4 ♗b5!?   83

4 exd5 ♕xd5 5 d4 allows Black the option of transposing to Chapter 9, Line A with 5...exd4 6 cxd4, while the immediate 5...♗g4 could be considered. Also possible is 5...♗f5, when 6 ♗e3?! (6 ♗e2 is stronger) 6...exd4 7 cxd4 ♗xb1! 8 ♕xb1 ♗b4+ gave White problems in Vlahović-Vujosević, Pula 1991.

A1)

4 ♕a4

Pinning the c6-knight and thus threatening ♘xe5.

4...♗d7!?

The most consistent follow-up to 3...d5. Black continues in aggressive fashion and gambits a pawn.

5 exd5

There is really no other choice. The cowardly 5 ♕c2? dxe4 6 ♕xe4 ♘f6 leaves White in a real mess after only 6 moves.

5...♘d4 6 ♕d1 ♘xf3+ 7 ♕xf3 *(D)*

In Turner-Hebden, Hastings 1995, White tried the ugly 7 gxf3?!, and following 7...♕h4 8 d4 0-0-0!? 9 ♗e3 ♖e8! 10 dxe5 ♖xe5 11 ♕d4 ♕xd4 12 cxd4 ♖xd5 White's shattered pawn-structure left Black with a very pleasant endgame.

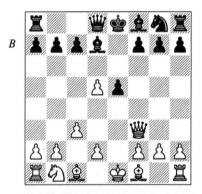

7...♗d6!?

Preparing to accelerate the development of the f-pawn. This seems logical, as in the other main line with 7...♘f6 Black often moves this knight to prepare ...f5. After 8 h3?! e4 9 ♕e3 ♗e7 10 c4 0-0 11 ♘c3 c6 12 ♗e2 cxd5 13 cxd5 ♗f5 14 ♗c4 ♖c8 15 b3 ♗c5 16 ♕e2 ♗d4 17 0-0 ♖e8 Black is in firm control, Rogers-Romanishin, Malmö 1993. White normally opts for 8 ♗c4 e4 9 ♕e2 ♗d6, and now:

a) 10 d3 0-0 11 dxe4 ♘xe4 12 ♗e3 f5 13 ♘d2 ♘xd2 14 ♕xd2 (or 14

♔xd2 f4 15 ♗d4 b5 16 ♗b3 ♕g5 with similar play, Ayas-Sulipa, Albacete 1995) 14...f4 15 ♗d4 ♕e7+ 16 ♔d1 ♕g5 with good compensation for the pawn, Kranzl-Blatny, Vienna 1991.

b) 10 d4 0-0 and then:

b1) 11 ♗g5!? h6 12 ♗h4 (12 ♗xf6 ♕xf6 13 ♘d2 ♕g6 14 0-0-0 ♖fe8 15 h3 f5 16 ♗b3 f4 17 ♘c4 ♗f5 18 ♘xd6 cxd6 19 ♖hg1 ♕g5 20 ♖de1 e3 21 f3 ♖ac8 and Black's monster of a passed pawn on e3 gave him the advantage in Florath-Breutigam, Bundesliga 1995/6) 12...♖e8 13 0-0 (after 13 ♘d2 I like 13...♗f4 14 ♘f1 g5! 15 ♗g3 ♗g4 and 16...♘xd5) 13...♗f4! 14 ♘d2 b5 15 ♗b3 g5 16 ♗g3 ♗g4 17 ♕e1 e3!, with a menacing attack.

b2) 11 h3 ♖e8 (or 11...b5 12 ♗b3 a5 13 a3 c6!?, as in Florath-Schirbel, 2nd Bundesliga 1994/5) 12 ♗e3 a6 (after 12...h6!? 13 ♘d2 ♘h7, 14 0-0-0 f5 15 g3 ♘f6 16 f4 a6 17 ♖dg1 b5 18 ♗b3 a5 gave Black a strong attack in Makropoulos-Tolnai, Dortmund 1988, but White should slow down the kingside offensive with 14 g4!) 13 ♘d2 ♖b8 14 ♗b3 b5 15 0-0 h6 16 f3 ♕e7 17 fxe4 ♘xe4 18 ♘xe4 ♕xe4 19 ♖ae1 ♕g6 20 ♕f3 ♖e7 21 ♗f2 ♖be8 and despite the simplifications, Black still has compensation for the pawn, Zelčić-Malaniuk, Montecatini Terme 1995.

8 ♗c4 f5 9 d3

After 9 d4, 9...e4 10 ♕e2 ♘f6 11 ♗g5 0-0 12 ♘d2 ♕e8 13 0-0-0 ♘h5 14 g3 b5 15 ♗b3 h6 16 ♗e3 was unclear in T.Upton-Mannion, Scottish Ch (Largs) 1998, while Black can also consider 9...exd4!?; for example, 10 cxd4 ♕h4 11 ♗e3 ♘f6, planning ...f4.

9...♘f6 10 ♗g5 0-0 11 ♕e2 b5 12 ♗b3 a5 13 a3 ♕e8 14 0-0

Black's pawn-fronts on both wings present him with more space and chances to attack. We are following Van Gelderen-Bisguier, Los Angeles 1991, which continued 14...♘h5 15 ♗d1 ♘f6 16 ♗b3 a4! (after an unusual repetition Black plays for more than a draw; now the immediate 17 ♗a2 allows 17...♘h5 and there is no longer the option of ♗d1) 17 ♗xf6 ♖xf6 18 ♗a2 f4 19 ♘d2 f3! with a promising kingside attack.

A2)

4 ♗b5 *(D)*

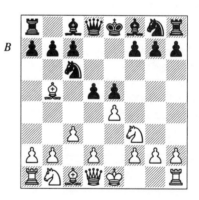

As with 4 ♕a4, this move pins the knight and threatens ♘xe5. The difference here is that this move can lead to unfathomable complications.

4...dxe4 5 ♘xe5 ♕g5 6 ♕a4

6 ♘xc6? ♕xb5 7 ♘d4 ♕g5 is good for Black, while 6 ♗xc6+ bxc6 7 ♕a4

♕xg2 8 ♕xc6+ ♔d8 transposes to the main line. 6 d4 is an independent try, which doesn't look too bad. Following 6...♕xg2 7 ♖f1 ♗d6, Black gained an advantage after 8 ♘xc6 ♗d7 9 ♕a4 bxc6 10 ♗xc6 ♖d8 11 ♘d2 ♘f6 12 ♘c4 0-0 13 ♗xd7 ♘xd7 14 ♗e3 ♗xh2 15 0-0-0 ♘b6 16 ♘xb6 axb6 in Glick-Karklins, Chicago 1994, but 8 ♕h5!? may be an improvement. Velimirović-Boudiba, Lucerne Wcht 1989 continued 8...g6 9 ♕h4 ♗xe5 10 dxe5 ♗d7 11 ♗f4 g5!? 12 ♗xg5 ♘xe5 13 ♗xd7+ ♔xd7 with an unclear position, although Black's chances appear to be at least equal.

6...♕xg2

The main line, although Black can also sacrifice the exchange with the enterprising 6...♕xe5. This has been tried by Ivan Sokolov, although it's difficult to tell how much faith he has in it, as he was only playing a rapidplay game. Following the forced line 7 ♗xc6+ bxc6 8 ♕xc6+ ♔d8 9 ♕xa8 ♘f6 10 ♘a3 (D) we have the following possibilities:

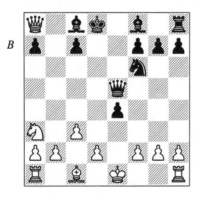

a) 10...♕g5!? was certainly a success for Black in the earlier game Nikitin-Izvozchikov, USSR 1968, which continued 11 g3 ♕h5 12 ♘c4? ♗d6 13 ♘xd6 cxd6 14 d3 ♖e8 15 0-0 ♘g4 16 h4 ♘e5 17 dxe4 ♘f3+ 18 ♔g2 ♘xh4+ 19 ♔h2 (19 gxh4 loses to 19...♕g4+ 20 ♔h1 ♕xh4+ 21 ♔g2 ♕g4+ 22 ♔h1 ♖e5) 19...♔e7 20 ♖h1? ♔f8 21 ♕xa7 ♕f3 22 gxh4 ♖xe4 0-1. However, you probably won't be surprised to learn that there are improvements for White in this line, starting with Keres's recommendation of 12 0-0, with a large advantage for White.

b) 10...♗c5 (Sokolov's choice) 11 b4 ♗xf2+!? 12 ♔xf2 e3+ 13 dxe3 ♘e4+ and now 14 ♔e2? loses a tempo over the main line; after 14...♔e7! 15 ♕c6 ♖d8 16 ♔e1 ♗g4 17 ♗b2 ♖d2 Black was already winning in *Virtual Chess*-Zsu.Polgar, The Hague AEGON 1995. Therefore White should play 14 ♔e1, with a further split:

b1) 14...♔e7 15 ♗b2 ♖d8 (if Black plays 15...♗a6, then not the greedy 16 ♕xh8?, which loses to 16...♕g5!, but the sober 16 ♕xa7, when I can't find anything for Black) and now in Yusupov-I.Sokolov, Nuremberg rpd 1994 White blundered with 16 ♖d1?? and after 16...♘xc3 Black was winning. However, after the infinitely superior 16 ♕c6! I can't find a way forward for Black; e.g., 16...♖d2 17 ♘c4 ♕f5 18 ♖f1 ♖f2 19 ♕xc7+ ♗d7 20 ♕e5+ and White wins.

b2) 14...♕xc3+!? is my attempted improvement over the last line, the point being that after 15 ♔e2 Black replies with the 'quiet' 15...♘f6, when White is rook up, but still facing problems. Now 16 ♖b1? ♔e7! threatens the decisive ...♗g4+, so it seems White should sacrifice a piece back with 16 ♗d2 ♛xa3. Now Black is still well in the game; e.g., 17 ♖hd1 ♔e7 18 ♔e1 ♗g4!? 19 ♛xh8 ♛d3 20 ♔f2 ♘e4+ 21 ♔g1 ♗xd1 22 ♖xd1 ♛e2 23 ♖c1 ♛xd2 24 ♖xc7+ ♔f6 25 ♖c6+ ♔e7 and here White has nothing better than to give (or else allow) perpetual check.

This last line could certainly do with more practical tests and some serious home study. As a substitute, it was given a good going over with the latest chess-playing program on a powerful computer – no significant improvements were found. In any case 6...♛xe5 certainly looks worth a try, if only in the occasional blitz or rapid-play game.

Returning to the position after 6...♛xg2 (D):

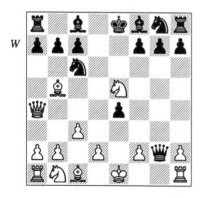

7 ♗xc6+

Or 7 ♖f1 ♗h3:

a) 8 ♗xc6+ bxc6 9 ♛xc6+ ♔d8 transposes into the main line after 10 ♛xa8+ ♔e7, while 10 ♘xf7+? ♔e7 11 ♛c4 ♛xf1+ 12 ♛xf1 ♗xf1 13 ♘xh8 ♗d3! is winning for Black.

b) An attempt to steer away from the main line with 8 d4 allows 8...exd3! (*ECO* gives the far weaker continuation 8...♗d6 9 ♗f4 ♗xe5 10 ♗xe5 0-0-0 as unclear, J.Claesen-Henris, Belgian Cht 1996) 9 ♘d2 ♘ge7 10 ♗xd3 ♛d5! and Black is already close to winning.

7...bxc6 8 ♛xc6+ ♔d8 9 ♖f1

9 ♛xa8?! ♛xh1+ 10 ♔e2 ♗d6 11 ♘xf7+ ♔e7 12 ♛xc8 ♔xf7 is clearly better for Black, who is closer to completing kingside development than White is on the other side.

9...♗h3 10 ♛xa8+ ♔e7 11 ♔d1!

11 ♘c6+ loses to the clever reply 11...♔d6! 12 ♛xf8+ ♘e7! 13 ♛xe7+ ♔xc6, when Black wins on the light squares after 14 ♔d1 ♛xf1+ 15 ♔c2 ♛d3+ 16 ♔b3 ♖b8+.

11...♛xf1+ 12 ♔c2 (D)

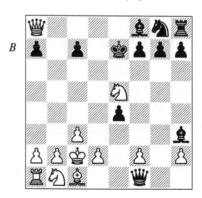

We have reached a bizarre position. The demolition of White's kingside and Black's queenside has amazingly left the body-count even. At the moment both sides are attacking with just queen and minor piece, and both sides are also struggling to introduce the rest of their army.

12...♗f5!

In my opinion, this move, which prepares a nasty discovered check with ...e3+, is Black's strongest move here. Other moves allow White to consolidate; for example, 12...f6 13 b3!, preparing ♗a3+. Following 13...fxe5 14 ♗a3+ ♔f7 15 ♕xf8+ ♔g6 16 ♕e8+ ♔f5 17 ♗c5! White held the advantage in Garcia Larrouy-Lane, Benidorm 1989.

13 ♘a3

Other moves:

a) 13 b3? e3+ 14 ♔b2 e2 is obviously what Black wants.

b) 13 ♕d5 ♘h6 14 ♘c6+ ♔f6 15 ♕d4+ ♔g6 16 ♘e5+ ♔h5 17 ♕e3 ♗c5! 18 ♕g3 ♗xf2 19 ♕xg7 e3+ 0-1 Soderberg-P.Smith, corr 1987.

13...f6! *(D)*

The other choice here is the tempting 13...e3+!? 14 d3. For example:

a) 14...♕xf2+ 15 ♔b3 ♗e6+ 16 c4 e2 17 ♗d2! ♕b6+ (Berg-Müller, corr 1991) and now 18 ♔c2! ♘h6 19 ♗b4+ ♔f6 20 ♗c3 ♔e7 21 ♖e1 looks very good for White.

b) 14...e2 15 ♗g5+ f6 (15...♘f6 16 ♕d5! wins) 16 ♕d5 and now:

b1) 16...♗e6 17 ♕c5+! (Müller only gives 17 ♘c6+ ♔f7, with perpetual

check) 17...♔e8 18 ♕c6+ ♔e7 19 ♕xc7+ ♔e8 20 ♕b8+ ♔e7 21 ♘ac4! and White has a winning attack; for example, 21...♕xa1 22 ♘c6+ ♔d7 23 ♘4e5+ fxe5 24 ♘xe5#.

b2) 16...♘h6 17 ♗xh6! e1♕ (after 17...♕xa1 White can mate by 18 ♕f7+ ♔d8 19 ♘c6+ ♔c8 20 ♕e8+ ♔b7 21 ♘a5+ ♔b6 22 ♕b5#) 18 ♘c6+ ♔e8 19 ♖xe1+ ♕xe1 20 ♕xf5 gxh6 21 ♕xf6 and White keeps the advantage.

c) 14...♕e2+! 15 ♔b3 exf2 16 ♘c6+ ♔d7, with unclear play, looks like Black's best bet here.

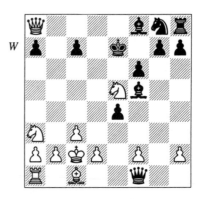

14 ♘c6+

This looks forced, as 14 ♘ec4 e3+ 15 ♔b3 ♕d1+ 16 ♔b4 exf2 wins for Black.

14...♔f7 15 ♘d4

Or 15 ♘d8+ ♔g6 16 ♕d5 ♘h6 and Black wins the crucial development race.

15...♘e7 16 ♘xf5

16 b3 and 16 b4 can both be met by 16...♗g6.

16...♕d3+ 17 ♔d1 ♘xf5

This position looks very promising for Black (for example, 18 ♕b8? ♗xa3 19 ♕xh8 e3! winning), while 18 ♕xa7 ♗d6 and 18 ♕c6 ♗d6 also see Black in control. In conclusion I would say that it's definitely White who needs an improvement in this line.

B)

3...♘f6

This is undoubtedly Black's safest and most reliable defence to the Ponziani.

4 d4 ♘xe4

This is the most common choice here, but if Black wishes to avoid the endgame that arises in the main line, then he could do worse than try the underrated 4...exd4 here. After 5 e5 ♘d5 *(D)* we have a position which has many similarities to the popular c3 Sicilian line 1 e4 c5 2 c3 ♘f6 3 e5 ♘d5 4 d4 cxd4 5 ♘f3 ♘c6, the only difference being that Black has a c-pawn instead of an e-pawn. In some ways this helps Black as he is nearer completing kingside development.

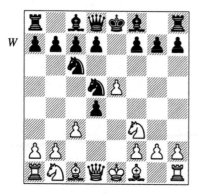

White has quite a few possibilities:
a) 6 ♗b5 a6! and now:
a1) 7 ♗xc6 dxc6 8 ♕xd4?! (8 ♗g5 is stronger, although Black is still very comfortable after 8...♗e7 9 ♗xe7 ♕xe7 10 ♕xd4 ♗f5) 8...♗f5 9 0-0 c5 10 ♕d1 ♕d7 11 ♕b3 ♕c6 and the exchange of his f1-bishop has left White suffering on the light squares, Sermek-Rogić, Dresden Z 1998.
a2) 7 ♗a4 ♘b6 8 ♗b3 (now we reach variation 'c' with Black having the extra move ...a6) 8...d5 9 exd6 ♗xd6 10 0-0 0-0 11 ♗g5 ♗e7 12 ♗xe7 ½-½ Velimirović-Spassky, Reggio Emilia 1986/7.
b) 6 ♕b3 ♘b6 7 cxd4 d6 8 ♗b5 ♗e6 9 ♕c3 ♗d5 10 0-0 ♗e7 11 ♘bd2 0-0 and Black was fine in Lakos-Krivec, Croatian Cht 1998.
c) 6 ♗c4 ♘b6 7 ♗b3 d6 (7...d5!?) 8 0-0 ♗e7 9 exd6 ♕xd6 10 ♘xd4 ♘xd4 11 cxd4 ♗e6 12 ♗xe6 ♕xe6 13 ♖e1 ♕d7 14 ♕e2 ♘d5 15 ♘c3 ♘xc3 16 bxc3 0-0! with equality in Sermek-Mikhalchishin, Ljubljana Vidmar mem 1993, since 17 ♕xe7? runs into 17...♖ae8!.
d) 6 cxd4 d6 (this position can also arise via 1 e4 ♘f6 2 e5 ♘d5 3 c4 ♘b6 4 c5 ♘d5 5 d4 d6 6 cxd6 exd6 7 ♘f3 ♘c6) 7 ♗b5 ♗e7 8 ♘c3 ♘xc3 9 bxc3 0-0 10 0-0 ♗g4 11 ♕d3 ♕c8! 12 ♗f4 ♕f5 13 ♕xf5 ♗xf5 and Black was OK in Lukin-Tseshkovsky, Russian Ch (Elista) 1995.

Now we return to the position after 4...♘xe4 *(D)*:

5 d5

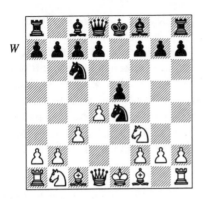

Overwhelmingly White's most popular choice here. After 5 dxe5 Black can play it safe with 5...d5; for example, 6 ♗b5 ♗c5 7 0-0 0-0 8 b4 ♗b6 9 a4 a5 10 bxa5 ♘xa5 11 ♗a3 ♗c5 with equality, Ljubojević-Filip, Nice OL 1974, or try for more with 5...♗c5. After 6 ♕d5 ♗xf2+ 7 ♔e2 f5 8 ♘bd2 ♘e7! 9 ♕b3 d5 10 exd6 ♕xd6 11 ♘xe4 fxe4 Black looks at least OK. 5 ♗d3 is another move that shouldn't put you off. Simply 5...d5 6 dxe5 ♗c5, and Black develops very smoothly.

5...♘e7

It should be pointed out that 5...♘b8 is also playable, but I preferred to recommend this more popular retreat. If Black wants to stir things up early on (but dislikes the complications resulting from 3...d5) then he could try the interesting piece sacrifice 5...♗c5!? 6 dxc6 ♗xf2+ (6...♘xf2 7 ♕d5! is good for White) 7 ♔e2 bxc6 and now:

a) Both 8 ♘bd2 ♘xd2 9 ♗xd2 ♗b6 and 8 ♕c2 d5 9 ♘bd2 ♘xd2 10 ♗xd2 ♗b6 look quite promising for Black.

b) 8 ♕a4! (the critical test) 8...f5 9 ♘bd2 0-0 10 ♘xe4 fxe4 11 ♕xe4! *(D)* (11 ♔xf2?! d5! 12 ♔e1? {12 ♕xc6} 12...exf3 13 gxf3 c5! left Black in command in Minev-Sax, Baja 1971) and now we have a further split:

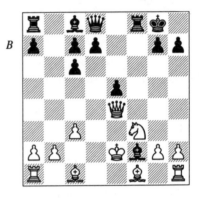

b1) 11...d5 12 ♕xe5! ♖e8 13 ♕xe8+ ♕xe8+ 14 ♔xf2 and the rook and two minor pieces outweigh the queen and pawn, Hector-P.H.Nielsen, Tåstrup 1992.

b2) 11...♗b6!? (recommended by Sax) 12 ♔d2!? (12 ♔d1 d5! 13 ♕xe5 ♗f5, with the idea of ...♕d7 followed by ...♖ae8, gives Black an attack for his piece; in Menacher-Bräuning, German Team Cup 1992 Black was successful after 14 ♗g5 ♕d7 15 ♕e7 ♕c8 16 ♕a3? ♗e4! 17 ♔d2 ♕g4 18 h4 h6 19 ♗e7 ♖xf3 20 gxf3 ♕f4+ 21 ♔e1 ♕xf3 22 c4 ♕f2+ 0-1, but White's 16th move did leave his queen very redundant) 12...d6?! (again 12...d5!? 13 ♕xe5 ♗f5 looks like the critical test) 13 ♗d3 ♗f5 14 ♕xc6 ♕f6 15 ♗xf5 ♕xf5 16 ♖e1 and White successfully beat off the attack in Hector-Sandström, Copenhagen 1991. Black is in need of an improvement in this line.

6 ♘xe5 ♘g6 (D)

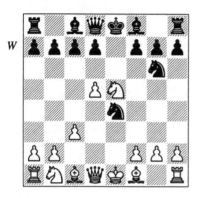

7 ♕d4

White has other options here:

a) 7 ♕e2 ♕e7 just leads to the main line after 8 ♕xe4, and 8 ♘xg6 hxg6 shouldn't worry Black.

b) 7 ♘xg6 hxg6 8 ♕e2 ♕e7 9 ♘a3 (9 ♗f4 d6 10 ♘a3 ♖h5! 11 0-0-0 ♗f5! 12 ♕e3 ♘f6 13 ♗b5+ ♔d8 14 ♕f3 ♕e4 15 ♕xe4 ♘xe4 and Black was doing well in Hector-Khalifman, London 1991) 9...c6 10 ♗e3 ♘f6 11 dxc6 dxc6 12 0-0-0 ♗g4 13 f3 ♗e6 14 c4 ♕c7 and Black was at least equal in Dreev-Malaniuk, Simferopol 1988.

c) 7 ♗d3 ♘xe5 (one trick to be aware of is 7...♘xf2?, which loses to 8 ♗xg6! ♘xd1 9 ♗xf7+ ♔e7 10 ♗g5+ ♔d6 11 ♘c4+ ♔c5 12 ♘ba3! ♘xc3 13 ♗xd8) 8 ♗xe4 ♗c5 and now:

c1) 9 0-0 d6 10 a4 (10 ♕c2!?) 10...a5 11 ♘d2 ♕h4 12 g3 ♕f6 is equal, Hamberger-Mandl, Werfen 1992.

c2) 9 ♕h5 d6 10 ♗g5? (White should choose 10 h3, with a roughly level position) 10...♗g4! 11 ♕h4? (damage limitation can be achieved by 11 ♗xd8 ♗xh5 12 ♗g5 {12 ♗xc7?! ♖c8 13 ♗a5 b6 14 b4 ♗xf2+ 15 ♔xf2 bxa5 is good for Black} 12...0-0 13 ♘d2 f5 14 ♗c2 ♖ae8, when Black was only slightly better in Oppitz-Wells, 2nd Bundesliga 1990) 11...f6! and White was already in grave danger in Kuijf-Anand, Wijk aan Zee 1990. Both 12 ♗d2 ♕e7 13 0-0 g5 14 ♕h6 ♘f7 15 ♕g7 ♕xe4 16 ♖e1 ♕xe1+ 17 ♗xe1 ♔e7! and 12 ♗e3 g5 13 ♕h6 ♕e7 14 0-0 ♘f7 15 ♕g7 0-0-0 16 ♗xc5 ♖dg8 17 ♖e1 ♗d7 win for Black. Kuijf tried the desperate continuation 12 ♗c1, but after 12...♕e7 13 0-0 g5 14 ♕g3 f5 White's position was hopeless.

7...♕e7

7...♘d6!? is an untried suggestion from Haba.

8 ♕xe4 ♕xe5 9 ♕xe5+ ♘xe5 (D)

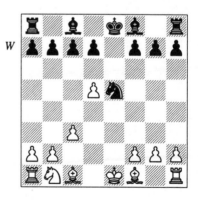

10 ♗f4!?

If White is looking for total sterility, then 10 ♘d2 does the job. Following 10...d6 11 ♘c4 ♘xc4 (11...♗f5!?) 12 ♗xc4 ♗e7 13 0-0 0-0 14 ♖e1 ♗f6 we have reached a dead-level ending, Velimirović-Smejkal, Rio de Janeiro IZ 1979.

10...♗d6! 11 ♘d2 0-0

Also possible is gaining the bishop-pair with 11...♘f3+!? 12 ♘xf3 ♗xf4 13 g3 ♗h6 14 ♘d4 d6 15 ♗b5+ ♗d7 16 f4 ♗xb5 17 ♘xb5 ♔d7 18 0-0-0 g6 19 ♖he1 ♗g7 with equality, Managadze-Ibragimov, Novgorod 1995.

12 0-0-0 b6!? *(D)*

Gaining the bishop-pair now is not such a good idea. After 12...♘d3+?! 13 ♗xd3 ♗xf4 14 ♖he1 White is well centralized and Black remains undeveloped.

The diagram position occurred in the game Dückstein-Donev, Vienna

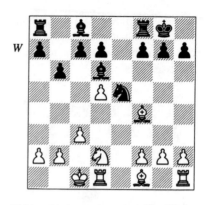

1991, which continued 13 ♖e1 ♖e8 14 ♗xe5 ♖xe5 15 ♖xe5 ♗xe5 16 g3 ♔f8 17 ♗h3 ♗b7 18 ♗xd7 ♗xd5 19 ♖e1 ♗f6 20 ♔c2 ♖d8 21 ♗b5 ♗e6 and Black's bishop-pair gave him a small edge.

In conclusion, Black has greater chances to stir things up against 10 ♗f4 than against the super-solid 10 ♘d2.

9 The Göring Gambit

1 e4 e5 2 ♘f3 ♞c6 3 d4 exd4 4 c3 *(D)*

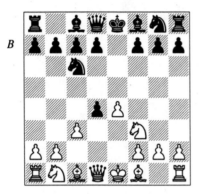

The Göring Gambit is very similar to the Danish Gambit, in that White offers either one or two pawns for a substantial lead in development. It's true that the double pawn sacrifice is extremely dangerous, and one defensive slip by Black can lead to a disaster. However, the Göring suffers from a major flaw, in that Black can safely decline the gambit to reach a very comfortable position.

A Quick Summary of the Recommended Lines

I've chosen to study both the declined and accepted versions of the Göring, to cater for two styles of play. The solid-minded player will prefer Line A, which has been known for a long

time to be at least satisfactory for Black. The only real problem with this line is that best play probably leads to an endgame in which Black's winning chances should not be that great. On the other hand, at least they seem to be greater than White's and in practice Black has scored well.

For the braver soul there's Line B, in which Black accepts material and then attempts to defuse White's initiative. Line B1 looks relatively harmless, but Line B2 remains the sternest test of Black's play. It goes without saying that the defender really needs to know his stuff in these lines, but those who get through the maze unscathed can look forward to rich rewards.

The Theory of the Göring Gambit

1 e4 e5 2 ♘f3 ♞c6 3 d4 exd4 4 c3

Before moving on, let's take a look at other 4th moves for White.

a) 4 ♘xd4 gives us the Scotch Game (see Chapter 10).

b) 4 ♗c4 gives us the Scotch Gambit. Black can transpose to the Two Knights Defence with 4...♞f6 (see Chapters 15-17).

c) 4 ♗b5 doesn't make much sense, as the bishop is clearly better placed on c4. Black can simply play 4...♗b4+ 5 c3 dxc3 6 0-0 ♘ge7 7 bxc3 ♗c5, with an extra pawn and a comfortable position.

After 4 c3 Black has two main lines:
A: 4...d5   92
B: 4...dxc3   94

It should also be pointed out that Black can play 4...♘f6, transposing to Chapter 8, Line B.

A)

4...d5

This is Black's solid way of meeting the Göring. Black shows no interest in grabbing pawns, but concentrates instead on the swift mobilization of his forces.

5 exd5 ♕xd5 6 cxd4 *(D)*

6 ♘xd4?! merely simplifies the position to Black's advantage. After 6...♘xd4 7 cxd4 (7 ♕xd4 ♕xd4 8 cxd4 just leaves White with a weak isolated d-pawn on which Black can feast in the endgame) 7...♗d7 8 ♘c3 ♗b4 9 a3 ♗xc3+ 10 bxc3 0-0-0 11 ♕f3 ♕a5 12 ♗d2 ♘f6 13 ♗d3 ♖he8+ 14 ♔f1 ♗g4 Black was well on top in J.Houska-L.Cooper, London 1993.

6 ♗e2 is tricky. White is trying to develop before recapturing on d4. However, in Velimirović-Malaniuk, Yugoslav Cht (Cetinje) 1993, Black responded with 6...♗f5 7 cxd4 ♗xb1! 8 ♖xb1 ♗b4+ 9 ♗d2 ♗xd2+ 10 ♕xd2 ♘ge7 11 0-0 ♖d8 12 ♕f4 ♕d6 13 ♕e4

0-0 and once again White is saddled with the weak d-pawn for no apparent compensation.

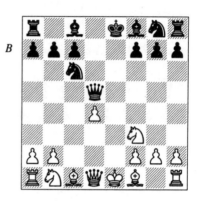

6...♗g4 7 ♗e2

After 7 ♘c3 Black can simply transpose into the main line with 7...♗b4 8 ♗e2. However, it's quite enticing to attempt to punish White for his slack move-order with 7...♗xf3!?. Now 8 gxf3 ♕xd4 simply leaves Black a pawn up, so White is forced to play 8 ♘xd5 ♗xd1 9 ♘xc7+ ♔d7 10 ♘xa8 ♗h5! 11 d5 ♘d4 12 ♗d3 *(D)*.

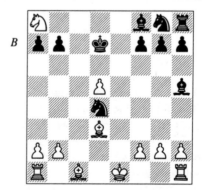

The assessment of this position revolves around whether Black can safely mop up the knight on a8. If he is successful, he can look forward to an advantage:

a) 12...♗b4+ 13 ♗d2 ♗xd2+ 14 ♔xd2 ♘e7 15 ♖ac1! ♖xa8 16 ♖c4! (this wins back material) 16...♘df5 17 g4 ♘d6 18 gxh5 ♘xc4+ 19 ♗xc4 ♔d6 20 ♖g1 g6 and despite White's extra pawn, this position looks very drawish, Pernutz-Michalczak, 2nd Bundesliga 1994.

b) 12...♗g6!? 13 ♗xg6 (13 ♔d2 ♗b4+ 14 ♔e3 ♘f5+ 15 ♗xf5+ ♗xf5 and White can do nothing to stop Black capturing on a8) 13...hxg6 14 ♔d1 ♘h6! 15 ♗e3 ♘hf5 16 ♔d2 ♗d6 17 ♔d3 ♘xe3 18 fxe3 ♘f5 19 e4 ♘h6 20 h3 ♖xa8 and Black is better, Coleman-Westerinen, Gausdal 1991.

7...♗b4+ 8 ♘c3 *(D)*

Other moves are no good. 8 ♗d2 ♗xf3 9 ♗xf3 ♕e6+ is embarrassing for White, while 8 ♘bd2 0-0-0 9 0-0 ♘xd4 10 ♘xd4 ♗xe2 11 ♘xe2 ♗xd2 leaves Black a pawn up.

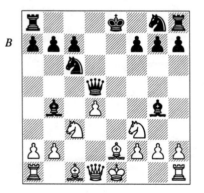

8...♗xf3 9 ♗xf3 ♕c4 10 ♗xc6+

White can also simplify with 10 ♕b3, but after 10...♕xb3 11 axb3 ♘ge7 12 0-0 a6 White's poor pawn-structure gives Black some advantage. 13 ♘d5 0-0-0 14 ♘xb4 ♘xb4 15 ♗f4 ♘ec6 left Black in charge in Raaste-Westerinen, Finland 1979, while 13 ♖a4 ♗d6 14 ♗g5 f6 15 ♗h5+ ♘g6 16 ♖e1+ ♘ce7 17 ♗d2 0-0-0 was also pleasant for Black in Ljubojević-Ree, Amsterdam 1972.

One of the earliest games in this line involved a World Champion: Marshall-Capablanca, Lake Hopatcong 1926. Marshall tried 10 ♗e3 and after 10...♗xc3+ 11 bxc3 ♕xc3+ 12 ♔f1 ♕c4+ 13 ♔g1 ♘ge7 14 ♖c1 ♕xa2 15 ♖a1 ♕c4 16 ♖c1 the players agreed to a draw. However, Black can actually play on in the final position and Bryson-Flear, British Ch (Edinburgh) 1985 continued 16...♕a2 17 ♖a1 ♕c4 18 ♖c1 ♕b4! 19 ♖b1 ♕d6 20 ♖xb7 0-0, when White was struggling to justify being a pawn down.

10...bxc6

The most popular move, although 10...♕xc6 is also fully playable. Prospects are roughly level after 11 0-0 ♘e7 12 ♕b3 ♗d6.

11 ♕e2+

Or 11 ♕b3 ♕xb3 12 axb3 ♘e7, when Black is just a shade better.

11...♕xe2+ 12 ♔xe2 ♘e7 13 ♗e3 0-0-0 *(D)*

Although *NCO* assesses this position as slightly better for Black, I must say that I've always believed it to be

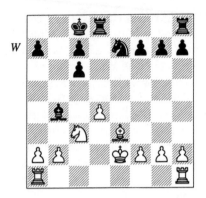

objectively equal. However, skimming through my database I noticed that Black has scored quite highly from this position. Indeed, from 31 games Black had achieved 14 wins (as opposed to a miserable 2 from White). In mitigation it should be said that the players with Black were in general higher rated, and in many cases it was obvious from the outset that White was playing for the draw (which is not always the best way to achieve a draw!). Anyway, here are a few possible continuations:

a) 14 ♖ac1 ♖he8 15 ♖hd1 ♘f5 16 ♔f3 h5 and Black had a small plus in Pirrot-Sturua, Biel 1996.

b) 14 ♖hd1 ♖he8 15 a3 ♗a5 16 ♔f3 ♗b6 17 ♘a4 ♘f5 and again Black is slightly better, Miles-Nunn, Islington 1970.

c) 14 ♔d3!?, planning to come to c4, may be White's strongest course. In Dolgov-Orlovsky, corr 1991, Black now strayed with 14...c5?! and following 15 ♔c4! ♗xc3 16 bxc3 it was White who was slightly better. Black

should keep his pawn on c6 and simply play 14...♖he8 15 ♔c4 ♗a5, which looks fairly level.

B)

4...dxc3

Despite Black's good results in the previous variation, one could still say that the real refutation of a gambit always lies in its acceptance! Now White has two choices, to recapture on c3 or to offer another pawn.

B1: 5 ♘xc3   94
B2: 5 ♗c4   97

B1)

5 ♘xc3 ♗b4

It is logical to develop the bishop first, as the immediate 5...♘f6 can be met by the awkward 6 e5. Now the plan is simply to play ...d6, ...♘f6 and ...0-0.

6 ♗c4 (D)

White's only plan is to use his development advantage to bear down on Black's Achilles' Heel, f7.

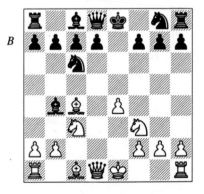

6...d6

This is the main move, but in my opinion Black should seriously consider inserting the moves 6...♗xc3+ 7 bxc3 and only then 7...d6. This doesn't seem to give White any new options, but does have the benefit of ruling out any recaptures with the queen on c3 (see the note to White's 9th move).

7 ♕b3 *(D)*

White cannot afford to waste any time; for example, 7 h3?! ♘f6 8 0-0 0-0 9 ♗g5 ♗xc3 10 bxc3 h6 11 ♗h4 ♕e7 12 ♖e1 ♘e5 left Black just a comfortable pawn up in De Graaf-Plasman, Dieren 1997.

White's main alternative to the text-move is 7 0-0. After 7...♗xc3 8 bxc3 the move 8...♘f6 leads us to the main line after 9 e5 ♘xe5 10 ♘xe5 dxe5 11 ♕b3 ♕e7. However, Black can also attempt to exploit the move-order by playing 8...♗g4, which prevents an immediate central push. After 9 ♕b3 Black can play 9...♗xf3! 10 ♗xf7+ ♔f8 11 gxf3 ♘e5 and although White has regained the pawn and prevented Black from castling, Black has excellent attacking chances against White's newly weakened kingside. 12 ♗xg8 ♖xg8 13 f4 ♘f3+ 14 ♔g2 ♘h4+ 15 ♔h1 ♕d7 16 f5 ♕c6! 17 f3 ♖e8 and now:

a) Ciocaltea-Karaklajić, Smederevska Palanka 1971 continued 18 ♕c2 g5! 19 fxg6 ♘xg6 20 ♗h6+ ♔e7 21 ♕f2 ♔d7 and Black went on to win (22 ♕xa7 b6 23 ♕a3 ♖xe4! is good for Black).

b) An attempt to improve on Ciocaltea's play was seen in Cargnel-Hegeler, corr 1986: 18 ♗g5 ♖xe4! 19 ♗xh4 ♖xh4 20 ♖ae1 ♖c4! 21 ♖e3 (21 f6 has been recommended in some sources, but simply 21...gxf6 22 ♕c2 ♖cg4! 23 ♕f5 ♖4g6 24 ♖e3 ♔g7 is good for Black) and now 21...♔f7! 22 ♖fe1 ♖f8 23 ♖e7+ ♔g8 24 ♖g1 ♖f7 leaves Black clearly better.

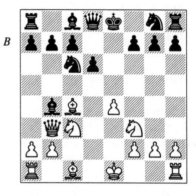

7...♕e7! *(D)*

Earlier sources recommended the continuation 7...♗xc3+ 8 bxc3 ♕d7 on the strength of Ciocaltea-Kovacs, Baja 1971, which continued 9 ♕c2 ♘f6 10 0-0 0-0 11 h3 ♖e8 12 ♗d3 h6, with an advantage for Black. However, the ambitious 9 ♘g5! causes Black many more problems, and following 9...♘e5 10 ♗b5 c6 11 f4! cxb5 12 fxe5 dxe5? 13 ♗a3 White had a vicious attack in Hoogendoorn-Van Wessel, Groningen 1995. Indeed, the game only lasted a further two moves: 13...a6? 14 ♖d1 ♕c7 15 ♘xf7! 1-0. It seems that if Black wants to play like this, then 12...h6 should be preferred to 12...dxe5?.

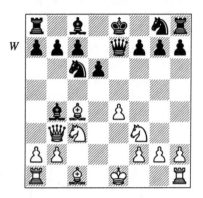

8 0-0 &xc3 9 bxc3

I can't find a single example of 9 ♕xc3 here, even though it may well be White's best move! The point is that after 9...♘f6 10 ♖e1 White prepares to blast open the position with e5, an action that will benefit his bishop-pair:

a) Attempts by Black to keep the position semi-closed are not all that convincing. For example, after 10...♘e5 White has the awkward 11 ♗b5+!, which is not easy to meet. I can't say Black is comfortable with 11...♗d7 12 ♗xd7+ ♔xd7 13 ♘d4, 11...c6 12 ♘xe5 cxb5 (12...dxe5? 13 ♗xc6+!) 13 ♘c6! ♕c7 14 ♘d4 or 11...♔f8 12 ♘d4.

b) So it seems that Black should simply play 10...0-0, allowing 11 e5 ♘xe5 12 ♘xe5 dxe5 13 ♖xe5. White obviously has some play for the pawn after 13...♕d6 14 ♗f4, while 13...♗e6!? 14 ♗xe6 fxe6 15 ♕b3 c6 16 ♕xe6+ ♕xe6 17 ♖xe6 ♔f7 bails out into a

level endgame. If no improvements can be found for Black here, then he should consider capturing on c3 earlier, forcing White to recapture with the pawn.

9...♘f6 10 e5

White must blast open the position, even at the cost of another pawn. Instead Minev-Matanović, Moscow OL 1956 went 10 ♗g5 0-0 11 ♖ae1 h6 12 ♗h4 ♘a5 13 ♕a4 ♘xc4 14 ♕xc4 ♗e6 15 ♕d3 ♖fe8 and Black was simply a pawn up.

10...♘xe5 11 ♘xe5 dxe5 12 ♗a3 c5 13 ♗b5+ *(D)*

13 ♕b5+ ♘d7 14 ♖ae1 0-0 15 f4 a6 16 ♕b3 e4 17 ♖e3 ♖e8 18 ♖fe1 ♘f6 19 ♕b6 ♗e6 20 ♗xc5 ♕d7 21 ♗xe6 ♖xe6 left Black in total command in Penrose-Unzicker, Leipzig OL 1960.

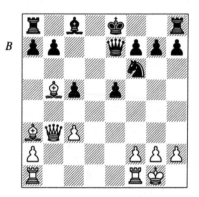

13...♔f8!

Stronger than 13...♗d7, when after 14 ♗xd7+ White has good chances to equalize following 14...♘xd7 15 ♕xb7 0-0 16 ♖ad1, while 14...♕xd7 15 ♗xc5 is unclear.

14 f4 e4 15 f5 ♔g8

Planning ...h6 and ...♔h7. White has some play, but not enough for the two-pawn deficit. Baer-Mitchell, corr 1971 continued 16 c4 b6 17 ♖ad1 ♗b7 18 ♗c1 h6 19 ♗f4 ♖d8 20 ♕g3 ♖xd1 21 ♖xd1 ♔h7 and Black went on to win.

B2)

5 ♗c4 (D)

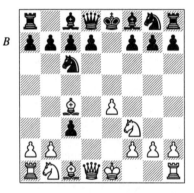

In my opinion this is far more dangerous for Black than 5 ♘xc3. OK, Black can grab an extra pawn, but White obviously has some compensation and if nothing else it's more difficult to assess the resulting positions.

5...cxb2

Of course Black could decline the second pawn, for instance with 5...d6, but after 6 ♘xc3 White would have an improved version of Line B1, as the f8-bishop is locked inside the pawn-chain. So the reasoning (for both sides) must be 'in for a penny, in for a pound!'

6 ♗xb2 d6 (D)

6...♗b4+ 7 ♘c3, followed by ♕c2 and 0-0-0, is considered very dangerous for Black.

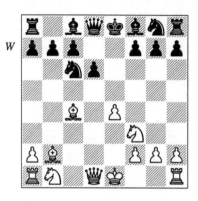

7 ♘c3

White has two other options here:

a) 7 ♕b3!? ♘a5 8 ♗xf7+ ♔e7 9 ♕d5 c6 10 ♕g5+ ♘f6 11 e5 (11 ♗b3 ♘xb3 allows Black to exchange his offside knight for one of White's menacing bishops) 11...♔xf7 12 exf6 gxf6 13 ♕h5+ ♔g8 14 ♘bd2 and White has some compensation for two pawns. Benavent-Esnaola, corr 1989 continued 14...♕e7+ 15 ♔d1 d5 16 ♖e1 ♕f7 17 ♕h4 and now Black should keep his f6-pawn with 17...♗g7.

b) 7 0-0 ♗e6! (this move, blunting the attack along the a2-g8 diagonal, is a well-known idea for Black) 8 ♗xe6 fxe6 9 ♕b3 ♕d7 10 ♘g5 ♘d8 11 f4 ♘f6 12 ♘d2 (after 12 ♘c3 Black should banish the knight with 12...h6!) 12...♗e7 (now 12...h6 could be met by 13 ♕h3) 13 e5 dxe5 14 fxe5 ♘d5. White obviously has lots of activity, but Black is still two pawns to the good, and has achieved some sort of blockade in the centre. L.Nun-H.Dunhaupt, corr 1975 continued 15 ♘de4 h6 16 ♕h3 ♕c6 17 ♗d4 ♖f8 18 ♖xf8+ ♗xf8 19 ♕h5+ ♔d7! 20 ♘h7 ♗e7 21 ♕g6 ♕c4 22 ♗f2 ♔c8 23 ♖e1 ♗b4 24 ♖d1 b6 and the black king has successfully fled to the safety of the queenside.

7...♗e6 8 ♘d5 (D)

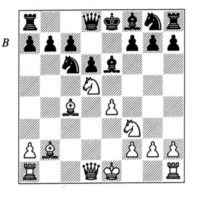

A crucial position in the assessment of the Göring Gambit Accepted. Ljubojević-Kovacs, Sarajevo 1970 continued 8...♕d7 9 ♖c1 ♘ge7 10 0-0 ♘g6 11 ♕a4 a6 12 ♖fe1 and White's pressure was becoming unbearable. In *NCO*, John Nunn gives two improvements over 8...♕d7:

a) 8...♘e5 9 ♘xe5 dxe5 10 ♗xe5 ♗xd5 11 exd5 ♗b4+ 12 ♔f1 ♔f8, which Nunn assesses as equal. This seems to be quite true, especially as White can recover the second pawn with 13 ♕b3 ♗d6 14 ♗xd6+ cxd6 15 ♕xb7, after which 15...♘f6 16 g3 ♕c8 does indeed look quite equal.

b) 8...♘a5 9 ♗e2 ♘e7, which Nunn assesses as "slightly better for Black". Once again I would say that positions like these are difficult to evaluate. White clearly has some play, but Black is under no immediate threat and after, for instance, 10 0-0 he can attempt to unravel with 10...c6 11 ♘f4 ♘g6.

10 The Scotch Game

1 e4 e5 2 ♘f3 ♘c6 3 d4 exd4 4 ♘xd4
(D)

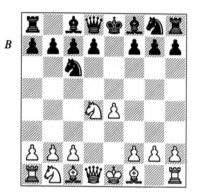

Garry Kasparov has stated that the Scotch Game is White's only serious alternative to the Spanish after 1 e4 e5, which I guess makes this one of the most important chapters of the book! Kasparov has himself been the chief reason for the resurgence of this logical opening, which for a long time remained unfashionable and a poor relation to the Ruy Lopez. His utilization of, and his success with, the Scotch in his World Championship battles have encouraged a whole new generation of chess-players to take up the opening themselves.

White's idea in the Scotch Game is very simple. By opening lines as early as move 3, White aims to develop

quickly and effectively. He also hopes that the pawn on e4 will give him a space advantage in the centre. When viewed in that light, it really is quite surprising that it remained so unpopular for so long. After all, what's White's normal plan against Black's other major response at move 1, the Sicilian Defence? Exactly! White continues 2 ♘f3 and 3 d4, the Open Sicilian. By the same logic we could label 1 e4 e5 2 ♘f3 ♘c6 3 d4 'the Open Open Game'!

Black has two different approaches against the Scotch. Either he counterattacks against d4, for example with 4...♗c5 or 4...♕f6, else he counterattacks against e4, with 4...♘f6 or 4...♕h4!?. In this book I'm plumping for the main line defence with 4...♘f6, a solid and reliable move, which, however, can lead to very complex play. For appellation buffs, 4...♘f6 is known as the Schmidt Variation, or the Zukertort-Berger Variation.

Activity versus Structure

If you were looking for a disadvantage of playing the Scotch Opening, then the main one would be that Black has generally no problems in developing his pieces to active squares. On the other hand, the price Black has to play for this is a weakening of his pawn-structure.

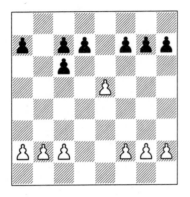

Here's the typical pawn-structure that arises in the 4...♘f6 variation of the Scotch Game. In simple terms White holds the advantage of having two 'pawn islands' against Black's three. If Black tries to gain space by eliminating (or bypassing) the e5-pawn, with ...f6, ...f5, ...d6 or ...d5, White will still possess fewer islands and a better structure. Sometimes the whole opening battle revolves around the importance of Black's activity and the importance of White's structural advantages.

A Quick Summary of the Recommended Lines

The reliability and diversity of 4...♘f6 means that I have no qualms in making this the only recommendation against the Scotch, although further down the main line I do give a choice of two continuations. Line A is not very common, but in my opinion it's quite underrated and I wouldn't be totally surprised if it suddenly became fashionable. Black needs to tread carefully here, as even some of the most innocuous-looking continuations contain just a drop of poison.

Line B2 is the variation in which there has been a great resurgence of interest after Kasparov's injection of new ideas. One of these is seen in Line B21, which may lead to an increase in popularity here. B22 remains the most popular variation, against which I'm advocating two possible defences. Line B221 is little played, but looks logical and direct, while B222 can lead to very complicated play, but I firmly believe Black has a full share of the chances.

The Theory of the Scotch Game

1 e4 e5 2 ♘f3 ♘c6 3 d4 exd4 4 ♘xd4 ♘f6 5 ♘xc6

5 ♘c3 transposes to the Scotch Four Knights Game (see Chapter 12). Other moves don't hit the mark; for example, 5 f3 ♗c5! when 6 ♗e3? loses a pawn to 6...♘xd4 7 ♗xd4 ♘xe4! (8 fxe4 ♕h4+ wins). White can play more strongly with 6 ♘xc6 bxc6 and 6 ♘b3 ♗b6, but in both cases Black has an easy position, while White has to worry about how to castle.

5...bxc6 *(D)*

Now we consider the two main moves for White:

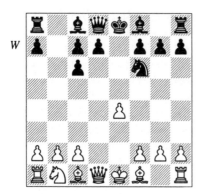

A: 6 ♗d3   101
B: 6 e5   104

6 ♘d2 is a quiet move, which is unlikely to cause Black any problems. Simple development with 6...♗c5 should be sufficient, after which 7 ♗d3 d5 transposes to the note to White's 7th move, while 7 e5 hasn't the same effect now that 7...♕e7! no longer blocks the dark-squared bishop (compare with 6 e5). Tartakower-Ed.Lasker, New York 1924 continued 8 ♕e2 ♘d5 9 ♘b3 ♗b6 10 ♗d2 a5 11 a4 0-0 12 0-0-0 and now both Alekhine's recommendation of 12...f6 and Euwe's of 12...♖e8, intending ...d6, give Black no problems at all.

After 6 ♘c3 Black can simply play 6...♗b4, transposing to the Scotch Four Knights. However, given that the dark-squared bishop often retreats of its own accord in that line, Black could also consider developing it to e7 or d6. Santo-Roman – Barbero, Lucerne Wcht 1985 continued 6...d5!? 7 exd5 (7 ♗d3!?) 7...cxd5 8 ♗b5+ ♗d7 9 0-0

♗e7 10 ♗g5 c6 11 ♗d3 and after 11...0-0 it could be argued that Black, having gained the extra moves ...♗e7 and ...♗d7, has a better version of the Scotch Four Knights (cf Chapter 12).

A)

6 ♗d3

6 ♗d3 doesn't enjoy the same popularity as 6 e5, but it's logical enough, defending the e4-pawn and preparing to castle.

6...d5 *(D)*

This move is by far the most common choice here, and theoretically speaking it doesn't give Black any major problems. Nonetheless, it does seem as though White is pulling the strings with regard to choosing the type of position, be it tactical with 7 e5, or super-solid and positional with 7 exd5. Because of this, ambitious players have been searching for ways to fight the battle on their territory and a reasonable alternative has come up in the shape of 6...d6 7 0-0 g6!? 8 ♕e1 (8 ♗g5 ♗g7 9 f4 0-0 10 e5 dxe5 11 fxe5 fails to 11...♕d4+) 8...♗g7 9 e5 dxe5 10 ♕xe5+ ♗e6. Now:

a) 11 ♗c4 ♕d6 12 ♕e2 was played in Oll-Ki.Georgiev, Groningen PCA qual 1993, and now Peter Wells in his excellent book *The Scotch Game* gives the variation 12...0-0 13 ♗xe6 ♖ae8! 14 ♘c3 (14 ♗xf7+ ♖xf7 15 ♕d3 ♕xd3 16 cxd3 ♘g4! gives Black serious threats) 14...♖xe6 15 ♕c4 (Oll stops here, claiming a slight edge for White) 15...♘d5 16 ♘e4 ♕b4 17 ♕xb4

♘xb4 18 ♘c5 ♖e2 19 c3 ♘d5 and Wells stops here, claiming a substantial advantage to Black!

b) An attempted improvement for White is 11 ♗g5, as in Zelčić-Rogić, Croatian Ch (Pula) 1996 (Zelčić is a seasoned campaigner of the 6 ♗d3 line). That game continued 11...♕d6 12 ♗f4 ♕e7 13 ♘c3 ♖c8 14 ♗e3 ♘h5 15 ♕a5 0-0 16 ♗e2 and Black's weak queenside pawns were beginning to feel the strain. However, there are improvements for Black too; for example, 12...♖b8!?, planning to meet 13 ♕e3 with 13...♘g4!, or earlier 11...0-0 12 ♖e1 ♘d5!? 13 ♕xg7+ ♔xg7 14 ♗xd8 ♖fxd8, when Black's piece activity should compensate for his structural deficiencies.

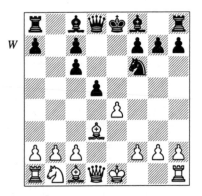

7 e5

After this aggressive push White must be prepared to sacrifice a pawn. 7 ♘d2 ♗c5 8 0-0 0-0 9 h3 ♖e8 10 exd5 cxd5 11 ♘b3 ♗b6 12 ♗g5 h6 13 ♗h4 ♕d6 14 ♕f3 ♘e4 left Black at least equal in Santo-Roman – Marciano,

French Ch (Strasbourg) 1992. Another quiet option is 7 ♕e2 dxe4 8 ♗xe4 ♘xe4 9 ♕xe4+ ♕e7 10 ♕xe7+ ♗xe7, when Black's bishop-pair compensates for the queenside pawn weakness.

The main alternative 7 exd5 cxd5 also appears rather sedate, although as I found out myself, line 'b' contains a surprising amount of venom.

a) 8 0-0 ♗e7 9 c4 0-0 (9...c6 10 cxd5 cxd5 11 ♘c3 0-0 12 ♗e3 ♗e6 13 ♗d4 ♕b8 is equal, Totsky-Gyimesi, Budapest 1996) 10 cxd5 ♗b7 11 ♗c4 ♗xd5 12 ♗xd5 ♘xd5 13 ♕f3 ♗f6 14 ♘d2 ♖b8 15 ♖b1 c6 ½-½ Totsky-Korneev, Moscow 1995.

b) 8 ♗b5+!? (it seems bizarre that White can move this bishop again so quickly and still hope for an advantage, but Black does have to be careful) 8...♗d7 9 ♗xd7+ ♕xd7 10 0-0 ♗e7 11 c4 and now:

b1) 11...0-0 12 cxd5 ♘xd5 13 ♘c3 ♖fd8 (13...c6 14 ♗e3 ♗f6 15 ♖c1 ♖fb8 16 ♘xd5 cxd5 17 ♗d4 gave White the smallest of edges in Zelčić-Emms, Montecatini Terme 1996) 14 ♘xd5 ♕xd5 15 ♕xd5 ♖xd5 16 ♗e3 ♗f6 17 ♖ac1 ♗xb2 18 ♖xc7 ♗e5 with complete equality in Borgo-Gyimesi, Elista OL 1998, as after 19 ♖xa7 ♖xa7 20 ♗xa7 Black has 20...♖a5.

b2) 11...dxc4!? looks ugly, but I can't see anything obvious against it. Black seems fine after either 12 ♕xd7+ ♔xd7 13 ♘d2 c3! or 12 ♕e2 ♕d3 13 ♕e5 ♕d5!, preparing to meet 14 ♕xc7?? with 14...♗d6.

7...♘g4 8 0-0 ♗c5 (D)

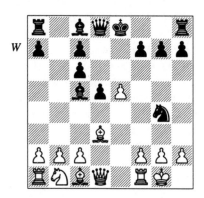

9 ♕e2

If White defends the pawn with 9 ♗f4, Black should immediately challenge the forward pawn with 9...f6!. Previously this position has either been ignored or written off as 'good for Black', but the following lines show there's more to it than meets the eye. In conclusion, though, I would still have to side with Black.

a) 10 exf6?! 0-0! gives Black a strong attack down the f-file.

b) 10 h3 and now 10...fxe5!? 11 ♗g3 (11 hxg4 exf4 12 ♖e1+ ♔f7 13 ♕d2 ♕f6 was good for Black in Reggio-Swiderski, Barmen 1905) 11...e4!? (11...♘f6 12 ♗xe5 0-0 looks level) 12 hxg4 exd3 13 ♖e1+ ♔f7 14 ♕xd3 is quite messy, but is probably not worse for Black. In any case there's also 10...♘xe5 11 ♗xe5 fxe5 12 ♕h5+ ♔f8 13 ♕xe5 ♗d6 14 ♕h5 ♖b8 15 b3 ♕f6 16 ♘d2 g6, which seems fine.

c) 10 e6 ♗xe6 and now White can play:

c1) 11 ♕e2 ♕e7 12 ♗xc7 0-0 (or 12...♘e3) 13 h3 ♘e5! 14 ♗a5 (14 ♗xe5 fxe5 15 ♕xe5 runs into 15...♖xf2! 16 ♖xf2 ♖f8) 14...♖fe8 15 ♘d2 ♕d7 and Black is more active, Gamboa-Barus, Erevan OL 1996.

c2) 11 h3 ♘e5 12 ♗xe5 fxe5 13 ♕h5+ ♔f8 14 ♕xe5 (this is similar to the line given at the end of note 'b', except Black has the extra move ...♗e6) 14...♕d6 15 ♕e2 ♖e8 16 ♕f3+ ♗f7 and once again the bishop-pair compensates for the slight draught around the black king, Belkadi-Ivkov, Malta OL 1980.

It should also be pointed out that 9 h3 ♘xe5 10 ♖e1 ♕f6 11 ♕e2 fails instructively to 11...0-0! 12 ♕xe5 ♕xf2+ 13 ♔h1 ♗xh3!! and Black wins. For example, 14 gxh3 ♕f3+ 15 ♔h2 ♗d6 16 ♖e3 ♕xe3! (this is a better deal than a queen for three pieces) 17 ♗xe3 ♗xe5+ 18 ♔g2 ♗xb2 and White will be hopelessly down on material.

9...♕e7!

In the early days of this variation 9...♕h4?! was the main move, but Krakops-Slucker, Latvia 1992 saw Black struggling to justify his early aggression after 10 h3 h5 11 ♘d2 ♕g3 12 ♘f3 h4 13 b4 ♗b6 14 c4 dxc4 15 ♗e4 ♗d7 16 e6!.

10 ♗f4 g5 11 ♗d2

Trying to hang on to the e5-pawn with 11 ♗g3 hands Black an attack on a plate with 11...h5!. Tomescu-Musat, Bucharest 1993 continued 12 ♗a6 ♗xa6 13 ♕xa6 ♕e6! 14 h3 h4 15 ♗h2 ♘xh2 16 ♔xh2 g4 17 hxg4 ♔d7 18

♘c3 ♖ag8 and the white king was already under intense fire.

11...♘xe5 12 ♖e1 ♗d6!

The popular opinion is that this is Black's strongest move. 12...♘xd3 13 ♕xd3 ♗e6 14 b4 ♗b6 15 ♘c3 0-0 16 ♘a4, as in K.Müller-Z.Almasi, Budapest 1991, gives White some degree of compensation due to the obvious pawn weakness on both sides of Black's camp. Black can also return the pawn with 12...f6 13 ♗xg5 fxg5 14 ♕xe5 ♕xe5 15 ♖xe5+ ♔d8, although after 16 ♘d2 ♖f8 17 ♖f1 h6 18 ♘b3 ♗d6 (18...♗b6!?) 19 ♖e2 a5 20 ♘d4 White keeps an edge, Kos-Roskar, Bled 1998.

13 f4 gxf4 14 ♗xf4 (D)

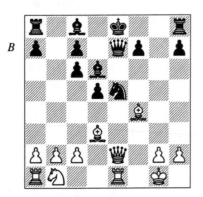

This is the critical position for the assessment of the 6 ♗d3 d5 variation. Obviously White has some compensation for the pawn, but the question remains whether it's insufficient, sufficient or more than sufficient (although the last scenario appears unlikely). From this point Black has two possibilities:

a) 14...f6 15 ♘d2 ♔d8 16 ♔h1 ♕g7 17 ♕f2 ♖g8 18 ♗f1 was unclear in Kaminski-Bacrot, Elista OL 1998.

b) 14...♗c5+ and now 15 ♔h1? ♘xd3 16 ♕xe7+ ♗xe7 17 cxd3 ♔d7 18 ♘d2 ♗a6 19 ♘f3 f6 20 d4 ♖he8 gave Black an obvious advantage in L.Webb-Lejlić, London (Lloyds Bank) 1994, but White's idea after sacrificing a pawn can hardly be to swap off into an endgame. 15 ♗e3! must be the critical test of this position, which certainly could do with a practical outing. I'll leave the reader to look at possible variations but I will point out that Black cannot solve all his problems with 15...♘xd3??, as 16 ♗xc5! wins immediately.

B)

6 e5 (D)

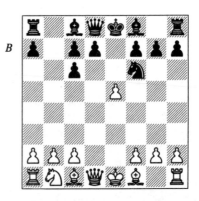

White's main choice. Immediately the question is put to the black knight.

6...♕e7! 7 ♕e2

This move is virtually forced. Wells called the last two queen moves "an exchange of inconveniences", which sums the position up very well. Now both sides suffer disruption to their normal kingside development, but Black counts on his disruption being less of a problem than White's. After all, Black's queen will be freer to move away and re-release the f8-bishop than will its counterpart, which has to make sure it's defending the e5-pawn.

7...♘d5 *(D)*

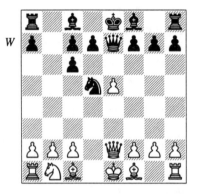

The natural square for the knight. Now we shall consider White's two main choices here:

B1: 8 ♘d2   106
B2: 8 c4   107

Other moves include:

a) 8 b3 should be met by 8...a5!, when White's most logical continuation seems to be 9 c4 ♘b6, which transposes to the line 8 c4 ♘b6 9 b3 a5.

b) 8 g3 is a tricky transpositional move, which is similar to 8 c4 ♘b6 9 g3!?. After 8 g3 White can meet the move 8...g6 with 9 c4, when 9...♘b6 10 b3 ♗g7 11 f4! reaches note 'b1' to White's 9th move in Line B2 and 9...♗a6 gives us a line usually reached via the move-order 8 c4 ♗a6 9 g3. As this falls outside our repertoire, I'm going to advocate 8...♕e6, with the following lines:

b1) 9 c4 ♘b6 10 b3 (10 ♘d2 a5 transposes to B2222) 10...a5 11 ♗b2 a4 12 ♘d2 ♗b4 13 ♗g2 and we have reached B2222.

b2) 9 ♗g2 ♗c5 (now the knight has the extra option of retreating to e7) 10 0-0 0-0 and Black can attack the e5-pawn with ...♖e8.

b3) 9 h4 ♘b4!? and now:

b31) 10 a3?! ♕d5 11 ♖g1 ♗a6 12 c4 should be met by Wells's suggestion 12...♗xc4, since 12...♕a5 13 ♘c3 0-0-0 14 ♕d1! is a substantial improvement over 14 ♖b1? (J.Diaz-Arencibia, Cuban Ch (Las Tunas) 1996).

b32) 10 c4 prevents ...♕d5, but Black can still keep the initiative with 10...♕f5!.

c) 8 h4!? is another invention of Van der Wiel's. White's almost child-like idea is to swing the rook across the third rank via h3. This can lead to some bizarre positions, but apart from the occasional outing, the move has never really caught on.

c1) 8...♕e6 9 g3 transposes to note 'b3' above.

c2) Van der Wiel-Timman, Amsterdam 1987 continued 8...f6!? 9 c4 ♗a6 10 ♖h3 fxe5 11 ♖a3!? ♘b4 12 ♘c3 (Wells's proposal 12 ♗g5 looks stronger) 12...♕xh4 13 g3 ♕d4 14 ♖xa6 ♘xa6 15 ♗f4 and now Wells suggests 15...♕c5 16 a3 ♕e7 as a way to defuse White's attack.

B1)
8 ♘d2 g6! *(D)*

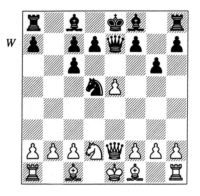

Preparing ...♗g7, which will attack the e5-pawn. White has two sensible replies:

B11: 9 ♘f3   106
B12: 9 c4   106

B11)
9 ♘f3 ♕b4+!
This is a very good move. Black makes use of the tactic 10 c3? ♘xc3! to put a large spanner in White's development.

10 ♕d2 ♖b8 11 c4
11 ♗d3 ♘f4! is embarrassing for White, while after 11 a3 ♕xd2+ 12 ♘xd2 ♗g7 the e-pawn is once again quite vulnerable.

11...♕xd2+ 12 ♗xd2 ♘b4 13 ♔d1 c5!

It is essential to create a good circuit for the knight. The horse would have an unhappy existence following 13...♗g7? 14 a3 ♘a6 15 b4!.

14 ♗c3 ♗g7 15 a3
After 15 e6 ♗xc3 16 bxc3 ♘c6 17 exd7+ ♗xd7 both sides possess pawn weaknesses, but Black is in a more favourable position to exploit them.

15...♘c6 16 ♗d3 d6 17 ♖e1
Or 17 exd6 ♗xc3 18 bxc3 cxd6 19 ♖e1+ ♗e6, and White's doubled c-pawns are potential targets.

17...0-0
Black can already claim a slight advantage. Schoellmann-Mikhalchishin, Bled 1995 continued 18 ♔c2 ♗g4 19 exd6 cxd6 20 ♗e4 ♗xf3 21 gxf3? (21 ♗xf3 is stronger, but 21...♘d4+ 22 ♗xd4 ♗xd4 23 ♖ab1 ♖fe8! is still better for Black) 21...♘d4+ 22 ♔d3 ♖b3 23 ♗d5 ♗f6 24 ♖ad1 ♖fb8 25 ♔e4 ♔g7 and Black's pressure on the b-file left him in total control.

B12)
9 c4 ♗a6! *(D)*
This is a good transposition into a line which could have also been reached via the move-order 8 c4 ♗a6 9 ♘d2 (9 b3 is a more popular continuation) 9...g6.

10 b3
10 ♘f3 and 10 ♘e4 can both be answered by the interfering 10...♕b4+!. White's only other alternative is 10 ♕e4, with the following possibilities:

a) 10...♘b6 11 ♗d3 ♗g7 12 0-0 0-0 13 f4 (Beliavsky-P.Nikolić, Munich

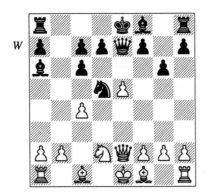

1994) and now 13...d6!? gives Black a good game.

b) After 10...f5!?, 11 ♕d4?! ♘b4 12 ♕c3 c5 13 ♗e2 ♗g7 14 f4?! d6! 15 ♘f3 ♗b7! left Black clearly better in L.B.Hansen-Z.Almasi, Tilburg 1994. 11 exf6 is stronger, but after 11...♘xf6 12 ♕xe7+ ♗xe7 Black's quick development and the half-open f-file offer him good chances.

10...♗g7 11 ♗b2 ♘b4 12 ♘f3 c5!

Resolving the problem of the knight by presenting it with a good circuit. Now it's ready to hop back to c6 and pressurize the insecure e5-pawn.

13 g3 0-0 14 ♗g2 d5

14...♖ae8 15 0-0 d6 16 ♘e1 ♕d7 17 ♕d2 ♗xe5 18 ♗xe5 ♖xe5 19 a3 ♘c6 20 ♘d3 ♖e7 was also slightly better for Black in Hjartarson-Portisch, Reykjavik World Cup 1991.

15 0-0 ♖ad8

This is stronger than 15...dxc4 16 bxc4 ♖ad8 17 ♖fd1 ♕e6 18 ♗f1 ♗b7 19 ♘g5 ♕f5 (Sveshnikov-Kharitonov, Leningrad 1991) and now 20 h4!? is unclear.

16 ♖fd1 ♖fe8 17 a3 ♘c6 18 ♕c2 d4

The e5-pawn is doomed. Svidler-Adams, Tilburg 1997 continued 19 ♖e1 ♕d7 20 b4 ♘xe5 21 b5 ♗c8 22 ♘xe5 ♖xe5 23 ♖xe5 ♗xe5 and Black was simply a pawn up.

B2)

8 c4 ♘b6 (D)

It's a straight choice between this move and 8...♗a6. Overall 8...♘b6 shades it in the preference stakes, if nothing else because I have far more experience with this move!

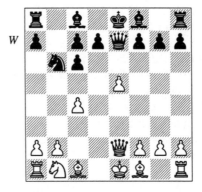

Now White has two principal continuations:

B21: 9 ♘c3!? 108
B22: 9 ♘d2 111

Other tries include:

a) 9 b3 and now:

a1) 9...a5 10 a4?! (White's best line is probably 10 ♗b2 a4 11 ♘d2, transposing to B2221, while Shirov gives the line 10 ♗a3 c5 11 ♘c3 a4 12

♘b5 ♔d8! as favourable for Black) 10...♕b4+! 11 ♘d2 ♕c3 12 ♖b1 ♗b4 (Shirov assesses this position as clearly better for Black) 13 ♕e4 (13 f4?! ♕d4 14 g3 0-0 15 ♕d3 ♕c5 16 ♗b2 d5 17 exd6? ♗f5 18 ♗d4 ♕xd6 19 ♕xf5 ♕xd4 20 ♕d3 ♖ad8 0-1 was a quick black victory in Weteschnik-Vajda, Balatonbereny 1996) 13...c5 14 ♗d3 ♗b7 15 ♕e2 0-0-0 16 0-0 f6 17 exf6 ♖he8 18 ♘e4 ♗xe4 19 ♗xe4 and now, instead of 19...gxf6?, as in Grosar-Matković, Makarska 1994, Black should simply play 19...♕d4!, against which I can find no good answer.

a2) 9...g6 (this also looks fine for Black) 10 ♗b2 (10 a4 a5 11 ♗a3 c5 12 ♘c3 ♗g7 13 f4 and now instead of 13...f6? 14 ♗xc5!, as in Van der Wiel-Piket, Dutch Ch 1992, Black should play 13...♗b7 14 ♕f2 d6 15 ♗e2 g5!) 10...♗g7 11 ♘d2 d6 12 f4 0-0 13 g3 dxe5 14 ♗g2 ♗g4! 15 ♕e3 ♖ae8 and White's compensation for the pawn was insufficient in Socko-Grabarczyk, Polish Ch (Warsaw) 1997.

b) 9 g3 is rarely played, but it doesn't look bad. Black's best option may be to try to steer the game into other variations by means of a transposition:

b1) Following 9...g6, Black was doing well after 10 ♘d2?! ♗g7 11 ♘f3 0-0 12 ♗g5 ♕e6 in Belotti-Grabarczyk, Pula Echt 1997. However, Mikhalevski suggests the stronger 10 b3 for White, which plans to meet 10...♗g7 with 11 f4 f6 12 ♗a3 ♕e6 13 ♗h3!.

b2) Therefore, my suggestion is 9...♕e6. Now 10 ♘d2 a5 transposes to B2222, as does 10 b3 a5 11 ♗b2 a4 12 ♘d2 ♗b4 13 ♗g2 0-0 14 0-0 d5.

B21)
9 ♘c3!? (D)

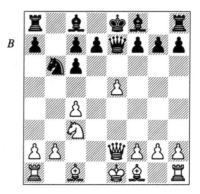

This move was given a new lease of life by a 1999 Kasparov win over Adams. We will now consider three possible moves for Black:

B211: 9...g6!?   108
B212: 9...♕e6   109
B213: 9...a5   110

B211)
9...g6!?

Planning an early attack on the e5-pawn with ...♗g7, followed by ...0-0 and either ...d6 or ...f6.

10 ♘e4!

This dynamic move was introduced by Van der Wiel. In fact it seems that White must play in this way, as routine moves simply allow Black to carry out his plan. For example, 10 ♕e4 ♗g7 11 f4 0-0 12 ♗d3 f6 13 exf6 ♕xf6 14 ♕e2 ♗a6 15 ♗e3 ♖ae8 16 0-0-0 ♕f7 left Black in total control in Ferčec-Pavasović, Pula 1999.

10...♕e6

Much stronger than 10...♗g7? 11 ♗g5 ♕b4+ (11...♕xe5?? loses to 12 ♗f6!) 12 ♕d2 ♕xd2+ 13 ♔xd2 ♗xe5 14 ♘f6+ ♗xf6 15 ♖e1+ ♔f8 16 ♗xf6 ♖g8 17 ♗d8 d5 18 c5 ♘c4+ 19 ♔c3 ♗e6 20 ♗xc7, when White's dark-square domination was clear in Feigin-Mikhalchishin, Dortmund 1999.

11 ♗d2!

This is an improvement over the tempting 11 ♘f6+, which only seems to help Black's king reach the safety of the queenside. After 11...♔d8 12 ♗d2 ♗a6 13 b3 d5 14 ♗c3 dxc4 15 ♕d2+ ♔c8 16 ♗e2 ♔b7 Black was better in Van der Wiel-Gild.Garcia, Wijk aan Zee 1996.

11...♗g7 12 ♘f6+ ♗xf6 13 exf6 0-0 14 0-0-0 ♗a6 *(D)*

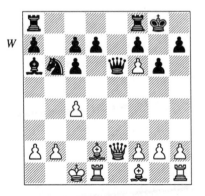

We are following Van der Wiel-Grabarczyk, Pula Echt 1997. In this position Van der Wiel slipped up with 15 ♕xe6?! fxe6 16 ♗g5 d6 17 c5 ♗xf1 18 ♖hxf1 ♘d5, when Black's strong knight on d5 gave him an edge. V.Mikhalevski suggests the improvement 15 ♕e3!?, with the following lines:

a) 15...♕xe3 16 ♗xe3 d6 (White is better after 16...♗xc4 17 ♗xc4 ♘xc4 18 ♖xd7) 17 g4! ♗xc4 18 ♗xb6 ♗xf1 19 ♗xc7 ♗e2 20 ♖xd6 ♗xg4 21 ♖e1 (Wells) and White is better, especially as 21...♖fe8 can be answered with 22 ♖e7!.

b) Perhaps Black should simply bite the bullet with 15...♕xf6. Naturally after 16 ♗c3 ♕e6 White has compensation on the dark squares, but after either 17 ♕d4 f6 or 17 ♕h6 f6 18 ♗d3 ♕f7, there's nothing obvious for White, and Black has ideas of his own, including ...♗xc4 and ...♘a4.

B212)
9...♕e6

This has been the traditional way for Black to meet 9 ♘c3, but an important innovation by Kasparov has cast doubt on its effectiveness. Note that 9...♗a6 10 ♕e4 ♕e6 reaches the next note.

10 ♕e4 *(D)*
10...♗b4

This is slightly more accurate than 10...♗a6, which can just transpose into the main line with 11 b3 ♗b4 12 ♗d2, but also gives White the added possibility of 11 c5!?. After 11...♗xf1 12 cxb6 f5!? 13 ♕e3 ♗xg2 14 ♖g1

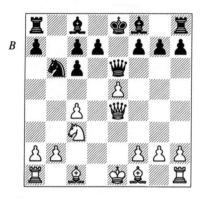

♗d5 15 b7 ♖d8 16 ♕xa7 ♕xe5+ (Mikhalevski) a very interesting position is reached. 17 ♗e3 f4 18 b8♕ ♖xb8 19 ♕xb8+ ♔f7 gives Black compensation for the exchange, but White's advanced b-pawn remains annoying after 17 ♔f1.

11 ♗d2 ♗a6 12 b3

Now 12 c5?! is less effective due to 12...♘c4 13 ♗xc4 ♗xc4 14 f4 ♗xc3 15 ♗xc3 ♗xa2, when Black has an extra pawn.

12...♗xc3 13 ♗xc3 d5

This move is the logical follow-up to Black's previous play.

14 ♕h4!?

This is Kasparov's prepared novelty. The older 14 ♕f3 has been seen in a couple of Spassky's games. After 14...dxc4 15 ♗e2 White uses the pin on the f1-a6 diagonal to try to drum up an initiative. Following 15...0-0 16 0-0 ♖fe8 17 ♖fe1 ♖ad8 we have:

a) 18 ♖ac1 c5 19 ♗f1 ♘d5 20 bxc4 ♘b4! 21 ♗xb4 cxb4 22 ♕e3 and a draw was agreed in Ljubojević-Spassky, Montreal 1979.

b) 18 ♗f1 c5 19 ♖ad1 h6 20 ♗a1 ♗c8 21 bxc4 ♗a6 was unclear in Ponomariov-Spassky, Cannes 1998.

I should also point out that 14 cxd5 only gives Black chances for the advantage, after 14...cxd5 15 ♕b4 ♗xf1 16 ♖xf1 (or 16 ♔xf1 ♘d7) 16...♘d7 17 0-0-0 c5 18 ♕b7 ♘b6!.

14...dxc4 15 ♗e2 ♘d5 (D)

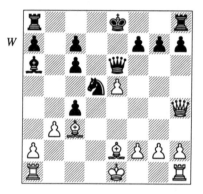

We have been following Kasparov-Adams, Sarajevo 1999, in which 16 ♗d4!? was met by 16...c5?! 17 ♗xc5 ♘c3 18 ♗xc4 ♕xe5+ 19 ♗e3 ♘e4 20 0-0 ♗xc4 21 bxc4 0-0 22 ♖fe1 with a slight plus to White. Kasparov offers 16...♘e7! as an improvement for Black, giving 17 0-0 ♘f5 18 ♕f4 ♘xd4 19 ♕xd4 0-0 as unclear. However, he also points out that White can keep a slight edge with 16 ♗xc4 ♗xc4 17 ♕xc4.

B213)

9...a5

This move is playable against 9 ♘c3, just as it is in the main line against 9 ♘d2.

10 ♕e4

This move, preparing to develop the f1-bishop, has been White's most popular choice. 10 b3!? has also been played, although it does seem to invite 10...a4. Maiorov-D.Frolov, Orel 1997 continued 11 ♖b1 axb3 12 axb3 ♕e6 13 ♕e4 g6 14 ♗d3 ♗g7 15 f4 0-0 16 0-0 and now 16...d5! looks promising for Black.

10 ♗d2 is a tricky move, planning to meet 10...g6 with 11 ♘e4!. Following 10...♕e6 11 ♕e4 White secured an advantage in Delchev-Ferguson, Benasque 1997 after 11...♗b4 12 ♗d3 ♖b8 13 0-0 ♗b7 14 f4 c5 15 ♕e2, so Black should consider playing in a similar fashion to the main line with 11...♗a6 12 b3 g6 13 ♗d3 ♗g7 14 0-0 0-0 15 f4 and now both 15...d5 and 15...f5 look interesting.

10...g6

With this move Black sets his sights on the e5-pawn. It's also possible to delay the fianchetto with 10...♗a6!?. After 11 ♗d3 ♕e6 12 b3 g6 13 0-0 ♗g7 14 ♗b2 0-0 15 ♖fe1 ♖fe8 16 f4 d5 17 ♕f3?! (17 exd6 ♕d7 18 ♕f3 cxd6 looks roughly level) 17...dxc4 18 f5 ♕d7 19 ♗e4 ♖xe5 White is struggling to justify his two-pawn deficit, Wieweg-Wedberg, Stockholm 1996/7.

11 ♗d3 ♗g7 12 0-0 0-0 13 f4 *(D)*

Black has completed his development and can now prepare to break with either f-pawn or d-pawn. Here are two examples from practical play:

a) 13...d5 14 cxd5 cxd5? (14...♖d8 looks better) 15 ♘xd5 ♕c5+ 16 ♗e3

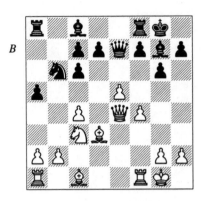

♕xd5 17 ♗xb6 ♕xe4 18 ♗xe4 cxb6 19 ♗xa8 ♗a6 20 ♗d5 ♗xf1 21 ♔xf1 with a clear plus to White, Yakovich-I.Sokolov, Oviedo rpd 1993.

b) 13...♗a6! (this looks more active than 13...♗b7, although that looks playable too) 14 ♖f2 (14 b3 d5 and 14 ♗d2 ♗xc4! favour Black) 14...f5 (or 14...f6!?) and now in Geenen-Lane, Leuven 1998, White erred with 15 exf6?! ♕xf6 16 ♕e2 ♖ae8 and Black had all the pressure. Stronger is 15 ♕e2, planning to meet 15...d6 with 16 c5! ♗xd3 17 ♕xd3 dxc5, with an unclear position.

B22)

9 ♘d2 *(D)*

The main line. Now we look at two moves for Black:

B221: 9...d6 111
B222: 9...a5 113

B221)

9...d6

With this direct move Black seeks to develop quickly, hoping that a swift

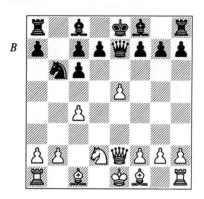

mobilization of his forces will counterbalance an inferior pawn-structure. So far 9...d6 has only been played fleetingly, but Wells predicted a bright future for it, and certainly White has yet to come up with anything convincing. It should also be pointed out here that 9...d5 should come to the same thing, as White's best move against that is also 10 exd6 (10 b3 g6 11 ♗b2 ♗g7 looks fine for Black).

10 exd6

Other continuations are not very effective:

a) 10 ♘f3 ♗g4! is comfortable for Black; e.g., 11 ♗f4 (Wells gives 11 c5 dxc5 12 ♕e4 ♕d7!) 11...dxe5 12 ♕xe5 ♗xf3 13 gxf3 ♕xe5+ 14 ♗xe5 ♗b4+! (A.Ivanov) and White's king will be vulnerable on the open central files.

b) 10 c5 dxc5 11 b3 ♘d5 12 ♘c4 ♕e6 13 g3 ♗e7 14 ♗g2 0-0 15 0-0 (Wells), and although White has structural compensation for the pawn, Black is well developed and has a strong knight on d5.

10...cxd6 11 b3

Or 11 ♘e4 ♗e6 12 b3 d5!, and Black develops rapidly.

11...♗g4 12 f3

An important alternative here is for White to exchange queens with 12 ♕xe7+ ♗xe7. However, experience in this line has so far shown that Black's initiative isn't dampened significantly by this trade. After 13 ♗b2 0-0 14 ♗d3 (or 14 ♗e2 ♖fe8 15 ♗xg4 ♗f6+ 16 ♔d1 ♗xb2 17 ♖b1 ♗d4, which is at least equal for Black, according to Wells) 14...d5 we have:

a) 15 f3?! ♗e6 16 0-0 ♖fd8 17 ♖fd1 a5 18 ♗f1 a4 and Black is slightly better, M.Müller-Wells, Bundesliga 1997/8.

b) 15 0-0 ♗b4! and the white knight doesn't have a useful square to go to.

c) 15 cxd5 ♗b4! (Wells) 16 f3 ♖ad8 17 fxg4 ♖fe8+ 18 ♔d1 ♘xd5 19 a3 ♗xd2 20 ♔xd2 ♘f4 and Black is better.

d) 15 h3 ♗h5 16 cxd5 ♗b4 17 g4 ♗g6 18 ♗xg6 fxg6! 19 0-0-0 ♘xd5 and Black's activity more than compensates for his bad pawn-structure, Shankar-Sorokin, Calcutta 1999.

12...♗e6 13 ♗b2

13 ♗a3?! ♕f6 14 ♖c1 d5 15 ♗xf8 ♔xf8, with ...♖e8 to come, only accelerates Black's development.

13...d5 14 cxd5 ♘xd5!

Black's motto must be 'activity over structure'. Black could improve his structure slightly with 14...cxd5?!, but this would leave him more passively placed. The knight belongs on d5, where it can eye other useful squares such as b4 and e3.

15 ♕e4

Making room for the f1-bishop. Madl-Akhmylovskaya, Manila wom OL 1992 continued instead with 15 ♖c1 ♖d8 16 a3 ♘f4 17 ♕e4 ♗d5 18 ♕xe7+ ♗xe7 19 b4 0-0 20 ♔f2 ♗g5 and once again Black's activity provides enough compensation for the pawn weaknesses.

15...♗f5!?

The choice so far, but maybe Black could also consider 15...♕g5, preparing to develop the f8-bishop, while attacking f2 and thus preventing White's own bishop from developing. The best I can see for White is 16 ♕e5 ♕xe5+ 17 ♗xe5 f6 18 ♗d4 ♗b4, which looks about level.

16 ♕xe7+ ♗xe7 *(D)*

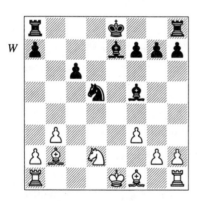

From this position we have:

a) 17 ♗c4 0-0 18 ♘e4 ♘e3 19 ♔f2 ♘xc4 20 bxc4 ♖ab8 21 ♗c3 and the players agreed a draw in I.Gurevich-A.Ivanov, St Martin 1992.

b) After 17 0-0-0 0-0 18 ♘e4 another quick draw was agreed in Grosar-Gostiša, Graz Z 1993.

c) 17 ♘e4!? ♗b4 18 0-0-0 ♘xa2+ 19 ♔b1 ♘b4 20 ♗xg7 is unclear, according to Alexander Ivanov.

d) Wells gives 17 ♗xg7 ♖g8 18 ♗e5 ♘e3 19 g4 ♘c2+ 20 ♔d1 ♘xa1 21 gxf5 ♖d8, which is good for Black.

e) 17 g4!? hopes to improve on the last line; the critical continuation looks to be 17...♗h4+ 18 ♔d1 ♗g6 19 ♗xg7 ♖g8 20 ♗d4 ♖d8, with compensation for the pawn.

B222)

9...a5 *(D)*

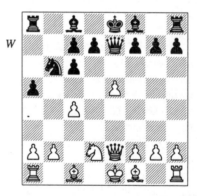

Mark Hebden first encouraged me to play this refined idea, which has become just as popular as Black's traditional tries (9...♕e6 and 9...♗b7). What are the attractions of this seemingly non-developing move? Well firstly, it obviously discourages White from playing b3, although this does in fact remain an option (see B2221).

Secondly, it prepares ...a4, which can be followed up with the imaginative ...♖a5!, which brings this rook into the game by attacking the advanced e-pawn. A final point is that if Black plays ...♗a6, this piece will be protected and will not block the a-pawn. As we shall see, in some lines ...♗a6 is important, as it puts pressure on White's vulnerable c4-pawn.

White's main choices against 9...a5 are the following:

B2221: 10 b3!? 114
B2222: 10 g3 116
B2223: 10 ♕e4 118

Before discussing these moves, let's take a brief look at two other alternatives:

a) 10 h4?! a4! 11 g3 (11 ♖h3?! d5!) 11...♖a5! 12 f4 ♗a6 13 ♖h2! (Shirov-Agdestein, Oslo (4) 1992) and now Shirov recommends 13...♔d8! (intending ...f6) 14 ♕e4 (or 14 ♔d1?! f6 15 exf6 ♕xf6! 16 ♘e4 ♕d4+ 17 ♕d2 ♕g1! 18 ♕xa5 ♕xf1+ 19 ♕e1 ♕xc4) 14...f6 15 ♖e2 fxe5 16 fxe5 ♔c8 with advantage to Black.

b) 10 ♕e3 d5!? (10...g6 also looks OK) 11 ♗e2 g6 12 b3 a4 13 ♗b2 axb3 14 axb3 ♖xa1+ 15 ♗xa1 ♗g7 16 ♗d4 ♕e6 17 f4 0-0 18 0-0 f6 with an equal position, Karatekin-Salazar, Calicut U-20 Wch 1998.

B2221)
　10 b3!?
This move seems to court trouble, as it invites Black to initiate a rapid attack with 10...a4. However, if White plays accurately he can withstand the early onslaught, and the positions that can arise demand positive play from both sides.

10...a4
Naturally Black attacks the pawn-chain.

11 ♗b2
Note that this position can also arise from the move-order 9 b3 a5 10 ♗b2 a4 11 ♘d2.

　11...axb3 12 axb3 ♖xa1+ 13 ♗xa1 ♕a3 *(D)*

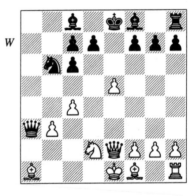

Revealing another point of 9...a5 (as opposed to 9...♕e6). The queen is able to join in the early activity on the queenside.

14 ♕d1
White has to be careful here. For example, 14 ♗c3?? loses immediately to 14...♕c1+, while 14 ♗d4? simply loses a pawn to 14...c5 15 ♗e3 ♕a1+.

　14...♗b4 15 ♗d3 ♕a5!
By adding extra pressure on the pinned knight on d2, Black prevents

White from castling. It's true that Black can force the white king to move after 15...♗xd2+?!, but following 16 ♔xd2 0-0 17 ♕c2 h6 18 ♗b2 ♕e7 19 f4, White's king is quite safe and Black has ceded the bishop-pair.

16 ♔e2 (D)

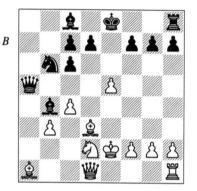

Reaching a critical position for the 10 b3 variation. Black has certainly been calling all the early shots and White has lost the right to castle. However, White has the usual structural advantage, and given time will consolidate with moves such as ♕c2, ♘f3 and ♗d4, preparing ♖a1. Black must react quickly in the centre in order to cause White as much discomfort as possible.

16...d6!?

16...d5, adding pressure to the c4-pawn, has been seen more often, but it seems to me that challenging the e5-pawn is more ambitious. After 17 ♕c2 (17 exd6? is too greedy – see the note to White's 17th move) we have three possibilities for Black:

a) 17...♗e6 18 ♗d4! (18 ♘f3 dxc4 19 bxc4 ♕a4 20 ♕xa4 ♘xa4 21 ♘d4 c5 22 ♘b5 gave White a token edge in Thorhallsson-S.Pedersen, Torshavn 1997) 18...dxc4 19 bxc4 ♗xd2?! 20 ♖a1! ♕b4 21 ♕xd2 ♕xd2+ 22 ♔xd2 and White had a clear plus in Palac-Marciano, Biel 1998. Both 18...♕a8 and 19...♕a8 are improvements for Black, although my general impression is still 'better for White'.

b) 17...♗g4+ 18 f3 and only then playing 18...♗e6 was suggested by Peter Wells, and does have the positive point of stopping White playing ♘f3. However, 19 ♗d4! is still a problem for Black.

c) 17...♕c5!? occurred in Magem-Hebden, Andorra Z 1998, which continued 18 ♘f3 ♗g4 19 ♖d1 g6 20 h3 ♗xf3+ 21 ♔xf3 0-0 22 g3 d4 23 ♗e2 ♗c3 24 ♗xc3 dxc3 25 ♕xc3 and now Hebden played 25...f6?, which allowed the clever 26 exf6!! ♕h5+ 27 ♔g2 ♕xe2 28 ♖e1 ♕h5 29 ♖e7, when, in view of the threat of ♖g7+ followed by f7, Black felt obliged to return the piece with 29...♘d5. Hebden suggests instead the simple 25...♖e8 26 ♔g2 ♕xe5 27 ♕xe5 ♖xe5, after which Black should draw the ending. More telling, however, was Hebden's later preference for 16...d6.

17 ♘f3

17 exd6? runs into 17...0-0!, when 18 dxc7 loses to 18...♖e8+ 19 ♘e4 f5!, while after 18 d7 ♗xd7 19 ♘f3 ♖e8+ 20 ♔f1 ♗g4, White's position is a mess.

17...♗g4 18 ♕c2

Once again 18 exd6 0-0! is too dangerous for White.

18...dxe5 *(D)*

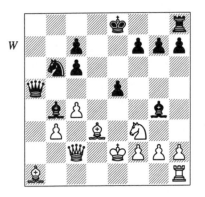

We arrive at another position that is difficult to assess. White has had to give up his central pawn, but at least he is now fully coordinated and Black certainly has some 'tidying up' to do before he can think about trying to exploit the extra material. At a push, I'd take Black, but I'm sure the last word hasn't been spoken on this line.

a) 19 ♖d1 g6 20 ♗e4 0-0! 21 ♗xc6 f6 was reached in Dovzhik-Ambrus, Szeged 1998. Black has returned the pawn, but has completed his development and his king now stands safer than his opponent's. After 22 h3 ♗f5 23 ♗e4 ♗xe4 24 ♕xe4 ♕a2+ Black had the advantage.

b) 19 ♗e4 and now 19...♘d7 20 h3 ♗xf3+ 21 ♔xf3 ♕c5 22 ♗f5 ♘f8 23 ♕e4 f6 gave White some compensation for the pawn in Butze-Poliansky, corr 1975. Black could consider giving

back the pawn immediately by playing 19...0-0!?. Following 20 ♗xh7+ ♔h8 21 ♗d3 (21 ♗f5? ♗xf5 22 ♕xf5 ♕a2+ wins for Black) 21...f5 22 h3 ♗h5 23 g4 e4 a very interesting position is reached.

B2222)

10 g3 *(D)*

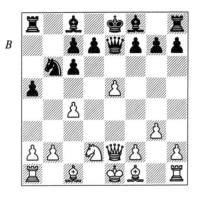

Completing kingside development with a fianchetto.

10...♕e6

Given that White's light-squared bishop is leaving the f1-a6 diagonal, it does seem logical to start an early assault on the c4-pawn. The slightly different plan begins with 10...a4!?, which keeps the option open of attacking the c4-pawn, but plans a cheeky attack on the e5-pawn with ...♖a5. Here are two possible lines:

a) 11 f4 ♗a6 12 b3 ♕b4 13 ♕d3 ♕a5! 14 ♗b2 ♗b4 15 ♕c2 d5! 16 exd6 0-0 17 0-0-0 cxd6 and now:

a1) 18 ♘e4 (Zapata-Sisniega, Linares (Mexico) 1992) 18...d5! 19 ♘g5 g6 20 h4 axb3 21 axb3 dxc4 22 bxc4 ♘a4 gives Black a very strong attack.

a2) Sisniega's suggestion 18 ♗d3 looks stronger, but even so Black can play 18...h6 and look to the future with confidence.

b) 11 ♗g2 ♖a5 12 f4 ♗a6 13 ♖b1 f6! (Black must nibble at White's e5-pawn; after the pedestrian 13...♕e6 14 b3 axb3 15 axb3 ♗b4 16 0-0 0-0 17 ♗b2 White has a clear advantage, Lakos-Ramon, Elista wom OL 1998) 14 b4 axb3 15 axb3 fxe5 16 b4 ♖a2 17 b5 cxb5 18 cxb5 ♗c8 19 fxe5 with a strange-looking position in Strange-McMahon, Sheffield 1996. Now Peter Wells's suggestion of 19...♘a4! 20 ♕e3 ♕e6 (preventing 21 0-0 due to 21...♗c5) 21 ♖f1 gives us a position that is still very murky, but my preference would be with Black.

We return to 10...♕e6 (D):

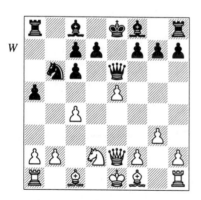

11 b3

A critical alternative to this obvious move is to offer a pawn sacrifice with 11 ♗g2 ♗b4 12 0-0!?. Black can choose to accept the pawn straight away, or keep the threat looming:

a) 12...♗xd2 13 ♕xd2 (13 ♗xd2!? ♘xc4 14 ♗c3 ♗a6 15 ♖fe1 ♘b6 16 ♕h5 ♗c4 17 ♗e4 g6 18 ♕h6 was unclear in Borge-Fedorov, Tåstrup 1992) 13...♕xc4 (after the game, Lautier proposed 13...♘xc4!? 14 ♕d4 0-0 15 f4 ♘b6 16 f5 ♕c4 as a good defence for Black and I agreed with him, but now I'm not so sure; after 17 ♕f2 White seems to have quite a menacing attack) 14 b3 ♕b4 15 ♕xb4 axb4 16 ♗d2 ♘d5 17 ♗xd5 (17 ♖fc1 ♖a5 18 a3 ♖xa3 19 ♖xa3 bxa3 20 ♗xd5 cxd5 21 ♖xc7 0-0 22 ♖a7 a2 23 ♖xa2 ♗b7 is equal) 17...cxd5 18 ♖fc1 c6 19 ♗xb4 and White has a minuscule edge, Lautier-Emms, Harplinge 1998.

b) 12...0-0!? (Wells) may well be more accurate. Now 13 b3 loses a pawn to 13...♗c3 and the threat on the c4-pawn remains. A possible line is 13 f4!? ♗xd2 (Black must grab the pawn; 13...♖e8? 14 b3 d5 15 ♗b2 a4 16 ♘f3 a3 17 ♗d4 c5 18 ♗f2 h6 19 cxd5 ♘xd5 20 ♕c2 gave White a clear advantage in Kreiman-Grinshpun, Budapest 1998) and now 14 ♗xd2 ♕xc4 15 ♕f2 leaves Black a tempo up on the line discussed in 'a'. This extra move can be put to good effect with 15...♖e8, preventing 16 f5. White can also play 14 ♕xd2, but after 14...♕xc4 15 b3 ♕c5+, Black is certainly more comfortable than in line 'a' and of course, we mustn't forget that extra pawn.

11...♗b4 12 ♗b2 a4 13 ♗g2 0-0 14 0-0 d5 (D)

An enticing idea is the exchange sacrifice with 14...a3 15 ♗d4 c5 16 ♗e3 ♕xe5 17 ♗xa8 ♘xa8. If Black could consolidate, he would certainly gain compensation on the light squares along the long h1-a8 diagonal. Unfortunately some powerful play by White in Shabalov-Yurtaev, Elista OL 1998 casts a big shadow over Black's idea. After 18 ♕f3 ♘b6 19 ♗f4 ♕e6 20 ♖fe1 ♕g6 21 ♗xc7! ♗xd2 22 ♖ed1 ♘xc4 23 bxc4 ♗b4 24 ♗d6 Black's position was not a pretty sight.

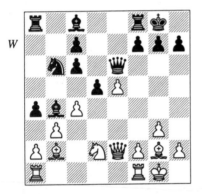

We are following P.H.Nielsen-Dautov, Bad Lauterberg 1991, which continued 15 ♘f3?! a3! 16 ♗d4 c5 17 ♗e3 ♗a6 and Black's pressure on the c4-pawn gave him the advantage. Dautov suggests 15 f4 as an improvement for White, but also mentions that then 15...♕g6! 16 ♘f3 ♕h5, keeping some control on the light squares, gives Black his full share of the chances.

B2223)
10 ♕e4 (D)

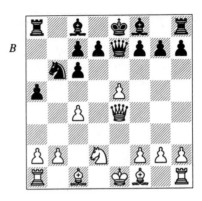

A sensible option. The white queen vacates the e2-square, thus allowing the light-squared bishop to develop.

10...g6

Preparing to fianchetto the dark-squared bishop and exert pressure on the advanced e-pawn. 10...♘a4 has also been tried, but, although the manoeuvre ...♘b6-a4-c5 is a central theme in this variation, playing it immediately is probably not the most accurate. After 11 ♗e2! ♘c5 12 ♕e3 g6 13 0-0 ♗g7 14 ♘f3 ♘e6 15 ♖e1 0-0 16 ♗d2 ♗b7 17 ♗c3 c5 White held a small advantage in A.Grosar-I.Sokolov, Portorož/Rogaška Slatina 1993.

11 ♗d3 ♗g7

Continuing to develop must be the most logical course, but now that White has committed his bishop to d3, there is also a reasonable argument for initiating the ...♘a4-c5 procedure. After 11...♘a4 I've had two different experiences, one successful, the other one not so, against the same opponent:

a) 12 0-0 ♘c5 13 ♕e2 ♗g7 14 ♘f3 ♘e6 led to equality in Lau-Emms,

Copenhagen Open 1992. Probably best for White here is simple development with 15 ♗d2, but my opponent played over-ambitiously with 15 h4?! 0-0 16 h5?! d6! 17 hxg6 hxg6 18 exd6 ♕xd6 19 ♖d1 ♘f4 20 ♗xf4 ♕xf4, after which the bishop-pair and pressure on the b2-pawn more than compensated for the wrecked structure on the queenside.

b) 12 ♘b3!? was an improvement lined up by Lau in a rapidplay tournament, also in Copenhagen, just a few days after our first encounter. The idea of this move is to hinder Black's plan of ...♘c5-e6. After 12...♗g7 13 0-0 0-0 14 ♖e1 ♗b7 15 ♖b1 f5 16 exf6 ♕xf6 17 ♗e3 we reached a position which was later assessed as 'better for White' in more than one source. However, I think this could be a case of the age-old author's disease of 'annotating by result'. Indeed I did lose this game, but had I chosen 17...♘xb2! here the result may have been different. The tactics seem to work for Black; for example, 18 ♗d4 ♕f7 19 ♗xg7 (or 19 ♗xb2 ♗xb2 20 ♖xb2 ♖ae8!) 19...♕xf2+ 20 ♔h1 ♘xd3 21 ♕xd3 c5! 22 ♖g1 ♔xg7 and Black is better, or 18 ♗e2 ♘a4 19 ♗d4 c5! 20 ♗xf6 ♗xe4 21 ♗xg7 ♔xg7 and again Black is happy.

I'd like to say that's the end of the story, but my general impression was that White should somehow be better in this line. Using another author's habit, 'annotating by Fritz', I've found that instead of 17 ♗e3, White can play

the solid 17 ♖e2, and indeed here does seem to keep a nagging edge. So the onus is still be on Black to come up with something new here.

12 0-0 0-0 *(D)*

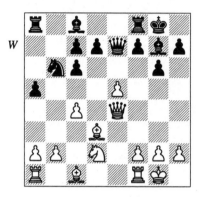

We've reached a critical position for the assessment of 10 ♕e4. Both sides have nearly completed their development and now that Black has castled, White must do something about the threat to the e5-pawn:

a) 13 f4? is a serious positional error, which was punished in Fogarasi-Hebden, Cappelle la Grande 1993. Black reacted positively with 13...d5 14 ♕e2 f6! and following 15 exf6 ♕xe2 16 ♗xe2 ♗xf6 Black was clearly on top.

b) 13 ♘f3 *(D)* looks much more sensible. White defends the e-pawn and unblocks the dark-squared bishop, which can now travel to g5. However, I still believe in Black's position, and here are a couple of possible lines:

b1) 13...♘a4 14 ♗g5 ♕b4 (14...f6 15 exf6 ♕xe4 16 ♗xe4 ♗xf6 17 ♗xf6

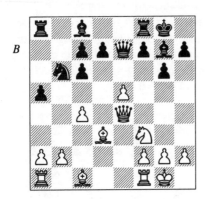

♖xf6 18 b3 ♞c5 19 ♗c2 leaves White with a slight edge in the endgame due to his better pawn-structure) 15 b3 ♞c5 16 ♕e3 ♞xd3 17 ♕xd3 a4, with an unclear position. Black is creating counterplay on the queenside, but must be careful against White's obvious chances on the other side of the board.

b2) 13...♗a6 (it makes sense to attack the c4-pawn, now that it only has two defenders) 14 ♗g5 ♕e6 15 ♖ac1 (15 b3!? d5 16 exd6 ♗xa1 17 ♖xa1 cxd6 18 ♕xc6 is an unclear exchange sacrifice) and now both 15...f5 16 exf6 ♕xe4 17 ♗xe4 ♗xf6 18 ♗xf6 ♖xf6 19 b3 d5 20 ♗d3 dxc4 21 bxc4 ♖d8 and 15...♞a4!? 16 ♕e2 ♞c5 17 ♖fd1 ♖ab8 18 b3 a4 look distinctly playable for Black.

11 The Belgrade Gambit

1 e4 e5 2 ♘f3 ♘c6 3 ♘c3 ♘f6 4 d4 exd4 5 ♘d5!? *(D)*

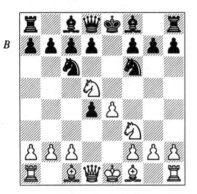

The Belgrade Gambit was introduced in the 1940s by Yugoslav masters. Also known as the Four Knights Gambit, at first sight this line makes a strange impression. Normally an opening gambit leads to a lead in development, but here White follows up his pawn sacrifice by moving a piece which has already been developed, offering his only other central pawn in the process. It's only after the position is studied a bit more that one realizes that Black has no easy way to refute White's play. Nevertheless, it should come as no surprise that Black has at least one continuation that should guarantee a satisfactory position from the opening.

A Quick Summary of the Recommended Lines

Once again, when dealing with a gambit, I've offered both a safe and not-so-safe solution. Line A is still quite rare and the theory is undeveloped. The positions that can be reached are quite fascinating, and the well-prepared player with Black has every chance of success. Line B is much better known and is seen as Black's most reliable defence to the Belgrade Gambit. Black has nothing to fear in Line B1, where more often that not it's White who's searching for equality. Line B2 has a better reputation, with best play leading to equal chances for both sides.

The Theory of the Belgrade Gambit

1 e4 e5 2 ♘f3 ♘c6 3 ♘c3 ♘f6 4 d4 exd4 5 ♘d5!?

We will now study my two recommendations against the Belgrade.

A: 5...♘b4!?   121
B: 5...♗e7   124

The former is adventurous, while the latter is solid and reliable.

A)

5...♘b4!?

Black prepares to capture on d5 with this knight, rather than the one on f6. White has two main courses of action:

A1: 6 ♗c4   122
A2: 6 ♘xd4!?   123

In contrast, 6 ♘xf6+?! is hardly a test for Black. Following 6...♕xf6 7 ♗c4 ♗c5 8 0-0 d6 9 ♘g5 0-0 10 e5 ♕g6! 11 a3 ♘c6 12 ♗d3 ♗f5 Black was fully mobilized and still a pawn to the good in Van der Weide-Golod, Groningen 1995.

A1)
6 ♗c4 ♘bxd5 7 exd5 ♗b4+! (D)

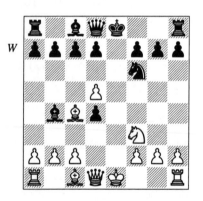

This move forces White into making some kind of concession.

8 ♗d2

8 ♔f1 is also possible, but I'm always happy if my opponent has to move his king in the opening, unless he has compensation for having to do so. In my opinion White's slight space advantage just about keeps the balance,

but just on psychological grounds I'd prefer Black here. After 8...0-0 9 ♕xd4 ♗e7 (9...h6 10 h4 d6 11 ♗g5 ♗c5 12 ♗xf6 ♕xf6 13 ♕xf6 gxf6 was equal in Hector-Karolyi, Copenhagen 1985) 10 ♗g5 d6 11 ♖e1 h6 12 ♗h4 ♖e8 13 h3 ♗d7 14 g4 c5! Van der Weide-Notkin, Groningen 1994 continued 15 ♕f4 b5 16 ♗d3 c4 and Black was clearly better. 15 dxc6 is probably stronger, although then Black is still spoilt for choice between 15...bxc6 and 15...♗xc6!?.

8...♕e7+ 9 ♕e2 ♗xd2+ 10 ♔xd2

After 10 ♘xd2?! ♕xe2+ 11 ♔xe2 b5! White will struggle to regain his pawn.

10...♕xe2+ 11 ♔xe2 c5! 12 dxc6 bxc6!?

Injecting some imbalance into the pawn-structure. Black plans gain time by attacking pieces with his c- and d-pawns. 12...dxc6 13 ♘xd4 would be dull and level.

13 ♘xd4 d5 14 ♗d3

Or 14 ♗b3 c5 15 ♗a4+ ♔e7 16 ♘b3 ♗a6+ 17 ♔f3 (or 17 ♔d2 ♔d6 18 f3 ♖ab8 with an edge to Black, Van der Brink-Van de Oudeweetering, Dutch Ch 1993) 17...♔d6 18 a3 ♖ab8 19 ♖ab1 ♗c4 20 ♖hd1 h5 and Black was more active in B.Ponomariov-Golod, Ukrainian Ch 1990.

14...c5 15 ♘b5

Black was also better after 15 ♗b5+ ♗d7 16 ♗xd7+ ♔xd7 17 ♘f5 ♖he8+ 18 ♔f3 ♖e5 in Eriksson-Sandström, Helsingborg 1991.

15...0-0 16 b3 ♗e6

We are following Van Haastert-Golod, Dieren 1998. Black's control of the centre gives him a small advantage.

A2)

6 ♘xd4!? ♘xe4 (D)

This is the most ambitious move. Psakhis gives 6...♘bxd5 7 exd5 ♗c5 as equal, whereas Nunn suggests that it may be slightly better for White after 8 ♕e2+. On this occasion I think I'll side with Psakhis, while adding that after 8...♕e7 9 ♕xe7+ ♔xe7, both 10 d6+ ♔f8 11 ♘b5 c6 12 ♘c7 ♖b8 13 ♗f4 ♘e4 14 0-0-0 g5! and 10 ♘f5+ ♔f8 11 d6 ♘e4 12 dxc7 are messy but I don't think Black is worse in the complications.

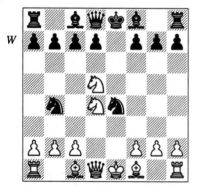

7 ♘f5

In *Informator* language, this is given the 'only move' symbol by Psakhis, but it seems that no one has paid much attention to 7 ♘b5!?. This is surprising, as ♘d4-b5 is a familiar theme in the Belgrade Gambit. Quite

apart from its obvious aesthetic value, this position is also quite important. This is because I would go as far to say that 7 ♘b5 could be White's most dangerous move here. Let's take a look at some of the variations:

a) 7...♗c5 and now:

a1) 8 ♗e3 ♗xe3 9 fxe3 ♘xd5 (or 9...♕h4+ 10 g3 ♘xg3 11 ♘dxc7+ ♔d8 12 hxg3 ♕xh1 13 ♘xa8 ♕h2 leading to an unclear position) 10 ♕xd5 ♘g5 11 ♘xc7+ ♕xc7 12 ♕xg5 0-0 13 ♗d3 d6 with a roughly level position.

a2) 8 ♘bxc7+! ♔f8 9 ♗e3! ♗xe3 10 fxe3 ♘xd5 (10...♕h4+ 11 g3 ♘xg3 12 hxg3 ♕xg3+ 13 ♔d2 ♘xd5 14 ♘xd5 is better for White) 11 ♕xd5 ♕xc7 12 ♕xe4 gives us a position where both sides have a weak pawn, but White gets the nod as Black has been forced to move his king.

b) 7...♘xd5 8 ♕xd5 and now:

b1) 8...♗b4+ 9 c3 ♕e7 10 ♘xc7+ ♔d8 11 ♗e3 ♔xc7 12 ♗d3 ♖e8 13 0-0 ♗d6 14 ♖fe1 and despite the extra piece Black is in some trouble, Gulbis-Meiers, corr 1985.

b2) 8...♕e7!? 9 ♘xc7+ ♔d8 10 ♗f4! d6 11 0-0-0 ♔xc7 gives us a position that could certainly do with a practical test. Black has the extra piece, but everything else is going for White.

b3) 8...♘c5 (the safest) 9 ♗e3 (9 ♗c4 ♘e6 10 ♗f4 c6 11 ♘d6+ ♗xd6 12 ♕xd6 ♘xf4 13 ♕xf4 ♕e7+ is clearly better for Black) 9...♘e6 (9...c6 10 ♘d6+ ♗xd6 11 ♕xd6 ♘e6 12 0-0-0 ♕e7 13 ♗c4 ♕xd6 14 ♖xd6 grants White compensation for the pawn in the shape of dark-square control) 10 ♘xa7 (it's time to recover material) 10...c6 11 ♕d2 d5 12 ♘xc8 ♖xc8, with a roughly level position. White has the two bishops, but Black can develop easily and has a good pawn-structure.

In contrast 7 ♗c4 should not worry Black. After 7...c6 8 ♘xb4 ♗xb4+ 9 c3 both 9...♗e7 and 9...♘xc3!? look good for Black.

7...c6! 8 ♘xb4 ♕a5

8...♗xb4+ 9 c3 ♕f6, as played in Tal-Averkin, USSR Cht 1954, may be even stronger. That game continued 10 ♕f3 ♘xc3 11 a3 and now Nunn suggests 11...♕e5+ 12 ♔d2 ♘e4+ 13 ♔c2 ♗f8, when White has nothing to show for the two pawns. After 10 ♘xg7+, Psakhis gives 10...♕xg7 11 cxb4 0-0 12 g3 as unclear, but Tal himself gave 10...♔d8! as the refutation of White's play and I can see no reason to disagree with this.

9 ♕f3 ♗xb4+ 10 ♔d1?

Psakhis gives 10 c3 ♘xc3 11 a3 ♘d5+ 12 ♔d1 as unclear, but Nunn adds that after 12...0-0 White is still struggling to justify his sacrifice; for example, 13 ♗h6 ♖e8 14 ♗xg7 d6! and Black is better.

10...♕e5! 11 ♘xg7+ ♔d8 12 ♘f5 d5

This position arose in Prié-Psakhis, Paris 1990. White has managed to restore material equality, but that's the end of the good news. Black is now fully coordinated and ready to take over the operation. Following 13 ♘h6!? ♕d4+

14 ♗d3 ♘xf2+ 15 ♔e2 ♖e8+ Black was on his way to a quick victory.

In conclusion, 5...♘b4 looks very playable, but it would certainly be interesting to see some practical examples of 6 ♘xd4 ♘xe4 7 ♘b5!?.

B)

5...♗e7 (D)

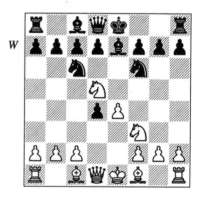

This is Black's most solid and reliable move. White now has two main choices:

B1: 6 ♗c4   125
B2: 6 ♗f4   125

Black has no problems after the pedestrian 6 ♘xd4. After 6...♘xd5 7 exd5 ♘xd4 8 ♕xd4 0-0 9 ♗e2 ♗f6 the bishop comes to the long diagonal and assures Black of at least equality.

6 ♗b5?! makes even less sense. After 6...0-0 7 0-0 d6 8 ♗xc6 bxc6 9 ♘xf6+ ♗xf6 10 ♘xd4 c5 11 ♘e2 ♗a6 12 ♖e1 ♖b8 13 c3 ♖e8 Black's bishop-pair gave him a commanding position in Fletzer-Zimmerman, Venice 1949.

B1)

6 ♗c4 0-0 7 ♘xd4

7 0-0 avoids Black's following pawn offer, but allows Black to snatch a pawn himself with 7...♘xe4! (7...d6 is level, but very dull). Following 8 ♖e1 ♘f6 White finds it tough trying to justify the pawn sacrifice:

a) 9 ♘g5? ♘xd5 10 ♘xf7 ♖xf7 11 ♗xd5 ♕f8 12 ♕e2 ♔h8 13 ♗xf7 ♕xf7 left Black with a winning position in Burton-Nunn, Oxford 1971.

b) 9 ♘xe7+ ♘xe7 10 ♗g5 (10 ♕xd4 d5! 11 ♗g5 ♘f5 12 ♗xf6 ♘xd4 13 ♗xd8 ♘xc2 14 ♗e7 dxc4 15 ♗xf8 ♔xf8 clearly favours Black) 10...c5! (10...♘g6 11 ♕xd4 gave White some compensation in Reefschläger-Carlhammar, Gausdal 1990) 11 ♗xf6 gxf6 12 ♕e2 d5! and once again Black comes out on top.

7...♘xd5 8 ♗xd5 ♘xd4 9 ♕xd4 ♗f6 10 ♕d3 c6 11 ♗b3 d5!? *(D)*

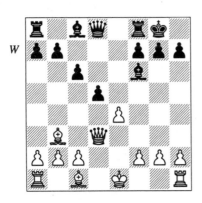

12 0-0

Accepting the pawn is extremely risky. After 12 exd5 Black throws in

12...♖e8+ 13 ♔f1 and then simply 13...cxd5 is sufficient. After 14 ♗xd5 Black's initiative carries on in the endgame after 14...♗e6 15 ♗xe6 ♖xe6 16 ♕xd8+ ♖xd8.

12...dxe4 13 ♕xe4 ♖e8 14 ♕f3 ♗e6 15 ♗xe6 ♖xe6 16 ♗e3 ♕a5

This position has been reached more than once. Black's pieces are slightly more active and White must work hard just to equalize. In M.Morris-Wedberg, New York 1991 White failed to do so and after 17 c3 ♕b5 18 ♖ab1 a5 19 ♖fd1 ♖e7 20 ♗d4 ♗xd4 21 cxd4 (21 ♖xd4 ♕xb2!) 21...♖d8 22 ♖d2 ♕g5 Black went on to win.

B2)

6 ♗f4

This is White's most popular move.
6...d6 7 ♘xd4 0-0 *(D)*

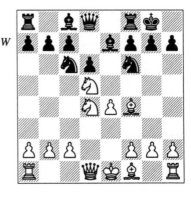

8 ♘b5

This move is virtually forced, otherwise White could be in danger of being worse. For example, 8 ♘xc6?! bxc6 9 ♘c3 ♖b8 10 ♖b1 ♖e8 11 ♗d3

♗g4 12 ♕d2 d5 13 0-0 ♗b4 and Black had the initiative in Bartek-Habinak, Slovakian Cht 1995.

8...♘xd5 9 exd5 ♘e5 10 ♕d2

Similar play develops after 10 ♗e2. For example, 10...♘g6 11 ♗g3 f5! 12 f4 ♗f6 13 c3 ♖e8 14 0-0 a6 15 ♘d4 ♗xd4+! 16 cxd4 ♗d7 17 ♖e1 ♕f6 and Black was better in I.Almasi-Bezgodov, Balatonbereny 1996.

10...c6 11 ♘c3

11 dxc6 bxc6 12 ♘d4 ♕b6 gives Black very active play.

11...♘g6!?

11...♗f5 isn't bad either. For example, 12 ♗e2 ♗f6 13 0-0 c5 14 ♖fe1 a6 15 a4 ♖e8 16 ♗f1 ♕b6 17 ♘d1 ♘g6 and Black was fine in Bellon-I.Ivanov, Benidorm 1982.

12 ♗e3 c5 13 ♗e2 f5 14 f4 ♗f6 15 ♘d1 ♕e8 16 0-0 b5 17 ♗f2 a6 18 ♗f3 ♖a7 19 g3 ♖e7

We are following Prié-Van der Wiel, France-Netherlands, Cannes 1990. Objectively the position must be equal, although there's still plenty to fight for, and Black can hope to exploit the slight weakness of the d5-pawn.

12 The Scotch Four Knights Game

1 e4 e5 2 ♘f3 ♘c6 3 ♘c3 ♘f6 4 d4
exd4 5 ♘xd4 (D)

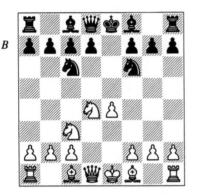

The *Oxford Companion to Chess* describes the Scotch Four Knights Game as "A combination of the Scotch Game and the Four Knights Opening". Had the second edition been more pushed for space, it could easily have just read "harmless" or "mostly harmless"! That said, the Scotch Four Knights remains a viable option for White and is good choice for those not interested in learning too much theory. Just like the Scotch Game, White opens up the position early on and plans rapid development and active piece play. The main disadvantage of the opening is that White does nothing to hinder Black's development, which is also swift and smooth. Often the lack of real pawn-breaks leads to a strategically sterile position, whereby the resulting middlegame is a just a battle between White's and Black's active pieces. It's no surprise that a fair number of games stemming from the main line end in draws.

A Quick Summary of the Recommended Lines

Line A is the traditional response to the Scotch Four Knights Game, and for a long time it has had a very trustworthy reputation. Line A1 really is harmless, which leaves with the ever-popular Line A2. The only real development in recent years has been Lautier's 11 ♘a4!? (Line A22), which for a while presented Black with some novel problems. In general, though, Black has been comfortably holding his own. The only defect is that in some positions it's hard for Black to play for a win.

This is the reason for my inclusion of Line B, which is still relatively fresh. Black has more chances to lead the game into uncharted territory here and this line can certainly benefit from some original analysis.

The Theory of the Scotch Four Knights Game

1 e4 e5 2 ♘f3 ♘c6 3 ♘c3 ♘f6 4 d4 exd4 5 ♘xd4

Now we consider my two recommended courses of action for Black:

A: 5...♗b4   128
B: 5...♗c5!?   137

The former is solid and respectable; the latter is less well-known, and somewhat under-rated.

A)

5...♗b4 (D)

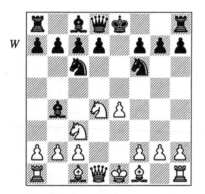

In my database 5...♗b4 was Black's choice in nearly 90% of the games reaching the position after 5 ♘xd4. Its popularity is not hard to understand. In one move Black develops a piece, attacks an important central pawn and prepares to castle. Moreover, 5...♗b4 leaves White with very little choice how to continue.

6 ♘xc6

This is virtually forced, as otherwise White has too much trouble defending both e4 and d4 at the same time. Alternative moves are very easy to deal with:

a) 6 ♘f5? 0-0! and the threats of ...d5 and ...♘xe4 mean that Black is already standing well.

b) 6 f3?! 0-0 and once more the thematic ...d5 cannot be prevented; for example, 7 ♗c4? d5! 8 ♘xd5? ♘xd5 9 ♘xc6 (or 9 exd5 ♕h4+) 9...bxc6 10 exd5 ♕h4+ 11 g3 ♖e8+ 12 ♔f1 ♕h3+ and Black wins, or 7 ♗e2 d5 8 ♘xc6 bxc6 9 e5? ♖e8! 10 exf6 ♗xc3+ 11 bxc3 ♗a6!. Relatively best is 7 ♗b5, although after 7...♕e7! 8 ♗xc6 Black can be optimistic whichever way he recaptures.

c) 6 ♗g5 h6 7 ♗xf6 (after 7 ♗h4 Black can simply grab the pawn with 7...g5 8 ♗g3 ♘xe4) 7...♕xf6 8 ♘db5 ♗a5 and Black will follow up with ...a6.

6...bxc6 7 ♗d3

Playing *à la* Scotch is no good here, because Black's bishop has already escaped to b4. Following 7 e5? ♕e7! 8 ♕e2 ♘d5 it's obvious that White is struggling.

The unusual 7 ♕d4, however, is playable and enjoyed a brief spell of popularity when Paulsen and Tarrasch adopted it in the 1880s. In those days the main line ran 7...♕e7 8 f3 and then 8...d5 9 ♗g5 c5?! 10 ♗b5+ ♔f8 11 ♕d3, with quite a good position for White, since 11...d4 can be answered by 12 0-0-0!. Black should instead play more steadily with 8...♗c5. After 9 ♕d3 a5 10 ♗g5 h6 11 ♗xf6 ♕xf6 12 ♘a4 ♗d6 13 g3 0-0 14 0-0-0 ♖b8 Black obtained good counterplay in Tartakower-Prins, Venice 1949.

One final try for White is the unpinning 7 ♗d2, but this does nothing to hinder Black's basic plan. Following 7...0-0 8 ♗d3 d5 the pressure on the e4-pawn virtually forces White to play 9 exd5, when the bishop on d2 is looking rather passive.

7...d5 *(D)*

This is by far the most popular choice here, but it should be pointed out that the refinement 7...0-0 is also fully playable, after which in my view White has nothing better than to return to the main line with 8 0-0 d5 9 exd5 (or 9 e5). Thorhallsson-Howell, Groningen U-20 Ech 1986 continued instead with 8 ♗g5, but Black obtained the advantage after 8...d5 9 exd5 (9 e5 ♕e8 10 f4 ♘g4 11 h3 is answered by 11...♘xe5!) 9...♖e8+ 10 ♔f1 ♗xc3 11 bxc3 cxd5 12 ♕f3 ♘e4! 13 ♗xd8 ♘d2+ 14 ♔g1 ♘xf3+ 15 gxf3 ♖xd8. The move-order with 7...0-0 does have the benefit of cutting out the 7...d5 8 exd5 cxd5 9 ♕e2+ variation, not that this line is particularly threatening (see the note to White's 9th move in Line A2).

White now faces his first major choice, whether to advance or to capture:

A1: 8 e5 129
A2: 8 exd5 130

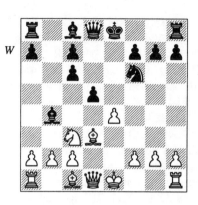

8 ♗g5 should be met with 8...h6, but not 8...dxe4?! 9 ♗xe4 ♕xd1+ 10 ♖xd1 ♘xe4?? 11 ♖d8#!

A1)

8 e5 ♘g4 9 0-0

In fact White is not obliged to defend the e5-pawn just yet as 9...♘xe5 would run into a pin with 10 ♖e1. That said, 9 ♗f4 is also an alternative here. White threatens to play h3, so Black should strike back at the centre with 9...f6!, when 10 exf6 0-0! 11 0-0 ♕xf6 transposes to the main line, while 10 h3 ♘xe5 11 ♗xe5 fxe5 12 ♕h5+ ♔f8 13 ♕xe5 ♗d6 slight favoured Black in Davie-Gligorić, Dundee 1967. Despite having lost the right to castle, Black can tidy up his king position with ...♕f6, ...g6 and ...♔g7, while the advantage of the bishop-pair is permanent.

9...0-0 10 ♗f4

Or 10 h3 ♘xe5 11 ♗xh7+ ♔xh7 12 ♕h5+ ♔g8 13 ♕xe5 ♖e8 14 ♕g3 ♗f5 15 ♗g5 ♕d7 16 ♖ac1 ♖e6! and Black was well on top in Pollock-Chigorin, New York 1889.

10...f6! 11 exf6 ♕xf6 12 ♗g3

Grabbing the c-pawn is too risky. Following 12 ♗xc7?! ♗c5! 13 ♗g3 ♘xf2 14 ♗xf2 ♗xf2+ 15 ♔h1 ♕h4, Black will improve his attack with ...♗g4.

12...♗d6

Also possible is 12...♗c5!?, planning to build up pressure on the f2-pawn. Korneev-Ibragimov, Ekaterinburg 1997 continued 13 ♕d2 h5!? 14 h4 ♗d7 15 ♖ae1 ♖f7 16 ♘d1 ♖af8 with a roughly level position.

13 ♗e2 ♘e5 14 ♘a4 ♗e6 15 ♕d2 ♘g6! 16 ♖ae1 ♘f4 17 ♗d1 ♖ae8 18 c3 c5

This position arose in Afek-Gyimesi, Kecskemet 1994. Black's active pieces and pressure along the half-open f-file give him at least an equal share of the chances.

A2)

8 exd5

White's usual continuation in this position.

8...cxd5 *(D)*

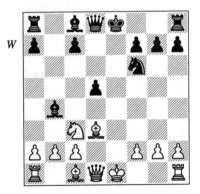

9 0-0

In recent years White has begun experimenting with 9 ♕e2+. Following 9...♗e7 there are two ways to play:

a) 10 ♗g5 0-0 11 0-0-0!? c6 12 ♖he1 ♗d6 (12...♗b4 13 ♕e5 ♘g4 14 ♕f4 ♗d6 15 ♕d2 f6 16 ♗f4 led to a quick draw in Rausis-Fyllingen, Gausdal 1995, while 12...♗e6?! 13 ♗f5! ♗xf5 14 ♕xe7 ♕xe7 15 ♖xe7 gives White the advantage) 13 ♕e3 h6 14 ♗f4 (14 ♗xh6 loses to 14...♘g4!) 14...♖e8 15 ♕d2 ♗e6 16 ♗xd6 ♕xd6 17 h3 ♖ab8 and with the half-open b-file, I prefer Black, Alonso-Gild.Garcia, Matanzas Capablanca mem 1993.

b) 10 0-0 0-0 11 ♖e1 ♗e6 12 ♗g5 h6 13 ♗h4 (13 ♗f4 ♗d6 14 ♗xd6 ♕xd6 15 ♘b5 ♕b6 16 ♕e5 ♖ac8 17 a4 ♗d7 18 ♕f4 c5 was equal in Rodin-Notkin, Moscow 1996) 13...c6 and now Pinter recommends 14 ♗g3 with an equal position. Instead after 14 ♘a4? ♖e8 15 ♗g3?! ♕a5! 16 b3 ♗f8 17 c3 c5! 18 ♗c2 ♖ad8 19 ♕f1 ♗d7! White's offside knight causes him many problems, L.B.Hansen-Pinter, Copenhagen 1995.

9...0-0 10 ♗g5

Pinning the knight to the queen is White's best and most natural continuation. Other moves fail to set Black any problems:

a) 10 ♘b5 ♗g4 11 f3 ♗c5+!? (after 11...♗e6 12 c3 ♗c5+ 13 ♔h1 ♗b6 14 ♘d4 c5 15 ♘xe6 fxe6 16 ♗f4 ♗c7 17 ♗xc7 ♕xc7 18 f4 ♖ae8 19 ♕d2 e5 20 fxe5 ♕xe5 21 ♖ae1 ♘e4 the position was level in Bojković-Nikolin,

Cetinje wom 1991) 12 ♔h1 ♗d7 13 c3 h6 (Mathe-Khuzman, Wijk aan Zee 1992) and here Khuzman suggests 14 b4!? ♗b6 15 ♗f4 ♖e8 with an equal position.

b) 10 ♘e2 ♖e8 11 c3 ♗d6 is very comfortable for Black. The brief but interesting game Piper-Gyimesi, Balatonbereny 1992 continued 12 ♘g3 ♘g4!? (12...c6 is a dependable alternative) 13 h3 ♘xf2! 14 ♖xf2 ♗xg3 15 ♗xh7+! ♔h8 16 ♖f1 ♕h4 17 ♗d3 ♗xh3 18 gxh3 ♕xh3 19 ♕c2 ♗d6 20 b4 ♕g3+ 21 ♔h1 g6 (21...♖e5!?) 22 ♕f2 ♕h3+ 23 ♔g1 ♕xd3 24 ♕f6+ ♔g8 25 ♕xf7+ with a draw by perpetual check.

10...c6 *(D)*

This is a fundamental move, which gives some much-needed protection to the d5-pawn.

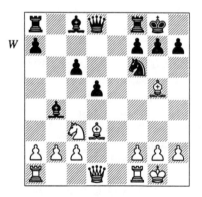

White is now at a major crossroads. Three different plans are available:

The first is sedate, the second is new, and the third is traditional.

A21)
11 ♘e2

White's plan is for the knight to hop to the kingside via d4, f4 or g3. While in general this is a good idea, an emphasis on just this plan fails to present Black with any immediate problems.

11...h6

Another active way to play for Black is 11...♖e8 12 ♘d4 ♕d6! (preparing ...♘e4), and now:

a) 13 ♗h4?! ♘e4 14 c3 ♗c5 15 f3 ♕h6! 16 fxe4 ♕xh4 17 exd5 (17 ♕f3? f5! 18 g3 ♕f6 19 e5 ♕xe5 20 ♖ae1 ♗xd4+ 21 cxd4 ♕xd4+ 22 ♔h1 ♗d7 was winning for Black in Leko-Winants, Nettetal 1992) 17...cxd5! 18 ♗f5 g6 19 ♗xc8 ♖axc8 leaves Black in command (Winants).

b) 13 c3 ♗c5 14 ♕a4 ♗d7 15 ♘b3 ♘e4 16 ♘xc5 ♘xg5 17 ♘xd7 ♕xd7 was equal in Afek-Zieher, Netanya 1987.

12 ♗h4 ♗d6!?

ECO gives as its main line 12...g5 13 ♗g3 ♘e4, which is also fine, but in my view there's no real need to weaken the kingside, especially with such a promising alternative available.

13 ♘d4 c5 14 ♘f5

After 14 ♘b5 ♗e5 it's not clear what White's prolonged knight manoeuvre has achieved.

14...♗xf5! 15 ♗xf5 ♖b8 *(D)*

White's knight manoeuvre has netted him the bishop-pair, but Black's

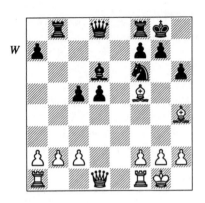

pieces are well coordinated and this factor is probably more important.

a) Lutz-Yusupov, Munich 1992 continued 16 b3? ♗e5 17 ♖b1 ♕d6 18 ♗g3 ♗xg3 19 hxg3 ♖fe8 20 ♖e1 ♖xe1+ 21 ♕xe1 ♖e8 22 ♕d2 ♕e5, when Black's control of the centre and the e-file gave him all the chances.

b) 16 ♗xf6?! ♕xf6 17 ♕xd5 ♖fd8 18 ♕f3 ♗e5 and Black is clearly better.

c) Yusupov suggests 16 ♖b1 ♖b4 17 ♗g3 ♗xg3 18 hxg3 and assesses it as equal, but I still prefer Black. In Alexei Ivanov-Liss, Tyniste ECC 1995 I witnessed first-hand White's suffering after 18...♕b8! 19 b3 ♕e5 20 ♕f3 g6 21 c3 ♖b6 22 ♗c2 ♖e8 23 b4 ♕g5 24 ♖fd1 (24 bxc5 ♖xb1! 25 ♖xb1 ♘g4 26 ♗a4 ♖e7 and White cannot cope with the threat of ...♕h5) 24...♘g4. Here White blundered with 25 ♕xd5?, allowing Black to win immediately with 25...♖e1+, but White was in bad shape anyway (25 ♖xd5 ♖be6! 26 ♖f1 ♖e1 27 ♖xg5 ♖xf1+ 28 ♔xf1 ♘h2+ 29 ♔g1 ♘xf3+ 30 gxf3 hxg5 gives Black excellent winning chances).

A22)
11 ♘a4!?

Eyeing the important dark squares on the queenside and releasing the c2-pawn, which may move to either c3 or c4. This ambitious move was brought to life by Lautier in the early 1990s. At first it enjoyed some success, but soon more than one way was found for Black to achieve a reasonable position.

11...h6 12 ♗h4 (D)

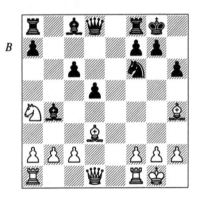

12...♖e8

Making use of the open e-file. A major alternative here is to retreat the bishop immediately with 12...♗d6!?:

a) 13 c4!? ♖e8 transposes into the main line. This may well be White's best option.

b) 13 ♖e1 ♖b8 leads to a further branch:

b1) 14 c3 c5 15 ♗c2 ♗d7 16 ♖b1 g5! (with two more sets of minor pieces coming off the board, Black can afford this minor weakness) 17 ♗g3 ♕c7 (17...♗xg3!? 18 hxg3 ♗xa4 19 ♗xa4 ♕d6 20 ♕d3 ♔g7 gives a similar position) 18 b4 ♗xa4 19 ♗xa4 ♖fd8 20 a3 a5! 21 ♗c2 ♗xg3 22 hxg3 d4! 23 bxc5 ♖xb1 24 ♗xb1 ♕xc5 25 cxd4 ♖xd4 and Black has any advantage that is going, Ki.Georgiev-Nikolić, Brussels 1992.

b2) 14 b3!? ♗e6 15 ♕f3 ♖b4 16 ♗g3 c5 17 h3?! (17 ♗f5 ♗xg3 18 hxg3 ♕d6 looks roughly level) 17...♖b8 18 ♖ad1 ♖e8 19 ♘c3 ♗xg3 20 ♕xg3 ♕a5 21 ♘a4 c4 22 ♗f1 ♖bc8 and Black is in the driving seat, Rublevsky-Anand, Moscow PCA rpd 1996.

13 c4

This move is logical as it adds pressure to the black centre and prepares to inflict Black with an isolated pawn, albeit a passed one. The quieter option 13 c3 shouldn't give Black any headaches:

a) 13...♗f8!? 14 ♗c2?! (14 ♖e1 looks better) 14...♗a6 15 ♖e1 ♖xe1+ 16 ♕xe1 ♕d6 17 ♕e3 ♘g4 18 ♕h3 ♕e6 19 ♗d3 ♗b5 and Black was very happy in Afek-Kosashvili, Rishon le Zion 1993.

b) 13...♗d6 14 ♖e1 ♖xe1+ 15 ♕xe1 ♗d7 16 ♗g3 ♗xg3 17 hxg3 ♕a5 18 ♗c2 ♖e8 19 ♕d2 (Yandemirov-Korneev, Omsk 1996) and now the simple 19...c5 20 b4 cxb4 21 cxb4 ♕b5 looks fine for Black.

13...♗d6 14 cxd5

It is best to exchange first before moving the rook to the c-file. The immediate 14 ♖c1 ♗f4 15 ♖c2 ♗g4 (or 15...♕d6!?) looks more than satisfactory for Black.

14...cxd5 15 ♖c1 (D)

15 ♘c3 ♗e5 gives Black a comfortable position and sets up a vicious trap, into which a young Peter Svidler fell headlong: 16 ♘xd5?? ♕xd5 17 ♗xf6 ♗b7! 0-1 was the end of Svidler-Malaniuk, St Petersburg 1993. Instead, 16 ♖e1 ♗b7 17 ♕d2 ♕b6 18 ♗g3 ♗xg3 19 hxg3 ♘e4 20 ♗xe4 dxe4 21 ♖ad1 ♖ad8 was a touch better for Black in Golubev-Malaniuk, Alushta 1994.

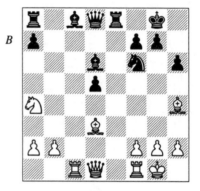

15...♗f4 16 ♖c5

Blatny gives 16 ♖c6 g5 17 ♗g3 ♗d7, assessing it as slightly better for Black, although after 18 ♖c5 ♕e7 19 b4 ♗xg3 20 hxg3 d4 I would veer more towards equal, with play revolving around how strong or weak Black's passed and isolated pawn becomes.

16...♕d6 17 ♗g3 ♗g4 18 ♕c2 ♖ac8 19 b4

The position is roughly level. Vokarev-Malaniuk, Bydgoszcz 1999 continued 19...♘e4 20 ♗xe4 dxe4 21 ♖xc8 ♗xc8 22 ♖d1 e3! (an amazing queen sacrifice; 22...♕f6 23 ♗xf4

♕xf4 24 ♕c6 looks better for White)
23 ♖xd6 e2 24 ♕xe2 ♖xe2 25 ♖d8+?
(25 ♖d1 looks stronger, although after
25...♗d2! 26 a3 ♗f5 Black has compensation for the pawn) 25...♔h7 26
♔f1 ♗a6 27 ♘c5? (27 b5) 27...♗xg3
28 ♘xa6 ♖xf2+ 29 ♔g1 ♗h4 30 ♖d4
♖xa2 31 ♖xh4 ♖xa6 and Black won.

A23)

11 ♕f3 *(D)*

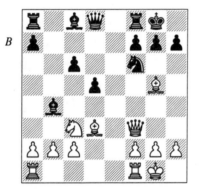

Historically this has been the main
choice for White. White steps up the
pressure on the pinned knight and now
has the option of inflicting Black with a
set of doubled pawns. Black can either
do something about this, or choose to
ignore the 'threat'. We will look at
both approaches in turn:
A231: 11...♗d6 134
A232: 11...♗e7 135

A231)

11...♗d6

Offering White the chance to exchange pieces on f6, although he will

usually wait until his hand is forced
with ...h6.

12 ♖ae1

Alternatively:

a) 12 ♖fe1 ♖b8 13 ♘a4 (13 ♖ab1
h6 14 ♗xf6 ♕xf6 15 ♕xf6 gxf6 is
equal) 13...h6 14 ♗xf6 ♕xf6 15 ♕xf6
gxf6 16 ♖ad1 ♗g4 17 f3 ♗e6 was
equal in Nunn-S.Sulskis, Moscow OL
1994.

b) 12 ♘a4 h6!? (12...♖e8 13 h3
♕a5!? 14 ♗xf6 ♕xa4 15 b3 ♕f4 16
♕xf4 ♗xf4 17 ♗d4 ♗d6 was comfortable for Black in Adams-Piket,
Dortmund 1992) 13 ♗xf6 ♕xf6 14
♕xf6 gxf6 15 c4 ♗a6 16 ♖ac1 ♖ab8
17 g3 ♖b4 18 b3 dxc4 19 ♗xc4 ♗xc4
20 ♖xc4 ♖xc4 21 bxc4 (Sutovsky-
Z.Almasi, Tilburg 1996) and here
Almasi claims a slight plus for Black.

c) 12 h3 ♖b8 13 ♖ab1 (13 b3 ♗e6
14 ♘e2 ♗e5 15 ♖ae1 h6 16 ♗h4 ♕d6
17 ♗g3 ♗xg3 18 fxg3 c5 19 c3 ♗d7
20 ♘f4 ♗c6 21 ♖d1 ♖be8 was equal
in Acs-Lukacs, Szekszard 1994, the
first battle in an ongoing series between these two players) 13...h6 and
now:

c1) 14 ♗h4 ♖e8 15 ♖fe1?! ♖xe1+
16 ♖xe1 g5 17 ♗g3 ♖xb2 18 ♘e2 c5
19 ♗xd6 ♕xd6 20 ♘g3 and Black was
simply a clear pawn up in E.Berg-
Leko, Gran Canaria U-16 tt 1995. In
this position the Hungarian prodigy
blundered with 20...♕f4?, allowing
the brilliant 21 ♕xd5!!. However, the
simple 20...♗d7 would have been sufficient to give Black a virtually winning position.

c2) 14 ♗f4 ♖e8 15 ♘e2 c5 16 c4?! (16 c3 ♗b7 17 ♗xd6 ♕xd6 was comfortable for Black in Acs-Lukacs, Budapest 1995, while after 16 ♗xd6 ♕xd6 17 ♖fe1 c4 18 ♗f5 ♗xf5 19 ♕xf5 d4 Black's d-pawn could become menacing) 16...♗b7! 17 ♗xd6 dxc4! 18 ♗h7+?! ♘xh7 19 ♕g3 ♖c8 20 ♖fe1 ♖e6! 21 ♖bd1 ♖g6 and Black was winning in Acs-Lukacs, Budapest 1996.

c3) 14 ♗xf6 (this seems the most obvious move) 14...♕xf6 15 ♕xf6 gxf6 16 ♖fe1 ♗e6 leads to a typical Scotch Four Knights endgame position. Objectively the position must be level, but preference for either side depends on taste. I would just say that many GMs, at a push, would opt for the bishop-pair and the luggage of the doubled pawns.

12...♖b8

It seems sensible to play this useful preparatory move before asking the question to the bishop on g5, although having said that, the immediate 12...h6 is also not bad. Nadyrkhanov-Malaniuk, Krasnodar 1997 continued 13 ♗xf6 ♕xf6 14 ♕xf6 gxf6 15 ♘e2 (15 ♘d1!?) 15...c5 16 b3 ♖b8 17 ♘g3 ♗e5 with equality.

13 ♘d1 h6 14 ♗xf6 ♕xf6 15 ♕xf6 gxf6

This position has occurred quite a few times in practice. Most games have ended in draws, but there is the occasional decisive result, which means there's still plenty to fight for. Here are a couple of examples:

a) 16 ♖e2 ♗g4 17 f3 ♗e6 18 c3 c5 19 g3 c4 20 ♗b1 ♗c5+ 21 ♔g2 ♖b6 with equality, Zhuravliov-Butnorius, St Petersburg 1992.

b) 16 b3 ♗d7 17 ♘e3 ♖fe8 18 ♘f5 ♗f8 19 g4 ♖e5 20 f4 ♖ee8 21 ♔g2 ♗xf5 22 ♗xf5 ♖xe1 23 ♖xe1 ♗d6 24 ♗d7 ♔f8 25 ♗xc6 ♖c8 26 ♗xd5 ♖xc2+ 27 ♔g3 ♖xa2 28 ♗c4 ½-½ Stavrev-At.Kolev, Bulgarian Ch 1994.

A232)
11...♗e7 *(D)*

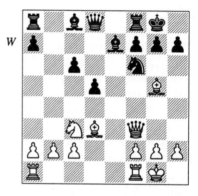

In a way this is Black's most ambitious move, as, unlike 11...♗d6, it doesn't offer White the chance to bail out into a drawish endgame by inflicting doubled f-pawns on his opponent. On the other hand, Black has to careful of tricks involving the slightly vulnerable bishop on e7.

12 ♖ae1 *(D)*

White's most aggressive option, putting pressure on the e-file and preparing for a kingside offensive. This can be augmented by manoeuvres such as ♘d1-e3 or ♘e2-g3/f4. Alternatively:

a) 12 h3 (preventing ...♗g4, but the lack of urgency in this move means that Black can defend comfortably) 12...h6 13 ♗f4 (or 13 ♗h4 ♖b8 14 b3 ♖b4 15 ♗g3 ♗d6 16 ♘e2 c5 17 c3 ♖b6 18 ♗xd6 ♖xd6 19 ♘g3 ♖e8 and Black was at least equal in Shtyrenkov-Tkachev, Cappelle la Grande 1995) 13...♘h7!? (13...♗e6 14 ♖ad1 ♕a5 15 ♖fe1 ♖fe8 was level in Sutovsky-Liss, Rishon le Zion 1994) 14 ♖fe1 ♘g5 15 ♕g3 ♘e6!? 16 ♗e5 (after 16 ♗xh6 Black regains his pawn with 16...♘h4! 17 ♕g4 ♗xf2+ 18 ♔xf2 ♕f6+ 19 ♔g1 ♕xh6) 16...♖e8 17 ♖ad1 ♗d7 18 ♗f5 ♗f8 is equal. This position looks very tame, but Pavasović-Beliavsky, Portorož Vidmar mem 1999 was an example of the dangers lurking if White is complacent: 19 ♘a4?! ♘g5 20 ♗d3 ♕a5 21 b3 ♗d6!, and suddenly White was struggling.

b) 12 ♖fe1 leads to variations similar to the main line. Black could play 12...♖e8 or try 12...♖b8!?, with the following lines:

b1) 13 ♖ab1 ♖e8 (after 13...h6, 14 ♗xh6!? gxh6 15 ♕e3 ♗d6 16 ♕xh6 ♖b4 17 ♕g5+ ♔h8 18 ♕h6+ is a draw by perpetual check; Black has to watch out for this tactic) 14 h3 ♗e6 15 ♘e2 c5 16 b3 h6 with a level position, Rosandić-Rogić, Vinkovci 1995.

b2) 13 ♘a4 h6 (13...♗e6 14 b3 ♖e8 15 h3 h6 16 ♗f4 ♗d6 17 ♗xd6 ♕xd6 18 ♕e3 ♕c7 19 ♕d4 saw White

achieving a dark-square clamp on the queenside in K.Müller-Mainka, German Ch (Dudweiler) 1996) 14 ♗f4 (now 14 ♗xh6 gxh6 15 ♕e3 doesn't work owing to 15...♖b4! 16 ♕xh6 ♘e4) 14...♗d6 15 ♗xd6 ♕xd6 16 ♕e3 ♘g4 17 ♕g3 ♕xg3 18 hxg3 ♗e6 19 b3 ♖fe8, with equality.

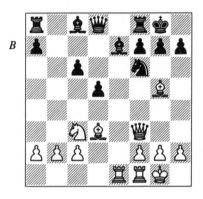

12...♖e8

This move prepares ...h6. The immediate 12...h6?! is met by the usual trick 13 ♗xh6! gxh6 14 ♕e3, after which White will achieve a perpetual check at the least (and maybe more). 12...♖b8, however, is a fully playable move and it gave Black a comfortable position in Gusev-Naumkin, Riga 1988 after 13 ♘d1 ♗e6 14 h3 h6.

13 ♘e2

Re-routing the knight to the kingside. The main alternative is 13 h3 h6:

a) 14 ♗h4 ♗e6 (or 14...♖b8!?) 15 ♗f5 ♗xf5 16 ♕xf5 ♘d7 17 ♗xe7 ♖xe7 18 ♖e2 ♖xe2 19 ♘xe2 ♘f6 with equality, Marquinez-Korneev, Leon 1998.

b) 14 ♗f4!? ♗e6 15 ♘d1 ♗d6 16 ♗xd6?! (16 ♘e3 ♗xf4 17 ♕xf4 ♕a5 18 a3 ♖ab8 19 ♖b1 is safer) 16...♕xd6 17 ♘e3 ♕b4 18 b3 ♕a3 and Black is better due to the weakness of a2. After 19 ♘f5 ♗xf5 20 ♕xf5 ♕xa2 21 f4 ♕a5 22 ♖e5 ♕c5+ 23 ♔h1 ♕d6 White had nothing to show for the pawn in Nadyrkhanov-Malaniuk, Smolensk 1997.

13...h6 14 ♗f4 ♗d6 15 ♘d4 ♗g4 16 ♕g3 ♗xf4 17 ♕xf4 ♕b6

Black is well coordinated and has no problems. *Deep Blue*-Kasparov, Philadelphia (5) 1996 continued 18 c4 ♗d7 19 cxd5 cxd5 20 ♖xe8+ ♖xe8 21 ♕d2 ♘e4 22 ♗xe4 dxe4 23 b3 ♖d8 24 ♕c3 f5 25 ♖d1? (25 g3 ♖c8 26 ♕e3 and "the game would end in four or five moves in a draw" – Kasparov) 25...♗e6 26 ♕e3 ♗f7 27 ♕c3 f4 28 ♖d2 ♕f6 29 g3 ♖d5 and Kasparov eventually converted his pressure on the d-file into victory.

B)
5...♗c5!? *(D)*

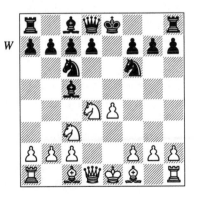

While 4...♗c5 has always been a popular reply to the Scotch Game (after 1 e4 e5 2 ♘f3 ♘c6 3 d4 exd4 4 ♘xd4), this similar line has been rather neglected. It's really not clear why the insertion of the moves ♘c3 and ...♘f6 should benefit White. Although it's true to say that Black no longer has the resource ...♕f6, there are also plus-points (in the line 6 ♘b3 ♗b4!, for example). White has two principal ways to deal with the threat to d4:

B1: 6 ♘xc6 138
B2: 6 ♗e3 139

6 ♘b3 ♗b4 doesn't look especially frightening, but I should warn you that it contains a drop of poison in the shape of a dangerous-looking pawn sacrifice. 7 ♗d3 (7 ♗d2 0-0 8 ♗d3 ♘e5 9 0-0 d5 was fine for Black in S.Arkell-Hebden, London 1988) and now:

a) 7...d5 8 exd5 ♘xd5 9 0-0 ♘xc3 10 bxc3 ♗xc3 11 ♗a3!? gives White some play for the pawn. After 11...♗e6 (11...♗xa1 12 ♕xa1 is also playable, albeit very risky) 12 ♖b1 ♗b4 we reach Afek-Votava, Rishon le Zion 1992 and here White could simply play 13 ♗xb4 ♘xb4 14 ♘c5 ♘xd3 15 cxd3, when I can't find a wholly satisfactory solution for Black. 15...0-0 16 ♘xe6 fxe6 17 ♖xb7 leaves White a little better, as does 15...♗d5 16 ♘xb7 ♕g5 17 ♕e2+ ♔f8 18 f4.

b) If Black is looking for something safer, there's a lot to be said for 7...0-0 8 0-0 ♖e8, intending ...♘e5 and eventually ...d5.

B1)

6 ♘xc6

Following the same recipe as against 5...♗b4.

6...bxc6 7 ♗d3 d6

It pays Black to be more restrained with his d-pawn here, as opposed to the 5...♗b4 variation. The point is that with the bishop on c5, there is less pressure on e4 after 7...d5. Because of this, White isn't forced into a quick exchange on d5, and this works to his advantage. Following 8 0-0 Black finds it hard to equalize after both 8...0-0 9 ♗g5 and 8...dxe4 9 ♘xe4 ♘xe4 10 ♗xe4.

8 0-0 *(D)*

Alternatively:

a) 8 ♗g5 (this is not so effective if Black hasn't committed himself to castling) 8...h6 9 ♗h4 ♕e7 10 ♕e2 ♖b8 11 ♘a4 ♗d4 12 f4 g5! 13 fxg5 ♘g4 14 0-0-0 hxg5 15 ♗g3 ♖b4 and Black has a very active position, Ankerst – Kachiani-Gersinska, Baden-Baden 1993.

b) 8 ♘a4 (going for the immediate elimination of the troublesome dark-squared bishop) 8...♘d7 (this seems the most solid; 8...♖b6 9 ♗g5 0-0 10 0-0 h6 11 ♗h4 ♖e8 12 ♘xb6 axb6 13 f4 ♗b7 14 c4 c5 15 ♕c2 ♖e6 16 a3 gave an edge to White in Rozentalis-Adams, Køge 1997) 9 ♘xc5 ♘xc5 10 0-0 0-0 11 ♗e3 ♘xd3 12 ♕xd3 ♗e6 (or 12...♖e8 13 ♖fe1 c5 14 ♗d2 ♗b7 15 ♖e3 ♖e6 16 ♖ae1 ♕e7 17 f3 ♖e8 18 c4 ♕h4 19 ♖3e2 g5 20 h3 h6 21 ♗e3 ♕g3 22 ♕c3 ½-½ V.Gurevich-Hebden, Cappelle la Grande 1996) 13

♖ad1 f5 and the players agreed a draw in this very level position in M.Ginzburg-Slipak, Villa Martelli 1998.

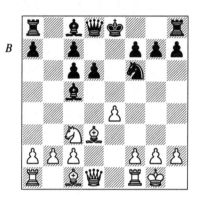

8...♘g4!?

An active move, which prevents the annoying pin with ♗g5 and prepares to begin a counterattack on the kingside. 8...♘d7 also prevents the pin, but is less direct. White obtained a small advantage after 9 ♗e2 0-0 10 ♘a4! ♗b6 11 b3 ♕h4 12 ♘xb6 axb6 13 f3 ♗a6 14 c4 in Miles-Hebden, London Lloyds Bank 1994.

9 ♗f4

The main alternative here is to harass the knight with 9 h3. After 9...♘e5 10 ♘a4 ♗b6 we have:

a) 11 ♗e2 g5!? (aggression is the order of the day, as otherwise White simply captures on b6 and plays f4) 12 ♘xb6 axb6 13 f4 gxf4 14 ♗xf4 ♕f6 15 ♗h5 ♗e6 16 a4 ♖g8 17 ♔h1 ♕h4 with an unclear position, M.Ginzburg-Sorin, Salta 1995.

b) 11 ♘xb6 axb6 12 ♗d2 0-0 13 ♗c3 ♘xd3 14 ♕xd3 ♕h4 15 ♖fe1

♗a6 16 ♕f3 ♖fe8 17 a4 ♗b7 18 ♕g4 ♕xg4 19 hxg4 c5 20 f3 f6 was equal in Volzhin-Hebden, Hastings 1993/4.

9...g5!?

Once again aggression is the key to Black's opening success.

10 ♗d2

This is sensible. There is certainly no need to encourage Black with 10 ♗g3? h5!.

10...♕f6 11 ♕e2 ♕e5 12 g3 *(D)*

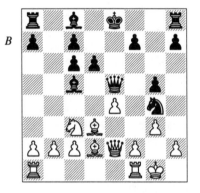

This is a critical position for the 6 ♘xc6 variation. Black looks active, but White's position is solid, and Black's weaknesses may become important later on:

a) In Miles-Sorin, Matanzas 1995 Black went wrong immediately with 12...♕e6?!, allowing White to gain the advantage with 13 ♘a4! (simply threatening to eliminate the dark-squared bishop) 13...♗d4 (13...♘xh2 14 ♘xc5 is good for White) 14 c3 ♕h6 15 h4 ♗f6 16 e5!. Following 16...♘xe5 17 hxg5 ♗xg5 18 f4 ♕h3 19 ♗e4! ♕xg3+ 20 ♕g2 ♕xg2+ 21 ♗xg2 ♗h6 22 fxe5

♗xd2 23 ♗xc6+ ♗d7 24 ♗xa8 ♗xa4 25 exd6 cxd6 White reached a winning endgame.

b) 12...a5 is a suggested improvement from Miles, and it was successful in the Szuk-Husar, Budapest 1999 after 13 ♘d1?! h5! 14 ♘e3? ♕xb2 15 ♘c4 ♕g7 16 ♘e3 ♘e5 17 ♗c3 g4 18 ♔g2 h4 19 ♘f5 ♗xf5 20 exf5 f6 21 ♗c4 ♔e7 22 ♗e6 hxg3 23 fxg3 ♖xh2+! and White resigned as it's mate in two. It would be interesting to see what would happen if White played the stronger 13 ♔h1, preparing f4.

B2)

6 ♗e3 *(D)*

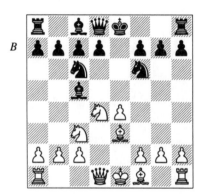

6...♗b6 *(D)*

The paradoxical 6...♗b4 is also possible. At first this seems quite strange, as we transpose to positions similar to Line A, except that White has the move ♗c1-e3 for free. However, it's not clear how useful this move is, and in some cases the bishop is even better off on c1, as on e3 it can be hit by a timely ...♘g4. Then White can continue:

a) 7 ♗d3 0-0 8 0-0 ♘e5! 9 h3 d5 10 ♘xd5 ♘xd5 11 exd5 ♘xd3 12 ♕xd3 ♕xd5 was fine for Black in Szobris-Mordhorst, Germany 1994/5, although White's play was a bit passive.

b) 7 ♘xc6 bxc6 8 ♗d3 (8 ♕d4!?) 8...d6 9 f3 (9 ♗g5 ♕e7 10 0-0 ♕e5 11 ♕d2 0-0 12 ♖fe1 ♖b8 13 a3 ♗xc3 14 bxc3 ♘d7 15 f4 ♕a5 16 ♔h1 f6 17 ♗h4 ♗a6 was level in Goldgewicht-A.David, Cannes 1996, while 9 0-0!? ♘g4 10 ♗d4 looks critical) 9...d5! 10 exd5 ♘xd5 11 ♗d2 0-0 12 0-0 ♖b8 13 ♘xd5 cxd5 with an equal position, Votava-Hebden, Rishon le Zion 1992.

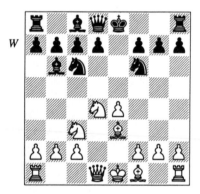

W

7 ♘xc6
Or:

a) 7 g3 0-0 8 ♗g2 d6 9 h3 ♖e8 10 0-0 ♗d7 11 ♖e1 h6 12 g4 ♘e5 was unclear in Lane-Hebden, London Lloyds Bank 1994.

b) 7 ♕d2!? 0-0 8 0-0-0 ♖e8 9 f3 d6 10 g4 ♘xd4 11 ♗xd4 ♗e6 12 ♖g1 ♗xd4 13 ♕xd4 c5 14 ♕d2 ♕a5 15 a3

a6 16 g5 ♘d7 17 f4 b5 18 f5 was very good for White in Reefat bin Satter-Hebden, Dhaka 1995, but Black played too passively. Playing ...d5, either on move 8 or 9, looks more critical.

7...bxc6 8 e5

This is the most testing move, after which Black is obliged to sacrifice a pawn. In Kozakov-Adams, French Cht 1996/7 White played timidly with 8 ♗xb6 axb6 9 ♗d3 0-0 10 0-0 d6 and after 11 ♖e1?! ♘g4! 12 h3 ♘e5 13 f4 ♘xd3 14 ♕xd3 ♕h4 15 ♕f3 ♗b7 16 a3 ♖ae8 Black's potential pressure on the e4-pawn gave him an edge. 11 ♕d2 is stronger, planning to meet 11...♘g4 with 12 f4, but even this shouldn't worry Black unduly.

8...♗xe3 9 fxe3 ♘d5 10 ♘xd5 cxd5 11 ♕xd5 ♕h4+ 12 ♔d1 *(D)*

Alternatives give Black an easy game:

a) 12 ♔d2 ♕b4+ and Black wins his pawn back.

b) 12 g3 ♕b4+ 13 ♕d2 ♕xb2 is favourable for Black, Faust-Rauber, Pizol 1997.

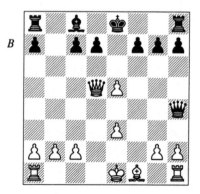

B

12...♖b8 13 ♗c4 *(D)*

Black obtained a vicious attack in Kecić-Potocnik, Slovenian Cht 1996 after 13 ♕d4 ♕h6 14 ♗c4 0-0 15 ♔d2 d5! 16 ♗b3 c5 17 ♕xc5 d4! 18 ♖ae1 ♗f5 19 ♔c1 d3.

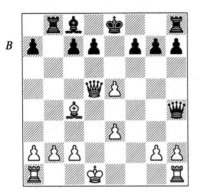

13...0-0

White has an extra pawn, but it's doubled and isolated and his king is still seeking security. All in all, Black has enough compensation.

a) 14 ♕d4 ♕g5 15 g3 d6 16 exd6 cxd6 (or 16...♖d8!?) 17 ♔d2 ♕a5+ 18 ♕c3 ♕h5 19 h4 ♗e6 with an unclear position, Andres-Slipak, Buenos Aires 1995.

b) After 14 b3, 14...♖b6 15 ♔c1 ♕e7 16 ♖f1 d6 17 ♔b2 dxe5 18 ♖ad1 worked out well for White in Rohl-Ramon, Santa Clara 1998, as he has returned the pawn for a favourable position. However, Black has many other enticing options, including 14...♗b7!? and 14...♕g5!?.

13 The Spanish Four Knights Game

1 e4 e5 2 ♘f3 ♘c6 3 ♘c3 ♘f6 4 ♗b5 *(D)*

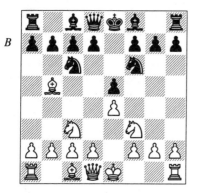

The Spanish Four Knights is another opening with a very long history, throughout which it has drifted in and out of fashion. Its latest comeback was fashioned by Nigel Short, who utilized it as a surprise weapon against Jonathan Speelman in their 1991 Candidates match. Spurred on by Short's good results with the opening, other English grandmasters such as John Nunn and Murray Chandler introduced it into their opening weaponry and the Spanish Four Knights was once again back into the limelight. Alexei Shirov has also used it to good effect, while more recently, young, up-and-coming players such as Sergei Movsesian and Ruslan Ponomariov have taken up its mantle.

As you would expect, the Spanish Four Knights is very similar to the Spanish Opening (i.e. the Ruy Lopez) in that White puts immediate pressure on the e5-pawn (in fact one can transpose to the other via the move-order 1 e4 e5 2 ♘f3 ♘c6 3 ♗b5 ♘f6 4 ♘c3). However, in some ways it causes Black different problems from the main-line Spanish. With the move ♘c3, Black's counterattack on e4 has been blunted, leaving the defender having to make an early decision about his e5-pawn. On the other hand, White has lost the ability to create a pawn-centre via c3 and d4, a plan so typical in the Ruy Lopez.

A Quick Summary of the Recommended Lines

Against the Spanish Four Knights I'm recommending two different lines for Black. Line A is the reliable and yet dynamic 4...♘d4 (the Rubinstein Variation) which was the move that started to put White off the Four Knights early in the 20th century. Black starts an immediate counterattack and in some lines he is ready to sacrifice material to claim the initiative. Line A3 shows some signs of coming into fashion, but White's main test of the Rubinstein is still undoubtedly Line A4 (5 ♗a4), which virtually forces Black to sacrifice a pawn. The traditional response to this move has been 5...♗c5, but I'm recommending the modern 5...c6, which has overtaken the old move in the popularity stakes.

Line A2, while being no threat to Black, will put some players off the Rubinstein Variation, as best play leads to a drawish ending. This is why I've also advocated the Classical Defence with 4...♗c5 (Line B). This line is not particularly approved at the moment, although I'm not exactly sure why. In my opinion it's an underrated defence, which is definitely worth a second look.

The Theory of the Spanish Four Knights Game

1 e4 e5 2 ♘f3 ♘c6 3 ♘c3 ♘f6 4 ♗b5

We should take a brief look at other variations of the Four Knights Game:

a) 4 g3 (this has been popularized by Igor Glek) 4...d5 5 exd5 ♘xd5 6 ♗g2 ♘xc3 7 bxc3 ♗d6 8 0-0 0-0 and we have transposed directly to the 3 g3 Vienna (see Chapter 3, Line A2).

b) With 4 ♗e2 White plans to develop his kingside before breaking in the centre. Black can meet this with

4...d5! (4...♗c5?! 5 ♘xe5! favours White) 5 exd5 ♘xd5 6 0-0 ♘xc3 7 bxc3 ♗d6 8 d4 0-0. Now 9 ♖b1 h6 10 dxe5?! ♘xe5 11 ♘xe5 ♗xe5 12 ♗a3 ♖e8 13 ♗f3 ♕h4 14 g3 ♕a4 was better for Black in Van der Wiel-Timman, Wijk aan Zee 1985, while 9 ♗b5!? transposes to the Scotch Four Knights with colours reversed. As Black you couldn't ask for too much more than to play a white opening, and if you look closely at my coverage of the Scotch Four Knights, you should be able to find a reasonably good equalizing line for White!

c) 4 a3 is similar to 4 ♗e2, in that it essentially prepares to play d4 (without allowing ...♗b4). Once again, Black's best policy is to go with the active 4...d5 5 exd5 ♘xd5 and once again we have the Four Knights Scotch with colours reversed and White having the relatively useless move a3 thrown in.

d) 4 d3 is really wet. Black's most active move is, you've guessed it, 4...d5!.

After 4 ♗b5, I'm recommending both:

A: 4...♘d4   143
B: 4...♗c5!?   155

The former is very popular, while the latter move is an underrated alternative.

A)

4...♘d4 (D)

The Rubinstein Variation. Black immediately moves on to the counter-offensive by attacking the bishop on

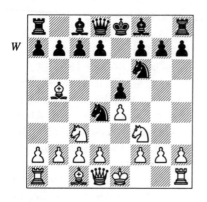

b5. White has four principal ways to continue:

A1: 5 0-0   145
A2: 5 ♘xd4   146
A3: 5 ♗c4   148
A4: 5 ♗a4   150

Other moves can be dealt with reasonably quickly:

a) 5 ♗e2!? ♘xf3+ (this is sensible, as the bishop will not be particularly active on f3) 6 ♗xf3 ♗c5 7 d3 d6 (perhaps 7...a6 is more accurate, preventing White's option on the next move) 8 0-0 (8 ♘a4!? would secure the bishop-pair, although whether this would be enough to give White an edge is another matter) 8...a6 9 ♘e2 0-0 10 c3 ♖e8 11 d4 ♗b6 12 ♘g3 ♗e6 with an equal position, Ivkov-Shamkovich, Polanica Zdroj 1970.

b) 5 ♗d3!? looks like a real beginner's move, but there is some point to it. White now threatens the e-pawn and after 5...♘xf3+ 6 ♕xf3, White's plan is to move the queen and perhaps arrange to play f4. That said, it does all

look a bit cumbersome and with natural moves Black can obtain a comfortable position; for example, 6...d6 7 ♗e2 ♗e7 8 ♕g3 0-0 9 d3 ♔h8 (or 9...c6 10 0-0 ♘e8 11 ♗g4 ♗e6 12 ♘e2 ♕d7 13 ♗xe6 fxe6 14 ♗e3 ♘c7 15 c3 ♗f6 16 ♖ad1 ♕e7 with equality, Lejlić-Hellsten, Limhamn 1998) 10 h4!? c6 11 f4 exf4 12 ♗xf4 d5 13 e5 ♘e8 14 d4 ♘c7 15 0-0-0 b5 16 ♗d3 a5 17 ♗g5 a4 18 ♘e2 b4 19 ♗xe7 ♕xe7 and Black has menacing counterplay on the queenside, Shabanov-Nizamov, Pardubice 1998.

c) 5 ♘xe5 ♕e7 and now:

c1) 6 ♘f3 can be viewed as an early draw offer, and it's true that following 6...♘xb5 7 ♘xb5 ♕xe4+ 8 ♕e2 ♕xe2+ 9 ♔xe2 ♘d5 a very level endgame is reached. However, the bishop-pair gives Black enough encouragement to battle on. One success story for Black in practical play continued 10 ♖e1 f6 11 d3 (11 c4 is answered by 11...a6) 11...♔f7 12 ♗d2 a6 13 ♘c3 ♘b4 14 ♖ac1 b6 15 a3 ♘c6 16 ♗f4 d6 17 ♔f1 (17 ♘d5 is met by 17...♖a7) 17...♘e5 18 ♘d2 ♗b7 19 ♖e2 h5 20 d4 ♘g6 21 ♗e3 ♘h4 22 f3 d5 23 ♗f4 c5 24 ♘a4 ♘f5! 25 c3? g5 26 ♗e3? ♗c6! 0-1 Kubbel-Grigoriev, USSR Ch (Moscow) 1920.

c2) 6 f4!? ♘xb5 7 ♘xb5 d6 8 ♘f3 (8 ♘d3?? loses to 8...♗g4!) 8...♕xe4+ 9 ♔f2 ♘g4+ and now White should probably settle for 10 ♔g1 ♔d8 11 h3 ♘f6 with an unclear position where both kings are misplaced. The more adventurous 10 ♔g3 can be answered with 10...♕g6!. Now 11 ♕e2+ ♔d8 12 ♖e1 ♗d7 13 ♘bd4 ♘e3+ 14 ♔f2 ♘xc2 15 ♘xc2 ♕xc2 was clearly better for Black in Spielmann-Rubinstein, Baden-Baden 1925. The critical line is 11 ♘h4 ♕h5 12 ♘xc7+ ♔d8 13 ♘xa8, but then Black goes on the attack with 13...g5! 14 fxg5 d5 15 d4 ♗d6+ 16 ♗f4 ♕xg5! and White's king is in big trouble.

A1)

5 0-0

This fresh move has been used almost exclusively by Emil Sutovsky. By not retreating his bishop from b5, White concedes the bishop-pair, but uses his development advantage to aim to play a quick d4.

5...♘xb5 6 ♘xb5 c6 7 ♘c3 d6 8 d4 ♕c7 (D)

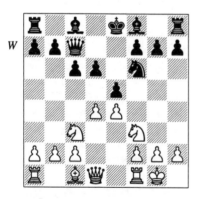

Reinforcing the e5-pawn. The stage is set for a tense struggle. The pawn-structure closely resembles that of the main-line Philidor Defence (1 e4 e5 2 ♘f3 d6 3 d4 ♘f6 4 ♘c3 ♘bd7 5 ♗c4

♗e7 6 0-0 0-0 7 ♖e1 c6). The Philidor is considered slightly better for White. The difference here, however, is that Black possesses the latent power of the bishop-pair, and this fact should give him a reasonable game.

9 ♗g5

Alternatively:

a) 9 ♘e1?! ♗e7 10 ♔h1 b5 11 a3 ♗b7 12 f4 exd4 13 ♕xd4 c5 14 ♕d3 a6 15 ♘f3 ♖d8 16 ♗d2 0-0 17 ♖ae1 ♖fe8 and I prefer Black, Euwe-Bogoljubow, Holland (10) 1928/9.

b) 9 h3 ♗e7 10 a4 h6 11 ♗e3 0-0 12 ♕d3 a5 13 ♖fd1 ♗e6 14 d5 cxd5 15 exd5 e4 16 ♘xe4 ♘xd5 17 ♗d2 ♖fc8 18 ♘d4 ♕c4 19 ♕xc4 ♖xc4 20 c3 ♘f6 21 ♘g3 ♗f8 22 b3 ♖cc8 with an equal position, Nunn-Parker, British League (4NCL) 1998/9.

9...♗e7 10 h3

This is necessary; otherwise Black's light-squared bishop would find a nice home on g4.

10...0-0

10...h6 11 ♗h4 and now 11...g5?! 12 dxe5 gxh4 13 exf6 ♗xf6 14 ♖e1 ♖g8 15 ♔h1 ♖g6 16 e5 ♗e7 17 ♘xh4 ♖e6 18 exd6 ♖xe1+ 19 ♕xe1 looked better for White in Sutovsky-Piket, Elista OL 1998, but 11...♘h5! 12 ♗xe7 ♕xe7 13 ♘xe5 dxe5 14 ♕xh5 exd4 15 ♘e2 0-0 16 ♘xd4 ♕xe4 17 ♖ad1 ♖e8 gave Black an equal game in Sutovsky-Illescas, Pamplona 1998/9.

11 ♕d2 b5

11...♗e6 12 a4 ♖fd8 13 a5 h6 14 ♗xf6 ♗xf6 15 d5 ♗d7 16 a6 c5 17 axb7 ♕xb7 18 ♖a5 ♖dc8 led to a more or less equal position in Sutovsky-Nunn, Oxford 1998.

12 a3 a6 13 ♖fd1 ♖e8

This equal-looking position arose in Sutovsky-Zhang Zhong, Elista OL 1998. Play now livened up with 14 ♕e3 exd4 15 ♘xd4 c5!? 16 ♗xf6 ♗xf6 17 ♘d5 cxd4 18 ♘xc7 dxe3 19 ♘xe8 ♗xb2 20 ♖ab1 exf2+ 21 ♔xf2 ♗xa3 22 ♘xd6 ♗e6 and Black had very reasonable compensation for the exchange.

A2)

5 ♘xd4

This is certainly not the most interesting move on offer. White aims for nothing further than a mass simplification. As far as I can see there are two types of opponent you will face playing this move. One, for whatever reasons, will be searching for that early draw offer. These players should be punished by playing the game on until the very bitter end. If you beat them, they are less likely to reoffend with this move, and even if they scrape a draw, they'll have second thoughts.

The second type are those who actually enjoy playing the sterile positions that arise in this line. They should be pitied, but also respected, as it's probable that they have acquired very reasonable endgame technique.

5...exd4 (D)

6 e5

Nothing else should give Black anything to worry about. White is worse after 6 ♘e2?! ♘xe4 7 ♘xd4 ♗c5,

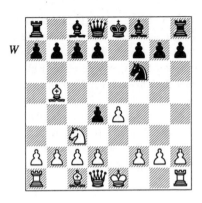

while 6 ♘d5 ♘xd5 7 exd5 ♕f6 8 0-0 ♗e7 9 f4 0-0 10 ♕f3 c5 was very comfortable for Black in Wolf-Alekhine, Karlsbad 1923.

6...dxc3 7 exf6 ♕xf6

It's true that Black can liven up the proceedings by grabbing a pawn with 7...cxd2+?!, but unfortunately it makes it rather more exciting for White than it does for Black. After 8 ♗xd2 ♕xf6 9 0-0 ♗e7 10 ♗c3 ♕g5 11 ♖e1! Black faces a vicious attack:

a) 11...♕xb5 12 ♕g4 ♖g8 13 ♖xe7+ ♔xe7 14 ♕e4+ ♔d8 15 ♕h4+ f6 16 ♗xf6+ ♔e8 17 ♖e1+ ♔f7 18 ♖e7+ ♔g6 19 ♗e5 d6 20 ♕g3+ ♔h5 21 ♕f3+ ♔h6 22 ♕f4+ g5 23 ♕f6+ ♖g6 24 ♖xh7+ ♔xh7 25 ♕h8# (1-0) was the conclusion to Shipman-Weber, New York 1985.

b) 11...0-0 12 ♖e5 ♕f6 13 ♗d3 g6 14 ♕e2! gave White a strong attack in Milev-Fuderer, Amsterdam OL 1954.

8 dxc3 ♕e5+

This is probably the most accurate move. After 8...♗c5 9 0-0 0-0, if nothing else White can play 10 ♗xd7 ♖d8

11 ♕h5 ♗xd7 12 ♕xc5, when it's probably going to be a draw, but if I had to choose, I'd take the extra pawn.

9 ♕e2

White's last chance to make the game slightly more interesting is with 9 ♗e2, but theoretically speaking this doesn't give White any sort of edge either. After 9...♗c5 10 0-0 0-0 we have:

a) 11 ♗d3 d5 12 ♕f3 (*ECO* gives 12 ♖e1 ♕f6 13 ♗e3 ♗xe3 14 ♖xe3 g6 as equal) 12...♗d6 13 g3 c6 14 ♗d2 (14 ♗e3 ♕e6 15 ♖fe1 ♕g4 16 ♕g2 ♕h5 is equal, Marshall-Ed.Lasker, New York 1931) 14...♕e6 15 ♕h5 (15 ♖fe1 ♕g4 16 ♕xg4 ♗xg4 is equal) 15...♕h3! 16 ♗xh7+ ♔h8 17 ♗g6+ ♔g8 18 ♗h7+ with a cute perpetual in Wittmann-Greenfeld, Thessaloniki OL 1984.

b) 11 ♗f3 c6 (11...♖e8!?) 12 ♖e1 ♕f6 13 ♗e3 ♗xe3 (13...d6 14 ♗xc5 dxc5 15 ♗e4 g6 looks equal) 14 ♖xe3 d5 15 ♗g4 ♗xg4 16 ♕xg4 ♖ad8 17 ♖ae1 d4 18 cxd4 ♖xd4 19 ♕c8! (this is a nice try, but Black has a way out) 19...g6 20 ♕xb7 ♖d2 21 ♖3e2 (or 21 ♖f3 ♕e5!) 21...♖xe2 22 ♖xe2 ♕d6 23 ♕e7 (23 ♖e1 ♖b8 24 ♕xa7 ♖xb2 25 c4 ♕f4 26 ♕c5 ♕e4 leaves Black very active) 23...♕d1+ 24 ♖e1 ♕xc2 25 ♕e2 ♕c5 26 ♕d2 a5 27 g3 ½-½ Gallagher-Korneev, Cannes 1998.

9...♕xe2+ 10 ♗xe2 ♗c5

10...d5 also gives a dead-level endgame; for example, 11 ♗f4 c6 12 c4 ♗e6 13 cxd5 ♗xd5 14 0-0 ♗c5 15 ♗d3 0-0 16 ♖fe1 ♖fe8 17 a3 f6 Alekhine-Capablanca, St Petersburg 1914.

11 0-0 d6 (*D*)

11...d5 12 ♗f4 c6 13 ♖fe1 ♗e6 14 ♗d3 0-0 15 a4 ♖ae8 was the prelude to another draw in Lanzani-Dorfman, Turin 1998.

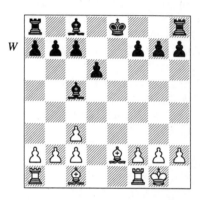

Well, what can one say about this position, except that it's totally level? Nevertheless, there's still just enough play to ensure that mistakes from either side can get punished. If Black is searching for a crumb of evidence as to why he should make his opponent suffer, then one can point to the very slightly weak c2-pawn. Here are a couple of examples, with Tony Miles taking the black pieces on both occasions. If anyone could grind out a win from this position, then England's first grandmaster would be just the man for the job.

a) 12 ♖e1 ♗e6 13 ♗d3 0-0 14 ♗e3 ♗b6 15 ♗xb6 axb6 16 a3 ♖fe8 17 ♖e3 ♗d7 18 ♖ae1 ♔f8 19 ♖xe8+ ♗xe8 20 f4 h6 21 ♔f2 ♗c6 22 h4 h5 23 g3 ♖a5 24 c4 ♗d7 25 ♖e3 g6 26 ♔e1 b5 27 cxb5 ♗xb5 28 ♗xb5 ♖xb5

29 b4 ♖b6 30 c4 ♖c6 31 ♖e4 ♖a6 32 ♖e3 c5 33 ♔f2 ♖a4 and Black's slight advantage was not enough to secure the full point in Lima-Miles, Linares open 1997.

b) 12 ♗f3 ♖b8 13 ♖e1+ ♗e6 14 ♗e3 ♗xe3 15 ♖xe3 0-0 16 ♖ae1 ♖fd8 17 ♗e4 d5 18 ♗d3 c5 19 ♖e5 g6 20 g3 ♖d6 21 ♗f1 ♖bd8 22 b3 ♔g7 23 c4? dxc4 24 ♖xc5 ♖d1! 25 ♖ce5 c3 26 ♔g2 ♖1d2 27 ♖1e2 ♗g4 28 f3 ♗f5 29 ♖c5 ♖xe2+ 30 ♗xe2 ♖d2 and Black went on to win in Shaked-Miles, Waikiki 1997.

A3)

5 ♗c4 *(D)*

This is still not as popular as the other bishop retreat, but there are signs that this move is being taken more seriously at the top level.

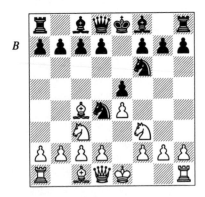

5...♗c5!?

This pawn-offer has been Black's traditional antidote to 5 ♗c4, although it now seems that Black is turning to other moves. A safer way to play is with the simple 5...♘xf3+!? 6 ♕xf3, which is not particularly exciting, but does offer Black a solid way of entering the middlegame:

a) 6...c6 7 0-0 d6 8 h3 ♗e7 9 ♖d1 b5 10 ♗f1 0-0 11 d4 ♕c7 12 ♗e3 ♗b7 with a level position, Sylvan-Lejlić, Tjalfe 1995.

b) 6...d6 7 d3 (or 7 0-0 ♗e7 8 ♕e2 0-0 9 d3 ♗e6 10 ♗b3 ♘d7 11 ♗e3 ♗f6 with equality, Keitlinghaus-Smejkal, Bundesliga 1996/7) 7...c6 8 0-0 ♗e7 9 h3 0-0 10 ♗g5 h6 11 ♗e3 ♗e6 12 ♗b3 c5 13 ♘e2 d5 14 exd5 ♘xd5 and Black is fine, Dobrowolski-Malaniuk, Polanica Zdroj 1999.

Another recent idea is the sacrificial move 5...c6!?. Black's plan is to develop rapidly after 6 ♘xe5 d5 7 exd5 ♗d6 8 ♘f3 ♘xf3+ 9 ♕xf3 0-0. Ivanchuk-Svidler, Linares 1999 continued 10 h3 (after 10 0-0 Black plays 10...♘g4!) 10...b5!? 11 ♗e2 b4 12 ♘e4 (after 12 dxc6 bxc3 13 c7 ♕xc7 14 ♕xa8 ♗a6 15 ♕f3 ♖e8 16 d3 ♗b7 17 ♕f5 ♖e5 White's queen is trapped) 12...♘xe4 13 ♕xe4 and now Ivanchuk suggests 13...♖e8 14 ♕f3 ♗a6 15 d3 cxd5 16 0-0 ♕e7 17 ♗d1 ♕e5 18 g3 ♖ac8, with compensation for the pawn.

6 ♘xe5 ♕e7

The enterprising 6...d5!? worked to perfection in Spangenberg-Tkachev, Villa Martelli 1997, which concluded swiftly after 7 ♘xd5 ♘xd5 8 ♕h5? (8 c3 is stronger) 8...g6 9 ♘xg6 ♘xc2+ 10 ♔f1 ♕f6 11 f3 hxg6 12 ♕xd5 ♖h5 0-1. However, Black needs something else in this line now, because a later game saw White achieving an advantage after 7 ♗xd5! ♘xd5 8 ♘xd5 0-0 (8...♕g5?! 9 ♘xc7+ ♔f8 10 ♔f1! ♖b8 11 ♘d3! ♗g4 12 f3 ♘xf3 13 ♘xc5 ♕xc5 14 gxf3 ♗h3+ 15 ♔e2 ♕xc7 16 ♔f2 is winning for White, according to Kramnik) 9 c3 ♖e8 10 cxd4 ♗xd4 11 0-0 ♖xe5 12 d3 c6 13 ♘f4! b6 14 ♕c2 ♖c5 (Shirov-Kramnik, Cazorla (6) 1998) and now 15 ♕a4!? ♖b5 16 ♖b1 a5 17 ♗e3 leaves White with a clear plus.

7 ♘f3

Or:

a) 7 ♗xf7+? loses a piece: 7...♔f8 8 f4 d6.

b) 7 ♘xf7 d5! 8 ♘xh8 (or 8 ♘xd5 ♕xf7 9 ♘b6 ♕g6 10 ♘xa8 ♕xg2 and Black wins) 8...dxc4 9 d3 ♗e6 and Black will follow up with ...0-0-0 and ...♖xh8.

c) After 7 ♘d3 Black continues powerfully with 7...d5!:

c1) 8 ♗xd5 ♘xd5 9 ♘xd5 ♕xe4+ 10 ♘e3 ♗d6 (or 10...♗b6 11 0-0 0-0) 11 0-0 ♗e6 with excellent value for the pawn, Nimzowitsch-Alekhine, St Petersburg 1914.

c2) 8 ♘xd5 ♕xe4+ 9 ♘e3 ♗b6 10 f3 (10 0-0 b5! 11 ♗b3 ♗b7 12 ♘e1 ♕h4 13 g3 ♕h3 14 c3 h5 15 cxd4 h4, Belsitzman-Rubinstein, Warsaw Ch 1917, 16 ♘f3 is very unclear – Burgess) 10...♕h4+ 11 ♘f2 0-0 12 0-0?! (12 g3 is more resolute, although after 12...♕h5 it's clear that Black has good compensation) 12...♘xf3+ 13 ♕xf3 ♗xe3 14 ♕xe3 (or 14 ♗xf7+ ♖xf7 15 ♕xe3 ♗d7, intending a combination

of ...♗c6 and ...♖e8) 14...♕xc4 15 ♕c3 (Keitlinghaus-Blatny, Lazne Bohdanec 1995) and now Blatny suggests 15...♕xc3 16 bxc3 ♗d7, intending ...♗a4, attacking the vulnerable c2-pawn, with an edge to Black.

7...d5 8 ♘xd5

8 ♗xd5?! ♘xd5 9 ♘xd5 ♕xe4+ 10 ♘e3 ♗g4! looks good for Black.

8...♕xe4+!

Much more ambitious and stronger than 8...♘xd5 9 ♗xd5 c6 10 ♘xd4 cxd5 11 ♘b3 dxe4 12 ♘xc5 ♕xc5, which has been quoted in at least one source as equal, but White has an obvious, albeit slight, pull after 13 d4 exd3 14 ♕xd3, Janowski-Marshall, Paris (10) 1905.

9 ♘e3 ♗g4 10 ♗e2 ♘xe2 11 ♕xe2 0-0-0 12 d3 ♕e6 (D)

12...♕g6? allows the simplifying 13 ♘e5! ♗xe2 14 ♘xg6 hxg6 15 ♔xe2, when White consolidates his extra pawn, Schubert-Hugolf, corr.

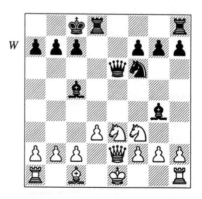

Black's development advantage on an open board now promises him sufficient compensation for the sacrificed pawn:

a) 13 0-0?! ♘d5 14 ♖e1 ♘f4 15 ♕d1 ♗h5 gave Black excellent prospects in Schubert-Henriksen, corr.

b) 13 ♘g5! is more testing. Following 13...♕d7 14 ♘xg4 ♘xg4 15 0-0 ♖he8 16 ♕d1 an unclear position was reached in Fruebing-Thorsteinsson, corr 1988. Black should also consider 13...♕c6!?, planning to answer 14 ♘xg4? with 14...♕xg2!. After 14 f3 ♗h5 Black retains the light-squared bishop.

A4)
5 ♗a4

This is White's main move. By keeping the pin on the d7-pawn, White makes it problematic for Black to defend e5.

5...c6!? *(D)*

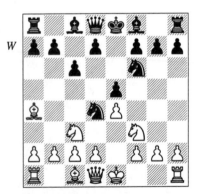

I believe it was Mark Hebden who popularized this move. Traditionally 5...♗c5, which also offers the e5-pawn, has been the main choice, but in recent years this move has been overtaken by 5...c6, which may have more to do with fashion than anything else (I believe the two are objectively of equal value). White now has three principal options:

A41)
6 d3

This quiet move shouldn't cause Black too many problems.

6...b5 7 ♗b3 ♘xb3 8 axb3 d6 9 0-0

Piket suggested immediately transferring the c3-knight with 9 ♘e2 ♗g4 10 ♘g3, which prepares to harass the bishop with h3. However, Black can react positively with 10...♘h5!, when 11 ♘xh5 ♗xh5 extinguishes the threat to the bishop and 11 h3 ♘xg3 12 fxg3 ♗d7 13 0-0 ♗e7 14 g4 0-0 was equal in Bosch-Van Gisbergen, Dutch Ch 1994. This leaves the knight retreat 11 ♘f1, which can be met by 11...♕f6!. The game P.H.Nielsen-Sobjerg, Copenhagen 1993 continued 12 h3 ♗xf3 13 ♕xf3 ♕xf3 14 gxf3 d5 15 ♘g3 ♘xg3 16 fxg3 ♗c5, and Black had nothing to worry about.

Another idea for White is to prevent the pin altogether with 9 h3!?. Short-Tkachev, Moscow OL 1994 continued 9...♗e7 10 0-0 0-0 11 ♘e2 ♖e8 (11...a5!?) 12 ♘g3 a5 13 d4 ♕c7 14 ♖e1 c5 15 c3 and here 15...h6!?, with the idea ...♘h7-g5, looks like a reasonable plan for Black.

9...♗e7 10 ♘e2 ♗g4!

An important move. White is probably a little bit better after the natural 10...0-0 11 ♘g3 c5 12 c4, as in Nunn-Bareev, Hastings 1992/3.

11 ♖e1

With this move White accepts the doubled pawns. 11 ♘g3 can be answered once more with 11...♘h5, or the more ambitious 11...h5!?, intending to reply to 12 h3 with 12...h4!.

11...♗xf3 12 gxf3 ♕d7 13 d4 ♕h3 14 ♕d3

After 14 ♘g3 g6 15 ♗e3 Black can play solidly with 15...a6, or sacrifice a pawn by 15...0-0!? 16 dxe5 dxe5 17 ♖xa7 ♖xa7 18 ♗xa7 h5!, with unclear play.

14...0-0 15 ♘g3 g6

We are following Nunn-Piket, Wijk aan Zee 1993. Objectively the position must be pretty level, but with White's wrecked pawn-structure on the kingside, I suspect most players would choose Black here.

A42)
6 0-0

This move has been favoured by Shirov. Importantly, White keeps the option open of playing d2-d4 in one go.

6...♕a5! *(D)*

Only with this move can Black prevent White from developing smoothly. When I first faced 6 0-0, in Nunn-Emms, London Lloyds Bank 1993, I continued with the natural enough 6...b5, but after 7 ♗b3 ♘xb3 8 axb3 d6 9 d4 ♕c7 10 ♗g5 ♗e7 11 b4! I

wasn't really satisfied with my position. White is planning to play a timely d5 and could wind up getting a juicy outpost on d5. I prevented this with the drastic 11...exd4, but after 12 ♘xd4 a6 13 f4 I was still a little worse.

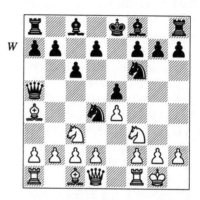

With 6...♕a5 Black eliminates, at least for the time being, any ideas White has of capturing on d4. Another point is that when the bishop retreats to b3 and is captured by the knight, White will have to recapture 'away from the centre' with the c2-pawn (not that this is always bad).

7 ♖e1

Alternatively:

a) 7 a3 ♗e7 8 b4 ♕c7 9 ♗b2 0-0 10 ♘xd4 exd4 11 ♘e2 ♘xe4 12 ♘xd4 d5 13 d3 ♘d6 14 ♘f3 ♗g4 15 h3 ♗xf3 16 ♕xf3 with equality, Shirov-Piket, Aruba (2) 1995.

b) 7 ♗b3 (it seems strange to retreat this before it's attacked, but White wants to force Black's hand over the d4-knight) 7...♘xb3 8 cxb3 d6 9 d4 ♗g4 10 ♗e3 ♗e7 11 h3 ♗h5 12 ♕e2

0-0 13 g4 ♗g6 14 ♘h4 ♖fe8 15 dxe5 dxe5 16 a3 ♘d7 17 ♘f5 ♕c7 ½-½ Ionov-Khalifman, Seville 1993.

c) 7 d3 b5 8 ♗b3 ♘xb3 9 cxb3 d6 10 ♘e2 ♗e7 11 ♘g3 0-0 12 d4 ♖d8 13 h3 ♕c7 14 ♕c2 ♗e6 15 ♗e3 ♖ac8 16 ♖ac1 h6 17 ♖fd1 c5 and again Black is fine, Vehi Bach-G.Georgadze, Ampuriabrava 1997.

7...d6 (D)

One amusing miniature continued 7...♗b4!? 8 ♘xd4 exd4 9 e5 ♘g8 10 ♕g4 dxc3 11 ♕xg7 cxd2 12 ♗xd2 ♗xd2 13 ♕xh8 ♗xe1 14 ♕xg8+ ♚e7 15 ♕g5+ ♚e8 16 ♕g8+ ♚e7 17 ♕g5+ ♚f8 18 ♕f6 ♗xf2+ 19 ♚xf2 ♕xa4 20 ♕d8+ ♚g7 21 ♕f6+ with a draw by perpetual check in Riemersma-Gausel, Gausdal 1993. It's difficult to recommend 7...♗b4, as I can't see any good way to avoid the perpetual check, and furthermore White may have some improvements; for example, 13 ♖e4!?.

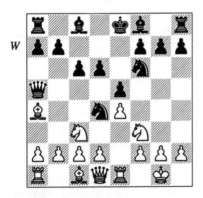

8 h3

This move, preventing the pin with ...♗g4, is the restrained way of playing

the position. Great complications arise from 8 ♘xd4!? exd4 9 ♘d5 ♘d7! (9...♕xa4?! 10 ♘c7+ ♚d8 11 b3! ♕a5 12 ♘xa8 is good for White) 10 b4 ♕xa4 11 ♘c7+ ♚d8 12 ♘xa8 b6!?. Smagin-Malaniuk, Tilburg 1993 continued 13 ♖b1 ♗b7 14 ♖b3 c5! 15 ♖a3 ♕c6 16 ♖xa7 ♗xa8 (16...♚c8!?; 16...cxb4!?) 17 b5 ♕c8 18 c3 ♕b8 with a real mess, although my suspicion is that Black is at least equal.

8...♗e7

8...b5 9 ♗b3 ♘xb3 10 cxb3 b4 11 ♘e2 c5 12 d3 ♗e7 13 ♘d2 ♕c7 14 ♘c4 0-0 15 f4 ♗d7 16 fxe5 dxe5 17 ♘g3 was a touch better for White in Shirov-L.B.Hansen, Moscow OL 1994.

9 a3

Preparing to play b4. Classical development with 9 d3 doesn't trouble Black. After 9...0-0 10 ♗e3 ♘xf3+ 11 ♕xf3 ♗e6 the position is roughly level.

9...0-0 10 b4 ♕c7

Now:

a) 11 ♘xd4 exd4 12 ♘e2 ♘xe4 13 ♘xd4 d5 looks equal.

b) 11 ♗b2 and then:

b1) Shirov-Piket, Aruba (8) 1995 continued 11...a5 12 ♘xd4 exd4 13 ♘e2 axb4 14 axb4 b5 15 ♗b3 ♖xa1 16 ♗xa1 c5 with an approximately level position.

b2) The simple 11...♘xf3+ 12 ♕xf3 ♗e6 also looks satisfactory for Black.

b3) Piket suggests 11...b5 12 ♗b3 c5!?; for example, 13 ♘xd4 cxd4 14 ♘xb5 ♕b6 15 a4 ♗b7 16 d3 a6 17 ♘a3 ♕xb4 18 ♘c4 ♕c5.

A43)

6 ♘xe5 *(D)*

Grabbing the pawn is the critical test of 5...c6.

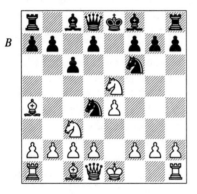

6...d6

The main alternative is to advance two squares immediately with 6...d5. Following 7 d3 ♗d6 we have:

a) 8 f4 0-0 9 0-0 b5! 10 ♗b3 b4 11 ♘e2 ♘xb3 12 axb3 ♕b6+ 13 ♔h1 dxe4 14 ♘c4 ♕c7 15 dxe4 ♘xe4 16 ♘xd6 ♘xd6 17 ♘g3 ♘f5 was fine for Black in Nunn-Piket, Monaco rpd 1994.

b) 8 ♘f3 and now:

b1) 8...♗g4 9 ♗e3 and then:

b11) 9...♗c5 10 ♗xd4 ♗xd4 11 ♕d2 ♗xf3 12 gxf3 b5 (Shirov-I.Sokolov, Linares 1995) and now Shirov recommends 13 ♗b3 a5 14 a4 b4 15 ♘e2 ♗xb2 16 ♖b1 ♗e5 17 d4 ♗c7 18 e5 ♘h5 19 c4, which he assesses as good for White.

b12) Black could play 9...♘xf3+ 10 gxf3 ♗h5, reaching the main line, but with the extra ...♗d6 thrown in free for Black. Unfortunately, this is a situation where the bishop would prefer to be at home on f8, because on d6 it allows White the possibility of 11 exd5!, as in Spraggett-A.David, Casablanca 1994. Black needs something new here.

b2) 8...♘xf3+ 9 gxf3 ♘h5!? 10 ♗e3 0-0 11 d4 ♗b4 12 ♕d3 ♕f6 13 ♗d2 ♘f4 14 ♗xf4 ♕xf4 15 ♕e3 ♕h4 16 0-0-0 a5 17 a3 ♗xc3 18 ♕xc3 dxe4 19 fxe4 ♕xe4 was fine for Black in Ferguson-Hebden, Hastings 1995, but this line could certainly do with more practical tests.

7 ♘f3 ♗g4 8 d3

Ponomariov has experimented with 8 h3!?, but not with any particular success. After 8...♗xf3 9 gxf3 Black can underline White's dark-squared weaknesses with 9...g6!, preparing a fianchetto. Here are two practical examples:

a) 10 ♔f1 ♗g7 11 ♘e2 ♘xf3 12 d4 ♕a5 13 ♘c3 ♘g5 14 e5 ♘fe4 15 ♗xg5 ♘xg5 16 ♕g4 ♘e6 was unclear in Ponomariov-Gomez Esteban, Pamplona 1996/7.

b) 10 ♘b1?! was an attempted improvement from the youngster later in the tournament, but after 10...♕a5 11 c3 ♘xf3+! 12 ♕xf3 ♕xa4 13 d4 ♗g7 Black had regained the pawn and was more comfortably placed in Ponomariov-Z.Almasi, Pamplona 1996/7.

8...d5! *(D)*

This move brought new life into this variation. Previously Black had played to regain the pawn immediately with 8...♘d7 9 ♗e3 ♘xf3+ 10 gxf3 ♗h5 11 d4 ♕f6, but the endgame arising after 12 ♖g1! ♕xf3 13 ♕xf3 ♗xf3 14 ♖g3 ♗h5 15 f3 is slightly in White's favour.

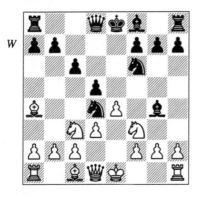

9 ♗e3

Less critical is 9 h3 ♘xf3+ 10 gxf3 ♗h5 11 e5 d4 12 exf6 dxc3 13 ♕e2+ ♔d7 14 ♕e4 ♕xf6 15 ♕d5+ ♗d6 16 ♕xh5 cxb2 17 ♗xb2 ♖ae8+ 18 ♔f1 ♕xb2 19 ♕xf7+ ♖e7 20 ♕f5+ ♔c7, when White's extra pawn is of no value, McShane-Pavasović, Lippstadt 1998.

However, there is an important alternative here in the shape of 9 0-0!?, which, despite a lack of practical experience, suggests itself as an obvious test of Black's play:

a) 9...b5 10 ♗b3 a5 11 a3 dxe4 12 dxe4 ♘xf3+ 13 gxf3 ♕xd1 14 ♖xd1 ♗xf3 15 ♖d3 ♗g4 16 ♗g5 looks slightly better for White.

b) 9...dxe4!? 10 dxe4 (10 ♘xe4 ♘xe4 11 dxe4 ♘xf3+ 12 gxf3 ♕xd1 13 ♖xd1 ♗xf3 is fine for Black) and we have a further split:

b1) 10...♗xf3 11 gxf3 and after 11...b5 12 ♗b3 ♗c5 13 e5 ♕d7? (the alternative 13...♘d7 is stronger, though I still prefer White) 14 exf6 0-0-0 15 ♔g2 White was winning in Nunn-Kristensen, Vejle 1994. In *NCO* Nunn gives 11...♗c5 12 ♗b3 as slightly better for White.

b2) 10...♘xf3+!? looks like Black's best bet. After 11 gxf3 ♕xd1 12 ♖xd1 ♗xf3 13 ♖d3 ♗g4 White's apparent lead in development shouldn't deter players from Black's situation, which is solid and has potential to improve. I'll leave you with a few lines that illustrate the resilience of Black's position: 14 ♗e3 ♘d7 15 ♗d4 ♗c5! 16 ♗xg7? ♖g8 17 ♗h6 b5 18 ♗b3 ♗f3+ 19 ♔f1 ♘e5 20 ♖d2 ♖g2 21 ♗f4 ♘g4 is a strong counterattack for Black. The line 14 h3 ♗e6 15 f4 ♗c5+ 16 ♔g2 ♖d8 also looks fine. This leaves 14 ♘d5, but I also think Black is OK here after 14...0-0-0 15 ♘xf6 gxf6 16 ♗e3 (or 16 ♖xd8+ ♔xd8 17 ♗e3 ♗f3 18 ♔f1 ♖g8!) 16...♖xd3 17 cxd3 ♗e2!.

9...♘xf3+ 10 gxf3 ♗h5 11 exd5?!

This move has been the most common, but it may not be the best. Alternatively:

a) 11 e5?! d4 12 exf6 dxc3 13 fxg7 (or 13 ♕e2 cxb2 14 ♖b1 ♕d5! 15 ♗b3 ♕f5 and Black can safely ignore the threat of the discovered check; for example, 16 ♗c5+ ♔d7 17 ♗xf8 ♖e8! 18 ♕xe8+ ♔xe8 19 fxg7 ♖xf8 20 gxf8♕+ ♔xf8 and Black should win) 13...♗xg7 14 ♖g1 cxb2 15 ♖b1 ♕a5+ 16 ♔f1 ♗f6 17 ♕e1 ♕xe1+ 18 ♖xe1

0-0-0 19 ♗xa7 ♗c3 20 ♖b1 ♖d5! 21 ♗b3 ♖f5 22 ♗e3 ♗xf3 and Black soon won in Istratescu-Malaniuk, Erevan OL 1996.

b) 11 ♗d4 dxe4 12 dxe4 ♗xf3 13 ♕xf3 ♕xd4 is given as equal by Onishchuk and Malaniuk. This assessment should be taken seriously as these two are well-known experts of this line for Black.

11...♘xd5

Now:

a) 12 ♗b3 ♘xc3 13 bxc3 ♕f6, hitting both f3 and c3, ensures a plus for Black.

b) 12 ♘e4 f5! 13 ♘g3 f4 14 ♘xh5 fxe3 15 0-0 ♕h4 16 f4 0-0-0 17 ♕f3 exf2+ 18 ♔h1 ♗c5 was another success story for Black in Bologan-Malaniuk, Nikolaev Z 1995.

c) 12 ♘xd5 ♕xd5 13 ♗b3 ♕xf3 14 ♕xf3 ♗xf3 15 ♖g1 bails out into an equal-looking ending and is probably White's best option.

d) 12 ♕e2 is supposed to be an improvement for White, but I have my doubts. Then:

d1) Daniliuk-Ulak, Litomysl 1995 continued 12...♗e7 13 ♗c5 0-0 14 ♗xe7 ♘xe7 15 0-0-0 ♘d5 16 ♕e5! ♗xf3 17 ♖hg1 g6 and here Daniliuk suggests 18 ♘xd5!? ♕xd5 19 ♕xd5 ♗xd5 20 c4 as being clearly better for White. I must say that after 20...♗e6 I think Black is doing perfectly well, but in any case, there may well be a big improvement for Black earlier on...

d2) 12...♘xc3!? has been dismissed on the grounds that after 13 bxc3,

13...♗e7? 14 ♗c5 is good for White, but once more I think Black should ignore the apparent threat of the discovered check and play 13...♕d5!. Now 14 ♗c5+ ♔d7 gets White nowhere and 14 ♗b3 ♕f5! (14...♕xf3 15 ♕xf3 ♗xf3 is only equal) 15 ♗f4+ ♔d7 leaves White struggling for a useful move. The onus is on White to come up with something new here.

B)

4...♗c5 *(D)*

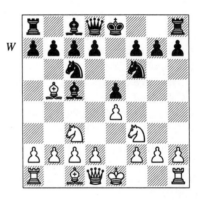

Strangely enough, this natural-looking move is not at all common, especially at the highest levels. Black is put off by lines involving the ♘xe5 fork trick, but as we see below, these lead to positions which have perhaps been overrated from White's point of view.

5 0-0

5 ♗xc6 is similar to the Delayed Exchange Variation of the Ruy Lopez, except that Black's bishop is more actively placed on c5, rather than e7. After 5...dxc6 we have:

a) 6 ♘xe5 ♗d4 7 ♘f3 ♗xc3, regaining the pawn.

b) 6 d3 0-0 7 h3 (7 ♘xe5?! ♕d4 8 ♗e3 ♕xe5 9 d4 ♕e6 10 dxc5 ♘xe4 looks good for Black, while 7 0-0 transposes into the note to White's next move) 7...♖e8 8 ♘e2 ♗f8 9 g4!? (Psakhis-Barua, Calcutta 1988) and now 9...♘d7 looks sensible, planning ...c5, followed by the knight manoeuvre ...♘b8-c6.

5...0-0 6 ♘xe5

This is White's major try for a theoretical edge in this line. Using the common 'fork trick' White hopes to gain the upper hand in the struggle for the central squares. Other moves are less critical:

a) 6 ♗xc6 dxc6 7 d3 (7 ♘xe5 ♖e8 8 ♘d3 ♗g4 9 ♕e1 ♗d4 regains the pawn) 7...♗g4 8 h3 ♗h5 9 ♗g5 (9 g4?! ♘xg4 10 hxg4 ♗xg4 is very dangerous for White) 9...h6 10 ♗xf6 ♕xf6 11 g4 ♗g6 leads to an equal position, Nimzowitsch-Rubinstein, San Sebastian 1912.

b) 6 d3 d6 7 ♗g5 h6 8 ♗h4 ♗g4 9 ♗xc6 (9 ♘d5?! g5! 10 ♗xc6 bxc6 11 ♘xf6+ ♕xf6 12 ♗g3 ♗xf3 13 ♕xf3 ♕xf3 14 gxf3 is a very good endgame for Black, as White finds it virtually impossible to get his dead bishop on g3 back into the game) 9...bxc6 10 h3 ♗d7 11 d4 exd4 12 ♘xd4 ♖e8 13 ♖e1 ♖b8 14 ♘b3 ♗b6 15 ♕f3 ♖e6 with a level position, Rozentalis-Ionov, Uzhgorod 1988.

6...♘xe5 7 d4 ♗d6 (D)
8 f4!

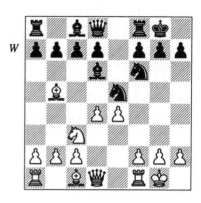

This is the move that gives White's system some bite. Instead of recapturing the piece immediately, White attempts to mow down Black's minor pieces with his row of central pawns. Black has no real problems after the insipid 8 dxe5 ♗xe5; for example, 9 ♗d3 ♖e8 10 ♘e2 d5 11 f4 ♗d6 12 e5 ♗c5+ 13 ♔h1 ♘e4! and now:

a) 14 ♗xe4?! dxe4 15 ♕xd8 (15 ♘c3 ♕xd1 16 ♖xd1 ♗f5 also looks good for Black) 15...♖xd8 16 ♘g3 ♗b6! 17 c3 (17 ♘xe4 ♗f5 is also pleasant for Black, so perhaps 17 h3!? is the best move) 17...e3! 18 ♖e1 ♖d3 19 ♘e2 ♗g4 and White has some problems.

b) 14 ♕e1 (Raszka-Macieja, Wisla 1992) 14...f5! 15 c4 dxc4 16 ♗xc4+ ♗e6 17 ♗xe6+ ♖xe6 18 ♘g3 is equal according to Kholmov and Macieja.

8...♘c6 9 e5 ♗e7 10 d5 ♘b4 11 exf6

White can delay recapturing the piece by a further move with 11 d6!?, a pawn sacrifice intending to damage Black's structure. Following 11...cxd6

12 exf6 ♗xf6 we have a position that is difficult to assess. Black is a pawn up, but his queenside pawns are a mess and it will take time to develop the c8-bishop. White has no development problems, but the pawn on f4 now looks a bit out of place and allows Black tricks involving ...♕b6+.

11...♗xf6 12 a3

12 ♘e4 c6 13 ♘xf6+ ♕xf6 14 ♗c4 ♕d6 15 ♗e3 ♘xd5 16 ♗xd5 cxd5 17 ♕d4 b6 18 ♖ad1 ♖e8 was equal in T.Taylor-Rizzitano, New York 1984.

12...♗xc3

This move forces some simplification. In Ferguson-Emms, Bury 1992 I tried 12...♘a6!? and after 13 ♘e4 d6 14 ♘xf6+ ♕xf6 15 c3 ♗f5 16 ♗e3 ♘c5 I was quite happy with my position. 14 f5, blocking out the c8-bishop, looks more of a test, although this might also be satisfactory for Black after 14...♘c5.

13 bxc3 (D)

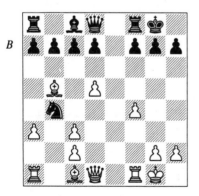

13...♘xd5 14 ♕xd5 c6 15 ♕d3 cxb5 16 f5 f6!

16...♖e8 17 f6! was most unpleasant for Black in Fedorov-M.Tseitlin, USSR 1978.

17 a4!?

Intending to swing the a1-rook into the action. White could also contemplate a more reserved approach with 17 ♗e3, although this shouldn't be too frightening for Black, who is still, after all, a pawn up. 17...d5 looks roughly equal.

17...bxa4 18 ♖xa4 d5 (D)

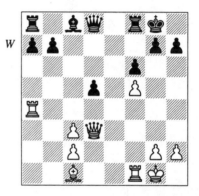

This is a very double-edged position. White is very active and Black has problems developing his c8-bishop. On the other hand, Black is still a pawn up, and if he completes his development then he can hope to exploit the weaknesses in White's pawn-structure. Here are two practical examples.

a) 19 ♖h4? ("looking for a non-existent mate" – Nunn) 19...♖e8 20 ♕d1? (20 ♕h3? ♕b6+ 21 ♔h1? ♕f2! is winning for Black, but 20 ♗e3! ♕e7 21 ♗d4 ♗d7 22 ♕h3 gives White some compensation) 20...♖e5 21 ♕h5?

♕b6+! 22 ♔h1 ♗xf5! and Black won quickly in Nunn-Hodgson, English Ch (London) 1991.

b) 19 ♖d4! *(D)* (both Hodgson and Nunn approved of this continuation; White regains the pawn and tries to prevent Black's bishop from entering the game):

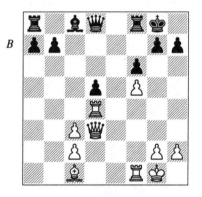

b1) 19...b6 20 ♖xd5 ♕e8 and now 21 ♖d1 ♗b7 22 ♖d7 ♗e4 23 ♕g3 ♖f7 24 ♕c7 ♖c8 25 ♕xa7 ♗xf5 26 ♖xf7 ♕xf7 27 ♕xb6 h5 28 ♖d8+ led to a draw in Ferguson-Belozerov, Zagan U-18 Ech 1995, but White can improve on this line significantly with 21 ♗a3! ♗b7 22 ♗xf8 ♗xd5 23 ♗xg7, and Black is in trouble.

b2) I prefer the disruptive 19...♕b6, preparing ...♗d7. White can prevent this with 20 ♗e3, but Black can continue to niggle with 20...♖e8. For example, 21 ♖e1 ♕c7 22 ♖xd5 b6! (Black must develop the bishop) 23 ♖e2 ♗b7 24 ♖d7 ♕c6 25 ♗h6!? ♕c5+ 26 ♔f1 (or 26 ♔h1 ♗xg2+ 27 ♔xg2 ♖xe2+ 28 ♕xe2 ♕c6+ 29 ♕f3 ♕xf3+ 30 ♔xf3 gxh6 31 ♔e4 a5! and the a-pawn is a runner) 26...♖xe2 27 ♖xg7+ ♔h8 28 ♕xe2 ♗c6! and Black has just as many threats as White. Perhaps best play from here leads to a draw by perpetual check after 29 ♖g3 ♗b5 30 ♗g7+ ♔g8 31 ♗h6+ ♔h8. Naturally there are many other continuations from move 19, but my suspicion is that Black is holding his own in the complications.

14 The Two Knights Defence: Introduction

1 e4 e5 2 ♘f3 ♘c6 3 ♗c4

We now move on to the traditional Italian Game. Throughout history this opening has always been very popular, although at the very highest levels the Ruy Lopez has gradually superseded it. Nevertheless, at all other levels, White's directness has a very appealing quality. With 3 ♗c4 White prepares to castle and puts his bishop on an ideal diagonal, where it bears down on Black's Achilles Heel on f7. The Italian Game is attractive to all types of players as it can lead to both attacking and sacrificial play, as well as slow, positional, manoeuvring games.

I'm recommending the Two Knights Defence:

3...♘f6 (D)

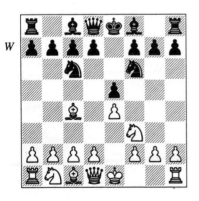

This is probably the most combative way of meeting the Italian Game. Black immediately counterattacks by hitting the e4-pawn, but in doing so allows White some enticing possibilities including 4 ♘g5 and 4 d4. In this chapter we consider all other moves.

A Quick Summary of the Recommended Lines

By far the most important of White's alternatives to the main lines (4 ♘g5 and 4 d4) is 4 d3 (Line C), which is the modern positional approach against the Two Knights. White defends the e4-pawn and plans to play the position in a similar way to the slow d3 lines of the Ruy Lopez. While not being immediately threatening to Black, these lines at least give White positions rich in possibilities, where the stronger player has a good chance of outplaying his opponent. Lines C1, C2 and C3 are all of about equal importance. In Lines C2 and C3, Black's main decision seems to be whether to lunge out with ...d5, or whether to restrict himself to ...d6. In lines with ...d5 Black can often try to claim the initiative, but must always be careful about attacks on his e5-pawn. Lines with ...d6 are safer, but are less likely to cause White immediate problems.

The Theory of the Two Knights Defence: 4th Move Alternatives for White

1 e4 e5 2 ♘f3 ♘c6 3 ♗c4 ♘f6

As well as 4 d4 (Chapters 15-17) and 4 ♘g5 (Chapter 18), White has:

A: 4 ♘c3   160
B: 4 0-0   162
C: 4 d3   163

Less important moves include:

a) 4 c3? (with good intentions of building a centre, but there are more pressing concerns, like the defence of the e4-pawn) 4...♘xe4 (naturally!) 5 ♕e2 d5 and now:

a1) 6 ♗xd5?! ♕xd5 7 c4 ♘d4 8 cxd5 ♘xe2 9 ♔xe2 ♗d6 and White's opening has been a disaster, Hennes-Kaestner, Hauenstein 1991.

a2) 6 ♗b5 tries to make the best of a bad job, but Black still retains everything after 6...f6 7 d4 ♕d6 8 dxe5 fxe5, as 9 ♘bd2 ♘xd2 10 ♕xe5+? loses to 10...♕xe5+ 11 ♘xe5 ♘e4 12 ♘xc6 a6 13 ♗a4 ♗d7.

b) 4 ♕e2 isn't a bad move, but it does commit the queen to e2 rather early. That said, e2 can be a reasonable square for the white queen, especially after ♖fd1, c3 and d4, so this plan must be treated with some respect. 4...♗e7 5 c3 0-0 6 0-0 and now:

b1) After 6...d6, Barua-Smejkal, Novi Sad OL 1990 continued 7 d3?! ♘a5! 8 ♘bd2 ♘xc4 9 ♘xc4 ♖e8 10 h3 ♗e6 and Black was absolutely fine. I don't really understand why White would want to give away the light-squared bishop so easily. Surely 7 d4 ♗g4 8 ♖d1 is more testing.

b2) Black could attempt to play a Marshall-style gambit with 6...d5!?. The early white queen move, coupled with c3, means that there is certainly some justification to Black's pawn offer. Following 7 exd5 ♘xd5 8 ♘xe5 ♘f4 9 ♕e3 ♘xe5 10 ♕xf4 ♗d6 Black has reasonable compensation.

A)

4 ♘c3 *(D)*

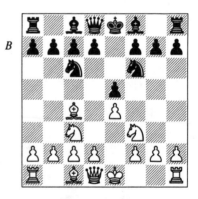

4...♘xe4!

Once again, the fork trick can be used to good effect.

5 ♘xe4

5 ♗xf7+?! just plays into Black's hands. The slight discomfort felt by the black king is easily outweighed by

the acquisition of the pawn-centre after 5...♔xf7 6 ♘xe4 d5. White is worse following both 7 ♘eg5+ ♔g8 8 d3 h6 9 ♘h3 ♗g4 and 7 ♘g3 e4 8 ♘g1 ♗c5.

5 0-0 is playable, and it transposes to 4 0-0 ♘xe4 5 ♘c3 (Line B).

5...d5 6 ♗d3

Other moves do not impress:

a) 6 ♗b5? dxe4 7 ♘xe5 ♕g5! and Black is clearly better.

b) 6 d4?! dxc4 7 d5 ♘d4! (much stronger than *ECO*'s 7...♘e7 8 ♘c3 c6 9 0-0 ♘xd5 10 ♘xe5 ♘xc3 11 ♕f3 ♗e6 12 ♕xc3, which was only equal in Cordel-Scupli, 1905) 8 ♘xd4 ♕xd5! 9 ♕f3 ♕xd4 10 ♗g5 f5! (West-Flear, British Ch (Edinburgh) 1985) and now Flear gives White's best try as 11 ♘c3 ♕g4 12 ♕xg4 fxg4 13 0-0-0 ♗d7 14 ♖he1 ♗d6 15 ♘e4 0-0 16 ♘xd6 cxd6 17 ♖xd6 ♗c6, although Black still holds the significant advantage of the extra pawn.

6...dxe4 7 ♗xe4 ♗d6 8 d4

After 8 ♗xc6+ bxc6 9 d4 Black can transpose into the main line with 9...exd4, or try 9...e4!?. Also possible is 8 0-0 0-0, after which we have transposed to the note to White's 8th move in Line B, Chapter 13 (with colours reversed).

8...exd4 *(D)*

8...♘xd4 is a very solid alternative. The variation continues 9 ♘xd4 exd4 10 ♕xd4 0-0 11 ♗e3 (not 11 0-0?? ♗xh2+!) 11...♕e7 12 0-0-0 and now:

a) 12...♖e8 13 ♖he1 ♗e6 14 ♕d3?! (*ECO* gives 14 ♗d5 as equal, while 14 ♗xb7!? ♖ab8 15 ♗c6 ♗a3!? 16 ♗xe8

♗xb2+ 17 ♕xb2 ♖xb2 18 ♔xb2 ♕xe8 looks quite unclear) 14...♖ad8 15 ♕e2 ♕f6 16 ♕h5 h6 17 ♕a5 ♗g4 18 f3 ♖xe4 19 fxe4 ♗xd1 20 ♖xd1 a6 21 e5 ♕f5 22 ♕c3 ♗e7 23 ♖xd8+ ♗xd8 and Black is slightly better due to White's isolated e-pawn, Tarrasch-Marshall, Breslau 1912.

b) 12...♗e5 13 ♕c4 ♕f6 14 ♗d4 ♗e6 15 ♕c3 ♗xd4 16 ♕xd4 ♕g5+ 17 ♔b1 ♖ad8 with an equal position, Tartakower-Szabo, Groningen 1946.

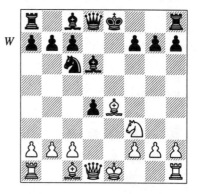

9 ♗xc6+

9 ♘xd4 is less accurate. For a start Black can consider the admittedly cheeky pawn-grab 9...♕e7!? 10 0-0 ♗xh2+ 11 ♔xh2 ♕d6+ 12 ♔g1 ♘xd4, against which I can't find anything really troubling. Alternatively Black can seize the initiative with 9...0-0!?:

a) 10 ♘xc6 bxc6 can become very dangerous for White; e.g. 11 ♕h5? g6 12 ♕f3 ♖e8 13 ♗e3 ♕h4 14 ♗xc6 ♗g4! wins for Black. Even after the stronger 11 ♗e3 ♖b8 12 ♖b1 ♕e7 13 ♗xc6 ♖d8 Black has menacing threats.

b) 10 ♗e3 ♛h4! 11 ♗xc6 bxc6 and now 12 g3?! ♛h3 13 ♕e2 c5 14 ♘b3 ♗g4 15 ♕f1 ♛h5 16 ♘d2 ♖fe8 was extremely grim for White in Tarrasch-Lasker, Berlin (3) 1916. Even after Lasker's suggested improvement of 12 ♕d2 ♖b8 13 0-0-0 c5 14 ♘f3 ♛a4 15 a3 I'd still take Black and the two bishops.

9...bxc6 10 ♕xd4 0-0 11 0-0 c5 12 ♕c3 ♗b7 13 b3 ♕d7 14 ♗b2 f6 15 ♖ad1 ♕f5 16 ♕c4+ ♔h8

Black's bishop-pair on an open board fully compensates for his slight structural defects, Tartakower-Bogoljubow, Bad Pistyan 1922.

B)

4 0-0 ♘xe4 (D)

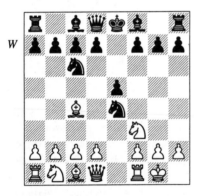

W

Why not grab a central pawn?

5 ♘c3

This move, which introduces the Boden-Kieseritzky Gambit, is probably White's most promising choice here. In fact other moves see White struggling to equalize:

a) 5 ♖e1? d5 6 ♗b5 ♗c5 7 d4 exd4 8 ♘xd4 0-0, with a clear advantage to Black, who is simply a pawn up.

b) 5 ♗d5 ♘f6 6 ♗xc6 dxc6 7 ♘xe5 ♗d6 and Black develops smoothly, with the bishop-pair in the bank.

c) 5 ♕e2 d5 6 ♗b5 ♗g4 7 d3 ♗xf3 8 gxf3 ♘f6 9 ♕xe5+ ♗e7 10 ♗xc6+ bxc6 11 ♖e1 ♕d6 12 ♗f4 0-0! 13 ♘d2 ♘h5 14 ♗g3 ♘xg3 15 ♕xd6 cxd6 16 hxg3 ♗f6 17 c3 ♖fb8 18 ♖ab1 ♖b7 and Black has a slight pull, Djurhuus-Gausel, Asker 1997.

d) 5 d4!? d5 (5...exd4 leads us to Chapter 16) 6 ♗b5 and now Black has a choice:

d1) 6...♗d7 7 ♗xc6 bxc6 8 ♘xe5 ♗d6 9 f3 ♗xe5 10 dxe5 ♘c5 11 b3 ♘e6 12 f4 f5 was roughly level in Gunsberg-Chigorin, Havana 1890.

d2) 6...exd4 7 ♘xd4 ♗d7 8 ♖e1 ♗d6 (8...♘xd4 9 ♗xd7+ ♕xd7 10 ♕xd4 c5 11 ♕e5+ is annoying for Black) 9 ♗xc6 bxc6 10 f3 ♗xh2+ 11 ♔xh2 ♕h4+ 12 ♔g1 ♕f2+ with a perpetual check.

d3) 6...♗g4!? looks reasonable, intending to meet 7 dxe5 by 7...♗c5, with active play.

5...♘xc3

The safest move. After 5...♘f6, 6 ♖e1 ♗e7 7 ♘xe5 ♘xe5 8 ♖xe5 d6 leads to equality, while 6 d4!? e4 7 ♗g5 d5 8 ♘xd5 ♗e6 (8...♘a5!?) 9 ♘xf6+ gxf6 10 ♗xe6 fxe6 11 ♘d2 fxg5 12 ♕h5+ ♔d7 13 ♘xe4 gave White some attacking chances for the piece in Z.Bašagić-Gligorić, Yugoslav Ch 1984.

6 dxc3 f6!?

With this move Black ambitiously tries to hang on to his extra pawn. For the more conservative, there's the safe option of 6...♗e7, when White can regain the pawn with 7 ♕d5, but after 7...0-0 8 ♘xe5 ♘xe5 9 ♕xe5 ♗f6 10 ♕h5 c6, followed by ...d5, Black has a fully level, albeit rather dry, position.

7 ♘h4

7 ♖e1 d6 8 ♘h4 is less accurate, as the rook is often better placed on f1, where it supports the f4 advance. After 8...g6 9 f4 ♕e7 10 f5 ♕g7 11 ♖f1 (this illustrates the point; White has lost two tempi) 11...♗d7 12 ♗d3 g5 13 ♕h5+ ♕f7 Black was clearly better in Canal-G.Thomas, Budapest 1929.

7...g6 8 f4 ♕e7! *(D)*

Sneakily threatening ...♕c5+, while also preparing to defend g6 with the queen.

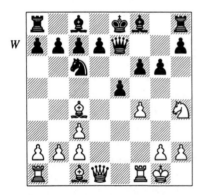

W

9 ♔h1

Another way for White to prevent the check is with 9 b4, which is similar to the text-move after 9...d6 10 f5 ♕g7 11 a4 ♗d7 12 a5 a6 13 ♗e3 ♘e7!.

9...d6

White has a lead in development, but this shouldn't quite compensate for Black's solid wall of pawns. I suspect that Black stands somewhat better, but White's 'swindling' chances should not be underestimated.

a) 10 ♘f3? (this is the wrong plan) 10...♗e6 11 ♗b5 ♗g7 12 ♗e3 0-0 and Black had consolidated his advantage in Engelbert-Stein, Hamburg 1989.

b) 10 f5! (putting pressure on g6) 10...♕g7 11 ♕f3 ♗e7 (11...♘e7!?) 12 ♗d5 ♗d7 13 b4 a6 14 a4 g5 15 g3 ♘d8 (not 15...gxh4?? 16 ♕h5+ ♔d8 17 ♗h6!) 16 ♘g2 c6 17 ♗b3 d5 18 ♗d2 ♘f7 19 c4 dxc4 20 ♗xc4 ♘d6 21 ♕h5+ ♔f8 and while Black still has the extra pawn, White's initiative has not been completely extinguished either, Amos-Jojart, Germany 1995.

C)

4 d3

This move introduces a quiet and respectable system for White, which has slowly enjoyed more and more popularity over the years. White aims to play the position in a similar fashion to the Closed Ruy Lopez, with a restrained d2-d3 (rather than an immediate d2-d4). Black can easily build a solid position, but chances for active counterplay are less obvious than in other lines, as White's structure is basically sound.

4...♗e7

Both this move and 4...♗c5 are of equal prominence and respectability.

I've chosen 4...♗e7 as it fits in neatly with the Two Knights Defence repertoire (after 4...♗c5 5 ♘c3 Black would also have to learn the extremely quiet Giuoco Pianissimo).

5 0-0 0-0 *(D)*

This is more flexible than 5...d6, as Black retains the option of both ...d5 and ...d6.

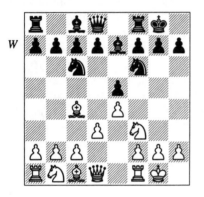

In this important position White has three main ways forward:

C1:	**6 ♖e1**	164
C2:	**6 c3**	167
C3:	**6 ♗b3**	169

Let's first dismiss other moves:

a) 6 h3?! is too slow. After 6...d6 7 ♖e1 ♘a5! Black succeeds in swapping off the light-squared bishop. Barua-Gild.Garcia, Manila OL 1992 continued 8 ♘bd2 c6 9 a4 ♘xc4 10 dxc4 ♕c7 11 b3 ♘d7 12 ♘f1 a5 13 ♘g3 ♘c5 14 ♗e3 b6 and Black had a very easy position to play.

b) 6 ♘c3 (a rare continuation, but certainly not that bad) 6...d6 7 a3

♘d7!? (7...♗e6 and 7...♗g4 look like worthwhile alternatives) 8 ♘d5 ♘b6 9 ♘xe7+ ♕xe7 10 ♗g5 ♕e8 11 ♗a2 ♗e6 12 ♗xe6 fxe6 13 a4 ♕g6 14 ♗h4 ♖f7 and Black can build up counterplay along the half-open f-file, Hauchard-Hebden, Cappelle la Grande 1989.

c) 6 ♘bd2 d6 7 c3 ♘a5 8 ♗b5 a6 9 ♗a4 c5 10 ♖e1 transposes to Line C1, note 'a' to White's 7th move.

d) 6 a4!? (this has been used by Adams recently) 6...d6 (6...d5 7 exd5 ♘xd5 8 ♖e1 ♗g4 9 h3 ♗xf3 10 ♕xf3 ♘b6 11 ♘d2 ♘xc4 12 ♘xc4 ♖e8 13 ♗d2 ♗c5 14 c3 a5 was equal in Malaniuk-Pavasović, Pardubice 1998) 7 ♘bd2!? (7 ♖e1 transposes to Line C1) 7...♔h8 8 a5 a6 (8...♖b8!?) 9 c3 ♘g8 10 d4 exd4 11 cxd4 f5 12 e5 d5 13 ♗d3 f4 14 ♘b3 ♗g4! and Black had good counterplay in Kovchan-Malaniuk, Swidnica 1999.

C1)

6 ♖e1

With this move White firmly dissuades Black from an early ...d5.

6...d6 *(D)*

7 a4

In the past few years this move has become established as White's main try for an advantage. White simultaneously expands on the queenside and creates a retreating space for the c4-bishop, should it be harassed by ...♘a5. Other moves here are:

a) 7 c3 ♘a5! 8 ♗b5 a6 9 ♗a4 c5 10 ♘bd2 ♕c7!? (10...b5 11 ♗c2 actually

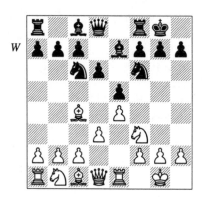

W

transposes to a line of the Ruy Lopez which is reached after the moves 1 e4 e5 2 ♘f3 ♘c6 3 ♗b5 a6 4 ♗a4 ♘f6 5 0-0 ♗e7 6 ♖e1 b5 7 ♗b3 d6 8 c3 0-0 9 d3 ♘a5 10 ♗c2 c5 11 ♘bd2; theoretically speaking this relatively quiet line is fine for Black, but there may even be more mileage in keeping the bishop on a4 for the moment) 11 ♘f1 ♗e6 12 h3 ♖ad8! 13 ♘g3 (13 ♗g5?! h6 14 ♗h4 g6! 15 d4?! ♘h5 16 ♗xe7 ♕xe7 17 b4 ♘c4 18 ♗b3 cxd4 19 cxd4 ♖c8 20 ♖c1 b5 left Black in charge in Yudasin-Vladimirov, Tilburg 1994) 13...b5 14 ♗c2 ♘c6 15 ♕e2 h6 and now:

a1) 16 ♘f5 ♗xf5 17 exf5 ♖fe8 18 ♘h2 d5 19 ♘g4 ♘xg4 20 ♕xg4 ♕d6 21 a4 ♕f6 22 axb5 axb5 and Black has taken over central operations, Mooney-Stephenson, Redcar 1995.

a2) 16 ♗b3 d5 17 exd5 ♘xd5 18 ♘h5 (18 ♘xe5 ♘xe5 19 ♕xe5 ♗d6! regains the pawn) 18...g6 19 ♘g3 ♘f4 20 ♗xf4 exf4 21 ♘f1 ♗f5 with a roughly level position, A.Dimitrov-Radulski, Bulgarian Ch 1996.

b) 7 ♗b3 ♘d7!? (7...♘a5 8 ♗a4 c5 9 c3 a6 transposes to line 'a') 8 c3 ♘c5 9 ♗c2 ♗g4 10 ♘bd2 d5 11 h3 ♗h5 12 ♕e2 a5 13 ♘f1 ♗xf3 14 ♕xf3 d4 15 ♘g3 ♗g5 and Black was doing very well in the game Yudasin-Kupreichik, Sverdlovsk 1984.

c) 7 a3 (this is an inferior version of the main line, as White does not make any headway on the queenside) 7...♔h8 8 ♗g5 h6 9 ♗h4 ♘h5 10 ♗xe7 (10 ♘xe5?? ♘xe5 11 ♗xe7 ♕xe7 12 ♕xh5 ♗g4 wins the white queen) 10...♕xe7 (but not 10...♘xe7? 11 ♘xe5!) 11 ♘c3 ♘f4 12 ♘d5 ♘xd5 and now 13 ♗xd5?! ♗g4 14 h3 ♗h5 15 c3 ♘d8 16 d4 exd4 17 cxd4 c6 18 ♗c4 ♘e6 was slightly better for Black in Kuijf-Nunn, Wijk aan Zee 1990. 13 exd5 is stronger, leading to an equal position after 13...♘d8 14 d4 f6.

7...♔h8

Intending to play ...♘g8, followed by the pawn-break ...f5. Black's other main plan here starts with 7...h6, intending to follow up by ...♘h7-g5. By doing this Black hopes to lessen White's control of d4, as well as pave the way for the f-pawn to move. Following 8 c3 ♘h7 White has the choice between:

a) 9 d4 ♘g5! 10 ♘xg5 ♗xg5 11 dxe5 ♘xe5 12 ♗e2 ♗xc1 13 ♕xc1 a5! 14 f4?! (now Black gets play against the e4-pawn; 14 ♘d2 looks pretty equal) 14...♘d7 15 ♕c2 ♘c5 16 ♗f3 ♗d7 17 ♘d2 ♕f6 18 g3 ♖fe8 19 b3 ♗c6 20 ♖e2 ♖e7 21 ♖ae1 ♕g6 22 ♘f1 ♖ae8 23 f5 ♕f6 24 h4 ♕e5 leaves

Black well in control, Eismont-Yan-demirov, Russian Club Cup (Maikop) 1998.

b) 9 a5!? (this move is more troublesome to Black) 9...a6 10 ♘bd2 ♘g5 11 ♕b3 (Speelman gives the line 11 d4 ♗g4 12 ♗e2 ♗xf3! 13 ♘xf3 ♘xe4 14 ♗d3 ♘g5 15 ♗xg5 ♗xg5 16 dxe5 ♘xe5 17 ♘xe5 dxe5 18 ♖xe5 as equal) 11...♖b8 12 d4 (Speelman-Malaniuk, Kropotkin 1995) and now Speelman suggests 12...♘xf3+!? 13 ♘xf3 ♗g4 14 d5 ♗xf3 15 dxc6 bxc6 16 ♕a4 ♗xe4 17 ♖xe4 d5 18 ♖xe5 dxc4 19 ♕xc4 ♕d1+ 20 ♕f1 ♕xf1+ 21 ♔xf1 ♗d6 22 ♖e4, when I suspect that Black's counterplay along the b-file compensates for the doubled and isolated c-pawns.

Returning to the position after 7...♔h8 (D):

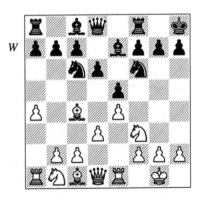

8 a5

With this move White continues to gain space on the queenside and prepares to answer 8...♘g8 with 9 a6!, giving Black serious light-squared weaknesses. White's alternative plan is to start making moves in the centre with 8 c3. Black's most aggressive response is to react with 8...♗g4 9 h3 ♗h5:

a) 10 ♘bd2 d5!? 11 exd5 ♘xd5 12 ♘f1 f5! 13 ♘g3 ♗g6 14 ♘xe5 ♘xe5 15 ♖xe5 ♘b6 16 ♕f3 f4 17 ♘f1 ♗d6 18 ♖e1 ♗e8! and Black had sufficient compensation for the pawn in the game Grosar-I.Sokolov, Bled/Rogaška Slatina 1991.

b) 10 a5!? ♖b8! (planning to answer 11 a6 with 11...b5; in comparison 10...a6 11 ♘bd2 d5 12 exd5 ♘xd5 13 ♘e4! f6 14 ♕b3 looks pleasant for White) 11 ♘bd2 d5 12 exd5 ♘xd5 13 ♘e4 f6 14 ♘g3 ♗f7 15 ♘h4 ♖e8 16 ♘hf5 ♗f8 17 ♕b3 ♕d7 18 ♘e3 ♖ed8 and Black had no reason to complain in Macieja-Pinski, Polish Ch 1999.

8...a6

Black should also consider 8...♖b8!? here, as after 9 c3 ♗g4 10 ♘bd2 d5 11 exd5 ♘xd5 12 h3 ♗h5 we have reached note 'b' to White's 8th move.

9 c3 ♘g8 10 d4 ♗g4

This position is well balanced. White has managed to erect a pawn-centre, but Black is very solid and is ready to strike back with a timely ...f5. Here are two practical examples:

a) 11 ♗e3 f5 12 exf5 exd4 13 cxd4 d5 14 ♗e2 ♗xf5 15 ♘c3 ♘b4 16 ♖c1 c6 17 ♕a4 ♘d3 18 ♗xd3 ♗xd3 was comfortable for Black in Degraeve-C.Bauer, Belgian Cht 1997/8.

b) 11 dxe5 ♘xe5 12 ♗e2 ♗xf3 13 ♗xf3 ♗g5 14 ♗e2 ♗xc1 15 ♕xc1 f5

16 f4 ♘c6 17 ♘d2 ♕d7 18 ♗d3 fxe4 19 ♘xe4 was level in Vratonjić-Nestorović, Yugoslav Cht 1994.

In conclusion it seems that both the plan with ...h6 and ...♘h7 and that with ...♔h8 and ...♘g8 are fully viable for Black.

C2)

6 c3 (D)

White prepares an eventual d3-d4, while giving the bishop an escape-route to c2.

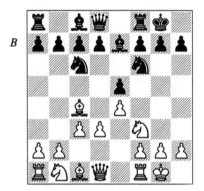

6...d5!?

Striking out in the centre is Black's ambitious attempt to wrest the initiative. With 6...d5 Black obtains the 'small centre' (e5 versus d3), which, with everything else being equal, is a positive acquisition. The drawback, however, is that White can put immediate and substantial pressure on the e5-pawn. If Black is looking for a more secure option, then he can transpose into other lines with 6...d6. Then 7 ♖e1 is C1, while 7 ♗b3 is C32.

7 exd5 ♘xd5 8 ♖e1

Attacking the e5-pawn is a natural follow-up plan. Alternatively:

a) 8 h3 (preventing the pin) 8...♗f5 9 ♖e1 ♗f6 10 ♗b5 ♖e8 11 ♘bd2 a6 12 ♗xc6 bxc6 13 ♘e4 ♘b6 14 ♕e2 ♘d7 15 ♘xf6+ ♕xf6 16 d4 e4 and Black will follow up with ...c5, with a roughly level position, An.Rodriguez-Zarnicki, Villa Gisell 1998.

b) 8 ♗b5 ♗d6 (8...f6!? also looks reasonable, now that White's light-squared bishop has left the a2-g8 diagonal) 9 ♖e1 ♗g4 10 h3 ♗h5 11 ♘bd2 and now 11...♘b6 transposes to note 'a' to Black's 10th move. This is probably Black's best option here, as 11...♔h8 12 g4! ♗g6 13 ♘c4 f6 14 d4 looked better for White in Psakhis-Geller, Sochi 1984.

8...♗g4 9 h3

9 ♘bd2 will often transpose to the main line, as White normally plays h3 sooner or later. For example, 9...♘b6 10 ♗b5 ♗d6 11 h3 ♗h5 gives us note 'a' to Black's 10th move. That said, there are occasions when White may try to do without playing h3. For example, 9...♘f4 10 ♘f1 ♘a5 11 ♗xf4 exf4 12 ♗b5 (12 ♘1d2?! c5 13 h3 ♗f5 14 ♘e4 ♘xc4 15 dxc4 ♕c7 16 ♕d5 ♗e6 was good for Black in Ipavec-V.Bašagić, Bled wom 1993) 12...a6 13 ♗a4 and now:

a) 13...b5 14 ♗c2 c5 leads us to the main line, but without h3 and ...♗h5. Here White can use this omission to his advantage with 15 d4 cxd4 16 ♕d3! g6 17 ♘xd4, with a plus to White.

b) Just as in the main line, Black should consider delaying ...b5 in favour of ...c5. After 13...c5 14 &c2!? &h5! Black is ready to meet 15 d4 cxd4 16 ♕d3? with 16...&g6!.

9...&h5 (*D*)

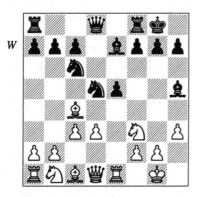

10 ♘bd2

This is not the best time for White to grab a pawn with 10 g4 &g6 11 ♘xe5 ♘xe5 12 ♖xe5. After 12...♘b6! the weakness of the d3-pawn gives White a big headache (compare with Line C31, where White has played &b3 instead of c3). Black is very happy after either 13 ♘d2 &f6 14 ♖e3 &g5 or 13 ♕f3 ♘xc4 14 dxc4 &d6 15 ♖e1 ♕h4, Walta-N.Høiberg, Pohja 1985.

10...♘f4

Black has a very reasonable alternative here in the outwardly less aggressive 10...♘b6:

a) 11 &b5 &d6 12 ♘e4 ♖e8! 13 ♘g3 &g6 14 a4 a6 15 &xc6 bxc6 16 a5 ♘d7 17 ♘e4 h6 18 ♕a4 c5 and Black was equal in Lazić-Gligorić, Yugoslav Ch 1990.

b) 11 &b3!? ♔h8 (11...♕xd3 12 ♘xe5 &xd1 13 ♘xd3 &xb3 14 ♘xb3 ♖fe8 15 &f4 looks a touch better for White) 12 ♘e4 f5!? (12...f6 is an alternative for those looking for a quieter life) 13 ♘g3 &g6 14 ♘xe5 ♘xe5 15 ♖xe5 f4 and Black has some compensation for the pawn, Radulov-Spassky, Slavija-Solingen ECC 1984.

11 ♘f1

Dolmatov suggests 11 ♘e4!?, after which Black should carry on in the same manner with 11...♘a5. Then 12 ♘g3? ♘xc4 13 ♘xh5 ♘xd3 left Black simply a clear pawn up in Duncan-Emms, London Lloyds Bank 1993. Stronger for White is 12 &b5, after which 12...a6 13 &xf4 exf4 14 &a4 c5 looks about level.

11...♘a5 12 &xf4

12 &b5 a6 13 &xf4 exf4 leads to the same thing.

12...exf4 13 &b5 a6 14 &a4 (*D*)

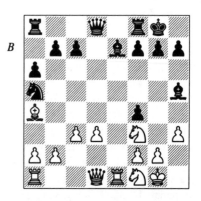

After 14...b5 15 &c2 c5 16 ♘1h2, Yudasin-Dreev, Lvov Z 1990 continued 16...♘c6 17 d4! cxd4 18 &e4 ♖c8

19 ♗xc6 ♖xc6 20 ♕xd4 (20 ♘xd4!?
♖c5 21 ♘c6! ♗xd1 22 ♘xd8 ♖xd8 23
♖axd1 also promises White an edge)
20...♕xd4 21 ♘xd4 ♖c7 22 ♖e4 and
White had a tiny advantage. In his notes
to the game Yudasin gave 16...♗f6!?
as an improvement for Black, quoting
17 ♘g4 ♗xg4 18 hxg4 h6 as unclear.
However, I have my doubts about this,
and the subsequent game Seils-Wells,
2nd Bundesliga 1992 reinforces this
disbelief. After 19 ♖e4 ♕d6 20 ♕d2
g5 21 ♕e2 ♘c6 22 ♖d1 ♖fd8 23 d4
cxd4 24 cxd4 ♕c7 25 d5 ♘a5 26 ♘d4
♖ac8 27 ♗b1 Black was clearly struggling and I'm finding it difficult to
come up with a worthwhile alternative.

In view of all of this, Black should
look earlier for improvements, and the
most obvious one which comes to
mind is 14...c5!? (there is no hurry to
chase the white bishop to where it
wants to go). Now 15 ♗c2 ♘c6 16
♖e4 ♕c7 is fine for Black. Perhaps
White can continue instead with 15
♕e2 or 15 ♘1h2, but in any case I
think Black is better off without playing ...b5 so early.

C3)
6 ♗b3 (D)

With this move White is trying to
get the best bits out of Lines C1 and
C2. By not weakening the d3-square
by playing c3, White discourages
Black from playing an early ...d5 (although as we will see below, it's still
just about playable). On the other hand

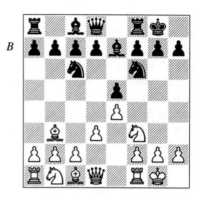

White is ready to play c3 once Black
has committed himself to ...d6, thus
assuring himself the light-squared
bishop and avoiding the time-consum-
ing manoeuvre ♗b5-a4-c2 seen in Line
C1.

Now we will study Black's two
most obvious tries:
C31: 6...d5 169
C32: 6...d6 171

C31)
6...d5

Despite the dissuasive argument
behind White's last move, Black goes
ahead and lunges two squares forward.
The big question is whether Black can
support his 'little centre'.

7 exd5 ♘xd5 8 h3!?

This little move has slowly overtaken its rivals as White's best shot at
gaining an advantage from this position. White uses a tempo to rule out
the annoying pin with ...♗g4.

The main alternative is the logical-
looking 8 ♖e1, immediately applying
pressure on the e5-pawn. Following

8...♗g4 9 h3 Black has two choices, to retreat or to capture:

a) 9...♗h5 (this is less effective here than against 6 c3, but it remains a viable move) 10 g4 ♗g6 11 ♘xe5 ♘xe5 12 ♖xe5 c6. White's weakened king-side pawn-structure promises Black some compensation in return for the lost central pawn. R.Perez-Gil d.Garcia, Santa Clara 1996 continued 13 ♕f3 ♗d6 14 ♖e2 f5 15 g5 f4 16 h4 ♔h8, with an unclear position.

b) 9...♗xf3!? 10 ♕xf3 ♘d4 11 ♕e4 (11 ♕xd5?! ♕xd5 12 ♗xd5 ♘xc2 13 ♗d2 ♘xa1 14 ♖c1 ♖ad8 15 ♘c3 c6 16 ♗f3 ♖xd3 17 ♗e3 ♗b4 was slightly better for Black in Dizdar-Mikhalchishin, Zenica 1989) 11...♘xb3 12 axb3 and now:

b1) 12...♘b4 13 ♘a3 ♘c6 14 ♗d2 f5 15 ♕c4+ ♔h8 16 ♗c3 ♗d6 17 ♕d5 ♕h4 18 ♘c4 and White had some pressure against the black centre in Biolek-Splosnov, Frydek Mistek 1998.

b2) 12...♗f6 is a suggestion of Mikhalchishin's, who assesses the resulting position as equal. My own view is that the little centre should give Black a comfortable position; for example, 13 ♘c3 c6 14 ♗d2 ♕d7, followed by ...g6 and ...♗g7.

Returning to the position after 8 h3 (D):

8...a5

This move is Mikhalchishin's idea. Black blatantly tries to force the bishop off the a2-g8 diagonal, so that the vulnerable e5-pawn can be supported by ...f6.

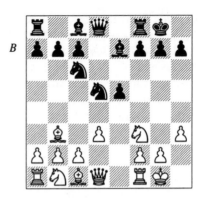

The only other option for Black is to defend the e5-pawn with his pieces, but this seems to tie Black down somewhat. After 8...♗f6 9 ♖e1 we have:

a) 9...♖e8 10 ♘bd2 ♘b6 11 ♘e4 with an edge to White, Titov-Mozetić, Vrnjačka Banja 1992.

b) 9...♗e6 10 ♘bd2 ♘f4 11 ♗a4! ♘d4 (Dolmatov proposes 11...♘g6!? 12 ♗xc6 bxc6 13 ♘e4 ♗e7 as giving Black counterplay, but I still prefer White after 14 ♘fg5 ♗d5 15 ♕h5 h6 16 ♘f3) 12 ♘e4 ♘g6 13 ♘xd4 exd4 14 ♕h5 and White's more active pieces gave him a slight pull in Bologan-Malaniuk, Novgorod 1995.

9 a3

Other moves are less effective:

a) 9 ♗a4 ♘d4 10 ♘xe5 ♘b6 11 c3 ♘xa4 12 ♕xa4 ♘e2+ 13 ♔h1 ♗f6 and Black was at least equal in Shirov-Mozetić, Tilburg 1993.

b) 9 ♖e1 a4 10 ♗xd5 (or 10 ♗c4 ♘b6 11 ♗b5 ♘d4) 10...♕xd5 11 ♘c3 ♕a5, which Mozetić assesses as unclear.

9...a4

Shirov suggests 9...♘d4, after which 10 ♘xe5?! ♘xb3 11 cxb3 ♗f6 gives White a horrible pawn-structure. After the stronger 10 ♗a2 the position is quite deceptive. Black looks active, but there are still some long-term problems regarding the safety of the e5-pawn. After 10...♘xf3+ 11 ♕xf3 c6 12 ♖e1 ♕c7 13 ♕g3 ♗f6 14 ♘d2 g6 15 ♘f3 ♖e8 16 d4 e4 17 ♕xc7 ♘xc7 18 ♘g5 ♗xg5 19 ♗xg5 White's bishop-pair gave him the edge in I.Almasi-Shabtai, Budapest 1994.

10 ♗a2 ♔h8

At first I was struck by the idea of 10...f5?, but now I realize it's just way too ambitious and even allows White a neat trick after 11 ♘c3 ♗e6 12 ♘xe5! ♘xe5 13 ♖e1 ♕d6 14 ♘b5.

11 ♖e1 f6 12 d4 exd4 13 ♘xd4

We are following Kramnik-Kasparov, New York rpd 1995. Slight weaknesses in the black camp give White an edge, which was retained after 13...♘db4 14 axb4 ♕xd4 15 c3 ♕xd1 16 ♖xd1 ♗f5 17 ♘a3, although Kasparov drew the game eventually.

C32)
6...d6

This move is Black's most reliable option.

7 c3 ♘a5 8 ♗c2 c5 *(D)*

After this move, play resembles the Closed Lopez, where White has played an early d3. The line in question is obtained by the move-order 1 e4 e5 2 ♘f3 ♘c6 3 ♗b5 a6 4 ♗a4 ♘f6 5 0-0 ♗e7 6 ♖e1 b5 7 ♗b3 d6 8 c3 0-0 9 d3

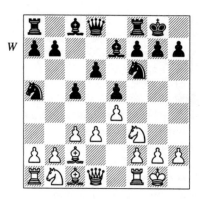

♘a5 10 ♗c2 c5. If we compare the variations directly, we see that on the negative side (from Black's point of view) is that White's bishop has only taken three moves to reach c2. As it takes four moves in the Lopez line we can say that White has effectively gained a tempo. However, this is not the end of the story. In the Lopez line, Black has played the moves ...a6 and ...b5 while chasing the bishop around. These moves are only of limited value (they gain some space, but also create a target of attack) and thus Black can be advised to put these two extra tempi to better use. The d3 Lopez is considered as playable for White, without giving any theoretical edge, and the same thing could be said about the line arising from the Two Knights Defence.

9 ♖e1

Alternatively:

a) 9 b4 cxb4 10 cxb4 ♘c6 11 b5 ♘a5 12 d4 (or 12 ♗b2 ♗g4 13 h3 ♗xf3 14 ♕xf3 ♖c8 15 ♕e2 ♕b6 with equality, Chandler-Romanishin, Biel

1987) 12...exd4 13 ♘xd4 ♗d7 14 ♘d2 ♖c8 with a roughly level position, Kramnik-J.Polgar, Moscow PCA rpd 1996.

b) 9 a3 ♘c6 10 b4 a6 11 ♘bd2 ♖e8! (11...♕c7 12 h3 b5 13 d4 was slightly better for White in Dolmatov – Sideif-Zade, Tashkent 1980, but Black should not bother with ...b5) 12 ♗b2 ♗f8 13 ♖e1 ♘h5 14 ♘f1 g6 15 ♘e3 (Bauer-Hebden, Andorra Z 1998) and now Hebden recommends the simple 15...♗g7, with the aim of an eventual ...f5.

9...♘c6 10 ♘bd2 (D)

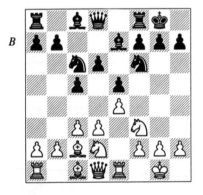

10...♕c7

With this move Black has a direct plan of ...♗e6, ...♖ad8 and ...d5. An important alternative is 10...♖e8, which aims for a similar plan of ...h6, ...♗f8 and ...d5. After 11 ♘f1 h6 12 h3 ♗f8 we have:

a) 13 ♘g3 d5 (or 13...g6 14 d4 cxd4 15 cxd4 exd4 16 ♘xd4 ♘xd4 17 ♕xd4 ½-½ Stean-Ciocaltea, Beersheba 1982) 14 exd5 ♕xd5 15 ♗b3

♕d6 16 ♘e4 ♘xe4 17 dxe4 ♗e6 18 ♗e3 ♕c7 19 ♗xe6 ♖xe6 20 ♕e2 ♖d8 21 ♖ed1 ♖ed6 ½-½ Gavrikov-Arlandi, Reggio Emilia 1991/2.

b) 13 d4 ♕c7 14 ♘e3?! (better is 14 d5 ♘e7 with equality) 14...exd4 15 cxd4 ♘xd4 16 ♘xd4 cxd4 17 ♕xd4 d5! (this trap is well known in Lopez circles) 18 exd5 ♖xe3 19 ♗xe3 ♕xc2 20 ♗xh6 ♗xh3! 21 ♖e3 ♗f5 22 ♖g3 ♗g6 23 ♗e3 ♗d6 24 ♖f3 ♖e8 and Black was clearly better in Gunnarsson-Olsen, Gentofte 1999.

c) 13 ♘3h2 d5 14 ♕f3 d4 15 ♘g3 g6 16 ♗b3 ♗e6 17 ♗xe6 ♖xe6 18 c4 ♖b8 19 ♗d2 b5 20 cxb5 ♖xb5 21 b3 a5 and Black was at least equal in Yudasin-P.Nikolić, Tilburg rpd 1993.

Returning to the position after 10...♕c7 (D):

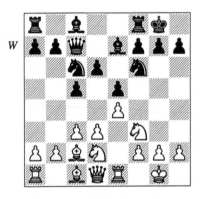

11 h3

11 ♘c4 doesn't prevent the black plan after 11...h6 12 ♘e3 ♗e6 13 ♗b3 ♖fe8 14 h3 ♖ad8, as in Kobaliya-Zsinka, Oberwart 1997. 11 ♘f1 ♗e6 12 ♘g3 d5 is similar to the main line

(in fact this was the move-order of Dolmatov-Timman below).

11...♗e6 12 ♘f1 ♖ad8 13 ♘g3

13...d5 would also be the answer to 13 ♗g5 or 13 ♘e3.

13...d5! 14 exd5

Beliavsky gives the line 14 ♘g5 d4! 15 ♘xe6 fxe6 16 ♗b3 ♕d7 17 ♘f5 ♔h8 18 ♘xe7 ♕xe7 as unclear, while 14 ♕e2 d4 15 c4 g6 16 ♗h6 ♖fe8 17 ♕d2 ♗f8 gave Black no problems in Dolmatov-Timman, Amsterdam 1980.

14...♘xd5

We are following Yudasin-Beliavsky, USSR Ch (Moscow) 1988, which continued 15 ♕e2 (the lines 15 ♘g5 ♗xg5 16 ♗xg5 f6 17 ♗d2 ♖fe8 and 15 ♗a4 f6 16 d4 cxd4 17 cxd4 ♘b6 are unclear according to Yudasin) 15...f6 (15...♘f4!?) 16 ♗d2 ♔h8! 17 a3 ♖fe8 18 d4 cxd4 19 cxd4 ♗f8 20 ♕e4 (20 dxe5 ♘xe5 21 ♘xe5? ♕xc2! favours Black) 20...♗g8! 21 dxe5 ♘xe5 22 ♗a4 ♘xf3+ 23 ♕xf3 ½-½.

In conclusion, I would say that 4 d3 gives White more chances to play for an advantage than either 4 ♘c3 or 4 0-0. On the other hand, if Black knows his stuff, then it would seem that he can reach a perfectly playable middlegame both using lines involving ...d6 and those with ...d5.

15 The Two Knights Defence: 4 d4 exd4 Introduction

1 e4 e5 2 ♘f3 ♘c6 3 ♗c4 ♘f6 4 d4 exd4 *(D)*

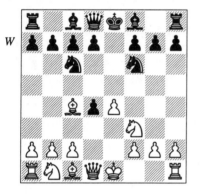

4 d4 is a very popular way of meeting the Two Knights Defence. This is especially so at club level, where White is often looking to take the initiative at the earliest possible stage. Black often comes under pressure very early and inaccurate defence can be punished severely. The following game is just one example of many in my database where Black goes under very quickly.

Clech – Verdun
Val Maubuée 1990

1 e4 e5 2 ♗c4 ♘f6 3 d4 exd4 4 ♘f3 ♘c6 5 0-0 ♗e7?!

Both 5...♘xe4 and 5...♗c5 are superior.

6 e5 ♘e4 7 ♗d5 ♘g5?

This just loses. Black had to try 7...♘c5.

8 ♘xg5 ♗xg5 9 ♕h5! g6 10 ♕xg5 ♘e7 11 ♗xf7+ ♔xf7 12 ♕f6+ ♔g8 13 ♗h6 1-0

The good news for Black is that there are much better ways to defend, and the even better news is that Black has nothing to worry about in the main lines, which I feel give Black at least as many chances as White to play for a win.

After 4 d4 exd4 White's most popular reply is 5 0-0, which we shall study in Chapters 16 and 17. In this chapter we will look at two other possibilities for White, which, while less popular, are still dangerous.

A Quick Summary of the Recommended Lines

Line A is not particularly popular (I've never faced it in a serious game). Nevertheless, it does contain a couple of tricks of which Black should be aware. Line B is seen much more frequently, and in my opinion is one of the most underrated lines against the Two Knights. Line B2 has always been Black's most popular defence, but in recent years Line B1 has also started to become important. In my opinion both lead to fully satisfactory positions for Black.

The Theory of the Two Knights Defence: 4 d4 exd4 without 5 0-0

1 e4 e5 2 ♘f3 ♘c6 3 ♗c4 ♘f6 4 d4 exd4

Apart from 5 0-0, which is the subject of the next two chapters, White has two other possibilities:

A: 5 ♘g5   175
B: 5 e5   177

5 ♕e2?! shouldn't worry Black. Following 5...♗c5 6 e5 0-0! 7 0-0 d5 8 ♗b5 ♘e4 Black was in command in Pietzsch-Masieev, corr 1967.

A)

5 ♘g5

This move, which has some similar properties to 4 ♘g5, is not especially popular or frightening. However, I should point out that it does contain some tricks of which Black should certainly be aware. Black's most dynamic response is to offer a pawn sacrifice himself.

5...d5

It is true that 5...♘e5, defending the pawn on f7 and attacking the bishop

on c4, looks like an appealing move. However, if White plays simply as in line 'b', then Black's chances of drumming up play in the endgame are minimal.

a) 6 ♗b3 h6 7 f4 hxg5 8 fxe5 ♘xe4 9 ♕xd4 ♘c5 10 ♘c3 d6 11 ♗e3 ♘xb3 12 axb3 dxe5 13 ♕xe5+ ♕e7 and now 14 ♕xg5 ♕xg5 15 ♗xg5 ♗d6 was slightly better for Black in the game Pfleger-Spassky, Hastings 1965/6, but 14 ♕xe7+ ♗xe7 15 ♘b5 ♗d8 16 ♗xg5 looks equal.

b) 6 ♕xd4 ♘xc4 7 ♕xc4 d5 8 exd5 ♕xd5 9 ♕e2+! (this check is rather annoying) 9...♗e6 10 0-0 0-0-0 11 ♘c3 ♕c4 12 ♘xe6 ♕xe2 13 ♘xe2 fxe6 with a dull position in which, if anything, White stands a bit better due to the isolated pawn on e6, J.Nagy-Kovacs, Balatonbereny 1994.

6 exd5 *(D)*

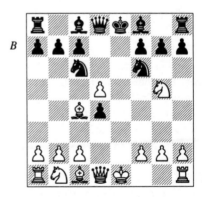

6...♕e7+!

The plausible 6...♘xd5?! falls into White's main trick. After 7 0-0 ♗e7 8 ♘xf7! White obtains the superior version of the Fried Liver Attack (see the note to Black's 5th move in Chapter 18), against which there is no escape.

7 ♔f1

After 7 ♕e2, *ECO* gives the strange line 7...♘b4 8 ♕xe7+ ♗xe7 9 d6 ♘xc2+ 10 ♔d2, with an assessment of 'unclear', but I can't see what's wrong with 7...♕xe2+ 8 ♔xe2 ♘b4, when Black just wins a pawn.

7...♘e5 8 ♕xd4 ♘xc4 9 ♕xc4 (D)

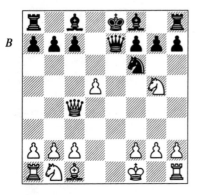

B

9...h6!?

This is the most ambitious way to play. The immediate 9...♕c5 is safer:

a) 10 ♕xc5 ♗xc5 11 ♘c3 ♗f5 12 ♗f4 0-0 13 ♗xc7 ♗xc2 (13...h6 14 ♘f3 ♗xc2 15 ♖e1 ♗f5 16 ♖d1 ♖ac8 17 ♗e5 ♖fd8 18 ♗xf6 gxf6 19 g4 ♗g6 20 f4 f5 21 g5 ♗b4 22 h4 ♗h5 23 ♖d4 ♗xc3 24 bxc3 ♖xc3 was equal in Sax-Lengyel, Budapest 1973) 14 ♖c1 ♗d3+ 15 ♔g1 ♖fe8 16 h3 ♖e7 17 d6 ♖d7 18 ♘ce4 ♗xe4 19 ♖xc5 h6 20 ♘f3 ♗xf3 21 gxf3 ♘e8 22 ♔g2 ½-½ Pfleger-Lengyel, Hamburg Echt 1965.

b) 10 ♕e2+ ♗e7 11 c4 (11 ♗e3 ♕xd5 12 ♘c3 ♕f5 was pleasant for Black in Karaklajić-Lejlić, Yugoslav Ch 1991) 11...♘xd5 12 ♘e4 ♕c6 13 ♗g5 ♗xg5 14 ♘xg5+ ♔f8 15 ♕e4 (or 15 cxd5 ♕c1+ 16 ♕e1 ♕xg5 17 ♘c3 ♗d7 18 ♕e3 ♕xe3 19 fxe3 with equality, Kiritsenko-Dobrovolsky, Karvina 1992) 15...♘b4 16 ♘c3 ♕xe4 17 ♘gxe4 ♗f5 18 f3 ♗xe4 19 ♘xe4 ♔e7 20 ♔e2 with a completely level endgame, Sax-Smejkal, Budapest 1975.

10 ♘c3!?

White is not forced to play this courageous piece sacrifice, but on the other hand 10 ♘f3 ♕c5! just seems to give Black a superior version of the previous note:

a) 11 ♕e2+ ♗e7 12 c4 ♘xd5 and Black is probably a touch better.

b) 11 ♕xc5 ♗xc5 12 c4 ♗f5 and Black's bishops cause White many problems; for example, 13 ♘e5 ♘d7 14 ♘xd7 ♗d3+! 15 ♔e1 ♔xd7 and the c4-pawn drops, or 13 ♔e2 0-0-0 14 ♗e3 ♖he8 15 ♘c3 ♘g4 16 ♘d1 c6! and the position opens to Black's advantage.

10...hxg5 11 ♗xg5 ♕c5 12 ♖e1+ ♔d8

Now:

a) 13 ♕e2?! ♗d7! 14 ♘e4 ♗b5! wins for Black.

b) 13 ♕f4. White has two pawns and some play for the piece, but this shouldn't be sufficient compensation. Carleton-Franzen, corr 1991 continued 13...♗e7 14 h4!? ♗d7 15 h5 ♔c8 16 ♖h4 ♗d6 17 ♕f3 ♘e8 18 h6 gxh6

19 ♗xh6 f5! 20 ♗e3 ♖xh4 21 ♗xc5 ♖h1+ 22 ♔e2 ♖xe1+ 23 ♔xe1 ♗xc5, when the material balance still favoured Black, while Franzen's suggestion of 13...♕d6!? also looks worth trying.

In conclusion, it seems that Black has more than one way to reach a fully playable position against 5 ♘g5.

B)
5 e5 *(D)*

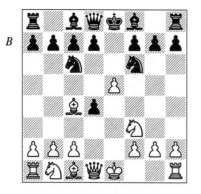

This move initiates the so-called Modern Attack. From White's point of view, it lacks the attacking thrill of the lines arising after 5 0-0, but on the other hand it's sounder in a positional sense and remains one of White's most underrated systems against the Two Knights Defence.

We will study Black's two main defences:

B1: 5...♘e4   177
B2: 5...d5   181

The former is solid, while the latter is more popular.

B1)
5...♘e4

In *Secrets of Grandmaster Chess*, John Nunn says of this move "Fashion has a profound influence on opening theory. In practice Black almost invariably plays 5...d5, yet there is a great deal of evidence to suggest that 5...♘e4 is a simple and effective equalizer". I have to admit that before I witnessed 5...♘e4 being played in a tournament by Zoltan Almasi, I was under the impression that 5...d5 was the 'only move'. This is certainly not the case, though, and recently many top players have been using 5...♘e4 with some success.

White has a varied choice here:

B11: 6 ♕e2   177
B12: 6 ♗d5   178
B13: 6 0-0   180

6 c3 is can be answered effectively with 6...d5!, when 7 exd6 ♘xd6 gains a tempo on the bishop.

B11)
6 ♕e2 *(D)*

White plans to round up the d4-pawn after 0-0 and ♖fd1.

6...♘c5 7 0-0 ♘e6!

This idea of Mikhalchishin's causes White considerable problems in regaining his pawn and thus is superior to the older 7...♗e7.

8 ♖d1

Alternatively:

a) 8 c3 d5! 9 exd6 ♗xd6 10 ♗g5 ♗e7 11 ♗xe7 ♕xe7 12 ♖e1 0-0!?

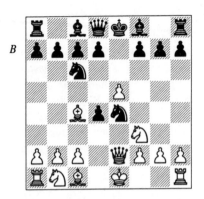

(Mikhalchishin gives 12...dxc3 13 ♘xc3 0-0 14 ♘d5 ♛c5 15 ♖ac1, when White certainly has some compensation for the pawn; the text-move gives Black an easier life) 13 cxd4 ♛f6! 14 d5 ♘cd4 15 ♘xd4 ♘xd4 16 ♛d2 ♝f5 and Black is very comfortable, while the isolated d-pawn may become a target.

b) 8 ♝xe6!? dxe6 9 ♖d1 ♝c5 10 ♘c3!? is another suggestion from Mikhalchishin. It looks as though it gives some compensation for the pawn, after, for instance, 10...0-0 11 ♘e4 ♝b6 12 c3. This line could do with a practical test.

8...d5 9 ♝b5

This move is Mikhalchishin's suggested improvement over 9 ♝b3, which led to a winning position for Black after 9...♝c5 10 c3 0-0 11 ♝c2 f6! 12 cxd4 ♘cxd4 13 ♘xd4 ♘xd4 14 ♖xd4 ♝xd4 15 ♛d3 ♝xf2+! in Voigt-Mikhalchishin, Dortmund 1992.

9...♝c5 10 c3

After 10 ♘bd2 0-0 11 ♘b3 ♝b6 12 ♝xc6 bxc6 13 ♘bxd4 ♘xd4 14 ♘xd4

Black can already think about expanding with 14...c5, when the bishop-pair gives him a nice edge.

10...♝d7 11 ♝xc6 ♝xc6 12 cxd4 ♝b6 13 ♘c3 0-0

Mikhalchishin assesses this position as unclear, which is about right. After, say, 14 b4 Black can strike out with 14...f5!, planning to re-route the light-squared bishop via e8 to h5.

B12)
　6 ♝d5 ♘c5 (D)

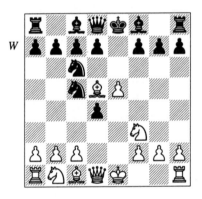

Now:
B121: 7 0-0　　179
B122: 7 ♛e2　　179

A third possibility is the pawn sacrifice 7 c3!? dxc3 8 ♘xc3, although in practice Black has scored well from this position. After 8...♝e7 9 ♝e3 0-0 10 ♛e2 ♘b4! 11 0-0-0 we have:

a) 11...c6 12 ♝xc5 ♝xc5 13 ♝b3 d5 14 a3 ♘a6 15 h4 b5, with a complicated position, but Black remains a pawn ahead, Hector-Nunn, Vejle 1994.

b) 11...♘xd5 12 ♘xd5 b6 13 h4 ♗b7 14 ♗xc5 bxc5 15 ♕c2 ♗xd5 16 ♖xd5 d6 17 ♔b1 ♖b8 again gives Black an advantage, B.Kristensen-Z.Almasi, Kopavogur 1994.

B121)
7 0-0 ♗e7

Black can attempt to hold on to the d4-pawn with 7...♘e6, but then White can sacrifice with 8 c3 dxc3 9 ♘xc3, when his lead in development certainly gives him some compensation for the pawn. For example, 9...d6 10 ♕a4 ♗d7 11 exd6 ♗xd6 12 ♘b5 0-0 13 ♘xd6 cxd6 14 ♕a3 was unclear in Bryson-D.Ledger, Newcastle 1995.

8 ♘xd4 ♘xd4

This is the safe method, which guarantees Black a reasonably comfortable position. The pawn-snatch 8...♘xe5 is more ambitious, although of course this also involves more risk. The only practical example I can find with this continued 9 f4 ♘c6 10 ♘f5 ♗f6 11 ♕g4 ♔f8 12 ♘e3 d6 13 ♕d1 ♘e7 14 ♗f3 ♘f5 15 ♘d5 ♗e6 16 ♘xf6 ♕xf6 17 ♘c3 h5 18 ♘d5 ♗xd5 19 ♗xd5 ♖e8 20 c3 h4 and Black eventually succeeded in converting his material advantage into victory in A.Cohen-Flear, Isle of Man 1994. I wouldn't be too surprised if there were improvements in White's play here.

9 ♕xd4 0-0 10 ♗e3 d6 11 ♕c3

Fahrni-Schlechter, Baden-Baden 1914 continued 11...♘d7 12 f4 ♘b6 13 ♗f3 c6 14 ♖d1 d5 with an equal position. Black could also consider

11...♘a4, planning to harass the bishop on d5 with ...♘b6.

B122)
7 ♕e2 (D)

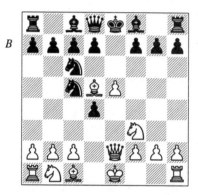

Once again planning 0-0 and ♖d1.

7...♗e7 8 0-0 0-0 9 ♖d1 ♕e8!?

This very clever move plans to exploit the pin on the e-file after 10 ♘xd4 ♘xd4 11 ♖xd4 ♗f6!.

10 ♘a3

Alternatively:

a) 10 ♗xc6 d3! 11 cxd3 dxc6 12 d4 ♘e6 and Black will continue with ...b6, ...♗b7, ...♖d8 and eventually ...c5.

b) 10 ♗f4 b6! 11 ♗xc6 d3! 12 cxd3 dxc6 13 d4 ♘e6 14 ♗g3 ♗b7 15 ♘c3 ♖d8! was good for Black in Khmelnitsky-Romanishin, Šibenik 1990. Once more Black plans ...♖d7, ...♕a8, ...♖fd8 and finally ...c5.

10...♘b4 11 ♗c4! d3 12 cxd3 d5 13 exd6 ♗xd6 14 ♕xe8

14 d4 ♕xe2 15 ♗xe2 ♘e6 gives Black an edge due to White's isolated d-pawn, according to Malaniuk.

14...♖xe8 15 ♘b5 ♗g4

This position, which occurred in Khmelnitsky-Malaniuk, Šibenik 1990, looks pretty even. White has an isolated d-pawn on a semi-open file, but is ready to saddle Black with one of his own after ♘xd6.

B13)
6 0-0

This is White's main continuation. Before undergoing any operations in the centre, he sensibly completes his kingside development.

6...d5 *(D)*

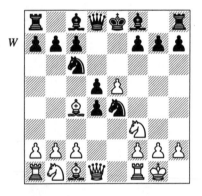

7 exd6

After 7 ♗b5 Black can transpose into Line B2 with either 7...♗c5 or 7...♗d7. However, it seems a bit odd to play 5...♘e4, only to offer White the chance to transpose into 5...d5 lines. Because of this, Black should consider playing the more ambitious 7...♗g4!?, clinging on to the d4-pawn, at least for the time being. Pachman-Gligorić, Leipzig OL 1960 continued

8 h3 ♗xf3 9 ♕xf3 a6 10 ♗xc6+ bxc6 11 ♘d2 ♘g5 12 ♕d3 ♘e6 13 f4 g6 14 f5 gxf5 15 ♕xf5 ♕d7 16 ♘f3 h6 17 ♗d2 c5 18 ♘h2 h5 19 ♖f2 0-0-0 20 ♕xf7 ♗e7 with an unclear position.

7...♘xd6 8 ♗d5

If White throws in 8 ♖e1+ ♗e7 and only then 9 ♗d5, Black can transpose into the main line with 9...♘f5, or play simply with 9...0-0. Then Reinderman-Van der Sterren, Dutch Ch 1996 continued 10 ♗xc6 bxc6 11 ♘xd4 ♕d7 12 ♘d2 ♗f6 13 ♘2b3 ♘c4 14 c3 ♕d5, when Black's activity compensated for his spoiled queenside pawn-structure.

8...♘f5!

This is the most challenging move. Once again 8...♗e7 9 ♗xc6+ bxc6 10 ♘xd4 is possible, although in this situation it's more favourable for White, who doesn't necessarily have to play ♖e1.

9 ♖e1+ ♗e7 10 ♗xc6+ bxc6 11 g4 *(D)*

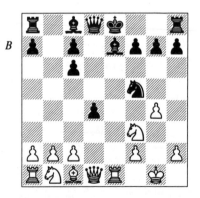

11...♘h6!?

This paradoxical move has breathed new life into this variation, especially as far as Black is concerned. Previously, only the more natural-looking 11...♘d6 was played. Theoretically speaking this may also be OK for Black, although practical results have not been too promising. After 12 ♘xd4 we have:

a) 12...♕d7 13 ♗g5 f6 14 ♗f4 ♔f7 15 ♘c3 ♖e8 16 h3 ♗f8 17 ♕f3 with an advantage to White, Sveshnikov-Arkhipov, Russian Ch (Elista) 1994. Evgeny Sveshnikov remains one of the leading advocates of this line from White's point of view.

b) 12...♗d7!? 13 ♕f3 0-0 14 ♘xc6 ♗xc6 15 ♕xc6 and now instead of 15...♗h4?!, as in Edelman-Kaidanov, New York 1994, Kaidanov suggests the immediate 15...f5!?, when Black has some chances to drum up play on the kingside.

12 ♗xh6

This may not be White's best choice here. Alternatives are:

a) 12 ♗g5 f6 13 ♗xh6 gxh6 14 ♕xd4 ♕xd4 15 ♘xd4 ♔f7 16 ♘xc6 ♗d6 and it's plain that Black's bishop-pair offers tremendous compensation for the pawn.

b) 12 ♕xd4!? may be preferable:

b1) 12...♗xg4 13 ♗xh6 ♗xf3 (or 13...♕xd4 14 ♘xd4 gxh6 15 ♘xc6 ♗e6, which looks about equal) 14 ♕xg7 ♔d7 15 ♔f1 ♗d5 16 ♘c3 ♗c4+ 17 ♘e2, with a very messy position, although White's king looks fractionally safer than Black's.

b2) 12...♕xd4 13 ♘xd4 ♘xg4 14 ♗g5 (or 14 ♘xc6 ♗e6 15 ♘xe7 ♔xe7 with equality) 14...♘f6 15 ♗xf6 gxf6 16 ♘xc6 ♖g8+ 17 ♔h1 and now Black can try 17...♗e6 18 ♘xe7 ♔xe7 19 ♘c3, which looks roughly level, or 17...♔f8 18 ♖xe7 ♗h3 19 ♖xc7 ♗g2+ 20 ♔g1 ♗h3+, which is a perpetual check.

12...gxh6 13 ♕xd4

13 ♘xd4 ♖g8 14 h3 ♖g6 also favours Black.

13...♕xd4 14 ♘xd4 ♔f8! 15 ♘xc6 ♗f6

15...♗d6!? looks like an enticing alternative.

16 ♘c3 ♗xc3

Or 16...♗xg4!?.

17 bxc3 ♗xg4

In this open position, Black's bishop is stronger than White's knight. Tzermiadianos-Agnos, Glyfada 1995 continued 18 ♖e3 ♖g8 19 ♔f1 ♗e6 20 ♘e5 ♖g5!, with an edge to Black. More tests are required, but at the moment 11...♘h6 may well be the way forward for Black.

B2)

5...d5

This counter-attacking response to 5 e5 is still Black's most popular choice, especially at club level. Black ignores the attack on the knight and strikes out in the centre, hitting the bishop on c4.

6 ♗b5

Moving the bishop again is White's only real try for an advantage. 6 exf6?

dxc4 is obviously very pleasant for Black as the g7-pawn is protected (compare with the Max Lange Attack, which we discuss in Chapter 17).

6...♘e4 7 ♘xd4 *(D)*

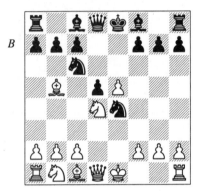

At this point Black has a major choice:

The former is solid and the latter adventurous, but it should be pointed out that these two lines often transpose.

B21)

7...♗d7

The safest move. In many cases we simply transpose into Line B223, but with this move-order, there are fewer options for both players.

8 ♗xc6

The loss of tempo involved after 8 ♘xc6 bxc6 leaves Black with no problems. After 9 ♗d3 Black can continue 9...♗c5, and if 10 ♗xe4 then 10...♕h4!.

8...bxc6 9 0-0

9 ♗e3 ♗c5 transposes into Line B223.

9...♗c5 10 f3

It's logical for White to push the f-pawn. After the mundane 10 c3 Black can simply carry on with 10...0-0 or 10...♗b6.

10...♘g5 11 f4

Or 11 ♗e3 ♗b6, when we are back to Line B2232.

11...♘e4

Most games now continue with 12 ♗e3 ♗b6, transposing to Line B2232.

The only independent path is 12 ♘c3; here are two examples:

a) 12...0-0 13 ♘xe4 dxe4 14 c3 ♕e7 15 ♗e3 f6 16 exf6 ♖xf6 was equal in Van Wijgerden-Geller, Plovdiv Echt 1983.

b) 12...♘xc3 13 bxc3 0-0 14 ♔h1 f6 15 ♘b3 ♗b6 16 a4 a5 17 ♗a3 ♖e8 and again the position is pretty level, Roofdhooft-Timmermans, Belgian Cht 1997/8.

B22)

7...♗c5!? *(D)*

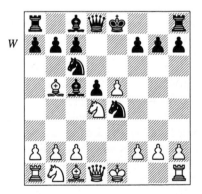

This move has been more popular than 7...♗d7 over the last few years, if nothing else because it contains a few clever tricks. However, some of the lines have not been assessed properly and so it's not clear who is tricking whom.

White has three plausible continuations:

B221: 8 ♘xc6!? 183
B222: 8 0-0 184
B223: 8 ♗e3 187

B221)

8 ♘xc6!?

Initially, this was roundly condemned, but John Nunn pointed out that it is in fact playable.

8...♗xf2+ 9 ♔f1 ♕h4 (D)

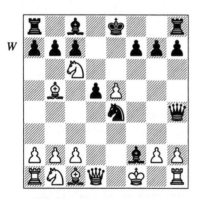

10 ♘d4+

This is not the only choice:

a) 10 ♕xd5 is probably just too greedy. After 10...♗c5! we have:

a1) 11 ♘b4+ c6 12 ♗xc6+ bxc6 13 ♕xc6+ ♔e7 14 ♘d3 ♘g3+ is probably good for Black.

a2) 11 ♘d8+? c6 12 ♗xc6+ bxc6 13 ♕xc6+ ♗d7 wins for Black.

a3) 11 ♕d8+ bails out into an endgame after 11...♕xd8 12 ♘xd8+ ♔xd8, but this is obviously more pleasant for Black.

a4) 11 ♘d4+ c6 12 ♗xc6+ (12 g3 loses after 12...♕h3+ 13 ♔e1 ♕g2 14 ♗xc6+ bxc6 15 ♕xc6+ ♔f8 16 ♖f1 ♗xd4 17 ♕xa8 ♗f2+ 18 ♔e2 ♘xg3+ 19 hxg3 ♕xa8) 12...bxc6 13 ♕xc6+ ♗d7! 14 ♕xa8+ ♔e7 15 ♗g5+ (or 15 ♘f5+ ♗xf5 16 ♕b7+ ♗d7 17 g3 ♕g4 18 ♔e1 ♗f2+ 19 ♔f1 ♕f3) 15...♘xg5 16 ♕d5 ♗xd4 with a clear plus for Black.

a5) 11 g3 was played in Bartolik-Malinin, corr 1991 and now 11...♗h3+! looks very strong: 12 ♔e1 (12 ♔e2 ♕g4+ 13 ♔d3 ♕f3+ 14 ♔c4 ♕e2+ 15 ♕d3 ♗e6#) 12...♗f2+ 13 ♔d1 (13 ♔e2 ♕g4+ 14 ♔d3 ♕f3+ 15 ♔c4 ♕xh1) 13...♗g4+ 14 ♗e2 ♗xe2+ 15 ♔xe2 ♕g4+ 16 ♔d3 ♕f3+.

b) 10 ♘xa7+!? (no mention has been made of this move, but as far as I can see, it leads to a draw) 10...c6 11 ♘xc8 ♖xc8 12 ♗e2 (12 ♗a4 also draws after 12...♘g3+ 13 ♔xf2 ♘e4++ 14 ♔e2 ♕f2+ 15 ♔d3 ♘c5+ 16 ♔c3 ♘xa4+ 17 ♔d3 ♘c5+, but 12 ♗d3? loses to 12...♘g3+ 13 ♔xf2 ♘e4++ 14 ♔f3 ♕f2+ 15 ♔g4 h5+ 16 ♔h3 ♕f5+ 17 ♔h4 g5+ 18 ♗xg5 ♕xg5+ 19 ♔h3 ♘f2#) 12...♗d4 13 ♕e1 ♗f2 14 ♕a5 ♗d4 15 ♕e1 and neither side can do better than repeating.

10...c6 11 ♘f3 ♘g3+ 12 ♔xf2 ♘e4++! (D)

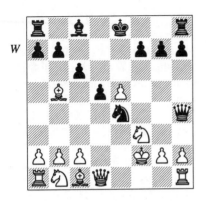

ECO stops here, assessing the position as clearly better for Black.

13 ♔e3 ♕f2+ 14 ♔d3 ♗f5

The most obvious move. White is happy after 14...cxb5 15 ♗e3 ♘c5+ 16 ♗xc5 ♗f5+ 17 ♔c3 ♕xc5+ 18 ♔d2, or 14...♕c5 15 ♖f1 ♕xb5+ 16 ♔e3.

15 ♘d4!

White loses after 15 ♗e3 ♘d6+, 15 ♗f4 cxb5 and 15 ♕e1 ♘d6+ 16 ♔c3 ♘xb5+.

15...♗g6

15...♘d6+ 16 ♘xf5 ♕xf5+ 17 ♔d2 ♘e4+ 18 ♔e2 ♕f2+ 19 ♔d3 ♕c5 20 ♖f1 ♕xb5+ 21 ♔e3 again looks good for White.

16 ♖f1 ♕xg2!?

Alternatively:

a) 16...♘d6+ 17 ♔c3 ♘xb5+ 18 ♘xb5 ♕c5+ 19 ♔d2 ♕xb5 20 ♕e2 and Black doesn't have enough compensation.

b) 16...♘d2+!? seems to force a draw after 17 ♔c3 ♕e3+ 18 ♗d3 ♘e4+ 19 ♔b3:

b1) 19...♕xd4 20 a3! ♘c5+ 21 ♔a2 ♘xd3 22 cxd3 ♗xd3 23 b3 and

suddenly White's king is looking very safe indeed on a2!

b2) 19...♘c5+! (Nunn) and now 20 ♔c3 ♘e4+ is a draw by perpetual check, which White is advised to take, as Black is winning after 20 ♔a3 ♕xd4, e.g. 21 ♘c3 a5! or 21 ♖f4 ♗e4!. Likewise, Black has nothing better after 20 ♔c3, as 20...♘a4+ 21 ♔b3 ♕xd4? 22 a3 ♘c5+ 23 ♔a2 would transpose into note 'b1'.

17 ♔e3 cxb5

At the moment, Black has two pawns for the piece and White's king has yet to find safety. This position could well do with a practical test, although it has to be said that not many players would find this fun to play with the white pieces. Another problem (and this applies for both White and Black) is that both sides can appear to force a draw earlier on.

B222)

8 0-0

Now we are back to something rather more sober. Ian Rogers has had some success with this move.

8...0-0!?

Offering a pawn. Instead, Black can play it safe with 8...♗d7, when after 9 ♗xc6 bxc6 10 f3 ♘g5 11 ♗e3 we transpose to Line B223.

9 ♗xc6

The other capture seems promising for Black. After 9 ♘xc6 bxc6 10 ♗xc6 ♗a6! we have:

a) 11 ♗xa8 ♗xf1 and now 12 ♕xd5 and 12 ♗xd5 both run into 12...♗c4!, while 12 ♗c6 ♗c4 13 ♗e3 ♗xe3 14 fxe3 ♕g5 is also strong for Black.

b) 11 ♕xd5 ♗xf1 12 ♕xe4 ♗b5! 13 ♘c3 ♗xc6 14 ♕xc6 ♗d4 15 ♗f4 ♖b8! (15...♗xc3 16 ♕xc3 ♕d5 looks roughly equal) 16 ♘d5 and now, instead of 16...♗xb2 17 ♖d1, which was unclear in Pitschka-Bräuning, 2nd Bundesliga 1990, I prefer 16...♖xb2!, planning to answer 17 ♖d1 with either 17...♕h4 or 17...♖a8!?.

9...bxc6 *(D)*

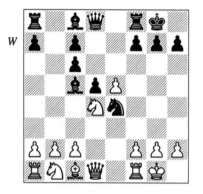

10 ♘xc6

Other moves are not dangerous for Black:

a) 10 b4?! ♗b6 11 ♘xc6 ♕h4! (in contrast to the main line, this now works, as the bishop is better placed on b6; in fact this point is quite crucial as 11...♕d7 now fails to 12 ♕xd5!) 12 ♗e3 ♗a6 13 g3 ♕h3 14 ♖e1 (14 ♗xb6 ♗xf1 15 ♕xf1 ♕xf1+ 16 ♔xf1 cxb6 17 ♘e7+ ♔h8 18 ♘xd5 ♖fd8 is a good ending for Black) 14...♗xe3 15 ♖xe3 ♘xf2! 16 ♔xf2 ♕xh2+ 17 ♔f3 ♕h5+ 18 g4 ♕h3+ 19 ♔f2 ♕h2+ 20

♔e1 (or 20 ♔f3 f5!) 20...♕h4+ 21 ♔d2 d4 22 ♘xd4 ♕f2+ 23 ♘e2 ♖ad8+ 24 ♖d3 ♕f3 25 ♔c3 ♗xd3 26 cxd3 ♖fe8 and Black went on to win in Corden-Nunn, Birmingham 1975.

b) 10 ♘c3 ♘xc3 11 bxc3 f6 12 ♗e3 ♖e8 13 ♘xc6 ♕d7 14 ♗xc5 ♕xc6 15 ♗e3 fxe5 and the pawn-centre gives Black an edge.

c) 10 f3 f6! 11 exf6 (11 fxe4 fxe5 12 ♖xf8+ ♕xf8 was clearly better for Black in the game Carr-Flear, British Ch (Southampton) 1986, while Black also stood well after 11 b4 ♗b6 12 e6 ♘g5 13 ♔h1 ♗xd4 14 ♕xd4 ♘xe6 in Minasian-Yakovich, Belgrade 1989) 11...♕xf6 12 ♗e3 ♗a6 13 ♖e1 ♖ae8 14 c3 ♗d6 15 g3 (15 fxe4 ♕h4 16 g3 ♗xg3 gives Black a winning attack) 15...♘xg3! 16 hxg3 ♗xg3 17 ♘a3 ♗xe1 18 ♕xe1 c5 19 ♘dc2 d4 20 cxd4 ♕g6+ 21 ♔f2 ♕g4 22 ♕h1 cxd4 0-1 Chiburdanidze-Mi.Tseitlin, Moscow 1989.

d) 10 ♗e3 ♕e8! 11 c3 (or 11 f3 ♘d6!) 11...f6 12 exf6 ♖xf6 13 ♘d2 ♖g6 14 ♔h1 ♗g4 gave Black an initiative in the game Vejcel-Poleshchuk, corr 1978, especially as 15 f3? loses prettily to 15...♘g3+ 16 hxg3 ♕xe3.

10...♕d7!

Originally the active 10...♕h4?! was considered as Black's best move, but Rogers-Wahls, Groningen 1990 altered the assessment of this line. Following 11 ♗e3! ♗a6 (the actual game went 11...♗xe3? 12 fxe3 ♕g5 13 ♖f4 ♗b7 14 ♕xd5 ♖ad8 15 ♕xe4 and White won quickly) 12 g3 ♕h3 13

♗xc5 ♗xf1 14 ♕xf1 ♕xf1+ 15 ♔xf1 ♘xc5 16 ♘e7+ ♔h8 17 ♘xd5 Rogers considers White to be slightly better in the endgame. I would add that Nunn's 16 ♘c3, keeping the black rooks tied down, looks even stronger.

11 ♘d4 (D)

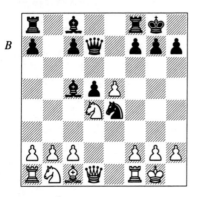

11...♕e7

Another interesting idea here is 11...♗a6!? 12 ♖e1 ♖ae8:

a) 13 ♗f4 f6 (13...♗b6!?) 14 exf6 ♖xf6 with some compensation for the pawn.

b) 13 f3 ♘d6 14 c3 ♘c4 15 b4 ♗b6 16 a4 and now instead of 16...♘xe5 17 b5 ♗b7 18 ♗a3 c5 19 a5, which was good for White in N.Høiberg-N.Pedersen, Århus 1993, Black should play 16...♖xe5.

12 ♗f4

12 ♗e3 ♕xe5 13 ♘c6 ♕xb2 is good for Black.

12...f6!?

This is the move suggested by Rogers, but once again there's some choice here:

a) 12...♗a6?! 13 ♖e1 and now 13...♘xf2 14 ♔xf2 ♕h4+ 15 g3 ♕xh2+ 16 ♔f3 doesn't quite work for Black.

b) 12...♗b6!? puts the bishop on a less vulnerable square and gives Black the option of ...c5. This move could well be worth a second look; for example, 13 ♘c3 ♘xc3 14 bxc3 c5 15 ♘b5 ♗a6 16 a4 ♕e6 gives Black compensation, or 13 c3 f6, when both 14 ♗e3 fxe5 15 ♘c6 ♕e6 16 ♕xd5 ♗xe3! and 14 ♘c6 ♕f7 15 ♕xd5 ♘xf2! are very messy indeed.

13 ♗e3 (D)

As far as I know, this tricky move is Rogers's latest word on this line. Alternatively:

a) 13 ♘b3? ♗xf2+! 14 ♖xf2 ♘xf2 15 ♕xd5+ ♗e6 16 ♕c5 ♕xc5 17 ♘xc5 ♖ae8 18 ♘c3 fxe5 19 ♗xe5 ♗f5 20 ♗d4 ♘g4 is clearly better for Black, Neuvonen-Timmerman, corr 1991.

b) 13 e6 ♗xe6 14 ♘xe6 ♕xe6 15 ♗xc7 is given as unclear by Rogers in *ECO*, but after 15...♖ac8 I quite fancy Black's chances; for example, 16 ♗g3 f5! 17 ♘d2 f4 18 ♗h4 ♕f5, preparing ...g5, or 16 ♗f4 ♘xf2! 17 ♖xf2 ♕b6 18 ♗g3 ♕xb2 19 ♘d2 ♗xf2+ 20 ♗xf2 ♖xc2 with advantage to Black.

The position after 13 ♗e3 (*see diagram*) is critical for the 8 0-0 line. Black must play carefully, as there are some hidden tricks:

a) 13...fxe5? 14 ♘c6! ♕d6 15 ♗xc5 ♕xc5 16 ♕xd5+! ♕xd5 17 ♘e7+ ♔h8 18 ♘xd5 ♗b7 19 ♘bc3 and White was simply a pawn up in Rogers-Wong Chee Chung, Singapore 1998.

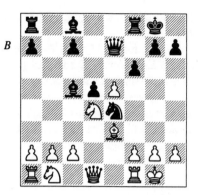

b) 13...♗a6 14 ♖e1 ♕xe5 (14...fxe5 15 ♘c6 ♕e6 16 ♗xc5 is again good for White) 15 f3! ♗d6 (15...♘d6 16 f4 ♕e7 17 ♘f5 ♘xf5 18 ♕xd5+ ♔h8 19 ♕xc5 ♕xc5 20 ♗xc5 and White still has the extra pawn) 16 g3! ♘c5 (or 16...♘xg3 17 f4!) 17 ♗f4 ♕h5 18 ♗xd6 cxd6 19 ♘c3 and White has the advantage because of Black's terrible pawn-structure.

c) 13...♗xd4 (the best move) 14 ♕xd4 (14 exf6? ♗xf6 15 ♕xd5+ ♕e6 16 ♕xa8 ♗a6 17 ♕xa7 ♗xf1 is good for Black) 14...♕xe5 15 f3 ♘d6 16 ♘c3 ♕xd4 17 ♗xd4 ♗e6 18 ♖ad1 ♖fe8 with a reasonably level endgame.

B223)
8 ♗e3
This is White's most popular reply to 7...♗c5. Now the threat to c6 is real.
8...♗d7
Black doesn't gain enough compensation after 8...0-0 9 ♘xc6 bxc6 10 ♗xc5 ♘xc5 11 ♗xc6 ♗a6 12 ♘c3! (rather than the risky 12 ♗xa8 ♕xa8). White threatens the d-pawn and can

organize kingside castling with ♗b5 or ♘e2.
9 ♗xc6 bxc6 (D)

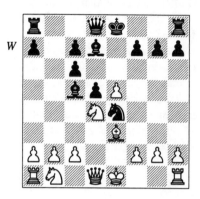

Once again White has a choice of moves:
B2231: 10 ♘d2 187
B2232: 10 0-0 188

B2231)
10 ♘d2
Putting immediate pressure on the e4-knight.
10...♕h4!
Black must be careful not to exchange into a worse position. After, for instance, 10...♘xd2 11 ♕xd2 ♕e7 12 ♘b3 ♗b6 13 ♕c3 0-0 14 0-0, White has a small but unmistakable advantage due to his control over the dark squares on the queenside.
11 ♘xe4
Given that Black seems to reach an untroubled position after this, White could do worse than look at the alternative 11 ♘4f3!?, which led to a roughly equal position after 11...♕e7

12 ♗xc5 ♘xc5 13 0-0 0-0 14 ♕e2 ♗g4 15 ♕e3 ♗xf3 16 ♘xf3 ♘e4 17 c4 f6 in R.Leyva-L.Perez, Santa Clara Guillermo Garcia mem 1998.

11...♕xe4 12 0-0 ♗b6 13 ♖e1 ♕g6 14 ♘b3 *(D)*

Battling for dark-square control on the queenside looks the logical way to play the position. In B.Kristensen-Hebden, Kopavogur 1994, White tried instead 14 a4 a5 15 ♖a3, but after 15...0-0 16 ♗c1 ♗g4 17 ♕d2 c5 18 ♘b5 ♕e6 Black was slightly better.

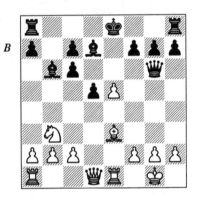

An important position for the 10 ♘d2 line. White has good chances of obtaining a dark-square bind on the queenside, but Black's counterplay on the light squares cannot be underestimated. Here are two possible continuations:

a) 14...0-0 15 ♗c5 (15 a4 ♗h3 16 ♕f3 ♗f5 looks pleasant for Black) 15...♖fe8 16 a4 ♗f5 17 ♖c1 ♖ab8 18 ♗xb6 (White really doesn't want to do this, but what else is there?) 18...axb6 19 ♘d4 ♗d7 and Black was more than

OK in Kotronias-Yilmaz, Pucarevo Z 1987.

b) 14...♗g4!? 15 f3 ♗h3 16 ♕d2 d4! 17 ♗f4 (both 17 ♗xd4 ♖d8 18 c3 c5 and 17 ♘xd4 ♗xd4 18 ♗xd4 0-0-0 are good for Black) 17...c5 18 ♔h1 ♗e6 19 c4 a5 20 ♕e2 a4 21 ♘d2 ♗a5 22 ♖ec1 ♗f5 23 ♘f1 a3 24 bxa3 ♗c3 and again Black is better, Illescas-Campos Moreno, Alicante 1989.

B2232)
10 0-0 *(D)*

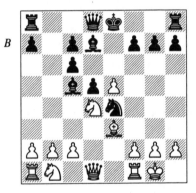

10...♗b6

10...♕e7!? is an important alternative, which is only at Black's disposal with the 7...♗c5 move-order. White has two possibilities:

a) 11 ♖e1 0-0 12 f3 ♘g5 and now:

a1) 13 ♘d2 ♗b6 14 a4 (Ljubojević-Averbakh, Palma de Mallorca 1972) and now Gligorić gives 14...♘e6 as slightly better for Black.

a2) 13 ♕d2 f6 14 ♔h1 h6! 15 ♗xg5 hxg5 16 ♘b3 ♗b6 gave Black an edge in J.Schneider-Yudovich, corr 1972.

a3) 13 f4 ♘e6 14 c3 (Sax-Smejkal, Vrbas 1977) and now Gligorić gives 14...♗b6 15 ♘d2 f6, again with a slight plus for Black.

b) 11 f3 (this move looks stronger) 11...♘d6 12 ♗f2 ♘f5 13 c3 0-0 14 ♖e1 ♖ab8 (or 14...♗b6 15 ♕c2 ♕g5 16 ♕d2 ♕g6 17 ♘a3 ♖ad8 with equality, Sveshnikov-Bjerke, Gausdal 1992) 15 ♕d2 ♖fe8 16 ♘b3 ♗b6 with a roughly level position, Borge-Lilja, Copenhagen 1993.

11 f3 ♘g5 12 f4

After 12 ♕d2, 12...♘e6 13 ♘c3 ♘xd4 14 ♗xd4 c5 15 ♗f2 ♗c6 16 ♕f4 ♕d7 17 ♖ad1 was slightly better for White in Rogers-Lin Ta, Shah Alam Z 1990, but 12...h6!? may be an improvement. After 13 a4 a5 14 ♘b3 0-0 15 ♘c3 ♘e6 16 f4?! d4! 17 ♘xd4 ♘xd4 18 ♗xd4 ♗g4 19 ♖ad1 ♗xd1 20 ♖xd1 ♕xd4+ 21 ♕xd4 ♖fd8! Black was clearly better in Nevanlinna-Sepp, Jyväskylä 1993.

12...♘e4 13 ♘d2 ♘xd2 14 ♕xd2 c5 15 ♘f3 d4 16 ♗f2 ♗c6 17 ♗h4

Or 17 ♕d3 ♕d7 18 ♖fd1 ♕g4 19 ♗g3 0-0 20 ♘g5 ♕h5 21 ♗f2 f6 22 ♕c4+ ♔h8 23 ♘e6 ♕g6 24 ♗g3 (½-½ Apicella-Boudre, Paris 1988) although here 24...♕e4 looks strong.

17...♕d7 (D)

Objectively this position is roughly level, although Black's bishop-pair

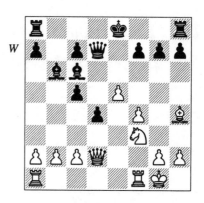

means that he can look to the future with some optimism:

a) 18 c4 0-0 19 ♕d3 ♕g4 20 ♗g3 ♖ae8 21 a4 ♗a5 22 ♘g5 ♕h5 23 ♘e4 ♖b8 24 ♖f2 ♗xe4 25 ♕xe4 ♖b3! was good for Black in Edelman-Czebe, Budapest 1996.

b) 18 f5 ♕xf5 leads to a further branch:

b1) 19 ♘g5 ♕g6 20 ♖xf7 0-0-0 21 ♕d3 ♕xd3 22 cxd3 h6 23 ♘e6 ♖de8 24 ♘xg7 ♖xe5 25 ♘f5 ♗e8 26 ♘e7+ ♔b7 27 ♘g6 ♗xf7 28 ♘xe5 ♗d5 29 b3 ♖e8 30 ♖e1 ♗a5 31 ♖e2 ♗b4 32 ♔f1 a5 and Black eventually won the endgame in Edelman-Klovans, Biel 1994.

b2) Klovans suggests 19 ♘xd4 ♕d7 20 ♘f3 as a possible improvement, giving 20...♕xd2 21 ♘xd2 0-0 as equal and 20...c4+ 21 ♔h1 ♕g4 as unclear.

16 The Two Knights Defence: 4 d4 exd4 5 0-0 ♘xe4

1 e4 e5 2 ♘f3 ♘c6 3 ♗c4 ♘f6 4 d4 exd4 5 0-0 ♘xe4 *(D)*

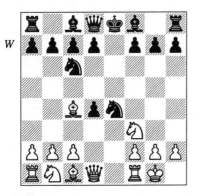

With 5 0-0 White completes his kingside development and offers Black a second pawn. In this chapter we deal with the acceptance of this pawn by 5...♘xe4. In my opinion this is Black's most reliable method of meeting 5 0-0.

A Quick Summary of the Recommended Lines

Line A is at worst harmless for Black and in all probability favours Black. As far as I can see, Line B1 offers Black the choice of either easy equality or playing for more with a slightly risky continuation. Traditionally, Line B2 has been Black's most popular defence, although I believe White has more chances to stir up complications in this line. Nevertheless, Black's resources are very good here as well. As far as I can see, the ball is very much in White's court.

The Theory of the Two Knights Defence with 4 d4 exd4 5 0-0 ♘xe4

1 e4 e5 2 ♘f3 ♘c6 3 ♗c4 ♘f6 4 d4 exd4 5 0-0 ♘xe4 6 ♖e1

This is White's only good move. Other tries simply allow Black to get away with his double pawn snatch.

a) 6 ♘c3? ♘xc3! (there's no need to get embroiled in the complications of 6...dxc3 7 ♗xf7+ ♔xf7 8 ♕d5+) 7 bxc3 d5 8 ♗b5 ♗e7 9 ♘e5 (or 9 ♘xd4 ♗d7 10 ♖b1 0-0 with a pawn plus for Black in Trajković-Trifunović, Yugoslav Ch 1952) 9...♗d7 10 ♘xd7 ♕xd7 11 cxd4 a6 12 ♗a4 b5 13 ♗b3 ♘a5 and Black has a clear advantage, S.Sokolov-Grodzenski, corr 1976.

b) 6 ♗d5? ♘f6 7 ♗g5 (7 ♘g5 ♘xd5 8 ♖e1+ ♗e7 9 ♕h5 g6 10 ♕h6 d6 11 ♕g7 ♖f8 12 ♘xh7 ♗e6 wins for

Black) 7...♗e7 8 ♗xf6 ♗xf6 9 ♖e1+ ♘e7 10 ♘xd4 0-0 11 ♘c3 c6 12 ♗f3 d5 and once more Black is a healthy pawn up, Venkataramanan-Gokhale, Calcutta 1994.

6...d5 (D)

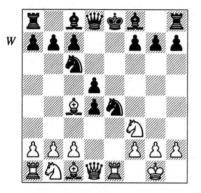

Now White has two options:
A: **7 ♘c3?!**   191
B: **7 ♗xd5**   191

A)

7 ♘c3?!

This is the Canal Variation. White's play, which looks just a bit too clever for its own good, was once thought to lead to an equal position. However, it looks like Black has a powerful resource that leaves White struggling.

7...dxc4 8 ♖xe4+ ♗e6 9 ♘xd4 ♘xd4 10 ♖xd4 ♕f6! 11 ♘b5

After 11 ♘e4, 11...♕xd4! 12 ♕xd4 ♖d8 wins back the queen and leaves Black a clear pawn up in the endgame. Keres assessed the position after 11 ♘b5 as slightly better for White but...

11...♖c8!

...puts a real spanner in the works. It seems that White has no really satisfactory reply.

12 ♗f4

12 ♘xa7 ♗c5! 13 ♖f4! ♖d8 and now 14 ♕e2? ♕e5! 0-1 was the conclusion of Lembeck-Klasmeier, German Cht 1987. 14 ♕f1 is relatively stronger, but 14...♕e5 still leaves Black in control.

12...♗c5 13 ♖e4 ♗b6 14 ♕e2 0-0 15 ♗e5 ♕g6

We are following Mindeguia Guruceaga-Estremera Panos, Pamplona 1995. Black is simply a pawn up for nothing.

B)

7 ♗xd5

This capture is White's strongest move.

7...♕xd5 8 ♘c3 (D)

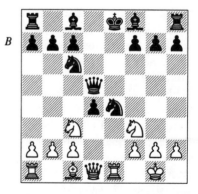

The point to all of White's previous play. Because of the two pins, White regains the piece. Black must decide which side of the board to put his queen.

I would add here that both options are satisfactory.

B1: 8...♕h5!?   192
B2: 8...♕a5   193

B1)

8...♕h5!? 9 ♘xe4 ♗e6 10 ♗g5

10 ♘eg5 makes less sense here with the black queen already positioned on the kingside. Following 10...0-0-0 11 ♘xe6 fxe6 12 ♖xe6 ♗d6! White is struggling to equalize:

a) 13 ♕e2? falls straight into the trap 13...d3!, when 14 cxd3 ♘d4 and 14 ♕e3 ♘d4 are both disastrous for White.

b) 13 ♗g5? allows another little trick with 13...♗xh2+!.

c) 13 ♗d2 is relatively best, although Black keeps a small edge with 13...♖he8 (compare with the 8...♕a5 line).

Black also need not worry about 10 ♘xd4. Following 10...♕xd1 11 ♖xd1 0-0-0 12 ♗e3 ♘xd4 13 ♗xd4 ♗f5 14 ♘g5 ♗g6 Black's bishop-pair gives him the edge.

10...h6!?

This looks like a very risky winning attempt, but I can't find anything wrong with it so I'm very happy to suggest it. If Black wants to play it safe there are a couple of sensible alternatives:

a) 10...♗d6!? and now:

a1) 11 c4!? h6 12 ♘xd6+ cxd6 13 ♗f4 0-0 (13...♕c5!?) 14 ♘xd4 ♕xd1 15 ♖exd1 ♗xc4 16 ♘f5 ♗e6 17 ♘xd6 ♖fd8 18 ♘xb7 ♖xd1+ 19 ♖xd1 ♗xa2

was equal in A.Simonović-J.Petronić, Ulcinj tt 1998.

a2) 11 ♘xd6+ cxd6 12 ♗f4 ♕d5 (this is objectively level, even though Black's practical results have been quite good) 13 c3 ♖c8 14 ♕d3 (14 ♘xd4 ♘xd4 15 ♕xd4 ♕xd4 16 cxd4 ♔d7 was slightly more comfortable for Black in Wikner-Wedberg, Österskars 1995) 14...0-0 15 ♘xd4 ♘xd4 16 ♕xd4 ♕xd4 17 cxd4 ♖c2 18 ♗xd6 ♖fc8 19 d5 ♗xd5 20 ♗e5 with dead equality, Blauert-Wedberg, Næstved 1988.

b) 10...♗b4 11 ♘xd4 ♕xd1 12 ♖exd1 ♘xd4 13 ♖xd4 ♗e7 14 ♗xe7 ♔xe7 15 ♘c5 ♖ad8 with another stone dead drawn position, which Black actually managed to win in Van der Tuuk-Piket, Dutch Cht 1993.

11 ♗f6 ♕g6 12 ♘h4

This is the usual recommendation for White, but perhaps we should look at a couple of alternatives:

a) 12 ♗xd4?! 0-0-0 and Black is very happy.

b) Black must be careful against 12 ♗h4 (Hebden), as after 12...♗b4 13 c3 dxc3 14 bxc3, 14...♗e7?! 15 ♗xe7 ♘xe7 16 ♘e5! looks promising for White. However, I can't find anything convincing against 14...♗a5; for example, 15 ♕b1 0-0 16 ♕xb7 ♗d5! is good for Black. Once again the ball is in White's court here.

12...♕g4!

It's very unusual to allow a double check in the opening, but this is exactly what this move does! In fact,

12...♕h7!? is also not so bad. B.Stein-Balshan, Israel 1979 continued 13 ♕h5 ♔d7 14 ♗xd4 ♖e8 15 ♕b5 ♔c8 with an unclear position.

13 ♕xg4

13 ♘d6+ ♔d7 14 ♕xg4 ♗xg4 transposes to the main line, while 13 f3 ♕h5! reveals the point of Black's play. After 14 c3 ♕a5 15 ♗xd4 0-0-0, White's position is close to falling apart.

13...♗xg4 14 ♘d6++ ♔d7 15 ♘xf7 ♖g8 *(D)*

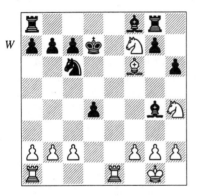

This could well be a critical position for the assessment of the entire 8...♕h5 line. As far as I can see, White has two options:

a) 16 ♗xd4?! g5 17 ♘f3 ♗xf3 18 gxf3 ♘xd4 19 ♖ad1 (K.Karlsen-Ernst, Gausdal Peer Gynt 1990) and now 19...♗g7 looks good for Black after 20 c3 ♖ge8 21 cxd4 ♖xe1+ 22 ♖xe1 ♖f8 23 ♘e5+ ♗xe5 24 dxe5 ♖xf3.

b) 16 ♘e5+ ♘xe5 17 ♗xe5 c5 (17...g5!?) 18 h3 ♗e6 19 ♘g6 ♗f5 20 ♘xf8+ ♖axf8 21 ♖e2 ♖f7 leads to a

position which looks like it should be drawn, although Black's pawn on d4 gives him a slightly more comfortable ride.

B2)

8...♕a5

This has traditionally been the main choice for Black.

9 ♘xe4

9 ♖xe4+?! ♗e6 10 ♘xd4 0-0-0 11 ♗e3 ♘xd4 12 ♖xd4 ♗b4 leaves Black well placed. Then 13 ♘e4 ♖xd4 14 ♕xd4 ♖d8 15 ♕xg7 ♕xa2! favoured Black in Mawla-D.Hamilton, Skopje OL 1972.

9...♗e6 *(D)*

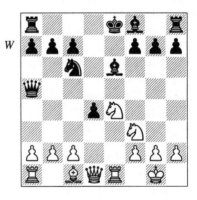

Now White must choose between:

B21: 10 ♗d2 194
B22: 10 ♘eg5 194

The former is tricky, while the latter is more popular.

Instead, 10 ♗g5?! h6 11 ♗h4 ♗b4 12 ♖e2 g5 13 a3 ♗e7 14 ♗g3 0-0-0 15 b4 ♕d5 left Black a pawn ahead for no compensation in Medina Garcia-Keres, Madrid 1943.

B21)

10 ♗d2 ♗b4!?

10...♕h5 is also possible, when it seems that White has nothing better than 11 ♗g5, transposing to Line B1.

11 ♘xd4 ♘xd4 12 c3 0-0-0!?

This is the most ambitious move. If Black prefers, he can play it relatively safe with 12...♗e7 13 cxd4 ♕d5:

a) 14 ♖c1 c6 15 ♗g5 ♗xg5 16 ♖c5 ♕xa2 17 ♘xg5 0-0-0 and White still has to justify being a pawn down.

b) 14 ♗f4!? c6 15 ♘c3 ♕d7 (not 15...♕f5? 16 d5 cxd5 17 ♕a4+ ♔f8 18 ♖e5, which looks promising for White) 16 ♕a4 b5 17 ♕a5 0-0 with an approximately level position, Greger-P.H.Nielsen, Valby 1991.

c) 14 ♗b4 ♗xb4 15 ♕a4+ ♕c6 16 ♕xb4 0-0-0 17 ♘c5 ♗d5 18 ♖ac1 ♕g6 19 g3 ♕b6 and with the dominating bishop sitting prettily on d5, I'd take the black pieces, Simonović-Malaniuk, Yugoslav Cht 1993.

13 cxb4 ♕f5 14 ♖c1

Other moves are less good:

a) 14 ♕c1?! ♗d5 15 ♗f4 ♗c6 16 ♗g3 ♖d7 17 f3 ♗xe4 18 fxe4 ♕b5 19 ♔h1 ♕xb4 and Black is well in control, R.Marić-Fuderer, Yugoslav Ch 1953.

b) 14 ♗c3? ♘b3! 15 ♕xd8+ ♖xd8 16 axb3 ♔b8 and Black's queen outweighs rook and knight, Huebener-Zimmer, St Ingbert 1987.

14...♗d5 15 ♘g3 ♕g6 *(D)*

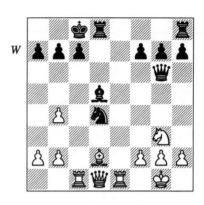

This position is extremely double-edged, as both kings can come under pressure. Here are some possible variations:

a) 16 ♖xc7+ (flashy, but not that effective) 16...♔xc7 17 ♗f4+ ♔c8 18 ♕xd4 b6 19 ♖e7 (19 ♕e5 ♔b7 20 ♕c7+ ♔a8 and 19 b5 ♖d7 also leave Black better) 19...♕b1+ 20 ♘f1 ♕xf1+ 21 ♔xf1 ♗xg2+ 22 ♔xg2 ♖xd4 23 ♖xa7 ♖e8 24 ♖c7+ ♔d8 25 ♖xf7 ♖d7 and Black has all the winning chances, Cubas-Cruz Lopez, Spanish Cht 1992.

b) 16 ♗f4 ♗c6 17 ♕h5 (17 ♖e7? ♘e6 18 ♕b3 ♘xf4 19 b5 ♕g5! 20 ♕e3 ♘e2+! wins) 17...♘e6 18 ♗e3 ½-½ Engbersen-Simmelink, corr 1988.

c) 16 ♗e3! (I suspect that this move causes Black most problems) 16...♘e6 (16...♘f5?? loses to 17 ♕c2, while 16...♘c6 17 ♕a4 and 16...♘b5 17 a4 also look promising for White) 17 ♕a4 a6 18 b5 axb5 19 ♕xb5 h5!, with a very unclear position.

B22)

10 ♘eg5

This is the most popular choice for White. The gambited pawn is regained immediately.

10...0-0-0 11 ♘xe6 fxe6 12 ♖xe6

It's strange that no one has paid much attention to the move 12 ♘g5!? here, which not only threatens ♘f7, but also allows the possibility of recapturing on e6 with the knight. Let's look at a couple of lines:

a) 12...♗b4 13 ♖xe6 ♕f5 and now 14 ♕d3?! ♕xd3 15 cxd3 ♖d5 16 ♘f3 ♗d6 17 ♗d2 ♖c5 18 ♖c1 ♖xc1+ 19 ♗xc1 ♘b4 left Black on top in Lane-Law, British Ch (Morecambe) 1981, so 14 ♕e2 looks stronger. Then 14...h6 15 ♘f3 d3 16 cxd3 ♕xd3 looks about equal, but not 14...d3? 15 cxd3 ♘d4, which fails to 16 ♕e4!.

b) 12...d3!? 13 c3 (13 cxd3 ♖xd3! is good for Black) 13...♕f5 14 g4!? ♕d5! 15 ♘f7 ♗e7 16 ♘xh8 ♖xh8 and Black has good compensation for the exchange.

12...♗d6 *(D)*

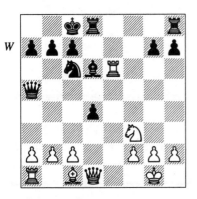

13 ♗g5!? *(D)*

In my opinion this is the most challenging move that Black can face. The question is put to the rook on d8, and it must decide between going to e8 or f8. In contrast, Black can be quite content after 13 ♕e2 ♕h5!; for example:

a) 14 ♗g5? d3! and now both 15 ♕e4 ♘d4! and 15 cxd3 ♘d4! are winning for Black.

b) 14 ♗d2? d3 is similar to line 'a'.

c) 14 ♕e4 ♖de8 15 ♗d2 ♘e5! 16 ♖xe8+ ♖xe8 17 ♘xe5 ♗xe5 18 f4 ♗d6 19 ♕d3 g6 20 ♖f1 b6 with an equal position, Kamsky-Ye Rongguang, Manila IZ 1990.

d) 14 h3 ♖he8 15 ♗d2 ♘e5! 16 ♖xe8 ♖xe8 17 ♘xd4 ♕xe2 18 ♘xe2 ♘c4 19 ♗e3 and now both 19...♘xb2 20 ♘d4 ♘c4 21 ♘f5 ♗e5 22 ♗d4 g6 (Michalczak-Klovans, Münster 1994) and 19...♘xe3 20 fxe3 ♗c5 21 ♔f2 ♖f8+ 22 ♔e1 ♗xe3 (Rogers-Adams, Bundesliga 1995/6) favour Black.

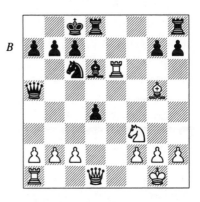

13...♖de8

If Black is concerned about heading into the intricacies of a very complex endgame, then 13...Rdf8!? is a useful alternative. 14 We2 h6 15 Bh4 g5 16 Bg3 Bxg3 17 hxg3 Rd8 18 We4 Wd5 19 Wxd5 Rxd5 gave a balanced position in Engelbert-Westerinen, Gausdal 1997.

14 We1!?

This move sets up the aforementioned ending. 14 We2 Kd7 15 Rxe8 (15 Re1?! Wxe1+! 16 Nxe1 Rxe6 and the two rooks are stronger than the queen) 15...Rxe8 16 Wd3 h6 17 Bd2 Wh5 18 g3 Wg4 led to equality in E.Berend-Potapov, Pardubice 1997.

14...Wxe1+ 15 Raxe1 Kd7 16 Rxe8 Rxe8 17 Rxe8 Kxe8 *(D)*

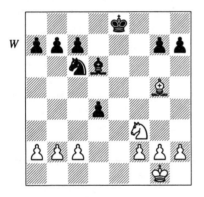

In my opinion this is one of the most critical positions in the 10 Neg5 variation. On first sight one could argue that the position should be dead drawn, but the respective pawn majorities for both sides ensure that there is still plenty of play left. In my database Black's practical results have been extremely good (9 wins, 7 draws and only 1 loss) but in mitigation Black was

generally the stronger player and some of White's play left something to be desired. My initial impression was favourable to Black, then favourable to White, and now I'm not sure at all! We could spend lots of pages looking at this position and still be no nearer the truth. I've restricted myself to just a few lines and observations:

a) 18 Kf1 Kf7 19 Ke2 (19 Kd2! transposes to line 'b') 19...Ke6 20 Bd2 (or 20 Kd3 Kd5 21 Nxd4? Nb4+! 22 Kc3 Nxa2+ 23 Kb3 Kxd4 24 Kxa2 Bxh2 25 Be3+ Kd5 26 Bxa7 b6 with a strange position which is winning for Black: White's bishop is trapped whereas Black's can escape) 20...Kd5 21 Kd3 b5! *(D)* and Black has at least the better of a draw here. Here are two practical examples:

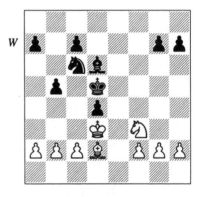

a1) 22 c3 Ne5+ 23 Nxe5 Bxe5 24 cxd4? Bxd4 25 Bc3 Bxc3 26 bxc3 a6 27 c4+ Kc5 28 f4 h5 29 g3 b4 30 h3 a5 31 g4 hxg4 32 hxg4 a4 33 f5 a3 34 g5 b3 35 f6 gxf6 36 g6 bxa2 0-1 Santos-Van Riemsdijk, Mercosul 1997.

a2) 22 h3 a6 23 g4 g6 24 ♗e1 ♗f4 25 ♗d2 ♗xd2 26 ♔xd2 ♞e5 27 ♞e1 c5 28 c3 ♔e4 29 cxd4 cxd4 30 ♔e2 d3+ 31 ♔d2 ♞c4+ 0-1 Skousen-Stempin, Copenhagen 1990.

b) 18 ♗d2! (a good move, patrolling the b4-square and setting up ideas of ♞g5) 18...♔f7 (18...♗e7!?) 19 ♔f1 *(D)* and now:

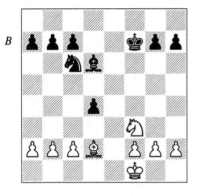

b1) 19...h6 20 ♔e2 ♔e6 21 ♔d3 ♞e5+ (21...♔d5? allows the trick 22 ♞xd4! ♞xd4 23 c4+ ♔e5 24 f4+ ♔f5 25 ♔xd4 ♗xf4 26 ♗xf4 ♔xf4, which

looks 'good to winning' for White; for example, 27 b4 h5 28 a4 h4 29 a5 a6 30 b5 g5 31 ♔d5 and White's pawns were faster in Wikner-Sylvan, Danish jr Ch (Tjele) 1995) 22 ♞xe5 ♔xe5 23 ♔c4, when White's chances are to be preferred, as he has prevented ...♔d5 and so his king is better placed.

b2) 19...♔e6!? 20 ♞g5+ ♔f5 21 ♞xh7 ♞b4 may well be Black's best bet. If White doesn't want to return the pawn on the queenside, he is forced to play 22 ♗xb4 ♗xb4, but then Black still regains the pawn after 23 h4 (forced, to give a square for the knight) 23...♗e7 24 g3 ♔g6 25 ♞g5 ♗xg5 26 hxg5 ♔xg5 and, as king and pawn endgames are the most complicated of all, I'll have to sit on the fence here and say that all three results are still possible!

In conclusion, both 8...♛a5 and 8...♛h5 achieve a fully playable position for Black, although at the moment I would say that 8...♛h5 gives White more chances to go wrong.

17 The Two Knights Defence: The Max Lange Attack

1 e4 e5 2 ♘f3 ♘c6 3 ♗c4 ♘f6 4 d4 exd4 5 0-0 ♗c5 *(D)*

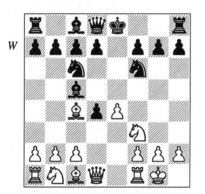

With 5...♘xe4 working out so well in the previous chapter, you might ask why Black would need a second defence to 5 0-0. Well, the honest answer is that he doesn't, but then again no survey of the Open Games would be complete without a look at the legendary Max Lange Attack, which offers both sides such rich attacking possibilities. I also fully believe in Black's chances in the Max Lange and all the other lines at White's disposal here. 5...♗c5 is a very reasonable alternative to the safer 5...♘xe4 and I can recommend it to the more adventurous player.

A Quick Summary of the Recommended Lines

Line A is uncommon but must be treated with some respect, as there are a few chances for Black to go wrong. Line B is the Max Lange. Line B21 is critical, and it seems at the moment that best play may well lead to a draw (a common occurrence in sharp lines). Line B22 is also important and here I present some largely ignored analysis, which may well overturn the original assessment.

The Theory of the Two Knights Defence 4 d4 exd4 5 0-0 ♗c5: 6 c3 and the Max Lange Attack

1 e4 e5 2 ♘f3 ♘c6 3 ♗c4 ♘f6 4 d4 exd4 5 0-0 ♗c5

Now we shall look at two ideas for White:

A: 6 c3!?   198
B: 6 e5   200

The former is underrated; the latter is the Max Lange Attack.

A)

6 c3!?

This is not played very often, but in my opinion it's quite underrated. While not being as 'glamorous' as the Max Lange Attack, this variation still offers Black chances to go wrong.

6...♘xe4 7 cxd4 d5!

Once again counterattack is the best form of defence.

8 dxc5 dxc4 *(D)*

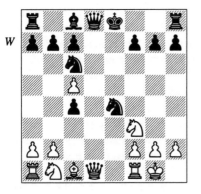

Here White has two possible lines:

A1: 9 ♕xd8+   199
A2: 9 ♕e2   199

A1)

9 ♕xd8+

This is not a particularly frightening move. In fact, it's White who now has to work hard to equalize.

9...♔xd8 10 ♖d1+

10 ♘g5?! ♘xg5 11 ♗xg5+ f6 12 ♗f4 ♘b4 13 ♘a3 ♘d3 14 ♖ad1 ♗d7 gave Black a clear edge in Gietl-Slobodjan, German Ch 1997.

10...♗d7 11 ♗e3

Or 11 ♘g5 ♘xg5 12 ♗xg5+ ♔c8 13 ♘a3 ♗e6 14 ♘b5 a6 15 ♘d4 ♘xd4

16 ♖xd4 a5 and despite the presence of opposite-coloured bishops, Black's extra pawn gives him reasonable winning chances, Blauert-Hebden, London Lloyds Bank 1991.

11...♔e7 12 ♘a3 ♗e6 13 ♘b5!

White can regain the pawn with 13 ♖dc1 ♖hd8 14 ♘xc4, but following 14...♖d5 15 ♘cd2 ♘xd2 16 ♘xd2 ♖ad8 17 ♘e4 ♖d4 18 ♘g3 a5 Black's control of the d-file gives him an endgame pull, Demarre-Korneev, Paris 1991.

13...♖hc8

Perhaps Black can consider playing 13...♖ac8!?.

14 ♘g5 ♘xg5 15 ♗xg5+ f6 16 ♗f4 ♘e5 17 ♗xe5 fxe5 18 ♖e1

Black will find it difficult to hold on to the extra pawn, but even so there's still plenty of play left in the position. Here are two practical examples:

a) 18...a6 19 ♘c3 ♔f7 20 ♖xe5 ♖e8 21 ♖ae1 ♖ad8 22 f4 g6 23 h3 ♖d3 24 ♖1e2 h6 25 ♔h2 ♗d7 26 ♖xe8 ♗xe8 with an equal position, although Black went on to win in Kisova – Kachiani-Gersinska, Antwerp 1992.

b) 18...♔f6 19 ♖e3 ♗d7 20 ♖f3+ ♔e6 21 ♘a3 b5 22 ♖e1 ♖e8 23 ♖fe3 ♔f6 24 ♖f3+ ♔e6 25 ♖fe3 ♖d5!? (of course Black can repeat moves with 25...♔f6) 26 ♖d1+ ♔c6 27 ♘xb5 ♔xb5 28 ♖xd7 ♖ad8 29 ♖xd8 ♖xd8 with a very unclear rook and pawn ending, Thorhallsson-Flear, London 1987.

A2)

9 ♕e2 *(D)*

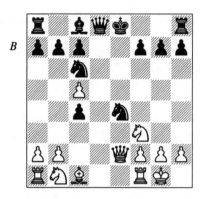

Graham Burgess resurrected this idea in his book *101 Chess Opening Surprises*.

9...♕d3 10 ♖e1 f5!

10...♕xe2 is not so good, as after 11 ♖xe2, 11...♗f5? drops a piece to 12 g4!, while 11...f5 12 ♘bd2 0-0 13 ♘xe4 fxe4 14 ♖xe4 gives White an edge.

11 ♘c3 0-0 12 ♘xe4 fxe4 13 ♕xe4 ♗f5 14 ♕h4

Naturally Black is happy if White presents him with a passed pawn after 14 ♕xd3? cxd3, but 14 ♕f4 is possible:

a) 14...♖ac8 15 ♕g3 ♗g6 16 ♗f4 ♕d5 17 ♗xc7 ♖xf3 18 gxf3 ♘d4 19 ♖e3 ♘f5 20 ♕e5 ♘xe3 21 fxe3 ♕c6 with a roughly level position, Baird-Schiffers, Vienna 1898.

b) 14...♖ad8!? 15 ♕xc7 ♗g4 16 ♘e5 ♘xe5 17 ♕xe5 ♖de8! 18 ♕xe8 ♖xe8 19 ♖xe8+ ♔f7 20 ♖e1 ♕c2 21 h3 ♗f5 and White has extra material but is tied up by the black queen, Ed.Holland-Lyell, British Ch (Plymouth) 1989.

14...♖ad8

Two other options come to mind:

a) 14...♖ae8 15 ♗f4 ♕d5 16 ♗xc7 ♕xc5 17 ♕g3 ♕d5 18 ♗d6 ♖xe1+ 19 ♖xe1 ♖d8 20 ♗e7 ♖e8 21 ♗f6 ♖xe1+ 22 ♘xe1 ♕d7 23 ♗c3 b5 with an equal position, Biolek-Keitlinghaus, Ostrava 1993.

b) 14...♕d5 attempts to reach the main line after 15 ♗e3 ♖ad8, without allowing White alternatives at move 15 (see the next note). Burgess suggests 15 ♗d2!? as an idea for White here, after which Black should probably grab the pawn and defend with 15...♕xc5 16 ♗c3 ♖f7.

15 ♗e3

Alternatively:

a) 15 ♗f4 ♖d7 16 ♘e5 ♘xe5 17 ♗xe5 ♕d5 18 ♖ac1 ♖e8 with an approximately level position.

b) 15 ♗g5!? (Burgess) 15...♖d5 16 ♖e3 ♕c2 17 ♖ae1 ♗d3 18 ♖e8 ♖f5! and again Black is holding his own.

15...♕d5 16 ♖ac1 ♗d3

Now in Vatter-Fleck, Bundesliga 1988/9 White allowed a promising sacrifice after 17 h3? ♖xf3! 18 gxf3 ♘e5 19 ♔g2 ♖f8, and Black's attack prevailed. As an improvement Burgess suggests 17 ♕g3, after which I consider 17...♖d7 to be the best move, with a level position.

B)

6 e5

Finally we delve into the maze-like complications of the infamous Max Lange Attack.

6...d5 *(D)*

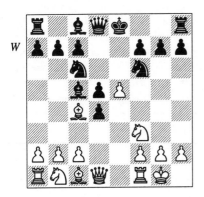

7 exf6

Most players cannot resist the temptation of entering the complexities of the Max Lange. However, it should be pointed out here that White can transpose into the slightly more tranquil waters of Line B222 in Chapter 15 by 7 ♗b5!? ♘e4 8 ♘xd4.

7...dxc4 8 ♖e1+

The universally played move, although perhaps White should look into the straightforward 8 fxg7 ♖g8 9 ♗g5, when 9...♕d5?! 10 ♘c3 ♕f5 11 ♘e4! is strong for White. Thus Black should play 9...♗e7 10 ♗xe7 ♔xe7:

a) 11 b4 cxb3 12 ♘bd2 ♖xg7 13 ♘xb3 ♗h3 14 ♖e1+ ♔f8 15 g3 ♕d5 and Black is clearly better, Balogh-Szabo, Hungarian Ch 1946.

b) 11 ♕e2+ ♗e6 12 ♘bd2 ♕d5 13 ♖fe1 d3 also looks good for Black, Gorodetsky-Gibentif, Moscow 1996.

c) 11 ♖e1+ (the critical move) 11...♗e6 12 ♖e4!? f5 13 ♖h4 ♔f7 14 ♖xh7 ♖xg7 15 ♖xg7+ ♔xg7 with an unclear position, Fahrni-Tartakower, Baden-Baden 1914.

8...♗e6 9 ♘g5

After 9 fxg7 ♖g8, 10 ♗g5 ♗e7 11 ♗xe7 ♔xe7 transposes to line 'c' of the previous note, while 10 ♘g5 ♕d5 gives us the main line.

9...♕d5!

Black has to be careful. 9...♕xf6? loses to 10 ♘xe6 fxe6 11 ♕h5+, picking up the bishop.

10 ♘c3 ♕f5 (D)

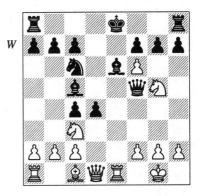

11 ♘ce4

Another line here is 11 g4 ♕g6! 12 ♘ce4 ♗b6 13 f4 0-0-0 14 f5 ♗xf5 15 gxf5 ♕xf5 and White's airy king gives Black enough compensation for the piece; for example:

a) 16 ♔h1 gxf6 17 ♕f3 ♕xf3+ 18 ♘xf3 ♘b4! and Black was better in Blackburne-Teichmann, Nuremberg 1896.

b) 16 ♖f1 ♕g6 17 ♕g4+ ♔b8 18 fxg7 (Kinzel-Miranda, Lugano OL 1968) and now 18...♖hg8 maintains Black's initiative.

c) 16 ♘xf7 ♖he8 17 ♘xd8 (or 17 ♘ed6+ cxd6 18 ♖xe8 ♕g6+ 19 ♔h1

♖xe8 20 ♘xd6+ ♔d7 21 ♘xe8? ♕e4+ 22 ♔g1 d3+ and Black wins) 17...♖xe4 18 ♖xe4 ♕xe4 and Black is better due to the threat of ...d3+, *Saitek*-Schouten, Dutch open Ch 1992.

11...0-0-0!

11...♗f8 is a playable alternative, but the text-move is the most reliable choice for Black.

12 g4!

Alternatively:

a) 12 fxg7 ♖hg8 13 g4 ♕e5 14 ♘xe6 fxe6 transposes to the main line (B2).

b) 12 ♘xe6 fxe6 13 fxg7 ♖hg8 14 ♗h6 ♗b4! and Black is doing well, Buchniček-Marek, Presov 1997.

c) 12 ♘xc5 ♕xc5 13 ♖xe6 fxe6 14 ♘xe6 ♕e5 15 ♘xd8 ♘xd8 16 fxg7 ♕xg7 and Black's powerful d4-pawn gives him an edge, R.Haag-C.Krämer, Weiler 1993.

12...♕e5 (D)

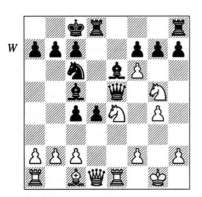

13 ♘xe6

13 fxg7 ♖hg8 usually just leads to a transposition after 14 ♘xe6 fxe6.

Attempts by White to improve on this are not particularly convincing. Smolnikov-Trofimokh, corr 1958-9 continued 14 ♘xc5?! ♕xc5 15 ♘e4 ♕e5 16 ♗h6 ♗d5 17 ♘g3 ♕f6 18 g5 ♕f4 19 ♘h5 ♕f5 20 ♘g3 and now instead of repeating moves, 20...♕h3 21 f3 f6! looks very strong.

There are two other moves which Black needs to know how to deal with. The first of these is 13 f4, which appears loosening but there is no obvious way Black can exploit this. After 13...d3+ 14 ♔g2 ♕d5 15 fxg7 ♖hg8 16 f5 (*ECO* gives 16 cxd3 cxd3 17 ♗d2 as unclear, but surely Black must be better after, for instance, 17...♗d4) 16...♗xf5 17 gxf5 ♖xg7 18 f6 ♖g6 19 ♔h1 ♖dg8, 20 ♘f3? ♕e5 21 ♗f4 ♘g4 22 ♗g3 ♘e3 led to a win for Black in Rossolimo-Medina Garcia, Malaga 1968, but 20 cxd3!? is a tougher defence.

However, the rarely-seen 13 ♘f3!? may well be good enough for a draw. After 13...♕d5 14 fxg7 we have:

a) 14...♖hg8 15 ♘f6 ♕d6 and now 16 ♘e4 ♕d5 17 ♘f6 is a draw by repetition which White is advised to take, as 16 ♘xg8?! ♖xg8 gives Black more than enough compensation for the exchange.

b) 14...♗xg4!? 15 gxh8♕ ♖xh8 (Black is a rook down but White is the one hanging on) 16 h3 (16 ♘f6 ♕xf3 17 ♘xg4 ♕xd1 18 ♖xd1 ♖g8! is good for Black) 16...♗h5 and now:

b1) 17 ♗f4? ♖g8+ 18 ♗g3 (18 ♔f1 ♕f5! 19 ♘g3 ♕xh3+ looks to be winning for Black after 20 ♔e2 ♖e8+ 21 ♔d2 ♗b4+ 22 c3 dxc3+ 23 bxc3 ♖d8+ or 20 ♔g1 d3) 18...♘e5 19 ♘xe5 ♗xd1 20 ♘f6 ♖xg3+ 21 fxg3 d3+ and Black won in Schoch-P.Littlewood, Winterthur 1986.

b2) 17 ♘f6! ♕xf3 18 ♘xh5 ♖g8+ 19 ♘g3 ♖xg3+ 20 fxg3 ♕xg3+ 21 ♔f1 ♕xh3+ 22 ♔f2 and Black probably has to take the perpetual check on offer, Acebal-Sanz Alonso, Spanish Ch 1993.

13...fxe6 *(D)*

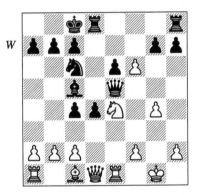

Now there are two lines:
B1: 14 ♗g5   203
B2: 14 fxg7   204

B1)

14 ♗g5

This move shouldn't worry Black. There's at least one way to reach a good position.

14...♗b6!

Also possible is another exchange sacrifice with 14...h6!? 15 ♘xc5 (15 fxg7 hxg5 16 gxh8♕ ♖xh8 gives Black

a ready-made attack, especially as 17 ♘xc5? loses to 17...♕xh2+ 18 ♔f1 ♕h3+ 19 ♔e2 ♕xg4+ 20 ♔d2 ♕f4+ 21 ♔e2 d3+ {or 21...♖h2!} 22 cxd3 ♘d4+ 23 ♔f1 ♖h1+ 24 ♔g2 ♕h2#) 15...♕xg5 and now:

a) 16 ♘xe6 ♕xf6 17 ♘xd8 ♖xd8. *NCO* assesses this as 'with enough compensation for the material', while the only practical example I can find continued 18 ♕e2?! d3 19 cxd3 ♘d4 20 ♕e7 ♘f3+ 21 ♔f1 ♘xe1 22 ♕xf6 gxf6 23 ♔xe1 ♖xd3 and Black is a pawn up in the rook ending, Krsek-Pridal, Czech U-16 Ch 1993.

b) 16 fxg7!, as suggested in *The Italian Game*, looks stronger. It's true that Black has compensation for the exchange after either 16...♕xc5 17 gxh8♕ ♖xh8 or 16...♕xg7 17 ♘xe6 ♕g6 18 ♘xd8 ♖xd8, but my suspicion is that it's not quite enough.

15 fxg7

15 f4?! d3+ 16 ♔h1 ♕xb2 gives Black a better version of the main line, as the b2-pawn has been bagged.

15...♕xg7 16 ♗f6 ♕g6 17 ♗xh8 ♖xh8

The extra pawn and White's weak kingside give Black ample compensation for the exchange. Here are two practical examples:

a) 18 ♘d2 ♗a5 19 f3 h5 20 ♖e4 hxg4 21 ♖xg4 ♕h5 with a menacing attack on the white king, Plijter-Markus, corr 1994.

b) 18 ♕e2 d3 19 cxd3 ♘d4 20 ♕d1 cxd3 21 h3 ♖f8 22 ♕xd3 ♘f3+ 23 ♔g2 ♘h4+! 24 ♔g3 ♖xf2!! 25 ♔xh4

♕h6+ 26 ♔g3 ♕f4+ 27 ♔h4 ♖f3 28
♕xf3 ♕xf3 29 ♖ad1 c6 30 ♘d6+?
♔b8 31 ♘e4 a6 32 a3 ♗c7 33 ♘g5
♕b3 34 ♖f1 h6 35 ♖f8+ ♔a7 36 ♘f3
♕xd1 0-1 Musil-Plsek, Moravian open
Ch 1994.

B2)

14 fxg7

This is the main continuation, which
leads us to some wild and wonderful
positions.

14...♖hg8 15 ♗h6 d3! 16 c3

White is forced to block things up,
since 16 cxd3 ♖xd3 leaves White in
trouble after 17 ♕c2 ♖h3! or 17 ♕c1
♘d4.

16...d2!

This is the most forcing move, but
16...♗e7!? is also not bad. Pikulski-
M.Baker, London 1993 continued 17
f4 ♕d5 18 ♕d2 ♖d7 19 ♖e3 ♘d8 20
b3 ♘f7 21 bxc4 ♕xc4 22 g5 ♕d5,
with an unclear position.

17 ♖e2

The only reply. Black wins after 17
♘xd2 ♗xf2+ 18 ♔xf2 ♕xh2+, while
17 ♗xd2 ♕xg7 18 ♘xc5 ♕xg4+ is
also very bad for White.

17...♖d3 (D)

A critical position for the assessment of the whole Max Lange. White
has two main options.
B21: 18 ♕f1   204
B22: 18 ♘xc5   205

18 ♘g5? ♕f4! 19 ♘xe6 ♕xg4+
was winning for Black in Poignant-
Rate, Torcy 1991.

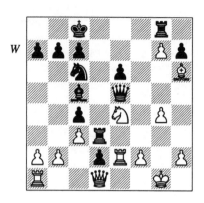

B21)

18 ♕f1

It is well known that queens are not
happy blockading passed pawns, so
White vacates the d1-square for the
rook and prepares to use the queen on
the kingside.

18...♕d5 19 ♖d1 ♘e5!

Once again Black's best strategy is
to prey on the weak light squares on the
kingside. 19...♖d8? 20 ♘xc5 ♕xc5 21
♖exd2 ♘e5 22 ♕g2 was good for
White in Balzar-Karaklajić, Dortmund
1988.

20 ♕g2

20 ♘f6!? seems to lead to a draw
with best play. 20...♘f3+? 21 ♔h1
♕d6 22 ♕g2 is winning for White.
Therefore Black must play 20...♕f3:

a) 21 g5? ♘g4 22 ♘xg4 (22 ♘xg8
♘xf2 23 ♘e7+ ♔d7 24 ♖xf2 ♗xf2+
25 ♕xf2 ♕xd1+ 26 ♔g2 ♕g4+ mates
quickly) 22...♕xg4+ 23 ♔h1 ♕f3+ 24
♔g1 ♗d6! and Black is better; for example, 25 h3 ♗f4 26 ♖xe6 ♗xg5 27
♗xg5 ♖xg7 28 ♖e8+ ♔d7 29 ♖d8+
♔c6 30 ♖xd3 ♖xg5+ 31 ♔h2 cxd3 32

♕h1 ♕xh1+ 33 ♔xh1 ♘d5 34 ♖xd2
♔e4!, and the difference in the activity of the two kings could hardly be
more marked.

b) 21 ♘xg8! gives Black nothing
better than to take the perpetual check
with 21...♕xg4+ 22 ♔h1 ♕f3+ 23
♔g1 ♕g4+ (Gligorić).

20...♘f3+ 21 ♔f1 ♘h4

Black can keep the battle for the
full point going with 21...♗e7!?, and
now:

a) 22 ♘xd2? ♗g5! 23 ♗xg5 ♕xg5
is very strong for Black.

b) 22 g5 (Martinek-Vajs, corr 1985)
22...♕f5, with an unclear position.
Note that 23 ♘xd2? ♘h4 24 ♕e4
♕h3+ is very strong.

22 ♕g1

After 22 ♕h1, 22...♗e7 23 ♖exd2
♗f6! wins the all-important g7-pawn.

22...♘f3

In this position White is advised to
take a draw by repetition with 23 ♕g2
♘h4 24 ♕g1, as 23 ♕g3 ♗d6 24
♘xd6+ cxd6 gives Black a vice-like
grip on the position. In conclusion, it's
difficult to see how either side can
vary from the two forced draw options.

B22)

18 ♘xc5

Getting rid of the powerful bishop.
This line has been seen a few times
with mixed results. Theory has stated
that with best play a draw should be
the outcome, but with the aid of some
new material I'm very confident of

Black's chances, at least in the main
line anyway.

**18...♕xc5 19 ♖xd2 ♘e5 20 ♖xd3
cxd3 21 ♔g2**

White has to counter the threat of
...♕d5/c6, followed by ...♘f3+. However, given the problems White has in
the main line, there may be something
to be said for 21 h3!? here, planning to
answer 21...♕d5 with 22 ♔h2. This
still looks rather shaky for White, but I
haven't found anything totally convincing for Black either. The position
is very hard to assess after 22...♘f7 23
♕d2 e5 24 ♖e1 ♕d6 25 g5.

**21...♕d5+ 22 ♔g3 ♘f7! 23 ♕d2
♕d6+ 24 ♔g2**

After 24 ♔h3 the white king gets
caught on the edge with 24...e5 25 g5
♕g6!, threatening 26...♖xg7! 27 ♗xg7
♘xg5+ 28 ♔g2 ♘e4+.

24...e5 25 g5 ♕g6!

This excellent move was suggested
in both *The Italian Game* and *The Two
Knights Defence*. Both books say the
game should end as a draw with perpetual check. 25...♘d8!? has also been
suggested in some books, but the English correspondence IM Mike Read
reckons that after 26 ♖d1 ♘e6 27 g6!?
White can achieve an advantage; for
example:

a) 27...hxg6 28 ♕xd3 ♕xd3 29
♖xd3 ♘f4+ 30 ♗xf4 exf4 31 ♖d4 g5
32 h4! and the endgame is clearly in
White's favour.

b) 27...♕c6+ 28 f3 (not 28 ♔g1??
♖xg7! 29 ♗xg7 ♘f4 30 f3 ♕xf3 and
Black wins) 28...hxg6 29 ♕xd3 ♖xg7

30 ♕d5! and again it's Black who is struggling.

26 ♔f1 ♕e4 27 ♔g1 ♕g4+ 28 ♔f1 ♕f3 29 ♔g1 ♕g4+ 30 ♔f1 ♕f3 31 ♔g1 *(D)*

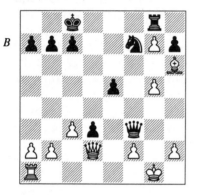

As far as I know, all sources have quoted this position as a draw. We are now following the little-known game J.Moore-M.Read, corr 1981. Black repeated to gain time on the 'clock' (!), but now unleashed a stunning novelty which seems to lead to a clear advantage for Black.

31...e4!

Preparing the way for the knight to reach f3 via the e5-square. It seems that, as so often in this line, Black can play around White's g7/h6/g5 cluster of pieces.

32 c4

Alternatively:

a) 32 ♖e1? ♘e5 33 ♖e3 ♕g4+ 34 ♔h1 ♘f3! and Black forces mate.

b) 32 ♕e3 ♕xe3 33 fxe3 ♘xg5! 34 ♖f1 (or 34 ♗xg5 ♖xg7 35 h4 h6 and the rook ending is winning for Black)

34...♔d7 and Read assesses this position as clearly favourable for Black, giving the line 35 ♖f8 d2 36 ♖f1 ♘f3+ 37 ♔f2 ♘xh2 38 ♖h1 ♘g4+ 39 ♔e2 ♘xh6 40 ♖xh6 ♖xg7 41 ♔xd2 ♔e8, followed by ...♖e7 and ...♔f8-g7.

32...♕g4+

This time there is good reason to give the check, because 33 ♔f1 loses to 33...♘e5, followed by ...♘f3.

33 ♔h1 ♕f3+ 34 ♔g1 b6!

So as to meet 35 ♕b4 with 35...c5. This move also gives Black's king some air, which is important later on.

35 c5 ♕g4+ 36 ♔h1

Again 36 ♔f1 ♘e5 wins for Black.

36...♘e5 37 cxb6

37 ♖g1 loses to 37...♕xg1+ 38 ♔xg1 ♘f3+.

37...axb6 38 ♕b4

Now 39 ♕f8+ is a real threat, but Black has some fantastic moves ready.

38...♕f3+ 39 ♔g1 ♘g6 40 ♖c1

After 40 ♕c4 Black calmly gives up the rook with 40...♘f4!! 41 ♕xg8+ ♔b7, when White cannot avoid the mate with queen and knight.

40...e3! 41 ♕xb6 ♕xf2+ 42 ♔h1 ♕f1+!!

A fitting finale to the game. Black uses his queen as a decoy.

43 ♖xf1 cxb6 44 ♔g2 e2 0-1

The black pawns are too strong. This was a wonderful exhibition, which shows the power of Black's resources in this line.

In conclusion, we can say that 18 ♘xc5 allows Black more chances than 18 ♕f1.

18 The Two Knights Defence: 4 ♘g5

1 e4 e5 2 ♘f3 ♘c6 3 ♗c4 ♘f6 4 ♘g5
(D)

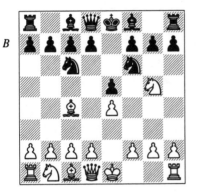

This is White's most direct, and in my opinion, the most critical response to the Two Knights Defence, a thought which is reflected by its use at the top level by players such as Kasparov, Short and Morozevich. White immediately attacks f7, leaving Black with an immense problem to solve. In fact there is no reasonable way to defend the weak pawn, so Black must once again turn to counter-attack. This can be achieved in the form of the complicated but probably unsound Traxler (or Wilkes-Barre) Variation (4...♗c5) or the traditional 4...d5, which is my recommendation against 4 ♘g5.

A Quick Summary of the Recommended Lines

Line A is rather uncommon and it seems to give Black plenty of counter-chances. Line B1 is also rare, as White tends to be afraid of grabbing the second pawn, but nevertheless, this is a sterner test for Black. This leaves us with the most popular variation, Line B2. White has an immediate decision to make about where to put his attacked knight. Although Line B22 is the traditional choice, many top players have shown a penchant for 9 ♘h3 (Line B21). This is a very tricky line, where Black has to play very accurately to keep an initiative for the sacrificed pawn. In the main variation the current choice for White seems to be B2221, which is another stern test for Black. However, White doesn't have all the choices. If Black wishes to avoid the main line, he would do well to study the positions in Line B221.

The Theory of the Two Knights Defence: 4 ♘g5

1 e4 e5 2 ♘f3 ♘c6 3 ♗c4 ♘f6 4 ♘g5 d5 5 exd5 ♘a5 *(D)*

Black has other choices here, including 5...♘d4 and 5...b5!?, which both lead to very interesting play, but I feel that 5...♘a5, Black's most popular choice, has more chance of standing up against the sternest scrutiny. Of course, before we go on, we should ask ourselves once more what's wrong with the very natural-looking recapture 5...♘xd5. Well, one of the first variations a budding chess-player will learn is the so-called 'Fried Liver Attack'. White sacrifices a piece for a raging offensive with 6 ♘xf7!? ♔xf7 7 ♕f3+ ♔e6 8 ♘c3. If this were the only problem, then there would be a chance to resurrect 5...♘xd5, as after 8...♘b4 it's by no means clear that the Fried Liver is winning, or even good for White. However, there is a rather larger spanner in the works, in the shape of 6 d4! exd4 7 0-0!. Black is now in some trouble as White is about to play a superior version of the Fried Liver. Following 7...♗e7 Black is hit with 8 ♘xf7!. Morphy-NN, New Orleans sim 1858 concluded 8...♔xf7 9 ♕f3+ ♔e6 10 ♘c3 (this is flashy and thus perfect for a simultaneous display; 10 ♕e4+ would allow Black to resign earlier) 10...dxc3 11 ♖e1+ ♘e5 12 ♗f4 ♗f6 13 ♗xe5 ♗xe5 14 ♖xe5+ ♔xe5 15 ♖e1+ ♔d4 16 ♗xd5 ♖e8 17 ♕d3+ ♔c5 18 b4+ ♔xb4 19 ♕d4+ ♔a5 20 ♕xc3+ ♔a4 21 ♕b3+ ♔a5 22 ♕a3+ ♔b6 23 ♖b1#. 7...♗e6 isn't much better. White wins after 8 ♖e1 ♕d7 9 ♘xf7 ♔xf7 10 ♕f3+ ♔g6 11 ♖xe6+!. You have been warned!

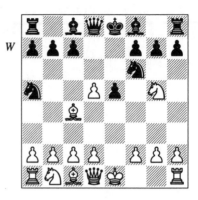

We now look at two options for White:

A: 6 d3   208
B: 6 ♗b5+   210

6 ♗b3? ♘xb3 7 axb3 ♘xd5 causes Black no problems whatsoever.

A)

6 d3 h6 7 ♘f3 e4 8 ♕e2

David Bronstein has played the piece sacrifice 8 dxe4, but while this is probably worth a go in blitz games, it shouldn't be too effective against accurate defence. Following 8...♘xc4 we have:

a) 9 ♕e2 ♘b6 10 c4 ♗b4+ 11 ♔f1 0-0 12 a3 ♖e8 13 e5 ♗f8 14 h3 c6 15 ♗e3 ♘xc4! 16 ♕xc4 ♘xd5 with a clear plus to Black, De Zeeuw-Timmerman, Dutch Cht 1992.

b) 9 ♕d4! ♘d6! 10 ♘c3 c6 (Euwe gives 10...♘fxe4!? 11 ♘xe4 ♕e7 12 0-0 ♘xe4 13 ♖e1 f5 14 ♘d2 ♕c5 with an advantage to Black) 11 0-0 cxd5 12 e5 ♘f5 13 ♕d3 ♘e4 14 ♘xd5 ♘c5 and White didn't have enough for the piece in L.Bronstein-Ra.Garcia, Mar del Plata Z 1969.

8...♘xc4 9 dxc4 ♗c5 10 h3

With this move White prevents any ideas of ...♗g4 and prepares to retreat the knight to h2. Alternatively:

a) 10 ♗f4 0-0 11 ♘fd2 ♗g4 12 ♕f1 c6 13 h3 ♗h5 14 g4 ♗g6 15 ♘c3 ♗b4 16 dxc6 bxc6 17 0-0-0 ♗xc3 18 bxc3 ♕a5 and Black had a menacing attack in Van der Weide-Medina Garcia, Amsterdam 1967.

b) 10 c3 b5!? 11 b4 ♗e7 12 ♘fd2 ♗g4 13 f3 exf3 14 gxf3 ♗h5 15 cxb5 0-0 16 0-0 ♖e8 and once again Black has a dangerous initiative, Grob-Keres, Dresden 1936.

c) 10 0-0 (this allows some kingside fireworks) 10...0-0 11 ♘fd2 ♗g4 12 ♕e1 ♕d7 13 ♘b3 ♗f3! 14 ♗f4 ♕g4 15 ♗g3 ♘h5 16 ♘xc5 (16 ♔h1 ♗xg2+! 17 ♔xg2 ♘f4+ 18 ♔g1 ♘e2+ is winning for Black, as is 16 ♘1d2 ♘xg3 17 hxg3 ♕xg3) 16...♘f4 17 ♘xe4 (alternatively, 17 ♕e3 ♘xg2 18 ♕d2 ♘f4!) 17...♕h3!! 0-1 Field-Tenner, USA 1923.

d) 10 ♘fd2 (apart from 10 h3 this is White's other principal move) 10...0-0 11 ♘b3 ♗g4 12 ♕f1 ♗b4+ 13 c3 (13 ♘c3 c6 14 h3 ♗h5 15 g4 ♗g6 16 dxc6 bxc6 17 ♗d2 e3! gave Black a big initiative in Luckis-Keres, Buenos Aires OL 1939) 13...♗e7 14 h3 ♗h5 15 g4 ♗g6 16 ♗e3 ♘d7 17 ♘1d2 ♘e5 18 0-0-0 ♘d3+ 19 ♔b1 b5! 20 cxb5 ♕xd5 21 ♘d4 (21 ♔a1 ♕xb5 22 f4 a5 was clearly better for Black in Salwe-Marshall, Vienna 1908, while *ECO*

gives 21 c4 ♕e6 22 ♘d4 ♕e5, again with a good position for Black) 21...a6 22 c4 ♕e5 23 ♘2b3 axb5 24 cxb5 ♖fb8 25 ♖d2 ♖xb5! 26 ♘xb5 ♕xb5 and Black's attack proved to be irresistible in Perschke-Emms, Wuppertal rpd 1993.

10...0-0 11 ♘h2 *(D)*

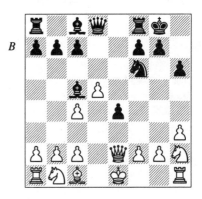

11...c6

11...b5!? is also possible:

a) 12 cxb5 ♘xd5 13 0-0 ♕e7 14 a3 f5 and Black can roll his kingside pawns forward.

b) 12 ♘c3 bxc4 13 ♕xc4 ♕d6 14 0-0 ♗a6 is fine for Black, Bird-Chigorin, London 1883.

c) 12 b3 bxc4 13 bxc4 ♗a6 14 0-0 c6 15 dxc6 ♕d4 16 c3 ♕d6 17 ♗e3 ♗xe3 18 fxe3 ♕xc6 19 ♘d2 ♖fd8 and White has many weaknesses, Baird-Chigorin, New York 1889.

12 dxc6 e3! 13 ♗xe3 ♗xe3 14 fxe3 ♘e4

White is three pawns up, but his position is a mess and the threats of ...♘g3 and ...♕h4+ are very difficult to deal with. Naftalin-Fridman, corr 1971 continued 15 ♖g1!? bxc6 16 ♘f3 ♕f6 17 c3 ♖b8 18 ♘d4 ♖d8 19 b4 c5! 20 bxc5 ♘xc5 21 ♘d2 ♖b2 and Black was in total control. It's probably better for White to offload the exchange with 15 0-0 ♘g3 16 ♕f3 ♘xf1 17 ♘xf1 (Kopylov-Kondratiev, USSR 1955) but even here Black stands slightly better.

B)

6 ♗b5+

The best and most popular choice.

6...c6

6...♗d7 is also playable, but the text-move is Black's most dynamic choice. Black secures a gain of tempo by attacking the bishop on b5.

7 dxc6 bxc6 *(D)*

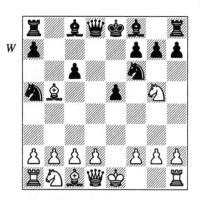

Now White chooses between:

B1: 8 ♕f3   210
B2: 8 ♗e2   212

Before looking at the main moves, here are some less important ideas:

a) 8 ♗a4?! (this is a common mistake amongst club players) 8...h6 9 ♘f3 e4 10 ♕e2 (10 ♘e5 ♕d4! 11 ♗xc6+ ♘xc6 12 ♘xc6 ♕c5 13 ♘xa7 ♖xa7 and with such a development advantage, Black's extra piece far outweighs three pawns, Arias-Mitkov, Orense 1997) 10...♗d6 11 ♘d4 (11 d3 may be stronger, but 11...0-0 12 dxe4 ♘xe4 13 0-0 ♘c5 14 ♗b3 ♗a6! still looks good for Black) 11...♕b6 12 c3 0-0 13 b4?! ♗xb4 14 cxb4 ♕xd4 15 ♘c3 ♕xb4 16 ♖b1 ♕d6 and Black is clearly better, B.Horwitz-E.Pindar, Manchester 1861.

b) 8 ♗f1?! looks very odd, but has actually been played in a World Championship match (twice!). Steinitz-Chigorin, Havana Wch (8) 1892 carried on 8...h6 9 ♘h3 ♗c5 10 d3 ♕b6 11 ♕e2 ♗g4 12 f3 ♗xh3 13 gxh3 0-0-0 and White's position was not a pretty sight.

c) 8 ♗d3!? ♘d5! 9 ♘e4 f5 (9...♘f4 10 ♗f1 f5 11 ♘ec3 ♗c5 12 g3 ♕d4 13 ♕f3 ♘e6 14 d3 0-0 15 ♘e2 ♕d6 16 ♘bc3 e4 17 ♕h5 g6 18 ♕h6 exd3 was also good for Black in E.Stefanović-D.Frolov, Orel 1997) 10 ♘g3 ♘f4 11 ♗f1 ♗c5 12 c3 ♗b6 13 d4 ♘g6 14 ♗d3 0-0 15 b4 ♘b7 16 ♗c4+ ♔h8 and Black has a dangerous initiative, Castaldi-Keres, Stockholm OL 1937.

B1)

8 ♕f3 *(D)*

This move, exploiting the pin on the h1-a8 diagonal, looks a little greedy, but there are also some hidden positional

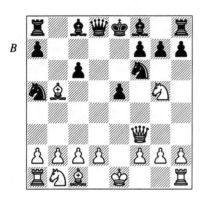

points to it. Black must play precisely in order to retain an initiative for the pawn(s).

We will consider two main moves for Black here:

B11: 8...♖b8   211
B12: 8...h6   212

8...♗e7!? is also worthy of attention. Black has definite compensation after 9 ♗xc6+ ♘xc6 10 ♕xc6+ ♗d7 11 ♕c4 0-0 12 ♘c3 ♗f5, while Carlier-Crawley, London GLC 1986 continued 9 ♘c3 ♗g4 10 ♗xc6+!? ♔f8 11 ♗xa8 ♗xf3 12 ♗xf3 ♘d7 13 ♘ge4 ♘c6 14 0-0 ♘d4 with another unbalanced position.

B11)
8...♖b8

Traditionally this has been the main choice for Black, who offers a second pawn in return for a further lead in development.

9 ♗d3!?

Van der Wiel was responsible for resurrecting this strange-looking move.

White tries to keep as much control as possible over the critical e4- and f5-squares, thus making it difficult for Black to arrange a kingside assault with his pawns. Other moves allow Black a fair share of counterplay; for example:

a) 9 ♗e2 c5 10 ♘c3 ♗e7 11 d3 0-0 12 0-0 ♖b6 13 ♕g3 ♘c6 14 ♘a4 ♖a6 15 b3 ♘d4 16 ♗d1 ♘d5 and Black is very actively placed, Paoli-Prins, Madrid 1959.

b) 9 ♗xc6+ (this is very gluttonous) 9...♘xc6 10 ♕xc6+ ♘d7! 11 d4 ♗e7 12 ♘e4 (12 h4?! h6 13 ♘xf7 ♔xf7 14 ♕d5+ ♔f8 15 dxe5 ♗b7 16 ♕e6 ♕a5+ 17 ♘c3 ♕xe5+ 18 ♕xe5 ♘xe5 was winning for Black in Papastavropoulos-Nenashev, Katerini 1993) 12...0-0 13 d5 ♖b6 14 ♕c4 ♗a6 15 ♕a4 f5 and White is made to suffer for his lack of development, Mutton-R.Jones, British Ch (Torquay) 1998.

9...h6 10 ♘e4 ♘d5 11 b3!?

This is Van der Wiel's little nuance in this line. Formerly Estrin had played 11 ♘g3, but without much success. Black can then develop with ...g6, ...♗g7 and ...0-0, before launching a kingside assault with ...f5.

11...g6 12 ♕g3 ♘f4

After 12...♗g7, 13 ♗a3?! ♘b4 14 ♔e2 0-0 15 c3? ♗g4+! was extremely strong for Black in Van der Wiel-Torre, Sochi 1980, but the alternative 13 ♗b2! ♘f4 transposes to the main line.

13 ♗b2 ♗g7 14 ♗a3 ♘b7

I can find two practical examples from this position:

a) 15 ♘bc3 f5 16 ♘e2 g5 17 ♘xf4 exf4 18 ♕f3 was a complete mess in Van der Wiel-Timman, Leeuwarden 1981.

b) 15 ♗a6 c5 16 f3 (this move is Van der Wiel's suggested improvement) 16...♘d6 (perhaps Black could try sacrificing a second pawn with 16...0-0 17 ♗xb7 ♗xb7 18 ♗xc5 ♖e8) 17 ♗xc8 ♘xe4 18 fxe4 ♕d4 19 ♘c3 ♖xc8 20 ♕f3 0-0 21 0-0-0 ♖fd8 22 ♖hf1 ♖d7 23 ♔b1 and Black probably doesn't have enough play for the pawn, Nielsen-Tiits, corr.

B12)

8...h6 (D)

This move was suggested by Gligorić.

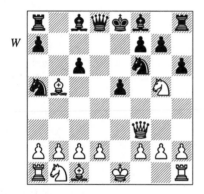

9 ♘e4 ♘d5

Once again we see this move, freeing the way for the f-pawn to advance and harass the knight on e4.

10 ♘bc3

Black's development advantage is very marked after 10 ♗a4 ♗e7 11 0-0

0-0 12 ♖e1 f5 13 ♘g3 e4 14 ♕d1 ♗a6, Stenzel-Brooks, Chicago 1994, while 10 ♗e2 ♗e7 11 ♕g3 0-0 12 d3 ♗h4 is also fine for Black, Taruffi-Rajna, Spain 1974.

10...cxb5 11 ♘xd5 ♗b7

11...♗e6!? 12 ♘e3 ♖c8 13 0-0 ♕d7 14 ♘g3 h5!? 15 c3 ♘c6 16 ♖d1 h4 was unclear in Gikas-Balashov, Lugano 1988, although I suspect there may be improvements for both sides in this line.

12 ♘e3 ♕d7 13 0-0 ♘c6 14 d3 0-0-0 15 c3 g6

Black is ready to play ...f5, prising open the important a8-h1 diagonal. Van der Wiel-Spassky, Reggio Emilia 1986/7 continued 16 a4 b4! 17 ♘f6 ♕e6 18 ♘fd5 f5 19 c4 ♘d4 20 ♕h3 g5 21 ♖e1 ♖g8 22 ♕h5 g4 and Black was well-placed for an attack.

B2)

8 ♗e2

This retreat is White's main continuation.

8...h6 (D)

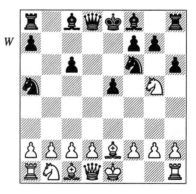

Now we have an important split:
B21: 9 ♘h3!?   213
B22: 9 ♘f3   215

B21)

9 ♘h3!?

This odd-looking move was the invention of Steinitz, who played it several times with some success. Fischer also liked the idea, while more recently it has been tried by Short and Kamsky, so it certainly must be given some respect.

The knight looks very awkward on h3, but the advantage of this move over 9 ♘f3 is that the knight at least cannot be harassed quickly by a black pawn. Of course Black can capture the knight with the c8-bishop and inflict a serious pawn weakness on White, but then this would deprive Black of the bishop-pair, quite an asset in an open position. Generally it is better for Black to play around the knight. At some point White will have to bring the knight back into the game and this will cost valuable time, which Black can use to improve his position.

Black has two different approaches at move 9. These are:
B211: 9...♗d6   213
B212: 9...♗c5   214

B211)

9...♗d6 *(D)*

10 d3

The general consensus has been that White should keep the position in the centre as blocked as possible, while

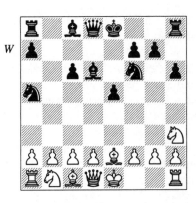

he catches up with his development. Fischer recommended that Black answer 10 d4 with 10...exd4!.

10...0-0 11 ♘c3

After 11 0-0 Black keeps up the pressure with 11...♘d5; for example, 12 ♘c3 ♘xc3 13 bxc3 ♕h4, with chances to attack on the kingside.

11...♘d5

Black can play to win back a pawn with 11...♖b8 12 0-0 ♖b4?! 13 ♔h1 ♗xh3 14 gxh3 ♖h4, but after 15 ♖g1! ♖xh3 16 ♖g3 (Short-P.Nikolić, Skellefteå 1989) White's king is safe and he enjoys the advantage of the bishop-pair. It's better for Black simply to complete development and improve his position slowly.

12 ♗d2

Alternatively:

a) 12 ♗g4 f5 13 ♗h5 ♘xc3 14 bxc3 ♕f6 15 0-0 g5 16 f3 ♗a6 17 ♗e3 c5 18 c4 ♘c6 19 ♖b1 ♖ab8 20 ♖xb8 ♖xb8 gives Black good compensation for the pawn, Megier-Read, corr 1992.

b) 12 ♗f3 ♘xc3 13 bxc3 ♕h4 14 ♘g1 f5 15 g3 ♕f6 16 ♘e2 e4 17 ♗g2

♗a6 with an unclear position, Tringov-Geller, Havana 1971.

c) 12 ♘e4!? ♗c7 13 c4 ♘e7 14 0-0 f5 15 ♘c3 g5 16 ♔h1 ♘g6 17 b4 ♘b7 and Black has chances to build up a kingside attack, Kamsky-Yusupov, Tilburg rpd 1992.

12...♖b8 13 b3

Lukacs mentions that after 13 ♕c1 the white queen is passively placed. Then after 13...♗xh3 (13...f5!?) 14 gxh3 ♘f4 15 ♖g1 f5 16 ♗f1 c5 17 ♗g2 ♘xg2+ 18 ♖xg2 (Bobkov-Korelov, corr 1975) there is no safe place for the white king.

13...♘b7 14 ♘g1

Finally White must improve the positioning of his weakest piece.

14...♘c5

Lukacs suggests 14...f5! as a possible improvement for Black; for example, 15 ♘f3 ♕e7 16 d4 e4 17 ♘e5 ♗xe5 18 dxe5 ♕xe5 19 ♘xd5 cxd5 20 ♗e3 f4 21 ♗d4 ♕e7, intending to continue ...f3.

15 ♘f3 ♘xc3 16 ♗xc3

Now Ivanchuk-Beliavsky, Dortmund 1998 continued 16...e4! 17 ♘d2 exd3 18 cxd3 ♗f5 19 ♘c4 ♖e8 20 0-0 ♘xd3! 21 ♗a5 (21 ♗xd3!?) 21...♕d7 22 ♗xd3 ♗xd3 23 ♘xd6 ♕xd6 24 ♗c7 ♕xc7 25 ♕xd3 ½-½.

B212)

9...♗c5 *(D)*

10 d3

10 0-0 0-0 11 d3 will usually transpose after 11...♘b7 12 ♘c3. A game which put 9 ♘h3 back in the limelight

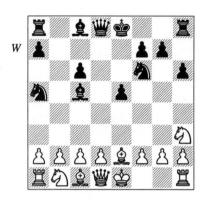

was Fischer-Bisguier, Poughskeepie 1963, which continued instead with 11...♗xh3?! (we've discussed before the drawback of this move) 12 gxh3 ♕d7 13 ♗f3! ♕xh3 14 ♘d2 ♖ad8 15 ♗g2 ♕f5 16 ♕e1 ♖fe8 17 ♘e4 and despite having regained the pawn, Black is worse as he has no real answer to White's bishop-pair.

10...0-0 11 ♘c3 ♘b7 12 0-0 ♗b6

An important alternative for Black here is 12...♘d5; e.g., 13 ♗f3 ♗b6 14 ♕e2 ♖e8 15 ♖e1 ♘xc3 (15...♘c5?! 16 ♘f4! ♘b4 17 ♘h5 ♘e6 18 ♗e3 and White has consolidated his extra pawn, Chandler-Speelman, Hastings 1989/90) 16 bxc3 ♗d7 17 ♗a3 ♖b8 18 ♖ab1 ♕c7 and White still has some problems over his knight on h3, Nunn-Hardicsay, Budapest 1978.

13 ♔h1

So that the knight can re-enter the game via g1.

13...♘c5 *(D)*

This is an important position for the assessment of 9...♗c5. In my opinion, Black just about has enough play to

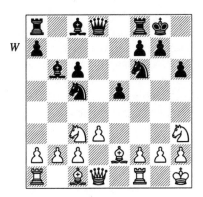

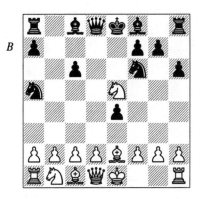

justify the pawn deficit. Here are two practical examples:

a) 14 f4 e4 15 ♘f2 exd3 16 ♘xd3 ♗f5 17 ♘xc5 ♗xc5 18 ♘a4 ♕a5 19 ♘xc5 ♕xc5 20 ♗d3 ♖ad8 and Black's pressure on the d-file is just about sufficient compensation, Hamann-Geller, Kislovodsk 1966.

b) 14 ♗f3 ♘d5 15 ♘g1 f5 16 ♘ge2 ♗a6 and Black is very active, Kuindzhi-Klovan, USSR 1973.

B22)
9 ♘f3

The most popular retreat.

9...e4 10 ♘e5 (D)

Here we will look at two ways for Black to play the position:

B221: 10...♗c5!?   215
B222: 10...♗d6   216

The latter is the more reliable.

B221)
10...♗c5!?

This rare move is an interesting attempt to steer clear of the main lines.

11 c3

This is the most popular move, but there is something to be said for the straightforward 11 0-0. If Black plays 11...♕d4 12 ♘g4 ♗xg4 13 ♗xg4 e3 then 14 ♗h3! exf2+ 15 ♔h1 looks good for White, who threatens c3, followed by d4 or b4. More testing is 11...♕d6 12 ♘g4 ♗xg4 13 ♗xg4 h5 14 ♗e2 ♘g4, but Black still has to justify his play after the solid 15 g3.

11...♕c7 (D)

After 11...♗d6 12 f4 Black is able to transpose into the main line with 12...♕c7. Chandler-Hebden, British League (4NCL) 1996/7 took a different route with 12...0-0 13 0-0 c5!? 14 d4 exd3 15 ♕xd3 ♗b7 16 ♖d1 ♘e4 17 ♘d2 c4!? 18 ♘dxc4 ♘xc4 19 ♘xc4 ♕h4 20 g3 ♗c5+ 21 ♗e3 ♘xg3 22 ♗xc5 ♘xe2+ 23 ♕xe2 ♖fe8 24 ♕f2 ♕h5 and Black actually wound up winning this game, although whether he has sufficient compensation for the piece here is very debatable.

12 f4

After 12 d4?! exd3 13 ♘xd3 ♗d6 we reach Line B2221, but with White

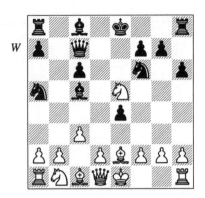

having the extra move c2-c3. This move actually changes the assessment in Black's favour, as the d3-square is weaker and a fianchetto with b3 and ♗b2 would leave the bishop blocked by the c3-pawn. Following, for instance, 14 h3 0-0 15 0-0 ♗f5 16 b4 ♘b7 Black would be able to look to the future with much confidence.

12...♗d6 13 d4 exd3 14 ♕xd3

White does best by offering the pawn back. After 14 ♘xd3?! 0-0 15 0-0 ♗f5, Black will follow up with the natural ...♖ad8 and ...♖fe8, with great pressure on the central files. Once more the inclusion of c2-c3 weakens d3 and thus hinders White's defence.

14...0-0

Black is better off delaying the recapture of the pawn. After 14...♗xe5?! 15 fxe5 ♕xe5 16 0-0, intending to continue ♗f4, White has a pleasant-looking position.

15 ♘d2

After 15 0-0 ♖d8 16 ♕c2 ♘d5 17 b4 ♘b7, *ECO* gives the line 18 ♘a3 ♘xf4 19 ♗xf4 ♗xe5 20 ♗xe5 ♕xe5

21 ♘c4 as equal (Gligorić). Herbrechts-meier-Read, corr 1985-6 saw White attempting to improve on this analysis with 18 ♗f3, but following 18...♗e6! 19 ♘a3 ♗xe5 20 fxe5 ♕xe5 Black was equal in any case. It seems that the real improvement is a move later: after 18 ♘a3 ♘xf4, there is 19 ♘xf7!, when I see no obvious answer. Black needs something here.

15...♗xe5 16 fxe5 ♕xe5 17 0-0

White possesses the bishop-pair, but Black's lead in development neutralizes this. Harding-Read, corr 1992 concluded 17...♖e8 18 ♗d1 ♗g4 19 ♘f3 ♕c7 20 ♘d4 c5 ½-½.

B222)
10...♗d6 (D)

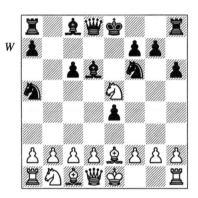

Now there are two main lines:
B2221: 11 d4   217
B2222: 11 f4   219

Alternatively:
a) After 11 ♘g4 Black can play many moves, but it seems to me that

it's best to win the pawn back immediately with 11...♘xg4! 12 ♗xg4 ♕g5! 13 h3 h5 14 d3 ♕g6 15 ♗xc8 ♕xg2 16 ♖f1 ♖xc8.

b) 11 ♘c4 ♘xc4 12 ♗xc4 0-0 and now White has little protection on the kingside. For example, the natural 13 0-0? walks into a typical 'Greek Gift' sacrifice with 13...♗xh2+! 14 ♔xh2 ♘g4+ 15 ♔g1 (15 ♔g3 is better but 15...♕c7+ 16 f4 exf3+ 17 ♔xf3 ♘e5+ is still horrible for White) 15...♕h4 16 ♖e1 ♕xf2+ 17 ♔h1 ♕h4+ 18 ♔g1 ♕h2+ 19 ♔f1 ♕h1+ 20 ♔e2 ♕xg2#.

B2221)
11 d4 exd3 12 ♘xd3 ♕c7 (D)

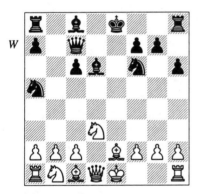

13 b3

As played by both Kasparov and Morozevich. For the moment White ignores the threat to h2 and begins developing his queenside. The bishop is well placed on b2, while the pawn on b3 prevents the black knight from entering the game via c4. There are quite a few alternatives, however:

a) 13 f4?! 0-0 14 0-0 ♗f5 15 ♘c3 ♖ad8 16 ♕e1 ♖fe8 17 ♕g3 ♘c4 18 b3 ♘d5 19 ♘xd5 cxd5 and Black's pieces are much more harmoniously placed than White's, Showalter-Chigorin, New York 1889.

b) 13 ♗e3 c5 14 ♘c3 ♘c4 15 ♕c1 0-0 16 ♗f4?! ♘xb2! 17 ♗xd6 ♘xd3+ 18 cxd3 ♕xd6 19 0-0 and Black has an edge, Roedl-Bogoljubow, Nuremberg 1931.

c) 13 b4 ♘c4 14 ♘d2 ♘xd2 15 ♗xd2 0-0 16 h3 ♗f5 17 0-0 and the players shook hands for a draw in Mikhalchishin-Geller, Dortmund 1991. Of course there's still plenty of play here, with again Black having just enough activity for the pawn.

d) 13 g3 0-0 14 ♗f4 ♗xf4 15 ♘xf4 and now 15...g5 16 ♕d4 ♕e7 17 ♘d3 ♗g4 18 ♘c3 ♖ad8 was unclear in Ljubojević-Van der Sterren, Wijk aan Zee 1988, but I like 15...♖b8 16 b3 ♖d8 17 ♕c1 and only then 17...g5. After 18 ♘d3 ♗h3 White has problems over where to put his king.

e) 13 h3 0-0 and now:

e1) 14 ♘d2 ♗f5 15 0-0 ♖ad8 16 ♖e1 ♘d5 17 ♗f1 c5 was unclear in Kholmov-Geller, Russian Ch (Elista) 1995.

e2) 14 0-0 c5 15 ♘c3 ♖b8 16 a3 (or 16 ♗f3 ♖d8 17 ♕e2 ♖e8 18 ♕d1 ♗e6 19 b3 c4 20 bxc4 ♘xc4 21 ♖b1 ♕a5 and Black is very active, Ekenberg-Keres, Lidköping 1944) 16...♖d8 17 ♕e1 ♖e8 18 ♕d2 ♘c4 19 ♕d1 ♗f5 with the same old story in C.Bauer-Anić, French Ch (Narbonne) 1997;

Black's active pieces compensate for White's extra pawn.

13...0-0

Against 13...c5 Nenashev recommends 14 c4!, which prevents Black from launching his own c-pawn. Of course I should also mention 13...♗xh2, but I cannot find enough counterplay for the piece after 14 g3! ♗xg3 15 fxg3 ♕xg3+ 16 ♘f2 ♘e4 17 ♕d4!.

14 ♗b2 (D)

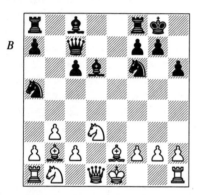

14...♘e4

Alternatively:

a) 14...♘d5 15 h3 ♗f5 16 0-0 ♖ad8 17 ♔h1 c5 18 ♘a3 c4 19 ♘b5 ♕d7 20 bxc4 ♘xc4 21 ♘xd6 ♘xb2 22 ♘xb2 ♕xd6 23 ♗d3 and by now White has consolidated his extra pawn, Morozevich-Balashov, Russia Cup (Novgorod) 1997.

b) 14...♖e8!? 15 h3 ♘d5 16 0-0 ♕e7 (preparing ...♕h4 and ...♕g5) 17 ♘c3! ♘xc3 18 ♗xc3 (Kasparov-Timman, Moscow rpd 1994), and now 18...♘xb3! 19 axb3 ♕xe2 is only minutely better for White.

15 ♘c3

15 ♘d2 should also be answered with 15...f5; for example, 16 ♘f3 c5 17 ♘de5 ♗b7 18 ♘c4 ♗f4 19 0-0 ♖ad8 20 ♕e1 ♘xc4 21 ♗xc4+ ♔h7 22 ♖d1 ♖de8 with annoying pressure on the e-file, Soos-Petran, Hungarian Cht 1991.

15...f5 (D)

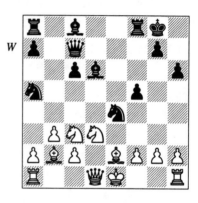

16 h3

Nenashev cites 16 f3 ♘c5 17 ♕d2 ♖d8!, intending to meet 18 0-0-0? by 18...♘xd3+ 19 ♕xd3 ♗f4+. Morozevich gives the line 16 f4 ♗a6 (not 16...♗xf4? 17 ♘xf4 ♕xf4 18 ♘xe4 fxe4 19 ♕d4, which is very good for White) 17 0-0 ♖ad8 and again Black's activity is enough for the pawn.

16...♗a6

Stronger than 16...♗b7 17 0-0 a6 18 ♕e1 c5 19 ♖d1 ♖ae8 20 ♘c1 ♗e5 21 ♘xe4 fxe4 22 ♗xe5 ♖xe5 23 ♕d2, when the position has simplified to White's advantage, Morozevich-Onishchuk, Alushta 1994.

17 0-0 ♖ad8 18 ♕e1 c5 19 ♔h1

The game Morozevich-Nenashev, Alushta 1994 continued 19...♘c6? 20 ♘xe4 fxe4 21 ♘xc5! ♗xc5 22 ♗xa6 and Black didn't have enough for the two pawns. Instead Morozevich recommends 19...♗b7! 20 ♗f3, assessing the position as unclear.

B2222)
    11 f4 exf3 12 ♘xf3 0-0 *(D)*

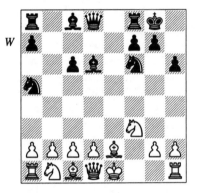

13 d4

White can also play in a more restrained manner, refraining from d2-d4 in favour of d2-d3. After 13 0-0 c5 14 ♘c3 we have:

a) 14...♗b7 15 ♕e1 ♘c6 16 ♕h4 ♘d4 17 ♗d1 ♖b8 18 ♘xd4 cxd4 19 ♘e2 d3 20 cxd3 ♕b6+ 21 d4 ♕c6 and White's two extra d-pawns are not very impressive, Havansi-Koskinen, Jyväskylä 1997.

b) 14...♘c6 15 d3 ♗b7 (or 15...♖e8 16 ♔h1 ♖b8 17 b3 ♘d4 18 ♘xd4?! cxd4 19 ♘b1 ♘d5 20 ♗f3? ♕h4 21 g3 ♗xg3 22 ♕d2 ♘e3 0-1 Zvan-Mikhalchishin, Nova Gorica 1999) 16 ♘e4

♘xe4 17 dxe4 ♕c7 18 ♗c4 ♘d4 19 c3 ♘xf3+ 20 ♕xf3 ♗xh2+ 21 ♔h1 ♖ae8 with an equal position, Sax-Lengyel, Hungarian Ch 1971.

13...c5 *(D)*

This offers White a chance to exchange queens, although Black still retains the initiative for the pawn. If he wishes, Black can also keep the queens on; for example:

a) 13...♖e8 14 0-0 c5 15 ♔h1 ♗b7 16 ♘c3 cxd4 17 ♕xd4 ♘c6 18 ♕h4 ♘e5 19 ♗d2 ♘g6 20 ♕d4 ♘e4 21 ♗c4 ♗f4 22 ♗xf4 ♘xf4 and Black's pressure on the kingside promises him compensation, Vukcevich-Romanishin, Hastings 1976/7.

b) 13...♕c7 14 0-0 c5 15 ♘c3 a6 16 d5 (16 ♔h1 ♗b7 17 ♗e3 ♖ad8 18 ♗g1 ♖fe8 19 ♖e1 ♘c6 was unclear in Spassky-Geller, Gothenburg IZ 1955) 16...♗b7 17 ♔h1 ♖ad8 18 ♗e3 ♖fe8 19 ♕d2 (Estrin-Jovčić, Yugoslavia-Russia 1967) and now the simple move 19...♘xd5! looks promising for Black.

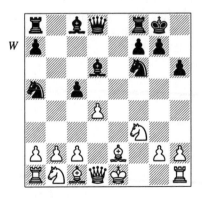

14 dxc5

After 14 0-0 Black can transpose into the last note with either 14...♕c7 or 14...♖e8 or try 14...cxd4!? 15 ♔h1 ♗c5 16 c3 dxc3 17 ♘xc3, which was equal in Estrin-Altshuler, corr 1964.

14...♗xc5 15 ♕xd8 ♖xd8 16 ♗d2

16 c3 ♖e8 17 ♔f1 ♖xe2!? (alternatively, 17...♘c6!?) 18 ♔xe2 ♗a6+ 19 ♔d1 ♘g4 20 ♔c2 ♘f2 21 ♖d1 ♘xd1 22 ♔xd1 ♖d8+ 23 ♗d2 ♘c4 turned out well for Black in Mednis-Bisguier, US Ch (New York) 1957/8.

16...♘c6 17 ♘c3 *(D)*

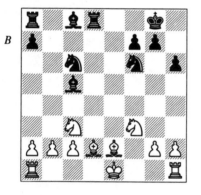

In spite of the exchange of queens, Black has sufficient piece activity to compensate for the pawn. Here are a few practical examples:

a) 17...♘b4?! 18 0-0-0 ♗f5 19 ♘e1 ♘g4 20 a3 ♘c6 21 ♘d3 ♗b6 22 h3 ♘e3 23 ♗xe3 ♗xe3+ 24 ♔b1 is a little better for White, Timman-Bisguier, Sombor 1974.

b) 17...♘g4! 18 ♘e4 ♗b6 19 0-0-0 (19 h3 ♘e3 20 ♗xe3 ♗xe3 21 ♗d3 ♖b8 22 b3 ♘b4 23 ♔e2 ♗b6 24 ♖hd1 ♗b7 25 ♘f2 ♘d5 26 ♖e1 ♘e3 27 ♖g1 ♖e8 puts Black in the driving seat, Hartoch-Bisguier, Sombor 1974) 19...f5 20 ♘g3 ♘f2 21 ♘h4 ♘d4 (21...♘xh1 22 ♖xh1 ♘d4 23 ♗d3 ♗e6 is unclear) 22 ♗c4+ ♗e6 23 ♗xe6+ ♘xe6 24 ♘hxf5 ♖d7 25 ♖de1 ♘xh1 26 ♖xh1 ♖ad8 is equal, G.Lee-J.Cooper, British Ch (Brighton) 1980.

In conclusion, I would say that Black's position is easier to play after 11 f4 than it is after 11 d4. If there were to be more developments I would expect them to be in the 11 d4 line, which is the choice of Kasparov and Morozevich. Meanwhile it remains difficult to reach a clear verdict on 9 ♘h3.

Index of Variations

Chapter Guide

1: Rare Second Moves for White

2: The Centre Game and the Danish Gambit

3: The Vienna Game (and the Bishop's Opening)